THE SPIRIT OF
THE OXFORD
MOVEMENT

Tractarian Essays

OWEN CHADWICK

The right of the
University of Cambridge
to print and sell
all manner of books
was granted by
Henry VIII in 1534.
The University has printed
and published continuously
since 1584.

CAMBRIDGE UNIVERSITY PRESS

Cambridge
New York   Port Chester
Melbourne   Sydney

Published by the Press Syndicate of the University of Cambridge
The Pitt Building, Trumpington Street, Cambridge CB2 1RP
40 West 20th Street, New York, NY 10011, USA
10 Stamford Road, Oakleigh, Melbourne 3166, Australia

First published 1990

Printed in Great Britain at the University Press, Cambridge

British Library cataloguing in publication data

Chadwick, Owen
The spirit of the Oxford Movement
1. Church of England. Oxford Movement
I. Title
283'.42

Library of Congress cataloguing in publication data

Chadwick, Owen.
The spirit of the Oxford movement / Owen Chadwick.
p. cm.
Bibliography.
ISBN 0 521 37487 1
1. Oxford movement. I. Title.
BX5100.C46 1990
283'.42'09034 – dc20   89–7071   CIP

ISBN 0 521 37487 1

CONTENTS

Preface   *page* vii
Acknowledgements   ix

1 The mind of the Oxford Movement   1
2 The limitations of Keble   54
3 The Ecclesiastical Commission   63
4 'Lead, Kindly Light'   86
5 The university on Mount Zion   99
6 Charles Kingsley at Cambridge   105
7 The Oxford Movement and its reminiscencers   135
8 Newman and the historians   154
9 Henri Bremond and Newman   167
10 The established Church under attack   198
11 The young Liddon   214
12 The choice of bishops   247
13 Edward King   256
14 A Tractarian pastoral ideal   289
15 Catholicism   307

Further reading   319
Index   321

v

PREFACE

The origin of this volume lies in a demand that the first essay in it, 'The mind of the Oxford Movement', be reprinted. This was published in 1960 as the introduction to some selected Tractarian documents in a series which reprinted classical texts of importance to the development of Christian thought. The documents themselves in that volume have been made easily accessible in other places, so that the volume as a whole is no longer needed. But it has been represented that the introduction itself, short though it is in relation to the weight of its subject, is still needed.

If it is reprinted it is easy to include with it various essays on similar or related themes, written at various times between 1954 and 1987. Most of these essays have been published before but are not now easily accessible. Most of them were written by request; for the centenary, or the centenary and a half, of institutions or of people; seven of them because particular institutions wished to commemorate Tractarians, or people engaged with Tractarians, who were prominent in the past of those institutions. One was written as a defence against a critic. One was written to correct an error which might otherwise be generally accepted. Two were reviews of books.

I have cheerfully altered the text that was originally printed, particularly to take out the local reference to the centenary or the institution; or in some cases to shorten, in two cases to lengthen; or in some cases to clarify for people who would not have the context; or in some cases to prevent overlap with another essay in the collection.

It is not to be supposed that so miscellaneous a group of essays will provide the reader with a systematic treatment of the Oxford Movement in its manifold aspects and its full place in the history of English religion. For that see the list of further reading at the end. This volume has no such intention. But it will be found that even the miscellany illuminates various sides of the movement and various of its leaders; and thus that despite the different origins and different dates of the pieces printed here, and the personal differences between several of the Victorians who are considered here, the portrait which emerges from the whole will not lack coherence.

My thanks to Andrew Robinson for his help in these studies. And thanks to those publishers, institutions and people who have allowed me to republish what I first wrote for them.

ACKNOWLEDGEMENTS

The author and publisher gratefully acknowledge permission to reproduce the following: 'The mind of the Oxford Movement', from *The Mind of the Oxford Movement*, (London, A. and C. Black, 1960); 'The limitations of Keble' and 'Catholicism', from *Theology*, (1964 and 1972 – this second was the Charles Gore Memorial Lecture in Westminster Abbey); the Church Commissioners for *Church and Historical Endowment in the Victorian Age* (London, 1986); 'Lead, Kindly Light', from *Ténèbres et lumière* (Paris, 1987; from essays in honour of a French scholar, Elisabeth Bourcier); 'The university on Mount Zion', from *Times Higher Educational Supplement* (1986); 'Charles Kingsley at Cambridge', *Historical Journal* (1975); 'The Oxford Movement and its reminiscencers', *Oriel Record* (1983; substance also printed in Richard Holloway (ed.), *The Anglican Tradition* (Wilton, Connecticut, 1984)); 'Henri Bremond and Newman', *Bulletin de l'Association Française des amis de J. H. Newman* (1988); 'The established Church under attack', in *The Victorian Crisis of Faith*, ed. A. Symondson (London SPCK with the Victorian Society, 1970); 'The young Liddon', *The Founding of Cuddesdon College* (1954); 'The choice of bishops', *Kirche, Staat und Gesellschaft im 19. Jahrhundert* (Munich, New York, London and Paris, Saur, 1984); 'Edward King', *Lincoln Minster Pamphlets* (second series, no. 4).

Chapter 1

THE MIND OF THE OXFORD MOVEMENT

The Oxford Movement was of decisive importance to the religion of the English, and not only to the Church of England, not only within the Church of England to the 'high church group' which gave birth to the movement, nurtured it, and was transformed by it.

Of decisive importance to the *religion* of the English – no doubt, not to their philosophy, perhaps not so markedly to their apprehension of Christian doctrine. The mind of the Oxford Movement is not a mind which can be best studied or examined by asking for its philosophical conclusions (if any); even though at least two of its principal thinkers had the training and the makings of a philosopher. Nor can it best be studied or examined by asking for a list of its doctrinal propositions – for example, by observing that its leaders at first suspected the doctrine that saints should be invoked in prayer. As well might we seek to comprehend John Wesley by asking what he thought of the theories of Locke and Berkeley, or by setting forth his hostility to Calvinistic doctrines as the key to understanding his whole work. Like its predecessor the Evangelical Movement, it was more a movement of the heart than of the head. If the generalization be allowed, it was primarily concerned with the law of prayer, and only secondarily with the law of belief. It was aware that creed and prayer are inseparable. It was not concerned for religious 'experience' while being unconcerned about religious language – on the contrary, it was earnestly dogmatic. But the movement, though dogmatic, was not dogmatic simply because it possessed or shared a particular theory of dogma. It always saw dogma in relation to worship, to the numinous, to the movement of the heart, to the conscience and the moral need, to the immediate experience of the hidden hand of God – so that without this attention to

I

worship or the moral need, dogma could not be apprehended rightly. The Creed was creed – the truth; not a noise of words to evoke prayer. But it roused the mind to prayer, and only through prayer and life was it known to be truth. The Oxford men did not affirm, that which helps men to be saints must be true. But they had much sympathy with the proposition, and would probably have agreed that it contained more than a seed of truth. And in this modified sense, it is right to see the Oxford Movement as an impulse of the heart and the conscience, not an inquiry of the head. Certainly the principal changes which it brought in English life were changes in the mode of worship, or in the understanding of sanctity, or in the consequent methods of religious practice; and the changes of theological or philosophical thinking were by comparison less far-reaching.

Though the leaders were not so extreme in their antagonism to Reason as their opponents sometimes believed, the Oxford Movement was one part of that great swing of opinion against Reason as the Age of Reason had understood it and used it. Through Europe ran the reaction against the aridity of common sense, against the pride of rationalism. There is little in common, of religion, between Keble and Goethe, between Pusey and Victor Hugo. The scepticisms of Hume and Kant, the romantic poets or novelists, the new historians, the shock of Robespierre and the temple of Reason, the Evangelical or pietistic theologians, the desire to justify the past and to value tradition and history in the face of the critical cuts of rationalism – the revolt against Reason and 'enlightenment' – cannot rightly be seen in terms of a few simple forces. But the Oxford Movement was part of this reaction. The leaders wanted to find a place for the poetic or the aesthetic judgment; their hymnody shared in the feelings and evocations of the romantic poets; they wished to find a place and value for historical tradition, against the irreverent or sacrilegious hands of critical revolutionaries for whom no antiquity was sacred; they suspected the reason of common sense as shallow; they wanted to justify order and authority in Church as well as State.

It is safe to say that the Movement would not have taken the form which it took without the impetus of ecclesiastical and secular politics. For example, one characteristic doctrine of the

Oxford men was that high doctrine of the episcopal and priestly ministry which is usually described in the phrase *apostolic succession*. This high doctrine of the ministry was lent power in Church and State because in 1833 dissent from the Church of England and Ireland seemed more potent than at any time since the surrender of King Charles I to the armies of the Scots. Irish Roman Catholics (or English Roman Catholics, but less commonly and less vociferously) had begun (since the Roman Catholic Emancipation of 1829) to sit in the Parliament at Westminster and to use their freedom against the Church of Ireland, still linked indissolubly to the Church of England. The Reform Act of 1832, in revising the constituencies and abolishing the rotten boroughs and extending the franchise, weakened the Tory traditions upon which ecclesiastical authority seemed to rest politically; and who knew what would happen when the Whigs began to 'reform' the Church according to their own notions? It was necessary, politically necessary, that the clergy of the Church of England should look to leaders who would declare that the authority of the church does not rest upon the authority of the State; that the Church possesses a divine authority whatever the State may do, even if the State should be represented by an indifferent or a persecuting government; that the authority of the bishop or the vicar rests not upon his national or his social position, but upon his apostolic commission. All this was politically necessary; it happened, *mutatis mutandis*, among the Presbyterians of the Church of Scotland for the same reasons, and among the Ultramontanes of the Church of France for similar reasons. If the government, which has for so long given privileges and fetters, seems to be at last neutral amidst the religious divisions of Ireland; if the government seems to lay rough hands upon ancient Church endowments without consulting the authorities of the Church; if the government must henceforth take serious account of the demands or even the prejudices of non-Anglicans in the House of Commons – then it is time to assert that even if the Church were disestablished and disendowed, even if there were a complete separation between Church and State, even if the State followed the example of the United States of America and became outwardly and constitutionally indifferent to religion, the Church of England has still a claim upon the allegiance of Englishmen; a claim upon their allegiance not simply because they are Englishmen and this is the Church of England; not simply because this religion is part of national tradition or is suitable to the national character; not simply because this is the religion of their forefathers. It still has a claim upon the allegiance of Englishmen because this Church is teaching Catholic truth, and as such is the authorized and commissioned agent of Christ and his apostles to the people of this country.

There was, then, a political impetus; a revolution in the relations between Church and State, even if the extent and consequences of this revolution were still half known or half perceived.

But a political impetus does not create religious thought. It affords it opportunity, gives it point and purpose, establishes it as effective. The high Anglicanism of the Oxford Movement was not quite identical with the high Anglicanism which had existed for two hundred years and more. But the difference was not the result of the political crisis. The power of the Movement's religious ideas sprang from somewhere deeper in men's souls and minds than their contemporary ideas of ecclesiastical expediency.

THE HIGH CHURCH TRADITION

The word *high* began to be used in this connexion shortly before the Revolution of 1688. It meant, in its original intention, strict; a man who was 'stiff for the Church of England'; rigid; careful and precise in observing the rules of the Church about prayer and fasting, even perhaps when those rules had begun to seem archaic; a man who stood for the privileges of the Church against the dissenters; a strong defender of the Establishment. The phrase *high churchman* had once a political tang to it, and was easily prefaced by the word *Tory*. This kind of high churchmanship was potent or impotent with the fortunes of the Tory party. In crude outline, it was weak under William and Mary, powerful under Queen Anne, impotent under the first two Georges, and rising to power again at the end of the century with the growing fear of radicalism and the dissent which radicalism was held, not without reason, to accompany.

But the high church tradition in religious thought contained more than this.

A 'high churchman' in (for example) 1800 would probably reverence King Charles I and keep the day of his death as a day of martyrdom. He would think that Charles died for the maintenance of the Church of England and its episcopal or apostolic ministry; that the responsibility for his death lay with the Roundheads who were the ancestors of the Whigs, and with the Presbyterians and independents who were the ancestors of the modern dissenter.

He would probably think that the Revolution of 1688 was far less 'glorious' than the Whig historians portrayed it; and he might well sympathize with those who, having taken their allegiance to King James II, refused to take an oath of allegiance to King William III – he might even have sympathies with the Jacobites, however archaic and dead their cause seemed by now to be. He might resent the safeguards for the Presbyterian religion of Scotland, established in consequence of the Revolution of 1688, and befriend or honour the little groups of Scottish Episcopalians.

He would probably think ill of any arrangement which might be held to suggest that the Protestants of the continental churches and the members of the Church of England were national allies, or equally, and without distinction, common members of a 'Protestant Church'. In the later years of the eighteenth century, the SPCK began to use German missionaries in India; some English high churchmen openly disapproved of the arrangement.

Here, at least, is a conviction which cannot be explained merely in terms of political churchmanship. Though there was some connexion between its growth and the suspicion of Dutch William and his natural affection for the Presbyterians, or of German George and his natural affection for his own Lutherans, the conviction would be inexplicable only on these terms. It is explicable only as a doctrine, as a conviction based upon principles of religious authority, and grounded not in political need but in theological thought.

How was it that an important wing of English churchmen, whose Reformation had accepted the impetus and influence of the Reformation in Germany and Switzerland, could so sharply distinguish between themselves and the contemporary heirs of the German and Swiss Reformations?

The first Elizabethan Archbishop of Canterbury, Matthew Parker, talked of a golden mediocrity (that is, a golden mean or *via media*) which his more continentally minded friends thought to be a leaden mediocrity, a mingle-mangle, an unfortunate compound of popery and the Gospel. In the intention of Parker, a golden mediocrity was aimed to preserve within the fold of the one Church both the extreme parties which divide English religion, the continentally trained Protestants who were faithful to their masters in Geneva or Zurich, and the leaders of Queen Mary's Church, who had been convinced by events in the reigns of Edward VI and Mary herself that Catholicism included allegiance to the See of Rome. To some extent moderation succeeded. A Protestant of 'Swiss Reformed' sympathies like John Jewel at first accepted it with reluctance and later, if not with enthusiasm, at least with loyalty. The number of persons who felt that their allegiance to the Pope prevented them from participating in the communion of the Church of England was at first comparatively small. But the decisive adherent of Geneva on the one side, and the decisive adherent of Rome upon the other, could do nothing else but work for change in the constitution and doctrine of the Church of England. Golden mediocrity never commanded the affections of the whole country. What is significant for our purpose, however, is that within the Protestantism of England, circumstances, political and religious needs, created more room for the traditionally minded than was possible anywhere outside Lutheranism. The church historian of the seventeenth century, Thomas Fuller, said that the Thirty-Nine Articles were like children's clothes, made of a larger size so that the children might grow up into them. Whether the original authors of the Articles were looking for that breadth and liberty, assigned to them by a more Latitudinarian age, is doubtful. The statement effectively represents the way in which Anglican moderation was seen to have room for persons attached, in mind or affection or devotion, to tradition. The more conservative and medieval elements in Cranmer's prayer books, or the continuation of the ancient mode of consecrating bishops, were perhaps important only to a few of the leaders of religion during the first twenty years of Elizabeth's reign. They became increasingly important thenceforth, to an always growing and influential section of English opinion.

One of the encouragements to the conservatives was the advance of scholarship during the later sixteenth century and after; especially the advances made by students of the early Church and the Fathers. It is hardly put too strongly if we say that scholarship discovered the Fathers to support the Calvinists less, and the conservatives more, than the scholars of the middle sixteenth century thought or expected. The great Reformers all appealed to the Fathers. Their appeal was subsidiary and secondary to the appeal to the Bible; but they had not supposed that the Christian Church had, from the very beginning, misunderstood the Biblical message, and therefore the evidence of the early Church possessed a theological and controversial importance. Calvin, indeed, won a measure of his influence through the depth and readiness of his patristic scholarship.

But, as the sixteenth century drew towards its end, patristic scholarship became more effective. The Lutherans led the way; the Catholics followed. Great editions of patristic sources were printed, better texts were slowly made available, newly discovered manuscripts were published. The critical methods were still in embryo; it was still, in 1600, difficult, if not impossible, to determine with security whether many of the works purporting to be ancient were, in fact, ancient or were spurious productions of a later age. Not until the second half of the seventeenth century was the scholarly method becoming sound in its treatment, assisted by printed collections, by comparison of texts, by study of linguistic style and environment, and all those means with which modern scholarship is familiar. But already, in 1600, the knowledge of the texts was making a momentous difference to the study of the early Church. St Augustine, to whom everyone looked back for guidance in the doctrines of justification, grace, and predestination, had once risen head and shoulders above the other teachers of the ancient Church. In 1630 he was still a giant; but he had been placed in a wider context of learning, and especially against a background of Greek thought. It was found that the Fathers, taken as a whole, were not so clearly unanimous upon the doctrine of predestination as some authors had at one time contended. It was found that St Jerome, who had contended for the essential parity between bishop and presbyter, was not in agreement with all other teachers of the ancient Church, and that in St Ignatius, and even in St Cyprian, the primitive Church had allowed high honour and order to the bishop as distinct from the presbyter. The ancient Church, when seen by the historians, was found to have valued the single life, thought private confession and spiritual direction to be useful, bestowed reverence upon the Blessed Virgin Mary and the saints, used formal and sometimes elaborate liturgies.

In short, it may be repeated, the advance of patristic scholarship befriended the conservative and traditional elements everywhere in Protestantism; and nowhere more significantly than within the Church of England.

If we look at the group of Anglicans between (say) 1610 and 1640, we find that they are Protestants, and, in many respects, within the normal inheritance of Reformed thought; just as Hooker, for all his knowledge of Aristotle and St Thomas Aquinas, and for all his desire to controvert Calvinism, had been unmistakably a disciple (though not an uncritical disciple) of Swiss Reformed thought. And yet the atmosphere was curiously different from the atmosphere anywhere else in Protestantism, even if parallels may be found among the Lutherans. In George Herbert, John Donne, Nicholas Ferrar, Lancelot Andrewes, John Cosin, Thomas Jackson, William Laud, there is an air which is somehow redolent of Catholicism while it is still Reformed. In Herbert, or in Donne, we may find some of the best of Reformed theology, whether pastoral or dogmatic. There is no question of repudiating the Reformation. And yet the air is fresh, and not blowing simply from the usual quarters in Protestant thought. Part of this freshness springs from patristic study; part from a measure of Platonic philosophy, which was infused into contemporary minds with revolutionary impact after the long reign of nominalism throughout the unmetaphysical epoch of the Reformation, and which (in this group of men) may be found at its most theological in Thomas Jackson. In their attitude to the visible world is a sacramentalism which is not easy to find among the Protestant authors of the sixteenth century.

The man that looks on glass
On it may stay his eye
Or, if he chooseth, through it pass
And then the heaven espy.

Both these elements – an appeal to the Fathers as interpreters of Scripture, and a sacramentalism of nature and the world, into which the sacraments of the Church fitted easily – were to be fundamental to the mind of the Oxford Movement. From this background came Laud's quest for the 'beauty of holiness', for altars in their old places, and protected by rails in a sanctuary; Andrewes's book of private prayers, wonderfully drawn from the ancient liturgies as well as from Scripture; Cosin's desire to utilize traditional ornaments in the chapel of Peterhouse or the cathedral at Durham.

The higher value placed upon the episcopal ministry in the Church of England came from the patristic background. But its contemporary importance arose from a more ecclesiastical and less theoretical question, the struggle with the Puritans.

The earliest Elizabethan bishops had not invariably exacted ordination by a bishop as a condition for holding posts in the Church of England. The known exceptions are very few, but they show, what would on other grounds be expected, that the bishops at first recognized the sufficiency for this purpose of (for example) Presbyterian ordination overseas. The Puritans, however, believed that the Presbyterian ministry was of divine right; and therefore that it was their duty to persuade the magistrate to overthrow the episcopal ministry among the other reforms to which he was called. In its extreme form, this programme created enemies for the bishops on grounds of conscience – or, at the practical level, trouble-makers in several dioceses. It was soon natural that the bishops, as administrators, should seek to control or restrain extremists. One chief measure of such control was to insist upon episcopal ordination; for otherwise an extremist, denied ordination in England, might seek it in Amsterdam or Geneva, and return. This control was, at first, an administrative act, based more upon pastoral expediency than upon theological doctrine. Only as the controversy sharpened did it seem necessary to assert the rightness of an episcopal ministry; and when (from 1589 or 1590 onwards) this was asserted against the Puritans,

Anglican theologians found the resources of the new patristic scholarship ready to hand. By 1610 there was an influential body of thought which believed, on grounds of historical study and historical continuity, that the episcopal ministry in its traditional form was 'God-given'. They did not deny that the ministries of the continental Protestants were good; but they believed that this ministry was the best, the complete ministry as God had intended his Church to be ordered.

The Civil War and the Commonwealth and the Protectorate achieved for this body of opinion a new and persuasive status. In the minds of non-Calvinists, Calvinism was now associated with disloyalty to the Church of England. Whatever might be said of extremists, this had not been true of Calvinists before 1640. Three out of the six Archbishops of Canterbury from Parker to Laud would not have disdained the theology of Switzerland: one of the most eminent English theologians of the early seventeenth century, Davenant, was a moderate Calvinist, and also Bishop of Salisbury. After 1640 there was not to be another Archbishop of Canterbury as 'Reformed' as Grindal, or Whitgift, or Abbot, until Sumner during the middle of the nineteenth century. This theology was associated, however unjustly and however faintly, with the killing of the King, with the overthrow of the constitution of the Church of England, with religious strife, and wrongheaded zeal and business, with disloyalty in Church and State. This was to have long consequences in English religious history. The descendants of the Puritans found it difficult to feel as fully at home in the Church of England as their ancestors had felt before 1640. There was a barrier of psychological association, too rarely recognized, for the Evangelical Anglicans of the eighteenth century to overcome. Many Evangelicals of 1800 were altogether loyal to the Church of England as they understood it, and for themselves felt completely at home in it. The high churchman had some half-conscious association in his mind which prevented him from recognizing them to be truly at home. To him they seemed to bring with them a touch of the alien intruder. The 'Anglican tradition' had come to be conceived as a tradition which did not include Calvinism. That tradition ran through Hooker, and Laud, and Thorndike, and Bull, and Jeremy Taylor; not through Whitaker, and Davenant, and Hall, and Baxter.

When the men of the Oxford Movement claimed to be representing the 'authentic' Anglican position in theology, they meant this. To them, Calvinism seemed by its history to have sacrificed any right which it might once have possessed to be counted an authentic portion of the tradition. And it has to be confessed that the rigidities of the Restoration settlement in 1660–2, by excluding men like Baxter from the ministry, and then by imposing severe restrictions upon dissent, had taken the most effectual step towards removing them.

The theology of the Church of England, though weakened by these rigidities, was preserved from impoverishment by a succession of remarkable thinkers. On the one side were the Platonists of Cambridge, continuing and extending brilliantly if sometimes perilously that Christian philosophizing which we have observed early in the century in minds like Jackson. On the other were the great students of the Fathers – Henry Hammond, Herbert Thorndike, Bramhall, Jeremy Taylor, Pearson, Gunning. The latter no longer looked for their inspiration to the school of Zurich, or of Geneva, or even of Wittenberg. They looked to antiquity, and systematically attempted to draw out the implications of antiquity for religious doctrine and religious practice. It was, therefore, natural that their thought should diverge increasingly from the thought of the continental Protestants; and thence begins that strange air of isolation which Clement Webb used to notice as a particular feature of much Anglican thought between 1650 and 1850.

The divergence was most marked, at the time, in Luther's key to the true church, the doctrine of justification. It was hardly conceivable that a church, Lutheran or Reformed, should not hold to the doctrine of justification by faith alone; and this is the interpretation of which the Thirty-Nine Articles of the Church of England are most readily patient. But Reformed theology was no longer the chief guide; and on the left of the Calvinists the anarchies of Civil War had thrown up a chaos of sects, few of them important (as the Quakers were to be) but some of them seeming to tend towards an antinomian interpretation of the doctrine of justification by faith – 'provided that I cling to Christ's Cross, it matters not what works I do'. To Luther and his contemporaries, the peril seemed to be a works-religion, to the neglect or destruction of the Gospel of faith. To the theologians of the Restoration the peril seemed to be an antinomian religion, to the neglect or destruction of good works.

They therefore attempted to frame their doctrine of justification in language which allowed more to the necessity of good works and human endeavour than had been common among Protestant divines. Few went as far as Jeremy Taylor, who minimizes the doctrine of original sin until it cannot be observed.

In the New Testament St Paul said that we are justified, not by the good which we do, which is always inadequate, but by our faith in God through Christ. St James said that we are justified by the good which we do and not by our 'mere' faith. Christian tradition always interpreted St James in the light of St Paul – put crudely, it saw that Paul was more right and that some of James's phrases, by themselves, were misleading. George Bull (1669) argued that St James was more right and some of Paul's phrases, by themselves, were misleading. Few high Anglicans went so far as George Bull, and none went so far as Jeremy Taylor.

But this veering away from the old, sharp, language of faith alone became, in some measure, characteristic of high Anglican thought in the later seventeenth century. Those divines sought to preserve what they believed the Reformation to have rightly defended; in particular, they eschewed the doctrine of merit. But they were eager to call attention to the needs of the soul's growth in sanctification, needs which they felt the extreme forms of the doctrine of 'faith alone' to have underestimated.

There were now three main differences of emphasis, therefore, between the non-Calvinist tradition of Anglican thought and the main stream of Protestant thought and practice upon the continent, whether Lutheran or Reformed. The English divines looked for their divinity in Scripture and the Fathers, and though they found Luther or Calvin to be sometimes useful, not inevitably more useful than (for example) St Thomas Aquinas. The continental divines (if it may be permitted thus to generalize, while we remember that any such generalization must be liable to exceptions) still saw the ancient Church through the eyes of the Reformation, and though they found the Fathers sometimes useful, not inevitably more useful than St Thomas Aquinas. The English divines believed in justification by faith in such language as to insist upon the necessity of good works; the continental divines might assent to the language as a matter of theory, but (when fully representative of their own tradition) preferred the more vigorous expressions of 'faith alone'. The English divines affirmed episcopacy to be, though not the only 'good' ministry (for the Reformation upon the continent, they said, had been less fortunate in its circumstances than ours), at least the best, the God-ordained ministry, and the historic mode of its transmission to be part of that divine ordinance. The continental divines (when they were rather Lutheran than Reformed) might recognize the episcopate to be a reasonable arrangement of the Church administration, might sometimes allow that, for purposes of reunion and peace, it could be good for a Lutheran Church to accept episcopal orders.

Together with these three main points of difference, there was a further difference between the high Anglican and the Reformed (though not between the high Anglican and the Lutheran). The Calvinist tradition wanted much simplicity in ritual and ornament, and anything that was not simplicity needed warrant from the Bible. Since Hooker's demonstration *Of the Laws of Ecclesiastical Polity* (1593–7), the high Anglican claimed with confidence that the Church could order 'things indifferent' to edification. Unless Scripture explicitly excluded a practice or ordered a practice, the Church might (under God) make arrangements for the due ordering of decent worship. It was no sound argument against the surplice, or incense, or the sign of the Cross in baptism, to affirm that the papists misused them. If that had once been a plausible argument when men and women were trained in erroneous ideas, it was a plausible argument no longer. And while no one wished the churches of the land to be clothed in a 'meretricious gaudiness', it was almost more important not to beware of an opposite extreme. And therefore high churchmen in the England of the later seventeenth century continued to desire that altars should be in their ancient places, and that confession might be available to those who wished it. These desires were not, however, exclusive to English high churchmen, among Protestants. They were still to be found among some of the Lutherans.

The gap between high English churchmen and the Protestants of the continent was widened by the age of reason. As the seventeenth century turned into the eighteenth, there came the age of Locke and of the reasonableness of Christianity. Reason, by its nature, is not kindly to history, or at least thinks little of arguments from history. The question that matters is not whether anyone has believed x in the past, but whether x is true. All that complex of new science, and mathematics, and invention, and empirical philosophy, worked the revolution throughout European divinity. Neither the Reformers nor the Fathers were any longer obligatory as spectacles with which to examine the Scripture, not even (according to some eminent thinkers) useful. Improved philosophy and improved knowledge of nature rendered these guides old-fashioned if not obsolete or misleading. We should find more help, in understanding St Paul, from Locke than from Luther or from St Augustine – so argued Latitudinarians in England.

The high churchmen, or their remnant, were sundered from the dominant Latitudinarians by a wide gulf. Their thought was now liable to the charge of archaism. But so far as they stood by the principles of their predecessors, they were further sundered, not only from the leading English divines of the Latitudinarian school, but from the equally rationalizing theology of the continent. During the eighteenth century even the Lutherans seemed to depart from their own tradition. Now, at last, the practice of confession fell into disuse in the Lutheran churches. Their sacramental theology grew less sacramental as it sought to become more rational. Their more daring men made tentative efforts at the higher criticism of the Bible. By 1800 the remnant of English high churchmen, though they avowed themselves still to be Protestant, saw little in common between their Protestantism and the Protestantism of Geneva or Wittenberg, which they were now inclined, more than at any previous epoch since the Reformation, to repudiate.

The Latitudinarian dominance in English thought widened the area of belief possible for English churchmen. It so reinterpreted the Thirty-Nine Articles as to make them no longer the doctrinal hedge or guide which once, perhaps (but only perhaps), they successfully formed.

The first widening was due, not to the Latitudinarians, but to the Laudian divines who wished for stronger language about the necessity of good works in the doctrine of justification, and were called by their opponents 'Arminians'. The Thirty-Nine Articles were intended, above all, to enshrine the doctrine of justification by faith alone. They were not intended to be rigid or exclusive upon the point; but such an article as number XIII, with its teaching that the works of the heathen cannot be good in God's sight, was only compatible with the idea of justification which Luther proclaimed. George Bull and others, in their attempt to interpret St Paul by St James, wished to find room for the good works of the heathen as truly good; and Bull manipulated the article by dividing the title from the text in order to discover in it what might later have been called a 'non-natural' sense. There was nothing dishonourable or even casuistical about this interpretation, for it was beginning to be agreed, by the end of the seventeenth century, that any dogmatic formula, at least of 'human' construction, may need reinterpretation in the light of future thought. The Latitudinarians continued to widen the opinion permissible to one adhering to the Thirty-Nine Articles – first, and moderately, in Gilbert Burnet's exposition of the articles, and later in the century by theologians like Blackburne or Paley or Hey or Watson, who held their places in the Church of England, subscribing to the Thirty-Nine Articles, but certainly not subscribing to all of them in their natural sense; and it was argued by some that the Articles could not have been intended to bind all English minds for all time, whatever the results of Scriptural study, and that they were, therefore, intended to be articles of peace in the Church, not to be articles exacting an *ex animo* assent to the doctrines individually contained therein.

The men of the Oxford Movement naturally disapproved of these endeavours, by a left wing, to widen the basis of communion. It seemed to them to be an attempt to weaken that authority of the Church which they were eager to proclaim. But it must be observed that this widening made it easier for them to affirm or even to speculate. It would have been anachronistic, or at least ineffectual, to accuse their doctrine of justification of incompatibility with the Thirty-Nine Articles, as once George Bull was accused by his opponents. When Newman published Tract 90 and showed, incidentally, that the Articles need not be so contradictory to all the doctrines of the Church of Rome as was formerly believed, he shocked a wide public, and faced charges of insincerity, and casuistry, and dishonesty. Whether or not Newman's method was sound is a question. But the novelty was not in his handling the Articles to extract the maximum breadth from their language. The novelty lay in his handling the Articles in a Catholic direction. It was natural that liberals like A. P. Stanley should support Newman's right so to interpret the Articles, and warmly resist any attempt by authority to condemn Tract 90.

The widening of the area of belief, and the turning of an assent or subscription to the Thirty-Nine Articles into a general assent rather than a particular adherence to every clause (even before such general assent received a measure of recognition by Parliament in the Clerical Subscription Act of 1865), were appropriate and perhaps necessary for the Oxford men. Their tradition long sought to draw its divinity from the wells of antiquity, and assumed that the Articles of the sixteenth century would be found to be in agreement with the divinity thence drawn. The mode of the Church's worship, and the forms of the Prayer Book, and the corporate mind of Church and bishops, were more important to them than the external propositions of faith declared by the divines of 1571, confronted as they were by particular circumstances and problems of the Reformation, not all of which were applicable to the nineteenth century. The Articles were not as expressive of the living mind of the Church as was its tradition of prayer; they must be conformable, but need not be directive.

The high churchmen of the Restoration had associated their churchmanship with another doctrine, declared to be derived from Scripture – the doctrine of the divine right of kings. King James I had said, 'No bishop, no king', and the Civil War seemed to prove the case. The doctrines of Calvinists had often included the right or duty of resistance to an ungodly sovereign; the restoration of King Charles II, in being the restoration of a truer religion, included as part of its orthodoxy the belief that resistance to a lawful sovereign was an offence against God as well as man.

In some circumstances, such a doctrine was near to being self-destructive. It needed only the accession of a Roman Catholic sovereign to put high churchmen into something of the predicament of a Cranmer, who believed in the supreme headship of the

Crown and was ordered by the Crown (in the person of Queen Mary) not to believe in the supreme headship of the Crown. After the Revolution of 1688, several of the best high churchmen believed that loyalty to the Stuart King was morally binding upon them. They went into the non-juring schism. Some were suspect of Jacobitism; and after the accession of George I in 1714, the whole high tradition was weakened.

The high church party was slow to perceive the consequence. It continued to revere King Charles the Martyr. But it was inevitable that some high churchmen should feel after a doctrine of a Church, as independent of the State. While the non-jurors were contending for the independent rights of the Church against the State, where the law of Caesar conflicted with the law of God, a few who would not carry their protest to the length of schism were concerned to state a doctrine like apostolic succession, which was a sign that the spiritual powers of the Church were not derived from the State and might have a claim upon the soul's allegiance superior to the claim of the State.[1]

For the most part, during the period from 1715 to 1830, the assertion of a spiritual independence from the State was not characteristic of the high tradition. That tradition was content to be conservative; still hostile to dissent, still politically Tory, still deeply attached to the Prayer Book, still concerned about sound doctrine – but it was coming, in the unemotional age, to be 'high and dry', as the Oxford leaders called it. Its ethics were guided by *The Whole Duty of Man*; and its piety tended to be sober, earnest, dutiful, austere, or even prosaic in expression. Take such a parson, and place him in the atmosphere of a new age, where feeling is permissible, where poetry is a high road to truth, and you would no longer find a 'high and dry' churchman. You would find a John Keble.

The Evangelicals contributed to the formation of the high church party both by influence and by reaction. As they preached their way into the hearts of rich and poor, neglectful of parish boundaries, friendly with dissent, calling for conversion, putting the Bible before the simplest people, teaching the necessity of faith, favouring the conviction of assurance in salvation, and

---

[1] E. G. Hill in *Municipium Ecclesiasticum* (1697), and cf. George Every, *The High Church Party 1688–1718* (1956), pp. 85ff.

distrusting language about good works, they encouraged by
reaction the 'stiff quality', the *high* element in high churchmanship. The high churchman believed that Evangelical language
about conversion might mislead Christian men into forgetting the
regenerating grace which had been bestowed upon them in
baptism; that their language about justification might minimize
the growth of the soul in sanctification; that their language of
assurance might lead to complacency, whereas the soul should
work out its own salvation in fear and trembling; that thus to set
forth the Bible, without reference to the historic community of
Christians, to whom the Scriptures had been given, was to breed
error and individualism; that the rights of the parish and of the
incumbent should be preserved.

On the other hand, the Evangelicals contributed more than any
other group to transforming the high and dry men into the new
high churchmen of the nineteenth century. There is a certain
continuity of piety between the Evangelical Movement and the
Oxford Movement. There were other reasons why the high
churchmen should learn not to be afraid of the feelings –
romantic literature and art, the sense of affection and the
sensibility of beauty pervading European thought, the flowering
of poetry, the medievalism of the novel or of architecture. But in
religion the Evangelicals taught the Oxford men not to be afraid
of their feelings. Both Newman and Pusey brought into the
movement a strong element of Evangelical sensibility and language, whether or not they may rightly have been called Evangelicals, at any stage of their lives (Newman, perhaps, more rightly
than Pusey). The poetry of Keble's *Christian Year* is the outward
sign of the new sensibility in the piety of high churchmen:

> Sun of my soul, thou Saviour dear,
> It is not night if thou be near –

such language would have seemed 'enthusiastic' and strained to
the old-fashioned high churchman, and to the piety of *The Whole
Duty of Man*. It was not difficult for an Evangelical like Samuel
Wilberforce, the son of the great slave-emancipator, to pass from
an Evangelical world to the world of high churchmanship, in the
crisis of the 1830s, when the revival of the Church as a divine

society seemed imperative in the face of a Parliament that was no longer wholly Anglican.

Probably it is this element of feeling, which marks the vague distinction between the old-fashioned high churchmen and the Oxford men, the desire to use poetry as a vehicle of religious language, the sense of awe and mystery in religion, the profundity of reverence, the concern with the conscience not only by way of duty, but by growth towards holiness. It was not so much a difference of doctrine. It was primarily a difference of atmosphere. It was a concern for the evocative and the reverent, a sense of the whispering beauty and truth of divinity as its presence surrounded the soul. The difference may be seen in a man who is regarded (and with reason) as a member of the Oxford Movement, William Palmer, Fellow of Worcester College. Palmer was one of the most learned high churchmen in Oxford, and by his liturgical studies enriched and inspired many of the Tractarians. He possessed a clear, cool head, a coherent and well-arranged mind, a knowledge of logic and of the scholastic method. In 1838 he published his treatise *Of the Church*, an exposition of the high doctrine of the Church which is formally the ablest exposition provoked by those times, and won the respect of Perrone, the leading theologian of the contemporary Roman schools. The book is marked by all the qualities of Palmer's mind, cool reasoning, system, relentless logic, such intelligibility as to be impossible to misunderstand. And yet it should be classed rather with the thought of the high and dry school than with the thought of the Tractarians themselves. Its scholastic qualities rely upon the clear proposition and the syllogism. There is no mystery, no sense of depth, no feeling – all is tidy, the mystery is cleared away, the system is propounded in its rigidities, the ends are rounded so that truth may not seem rugged. It is a conscientious book; but it is not what Newman, or Keble, or Pusey, or Froude, or Williams would have written. Apostolic succession is soberly stated; but it is stated somewhat as though it was a cold piece of machinery for averting heresy and schism, and in it there is nothing of the personal, nothing evocative of historical continuity in the power of the gospel.

In his *Apologia*, Newman painted an unfriendly picture of

Palmer, one of the few unfriendly pictures among the generous portraits of his former colleagues in the Church of England:

Mr Palmer had many conditions of authority and influence. He was the only really learned man among us. He understood theology as a science; he was practised in the scholastic mode of controversial writing; and, I believe, was as well acquainted, as he was dissatisfied, with the Catholic schools. He was as decided in his religious views as he was cautious and even subtle in their expression, and gentle in their enforcement. But he was deficient in depth; and besides, coming from a distance, he never had really grown into an Oxford man,[2] nor was he generally received as such; nor had he any insight into the force of personal influence and congeniality of thought in carrying out a religious theory – a condition which Froude and I considered essential to any true success in the stand which had to be made against Liberalism. Mr Palmer had a certain connection, as it may be called, in the Establishment, consisting of high church dignitaries, archdeacons, London rectors and the like, who belonged to what was commonly called the high-and-dry school. They were far more opposed than he was to the irresponsible action of individuals. Of course, their *beau ideal* in ecclesiastical action was a board of safe, sound, sensible men. Mr Palmer was their organ and their representative; and he wished for a committee, an association, with rules and meetings, to protect the interests of the Church in its existing peril.

Palmer had turned the artillery of his logic upon the thought of Newman during his last two or three years as an Anglican. Perhaps this application of cold scholasticism helped to create in Newman's mind the touch of bias which marks this brilliant portrait and renders it something of a caricature. But if allowance is made for the element of caricature, it is an excellent and illuminating example of a criticism of the high and dry by the high. They were shallow; their theory attempted to rest upon the reasoning of its propositions and took no account of the force of personality; they were far too concerned with defending the Church, maintaining the privileges of the establishment; they were sober, sensible men, suspicious of extremism or (in its eighteenth-century sense) enthusiasm. And by contrast, Newman thought of the Oxford men as men of personal influence and enthusiasm, suspicious of sobriety and common sense, anxious to strive after depth and to penetrate mystery even at the expense of clarity, content to be less coherent so long as they were not shallow, using propositions rather as means than as ends, more concerned with truth than with the defence of the Establishment,

[2]   Palmer came from Trinity College, Dublin.

more content even to let the Establishment go so long as truth prevailed. The contrast was exaggerated by Newman. But it represents a real and momentous difference in habit or cast of mind.

KEBLE

In trying to represent the mind of a movement, we are faced with the difficulty that movements have no mind. If we sought to present the mind of the Reformation, Bossuet would soon have something to say with his book on the variations of Protestantism. Froude, or Pusey, or Rose, or Newman, or Keble, each contributed something distinctive to a store which was not always common. Froude believed the doctrine of the Real Presence in the Holy Communion and brought Newman to value it; a poem in Keble's *Christian Year* seemed to deny it. Even the closest of associates may sometimes contradict each other, and on matters which are not unimportant.

Let us take, as a provisional guide, the principle that the mind of the Oxford Movement from 1833 to 1841 is not rightly illustrated by any speculation, doctrine, position, or argument which Newman, or Keble, or Pusey, would (at that date) have rejected. Such a principle is open to the accusation of leaving nothing but a lowest common denominator between the religion and theology of three men. It forces removal of Keble's earlier denial of the doctrine of the Real Presence in the Holy Communion. It forces the removal of those later arguments of Newman as he moved towards becoming a Roman Catholic. More seriously, it forces the removal of a few speculations or theories of real interest for religion but which were characteristic only of Newman's bold mind. But it is a sign that this was a movement of minds, and not an alliance of individual minds, that the doctrine and theology thus left between the three men has certain recognizable features, of details as well as of type; and this doctrine and theology forms the centre of a far wider group of writers and preachers, rooted in the old tradition of high churchmen, receiving fresh impetus both from the crisis of the times and from their leaders in Oxford, but so substantially coherent that it is not misleading to speak of 'the theology of the

Tract-Writers'. The writers of the Tracts issued lists of books declared by them to contain the principles which they were seeking to assert.

Each of these three – Keble, Newman, Pusey – contributed something characteristically his own, as to the success, so to the thought, of the Movement.

Newman believed that Keble was 'the true and primary author' of the Movement, although 'as is usual with great motive-powers', he was 'out of sight'. After achieving the highest rewards of scholarship which the University of Oxford had to offer, Keble retired to be his father's curate in Gloucestershire, and remained in country curacies until he became vicar of Hursley near Winchester in 1836; from 1823 Oxford knew him only as a visitor. But the visitor, though a country clergyman, did not share in the traditional obscurity of that profession after 1827. If he was 'out of sight', as Newman wrote, it was not in the sense that he was out of the public eye. In 1827 he published, with the utmost reluctance, the volume of poetry entitled *The Christian Year*. Its immense popularity as a handbook of devotion was a surprise to him and made no difference to his life or character. He was a deeply modest, quiet, meek man, with no trace of self-confidence, or assertiveness. He went about his country parish conscientiously, unobtrusively, unexcitingly, engaging otherwise only in the scholarship for which he was well fitted, but in which his modesty made him shrink from publication, and which issued, as its most appropriate fruit, in an excellent edition of Hooker's works.

He was not, in spite of Newman, 'out of sight' of the world. From 1831 to 1841 he held the (non-resident) Professorship of Poetry at Oxford. But it was a true judgment in a moral sense. He gave the impression of seeking obscurity, of being fearful of publicity. He eschewed all the arts that gain popular applause. He would allow nothing that might merely captivate, even in the sermons which he preached to his simple parishioners. And there was something about him, perhaps, connected with this, which unfitted him to be the author or leader of a movement. It was once said of him by one who had known and admired him that he had 'no go'. What is the force of the criticism, if it is a criticism? Was there just a hint of dullness being round the corner, to the lively minds which were his equals? Or was it that he seemed to dislike speculative fire and energy? For Keble, in spite of his poetry and his prayer of feeling, was a Tory high churchman of the old school, and thought it the supreme duty to stand in the ancient ways and avoid novelty. Was it the rigidity of the high churchman, who was hostile to dissent or to Evangelicals or to Whigs within the Church of England? If he was gentle and meek, he could nevertheless be roused to indignation by any person or policy that seemed to be trampling upon his Church, which he truly loved (the word is not too strong) as the authentic representative of his Master. And he identified the cause of the Church of England with the cause of Tory high churchmanship. If there is a distinction between decisive adherence to principles and rigidity, then, alone of the four original leaders of the Oxford Movement, Keble seemed at times to pass from the one into the other. It is evident in his university sermons. His own person was the chief link between the Oxford men and the high churchmen of 1688. He represented in the Movement that symbolical reverence for King Charles the Martyr which was one of the principal elements composing the traditional churchmanship of the school.

There was nothing in him to foreshadow the leader in a bold and wide-reaching movement. He was absolutely without ambition. He hated show, and mistrusted excitement. The thought of preferment was steadily put aside both from temper and definite principle. He had no popular aptitudes, and was very suspicious of them. He had no care for the possession of influence; he had deliberately chosen the *fallentis semita vitae*, and to be what his father had been, a faithful and contented country parson, was all that he desired . . . He had not many friends and was no party chief. He was a brilliant University scholar overlaying the plain, unworldly country parson; an old-fashioned English Churchman, with great veneration for the Church and its bishops, and a great dislike of Rome, Dissent and Methodism, but with a quick heart; with a frank, gay humility of soul, with great contempt of appearances, great enjoyment of nature, great unselfishness, strict and severe principles of morals and duty.[3]

His contribution to the mind of the Movement is more difficult of analysis than his personal place and influence within it. Newman kept the day of Keble's assize sermon upon *National*

---

[3] R. W. Church, *The Oxford Movement* (1891), pp. 21–3. I cannot think Church's use of the epithet 'brilliant' to be justified. It suggests qualities which Keble distrusted, and which should not be attributed to him by a sober judgment.

Apostasy (14 July 1833) as the day when the Oxford Movement began. Yet that sermon is untypical of the Movement as it later developed. It denounced the government for its neutrality between the religions of Ireland, represented by its plan for the suppression of Irish bishoprics. The sermon is more akin to the sermons of high churchmen in Queen Anne's reign than to the high churchmanship of Hurrell Froude or Newman. It is high churchmanship with regard to the State and dissent, a claim to retain the rightful privileges of the Establishment, and less markedly the type of high churchmanship which asserted the independent and divine status of the Church, whether the Church was established or disestablished. The sermon collected no disciples, raised no party-standard, asserted nothing but what other high churchmen were saying through the country. The importance of the sermon to the Movement was only in its signal within Newman's mind. The trumpet was sounded, and the warriors began to gather, when Newman started to publish the *Tracts for the Times*. Nor did the trumpet at first sound a sufficiently loud, or at least sufficiently distinctive, note to collect many warriors. The transformation of a few like-minded persons into a 'movement' was not the work of an instant.

Keble collected round him pupils — Isaac Williams, Robert Wilberforce, Hurrell Froude — and won their allegiance by personal stature. It was Froude who persuaded Keble that he ought not to be suspicious of Newman, despite Newman's dialectic, despite his friendship with the liberal philosopher Whately, despite the Evangelical forces in his early life. Keble distrusted dialectic. He had learned to think of Whately the logician as shallow, and irreverent. He was altogether out of sympathy with that school of rational theology which treated Christian truth as though it were a philosophy of life, God as though He were a theory to be demonstrated, and faith as though it were the assent of the mind to proven, or to highly probable, propositions. Faith was a gift, its source the Holy Spirit acting through the authoritative teaching of the Church, its medium the sacraments of the Church. Reason was to expound a given truth; to criticize, or to prove (supposing the latter possible) savoured to Keble of irreverence. In Keble this distrust of the dialectician was more a feeling than a clearly articulated conclusion. But in

Hurrell Froude he captured a mind, it is true from an old-fashioned high church family, resembling his own in its outlook, but a mind that was dialectical and critical and original. 'Froude was a bold rider', wrote Newman, 'as on horseback, so also in his speculations.' Rose said of him, 'with quiet humour' after a long conversation, 'he did not seem to be afraid of inferences'. He brought to bear upon the old tradition, represented by Keble, an inquiring and even revolutionary spirit, 'a free elastic force and graceful versatility of the mind, brimful and overflowing with ideas and views, which were too many and strong even for his bodily strength, and which crowded and jostled against each other in their effort after distinct critical expression', the opposite of all that could be described as 'wooden'. Keble alone could never have understood Newman, the dialectician who had helped Whately to compose his treatise upon logic. It was Froude who brought Newman to reverence Keble, and Keble not to be afraid of Newman.

In this way Keble helped to form the moral ideal of the Movement, more by his person than his thought; and the moral ideal was essential and integral to its theological development. The fact that he was not a don but a country pastor – this alone was momentous for the Movement. It was never to be a movement of mere speculation (which Keble abhorred), a mere movement of the upper mind. It was to be a movement of pastoral and moral care (without which the movement of the mind would stray). The mental picture of pastoral care was still, in the England of 1830, the parson in the country parish. Since 1714, or since 1688, the lower clergy of the Church of England had been 'higher' than their bishops and their flocks. *They* were confronted with the dissenter in their parish, or the itinerant preacher, as the bishop was not. *They* had sought vainly (and sometimes foolishly) to maintain the rights of Convocation. And the Church of England in 1830, despite the Industrial Revolution and the spreading populations of London and the North, was still pre-eminently (and too much) a church of country parishes. The Movement reached out so forcefully from Oxford because it understood the needs of the country parish, because its teaching passed into the shelves of the vicarage library and the ideas of its sermons (or the sermons themselves) into the village pulpit. Keble represented for the Movement this anchor in the parochial clergy of the country. In some ways the most 'typical' figure of the whole Movement is none of the leaders, but Isaac Williams – pupil of Keble; poet; quiet and obscure country parson; avoiding noise and publicity and controversy (though he found it without intending to find it). The truth, Keble had taught the clergy, will not be popular. We must not expect more than a remnant of faithful men. We must expect criticism and even abuse; that is always the way of truth. And we must go about our parishes quietly, diligently, unassertively, but faithful to our commission, leading our people into the community of Christ which is the Church, and therefore keeping from them nothing of that body of truth which the Church declares to us authoritatively, in such a manner as they are each able, in their moral and spiritual condition, to receive it.

The mode of receiving or apprehending doctrine is believed, by all these men, as they react against the 'merely' intellectual, the school of religious philosophy, to be related to moral and spiritual capacity. Though the full Gospel is to be declared, it can only be declared rightly to those who can apprehend it fully, and Christian teachers ought therefore to follow the apostolic example and begin with milk in order that the hearers may grow up and later receive meat. This was a doctrine which the Oxford Movement derived, or thought it derived, from the methods and practice of the primitive Church in instructing its catechumens, the keeping back of the creed until the convert had reached a stage of his Christian education, the exclusion of the unconverted from the holiest rites of the sacraments. Their patristic scholarship dwelt much upon the *disciplina arcani* of the ancients, the 'reserve in communicating religious knowledge', as two celebrated *Tracts for the Times* described it. But their interest in this patristic restraint arose from more contemporary considerations. They shrank from the newer methods of evangelism, used especially among dissenting bodies, where (so they thought) the preacher forcefully declared the holiest and deepest mysteries of the Christian religion before crowds in the effort to secure conversion. There seemed to them to be something irreverent in holding up (for example) the Cross of Calvary before persons whose impenitent or irreverent spirit caused them only to mock. How the impenitent were to be brought to penitence was another question, but they were sure that this was not the divinely given mode of doing so, and perhaps some of the old prejudices of the high church party of the last century also entered their dislike of these methods. Again, they possessed a strong theological interest in 'reserve'. Conscience, not logical reason – the ethical judgment rather than the argumentative judgment – is for all these Tractarians the chief road to religious knowledge. The soul is to grow into apprehending Calvary by doing right, by allowing grace to sanctify.

Despite these practical and theoretical reasons for an interest in the doctrine of reserve (apart from the interest aroused by the desire to follow an example in the early Church), Keble's person and outlook were powerful in this direction. 'Publicity', or anything of the kind, was abhorrent to him. Religious truth was an aweful judgment, to be approached like the burning bush with the shoes off the feet, to be approached with wonder and fear, not with the axe of the critical intellect, or the desire for novelty.

'Don't be original' was the advice which Keble gave to Newman when he read his sermon and found new ideas. Against the rough hands of reformers, he wished to preserve the traditions which he had received in the Church; and therefore to Keble and to many conservatives of this time the word *tradition* is a word of good omen. The Protestant fathers of the Church of England, mindful of medieval corruption, had thought tradition to be an ill-sounding word, to be admitted if at all only under strict safeguards, and had associated it with the traditions of the scribes and Pharisees. But now, at a time when the utility of all ancient institutions is in question, the value of tradition and custom is brought home to every Tory churchman. And among ancient institutions the Church was pre-eminent. It was natural that conservatives should again be ready to hear the word *tradition* upon the lips of theologians. The contemporary need of theology seemed to be a revival or reconsideration of the corporate authority of the Church. Men said, the Bible and the Bible only is the religion of Protestants; and they seemed to mean that every individual should extract from the Bible what his or her individual reason found there, without regard for the corporate judgment of the Christian community. It seemed to Keble, and to

Newman and Froude, imperative to teach the authority of the corporate judgment of the Church, and therefore to understand aright what is meant by Christian tradition.

It was denied by none of the Tractarians (until they were ceasing to be Tractarian) that all things necessary for salvation are found in Scripture. But this was not to confess the Bible and the individual reason to be the sole guides to religious truth. The individual reason strayed and misjudged. The Scriptures had been addressed to primitive congregations which already received a faith from apostolic men, and were therefore never intended to be systematic expositions of doctrine, were never intended to be understood apart from the common faith of the Christians who received them. If this is to be summarized in an epigram (as it was summarized by Dr Hawkins of Oriel College in a long and famous sermon of 1818, preached to a congregation which included the undergraduate Newman), we may say that the Church is to teach, the Bible to prove. The Christian does not first fetch his faith by applying his reason to the critical study of the Bible, but by apprehending the truth from other Christians and thereafter being led by them to find the evidence and proof of these truths in the Scriptures. The Church can neither teach what is contrary to the Scriptures nor add doctrines to the truth taught in the Scriptures. But the individual will not understand the profundities of Scriptural truth, will have but a shallow and misleading notion, until he or she has advanced in the Christian way of life – that is, by sharing in the life of the Christian community and allowing the grace of God to sanctify him through its teaching and its sacraments.

Therefore we may say (and Keble is not afraid of it, though he was much criticized for saying it) that in understanding the Bible it is indispensable to consider the tradition of the primitive Church. The Church not only puts the Bible before our minds. It puts the Bible in a certain light before our minds, and prepares our minds to penetrate into its truth. It arranges the doctrines of the Bible into a system as it delivers them, distinguishes the essentials from the inessentials, gives us help by its treasures of interpretation, and a mode of government and worship which forms the context in which the Scriptures are declared.

Therefore we need, according to Keble, to keep tradition

before us in three spheres: (1) the system and arrangement of fundamental articles – i.e. approach the Scriptures with the creed in mind; (2) the interpretation of Scripture – establishing by the consensus of the early Church, for example, that Melchizedek's feast is rightly seen to be a type of the Eucharist, or the Song of Songs rightly understood as an allegory of the mystical union betwixt Christ and His Church; (3) the discipline, formularies and rites of the Church – of which the New Testament taken alone gives but fragmentary notices – the observance of Sunday, the mode of consecrating the Eucharist.

There was a difference between Keble and Hawkins, not a difference of theory but of attitude, and it was a difference which divided the Tractarians from their predecessors, even from the highest of the high churchmen among their predecessors. Hawkins had a theory of tradition, because he believed it to be necessary if the existing teaching of the Church was to be defended against its adversaries, Unitarian or philosophical. His theory was conservative, preservative. Keble's theory is also, in a manner, preservative – keep the deposit of faith which you inherit. But it is not only preservative. He has begun to compare the teaching and practice, common or popular in the present Church of England, with the teaching or practice of antiquity, and to find the present Church wanting. Therefore the idea of primitive tradition is not only a preservative idea, but a quest for reform. It is a demand for the restoration of, or re-emphasis upon, those beliefs or practices approved or authorized by antiquity but wanting or fragmentary in the present age. 'Is there not a hope', asked Keble, 'that by resolute self-denial and strict and calm fidelity to our ordination vows, we may not only aid in preserving that which remains but also may help to revive in some measure, in this or some other portion of the Christian world, more of the system and spirit of the apostolical age? New truths, in the proper sense of the word, we neither can nor wish to arrive at. But the monuments of antiquity may disclose to our devout perusal much that will be to this age new, because it has been mislaid or forgotten, and we may attain to a light and clearness, which we now dream not of, in our comprehension of the faith and the discipline of Christ.' It is the more powerful in that it comes from the pen, not of Newman, whose mental processes certainly did not run in tram-lines, but of the old-fashioned, retrospective, Tory pastor of a humble country parish.

This concern for the 'tradition' of the ancient and undivided Church is the foundation of Tractarian thought. It is not that they were non-Scriptural, though Newman has been accused (unjustly) of being uninterested in Scripture. No one can read the sermons of Pusey or Newman without discerning how lovingly and reverently they turned the pages of their bibles. But they believed the Bible could only be approached with the proper spirit of reverence when it was approached not with the fallen, objective, detached, intellectualist mind of the individual, but with the eyes of the ancient and undivided Church for which the Biblical texts were in fact written, and which selected some to be Biblical and others not. For this reason they set out to make the Fathers available to the English reader, with something of the same religious spirit in which the Reformers had sought to make the Bible available in the language of the people.

Newman (in Tracts 38 and 41, published in 1834, and in the *Lectures on the Prophetical Office of the Church*, published in 1837) taught this theory in a lucid and extended form, amplifying it as vehemently against Rome as against the Latitudinarian Protestants towards whom its first formulations had looked. In Newman's exposition of the theory the new note of Tractarian thought, compared with the older high churchmen, is still more evident.

There were three charges (in particular) to which this theory of tradition was open: first that the difficulty of finding out what was tradition was worse than the difficulty of finding out what was in Scripture, the writings of the Fathers being a vaster, less coherent, less concordant body of material, and therefore that the argument from tradition removed the real authority in the Church from the faithful and from their pastors into the hands of the Church historians, who could declare with expert information the teaching of the early Church; secondly that it could easily be made to sound like a piece of ecclesiastical machinery for disposing of dissent, as sometimes it sounds when expounded by a schoolman like William Palmer of Worcester College; and thirdly, the practical difficulty of *applying* antiquity, as a reforming measure, to the beliefs and practices of the Church of England in 1835.

The second of these charges – that it is a device – misses the mark in the case of Newman and Pusey and Keble. It is not a negative, nor is it a mere form. It is (if the expression be allowed, for they would not have used it) a sacrament. The Church is seen to be like a living being, with its breath, and its limbs, and its head. And tradition is not like certain sentences spoken from the mouth, though the words of the mouth are part of tradition. It is more like the beating of the heart or the breathing of the lungs, or the character of the man, which is part hidden, part reflected in his appearance, part issuing in his conduct, part appearing in his words. 'Prophets or Doctors', wrote Newman,[4] 'are the interpreters of the revelation . . . Their teaching is a vast system, . . . pervading the Church like an atmosphere, irregular in its shape, from its very profusion and exuberance . . . This I call Prophetical Tradition, existing primarily in the bosom of the Church itself, and recorded in such measure as Providence has determined, in the writings of eminent men.' This atmosphere is best expounded by Newman, because he possessed the most acute and sensitive mind among the leaders, and above all because he possessed by nature and by musical ear, and had developed by practice, a gift of writing good prose. He was incapable of representing tradition as an ecclesiastical device. It was sacramental of the life of heaven, the Church visible as a sign of the invisible. It was an earthly story of the communion of the saints in heaven. His feeling for historical continuity, his affection for the past, his reverence for an otherworldly sanctity, his love of 'orthodoxy' not as orthodoxy or rigidity but as faithfulness to every truth revealed, his sense of the richness and exuberance of the Christian tradition – all these enabled him to set forth tradition as a kind of sacrament.

If Palmer was the clearest head, because the doctrine is mechanical, Newman, because the doctrine is not mechanical, gives most trouble to his commentators. Perrone, the leading schoolman of Rome, believed his expositions to be muddled – but unjustly. Everything is blurred, nothing has sharp edges;

[4] *Lectures on the Prophetical Office* (1838 edn), pp. 305–6.

everything is irradiated with the light from heaven, nothing is lit by the bare, drab, light of a dull afternoon. He saw mystery lurking at every turn; he had learned, intellectually from Bishop Butler, and emotionally from his quasi-evangelical upbringing and from the romantic environment of the day, that the mere intellect skims the surface of reality. He attributed to a mixture of influences from Butler and Keble his belief that 'material phenomena are both the types and the instruments of real things unseen'. Tradition is the life of the Church, which, though visible, is more invisible than visible. Tradition, apostolic succession, ministry, episcopate – despite the strength of his language against dissent, he seldom sees these as engines against dissent. He sees them as rungs in Jacob's ladder, where the angels ascend and descend.

NEWMAN AND FAITH

It is easy to exaggerate Newman's part in the Movement and indeed to think of him as the whole. We so often see the Tractarians through the spectacles of Newman's *Apologia*, and read it as the development of a single mind. Clement Webb wrote to the contrary that though Newman was the greatest figure in the Movement, he was not 'even typical' of it. I should not like to subscribe to this opinion, in spite of the authority of its progenitor. It appears to me that the Newman of the years until 1839 or 1840, even if (like any individual) he had idiosyncrasies which cannot properly be described as belonging to the Movement, represents all its qualities – its sacramentalism and sense of mystery, its controversial confidence, its doctrine of authority, its theory of religious knowledge, its pastoral impetus – are not the Parochial Sermons of Newman the 'typical' doctrine of the Movement at its highest, contributing to, rather than creating, a body of theological and devotional thought? It is of the essence of the Movement that its best writing should be enshrined in parochial sermons.

But (I have heard it said) he was a sceptic, not an honest doubter, not even a man with a faith seeking to understand itself.

This is one of the most intractable problems about his thought. He gives ground for the charge. There is a sceptical streak – the

Essay on Ecclesiastical Miracles at the lowest, a jumble of twisted dialectic about historical evidence, which it is not too strong to describe as repellent, in a man who possessed (as Acton later confessed) the potentialities of a historian.[5] James Froude, at one time his disciple, thought of him later as irrational and revolted against the irrationalism. Some of Newman's work upon the lives of the saints, and his Tract 85, show something of the same streak. He had learned (too much?) from Bishop Butler's *Analogy* – had he almost learned that we need not shrink from paradox because the world is in any case full of paradox and so we must expect it? He enjoyed argument, and occasionally there is too much argument, too much cleverness.

Yet Newman's was the most profound exposition of the Tractarian doctrine of faith. Doubtless there must be confessed to be a streak of scepticism, about the metaphysical realm, in Pusey and Keble and the others. The whole Movement was fighting the aridity (as it believed) of Paley and Whately and the school of religious philosophers, was engaged in showing the lack of value, *for religious purposes*, of the logical intellect. Newman was untypical in that he possessed a dialectical mind for his purpose. He was not untypical as he formulated the doctrine of conscience and faith in his university sermons upon religious belief.

Faith is not, as Paley and the religious philosophers had taught or implied, an assent to argument, an assent after weighing the probable evidences. According to the New Testament faith is the gift of God; it comes by hearing the testimony of God and accepting it. Though nothing can be claimed to be true in faith which is rejected by the reason, it does not therefore follow that faith is the result of reasoning in the mind. Reason tests, and verifies, faith; it does not create it.

A child may act savingly on faith, though he cannot give reasons, and knows nothing of logic or proof. Reason is always, for Newman, the analytical reason. And though faith is seen to be an act of the reason, he is anxious to demonstrate that it is no act of proof, or demonstration, or analysis, or syllogism; that it is an act, based partly upon the moral judgment of the conscience, which insists that we venture now because act we must, and

---

[5] See the study by T. S. Bokenkotter, *Cardinal Newman as a Historian*, in *Recueil de Travaux d'Histoire et de Philologie*, IV, fasc. 18 (Louvain 1959), especially pp. 98ff.

which is content (like every other practical decision of our lives) with evidence short of the demonstration, perhaps far short. Faith is more a principle of action than of intellectual assent. Something must be done, and done now. Faith is acting upon what we hope for or desire – though this hope and desire are not simply conjured from our own heart, but are formed in response to the circumstances which we find. Therefore the same evidence will be weighed differently by different minds, in the measure that they allow moral considerations to enter. Faith is created in the mind, not by proofs but by probabilities, and probabilities will appear different according to the moral judgment and values of the person perceiving them.

In declaring that faith is not assent to the Evidences of Christianity, and that such a notion creates an attitude of mind irreverent and irreligious and detached, Newman did not therefore declare evidences to be valueless. They are an encouragement to believers, a stay and confirmation of their faith or hope. Newman, in a momentous admission, named the idea that no reliable evidence is needed for the profession of Christianity 'a wild notion'. He allowed that there could (theoretically) be evidence sufficient to disprove. But he will not say that evidence is the source of faith; for faith, though confirmed by evidences, has another source – in the moral judgment and the religious feelings, acted upon by the grace of God. 'A mutilated and defective evidence suffices for persuasion where the heart is alive; but dead evidences, however perfect, can but create a dead faith.'

Then how is faith to be distinguished from credulity? How is faith to be seen as different from prejudice, bigotry, superstition, or fanaticism? The philosophers of religion replied, again, that as reason was the foundation of faith, so the safeguard was in reason. If the reason is cultivated, men will know why they believe, and how their belief differs from superstition or credulity. Educate men, and they will cease to be superstitious.

Newman denied it. Reason is not the safeguard of faith. Why not? Because he was afraid that, the moment reason is allowed to be the safeguard of faith, it will become detached from it, will hold the facts of religion at arm's length, instead of embracing them, will examine and dissect them, will pass into irreverence. God cannot be God if the proper human attitude is to dissect His qualities and prove His existence. Newman protested too much, for he had already allowed that reason had the duty of subsequently verifying faith, that nothing which reason rejected could be regarded as part of faith; and to verify faith by the reason is at the same time to safeguard it from fanaticism. He ought to have allowed that reason must enter into the appropriation or transmission of the Scripture and the Church's teaching. He ought, even upon his own principles, to have allowed some place for reason in his safeguard of faith, and his extreme statement is one of those which opened him to the charges of scepticism or fideism. But he was denying that reason is the safeguard of faith because he believed (with all the Tractarians) that there was a deeper and a better safeguard – a right state of heart. Holiness, or dutifulness, or love – that is the eye of faith, which keeps it from fastening upon unworthy objects; *fides formata*, faith working by love – there is the stability which prevents the faith from wandering after unworthy objects. Faith is 'a movement from something known to something unknown, kept in the narrow path of truth by the Law of dutifulness which inhabits it, the Light of heaven which animates and guides it ... It is perfected not by mental cultivation, but by obedience.'

Newman is only the most subtle expounder of this doctrine of faith and conscience, which is the second foundation (after the doctrine of authority) of all the Tractarian teaching. Keble and Pusey both taught it, in their different ways; W. G. Ward tried to codify it; Isaac Williams gave what is in some ways the most interesting account of it, even if the account is oversimplified, in his Tract on reserve in communicating religious knowledge. The doctrine of reserve, though much misunderstood and abused at the time, lies near the heart of Tractarian thought; partly because its connexion with Keble's own stamp of character is so intimate, and partly because it is inseparable from the doctrine that a right state of heart is the safeguard of faith.

Newman never expounded this doctrine of faith systematically, and it must be taken as a line of thought suggestive of the meaning of faith and its relation to evidence. There are those who see the systematic working out of this view in the much later *Grammar of Assent* (1870), and it is plain that the relation between the university sermons upon faith and reason and that book is close, so close that the later book cannot easily be understood without reference to the sermons. But by the time he came to write the *Grammar*, his change of allegiance and the development of his mind introduced new considerations, a concern for certitude, and for the nature of divine faith as distinguished from human faith. These later concerns are hardly present in the struggling paragraphs of the university sermons; and perhaps for this reason the sermons are more congenial to the mind of the twentieth century than the more systematic *Grammar*. We know more now of the relation of beliefs to attitudes, and are fully ready to go thus far at least with Newman, that evidences, however suggestive of faith, are not its source, and that in this kind of knowing the will is concerned as well as the intellect. Does a child believe in God simply because his parents tell him so? If that is all, then his belief in God is not faith: he may have learned of God on evidence (their authority) but the trust in God must be his own, formed through the parents upon Him whom the parents trust, formed upon their own faith and their attitude, reaching out with the heart towards someone but dimly comprehended; the evidence is subsequent, and even when subsequent is not weighed with the disembodied detachment of the pure contemplative intellect, studying its probabilities. And therefore said Newman (too forcefully): 'It is as absurd to argue men, as to torture them into believing'; and 'first shoot around corners, and you may not despair of converting by a syllogism'. For the deepest motive of faith is not the arguments presented to the head, but the harmony of Christian truth with the inner teachings, and inner growth, of the conscience. Faith is more a test of a man's heart than of his head.

Newman gave the Movement leadership, and coherence, and influence, the form of a party. He was the decisive kind, he made opponents and disciples. He gave them a beauty of language in sacramental apprehension, a concern for forms of worship and for the ascetic modes of holiness, a love of the Fathers and their thought. He was not essential to the Movement; none of the main ideas would have been hidden if Newman had not been its leader. But it can hardly be denied that from 1840 his veering away from its main fortress, his loss of confidence in his own leadership, his emotional (on top of his earlier intellectual) awareness that the

Tractarian Via Media was a paper religion, his resentment at episcopal and other attacks, his retirement from Oxford, and the rumour of his passage towards Rome, were (temporarily at least, probably more than temporarily) calamitous for the Oxford Movement.

PUSEY AND THE LANGUAGE OF MYSTICISM

Dr Pusey was not a speculative theologian, or the leader of a party by inclination, or the representative of the parochial clergy. He was as retiring and popularity-hating as Keble, and like Keble he had none of the arts which captivate the many. His contributions to the *Tracts for the Times* were long, solid, documented, not easily readable, and were partly responsible for turning the *Tracts* from short and popular pamphlets into treatises for theologians. His name was attached to the Oxford Movement because he had a recognizable and senior position in the university; he was a man of the aristocracy, a man of wealth and place; of rare and conscientious learning and accuracy, but withal a simple, unworldly, otherworldly soul, with a simple unquestioning faith. In the *Apologia* Newman ascribed to Pusey the power to be the centre of the party – 'He was able to give a name, a form and a personality to what was without him a sort of mob.' But this, as is evident from Pusey's career, is what Pusey could not, and what Newman himself could, do. Pusey could make disciples, but few, very few, and they profound and individual. Despite the name *Puseyite* which was so gratuitously bestowed upon the Tractarians, he could not lead a party. If he had thought a party to be following him, he would have shut himself in his house, said his prayers, and continued with his studies. Men looked upon him as somehow remote – beautifully strange, but still strange.

Newman did not recognize that Pusey had made any *intellectual* contribution to the Movement; or, if he recognized it, he was silent upon the subject. Most of what he attributed, in retrospect, to Pusey was but external – 'he furnished the Movement with a front to the world'. He allowed that Pusey had imported into it a weight of scholarship, a sobriety and a gravity which might otherwise have been lacking. Pusey looked, not for broadsheets, but convincing tomes, not for dialectic, but for massed information, not for controversial skill, but for a sense of responsibility. And it is true that at first sight Pusey's intellectual contribution was insignificant in comparison with that of Newman. He wished only to accept the teaching of the Bible as handed to him by the Church. He was content with an appropriation of it and fully shared, more than shared, Newman's view that to be critical and detached (and even argumentative) was to be guilty of irreverence. He was not subtle, had no intention of being subtle. His famous Tract upon Baptism, with its massed information, whatever its temporary success by way of confirming high churchmen in their belief that the ancient Church taught baptismal regeneration, succeeded only in clouding the issue for his successors; for amid all the texts and quotations about regeneration, he nowhere considered the meaning of the word *regeneration* itself, or defined carefully enough the sense in which he was using it, and thereby removed almost all permanent value from the volume, apart from its use as a work of reference. Like Keble, he distrusted originality and novelty. He desired only to stand in the ancient ways, and his sole intellectual weapon was information about the ancient ways. He was shocked to find that the professors in Germany seemed to read no book not published during the last twenty-five years. It was tragic that his biography should have been entrusted to the obvious author, the most intimate of his immediate disciples, H. P. Liddon. For Liddon treated Pusey's letters and papers with reverence, the reverence due to a great man (but not due to a great mind, for the mind is not that kind of mind), and the reiteration at inordinate length of detailed information succeeded in concealing Pusey's stature behind a pile of paper, and rendered the biography readable only by the student.

It would be too sharp a dissection, but not therefore without its truth, to say that Newman represented the moral and intellectual force in the Movement, Keble the moral and pastoral, Pusey the moral and devotional. Newman left the Church of England, Keble and Pusey remained; and though this single fact is in no way a cause but only a symbol, the pastoral and devotional power in the Movement proved to be far more effective, in the long run, than its intellectual power. If it altered the way of belief, it altered it by first transforming the way of prayer. If we think of the Catholic Movement in the Church of England as consisting in a doctrine of authority, a pastoral concern for worship, sacraments, and new modes of sanctification, derived from wider sources than those common within Protestantism (priestly ideals, retreats, confession, devotional books, ways of private prayer and the like), then Pusey should be principally associated with this last. He it was who in the years after 1841 and 1842 translated and adapted continental books of devotion for English usage. He did more than anyone to encourage the revival of the monastic life, and was in closest touch with the new foundations of nuns.

Upon the doctrinal plane, Pusey's language imparted a new note to the common language of the Tractarians. The Church is the Body of Christ – that is common to them all. But Pusey almost *feels* the individual's incorporation into the Body. His language is more mystical (in the modern rather than the contemporary sense) than the language of any other Tractarian, and in its dwelling upon the participation of the Christian in the divinity of Christ, the union of the soul with its Redeemer, can rise to heights of beauty. Brilioth, indeed, named him the *doctor mysticus* of the Movement. Pusey fetched this language not from the French writers of devotion, but from the Greek Fathers, and the Christian Platonism which they represented, though its roots went down into the pietism of the Evangelicals. He made many disciples of the Movement familiar with the classics of mystical writing, from St Bernard onwards. The language of his sermons breaks forth in contemplative rapture as he meditates upon the unity of God and man. Never would you naturally use the word *ecstatic* of the published writings of Keble or Newman, not even when reading their poetry. The word springs naturally to the mind of one reading the sermons of Pusey. He loved to contemplate the presence of Christ in the soul; he conceived obedience, less as action, than as a quiet resting in the will of God; he thought of the Eucharist as the gate through which the Lord came to take up His habitation in the soul. In this aspect of Tractarian thought is to be found the chief source of that greater emphasis upon the Incarnation in its relation to the Atonement, which has often been noticed as characteristic.

In one other respect the atmosphere of Pusey's teaching was unique. More than the others, he felt able to use strong language, indeed the strongest language, about the responsibility of the human will for its choice between good and evil.

Since the days of the seventeenth century when antinomian doctrines of good works had shocked more sober churchmen, the high church tradition had usually favoured a moderate theology of justification by faith; a theology which preferred to avoid the phrase 'faith alone', stressed the necessity of good works as an issue of faith, sometimes allowed that works could be 'good' before justification, or (in other words) that justification could be a process rather than a single act of God, asserted that righteousness could not be imputed without beginning to be inherent, eschewed merit and works of supererogation, attempting to avoid the charge of teaching 'salvation through good works' by recognizing the grace of God as the beginning and the accompaniment of the road to heaven, and by denying the doctrine that with the aid of grace, apart from the imputation of Christ's holiness, good works could qualify the soul for heaven. Newman, who, in his lectures on Justification (1837) reconsidered these traditional questions from the standpoint of the theologian, substantially taught this moderate or mediating doctrine. As a theologian, Pusey agreed.

But as a devotional writer, rather than as a divine, Pusey seemed prepared to attribute still more to the powers of the human will to choose the good. Like Keble and Newman, he believed that the contemporary teaching of the Evangelicals, by attributing so much to faith alone and assurance, underestimated the need to exhort men to obey, the need to show them that they were responsible for their lightest sin, that they could turn to God and could choose the right if they but would, that they were perpetually being confronted by the broad way which beckoned and the narrow way which appeared so steep. This moral earnestness is almost to be described as passionate. All the Tractarians, believing that sanctity had been undervalued by the latitude-men, were inclined to the other extreme, to press men to be saints quickly. Observers of the Roman Catholic Church, experienced in the guidance of monks and nuns, commented that Newman's rule of life for his little group at Littlemore was too severe. If Newman at times pressed the immediate claims of holiness too earnestly, this was still truer of Pusey. It was not that he failed to recognize the workings of grace, or man's incapacity, or justification by faith. But he was zealous to remind the soul of its aweful responsibility as it stands under judgment before God, and he could perhaps create a sense of strain. The nursery of his own family was not a natural nursery; his wife, as she declined in health, became subject to a painful over-scrupulousness; his immediate disciples sometimes laboured under a similar strain.

This concern for responsibility, this devotional (not theological) undervaluing of grace, this reluctance to recognize naturalness and 'the seed growing secretly', that sanctification was not only a supernatural life but a supernatural consecration of natural life, affected the young Liddon, Pusey's most intimate friend and follower. I have elsewhere written of the young Liddon's moral exhortations[6] – 'Even when the presuppositions of another age in theology are put aside, something perhaps is still missing. Sin, judgment, grace, redemption – he proclaims them from the rooftops. But he cannot quite bring himself to say, *O felix culpa quae talem ac tantum meruit habere Redemptorem!* The reason seems to lie in a weakening of the childlike quality in him. In the young Liddon you feel, sometimes, that the burden of responsibility has weighed down youth's simplicity.'

Dr Pusey, then, was not always wise. But he practised what he preached.

THE TEACHING OF THE TRACTS

Pusey once gave a simple summary of Tractarian teaching, in 1840, when the word *Puseyism* was beginning to be commonly used to describe the Oxford Movement. Part of his reply went thus[7] (the italics are original):

What is Puseyism?

It is difficult to say what people mean when they designate a class of views by my name; for since they are no peculiar doctrines, but it is rather a temper of mind which is so designated, it will vary according to the individual who uses it. Generally speaking, what is so designated may be reduced under the

[6] *The Founding of Cuddesdon* (Oxford University Press for Cuddesdon College, 1954), p. 43.
[7] Liddon, *Life of Pusey*, II, p. 140.

following heads; and what people mean to blame is *what to them appears* an excess of them.

(1) High thoughts of the two Sacraments.
(2) High estimate of Episcopacy as God's ordinance.
(3) High estimate of the visible Church as the Body wherein we are made and continue to be members of Christ.
(4) Regard for ordinances, as directing our devotions and disciplining us, such as daily public prayers, fasts and feasts, etc.
(5) Regard for the visible part of devotion, such as the decoration of the house of God, which acts insensibly on the mind.
(6) Reverence for and deference to the ancient Church, of which our own Church is looked upon as the representative to us, and by whose views and doctrines we interpret our own Church when her meaning is questioned or doubtful; in a word, reference to the ancient Church, instead of the Reformers, as the ultimate expounder of the meaning of our Church.

And after mentioning differences of attitude, and in the doctrine of justification, he continued:

I am, however, more and more convinced that there is less difference between right-minded persons on both sides than these often suppose – that differences which seemed considerable are really so only in *the way of stating them*; that people who would express themselves differently, and think each other's mode of expressing themselves very faulty, mean the same *truths* under different modes of expression.

This summary of Tractarian thought does not seem extreme, or extreme only in being unusually conciliatory. It is almost the old platform of the old high church tradition, and Pusey half-contended that it was nothing more when he said that they were 'no peculiar doctrines'. The traditional and conservative mode of expression may be seen in such phrases as 'the two Sacraments'. The only part of this platform which might have been expressed otherwise by Hammond, or Thorndike, and the divines of the seventeenth century, is the sixth section, with its implied antithesis between Fathers and Reformers. This, though only an implied antithesis, made a momentous difference to the nature of the 'temper' of mind. It might, for example, have a widely different effect upon section 5, upon which is intended by the phrase 'regard for the visible part of devotion'.

In the Tracts themselves, the conservative element is strongly marked, particularly because several of them are Catenas (Newman's idea, though probably under Pusey's general influence), that is, extracts from the Anglican divines of the high church tradition, illustrating for example how the doctrine of the Eucharistic sacrifice had frequently been professed by loyal members of the Church of England; and others are designed to prove that the doctrines professed are the doctrines of the Book of Common Prayer, that the doctrine of apostolic succession, for example, is contained in, or at least implied by, the service of ordination; to emphasize the duty of fasting or of frequent Communion; to exhort the clergy to refuse an alteration in one jot or tittle of the liturgy. There is practically no 'theology' properly speaking to be found among the Tracts, except in Isaac Williams's Tracts on Reserve, Pusey's on Baptismal Regeneration, or Newman's last few Tracts. There is nothing original in the polemic against Rome – transubstantiation, purgatory; it is no more effective, and no less effective, than the traditional criticisms by Protestants, even though one or two of the Tracts (Newman's number 75 on the Breviary, for example) might be held by the nervous to have a devotional influence towards a Roman world of thought. Among the productions of the Tractarians, *The Tracts for the Times* cannot be regarded as those most significant for their religious thought. They were too slight, or too sensibly designed for other purposes, devotional, controversial, ecclesiastical, historical.

The controversy with Rome led to Tract 90; and the publication of Tract 90 (1841) led to the end of the Tracts, shattered Newman's self-confidence, and hacked away at those roots in Protestant tradition out of which the Movement had grown.

The unusual nature of the last Tract has tempted some to regard it as one of Newman's later idiosyncrasies on his Rome-ward path, to be rejected when estimating the mind of the Oxford Movement, a thesis no more authentic to the Tractarians than his Essay of 1845 on the development of Christian doctrine. But this view would not be in accordance with the facts. The idea behind Tract 90 was integral to the theology of the Movement. It was defended and applauded by Pusey and by Keble, and still more by William Palmer of Worcester College, who had veered away in distrust from Newman since the publication of Froude's *Remains*, and who was the most solid, and among the most conservative, of the Oxford divines. These men did not agree with all the phrases of the Tract, and would have preferred alterations in detail. The principle behind the Tract they supported wholeheartedly. Indeed its seed was present in such a bare summary as Pusey's definition of *Puseyism* given above, with the phrase 'reference to the Ancient Church instead of the Reformers': the *instead of* which divided the high churchmen of the Oxford Movement from the high churchmen of the seventeenth century.

The aspect of the Movement which rankled in the public, or the academic, mind was the apparent hostility to the Reformation believed to be attributable to the Tractarians. This belief had been founded when after Hurrell Froude's early death, Keble and Newman published his *Remains* in 1838. There they had allowed to go forth to the world, together with sentences vehemently denouncing Rome, sentences which were shocking to the popular mind of the English. Froude had begun to study the Reformation at the beginning of 1832, during the constitutional crisis in the country. His visit to Italy in 1833 predisposed him to look upon reformers with a little more favour. By August 1833 he could write that 'odious Protestantism sticks in people's gizzard'; by December 1835 (now a dying man), 'really I hate the Reformation and the Reformers more and more'.

Newman, though he edited Froude's volumes, had not asserted publicly that he shared these extreme opinions (unless his editing of the *Remains* be taken as silent consent), and Pusey, who did not share them in this extreme form, was surprised when in 1841 he discovered Newman's deep dislike of the Reformers. It cannot be said that either Froude or Newman did more than dabble in the history of the Reformation, and neither was well qualified to make sound judgments upon the subject. But they had both formed an impression of an antithesis, perhaps an incompatibility, between the ancient Church and the Protestant leaders of the Reformation; and in Newman's more extreme, less sober disciples after 1838, like W. G. Ward and Oakeley, this 'hatred' of the Reformers created a genuine stumbling-block to subscription of the Articles *ex animo*. For subscription was not, to the Tractarians, a vague or general assent to articles of peace. They desired to reassert the authority of the Church, to adhere to the liturgy and the rubrics; and no one could deny that the Thirty-

Nine Articles were a significant part of the authority of their Church.

It was therefore necessary to prove that the Articles might be interpreted, and subscribed, in a sense compatible with the faith of the ancient Church, and not in the sense intended by their reforming framers (if it was assumed that those senses were not identical). Newman was forced into Tract 90 by extremists like Ward, but it must not therefore be believed to be an idiosyncrasy of Newman. Some such explanation would have been necessary, sooner or later, upon the most sober principles of the Oxford Movement. That was why William Palmer welcomed and defended the Tract when it was published. And since, as Newman was well aware, Arminians or latitude-men had for two centuries or more been extending the meaning of the Articles in various directions, and widening the number of opinions which might be professed under their shelter, it seemed to Newman that he was doing nothing disloyal to his Church in applying precisely the same principle to the particular needs of himself and his followers. Articles are the product of one age; and the theological needs of later ages make some readjustment or interpretation inevitable. The wisdom of the early Church must be allowed to speak to the contemporary mind. It must not be narrowed and restricted by promulgations drafted when the knowledge of the early Church was less broad and less well grounded.

In the prevailing state of popular opinion, which resented the alleged Tractarian hostility to the Reformation, and was peculiarly sensitive at the time because of its concern with the troubles in Ireland, this plan was delicate in execution. Newman was never imaginative in the realm of tact. In the introduction he described the Church as teaching 'with the stammering lips of ambiguous formularies', a phrase by no means palatable even to Pusey. But it is perfectly clear, both from the Tract itself and from the subsequent explanations which he gave, that Newman in no way intended Tract 90 to be a reconciliation with Rome; and the fact that some still believe he intended this cannot be based on a reasoned study of the relevant documents, but can only be an inference from what happened subsequently, in 1845, or from the joyous deductions based on the Tract by extremists like Ward. 'The only peculiarity of the view I advocate',

Newman explained in a public letter to Jelf, 'if I must so call it, is this – that whereas it is usual at this day to make the particular *belief of their writers* their true interpretation, I would make the *belief of the Catholic Church* such' (and by the Catholic Church he still meant the ancient and undivided Church). 'That is, as it is often said that infants are regenerated in Baptism, not on the faith of their *parents* but of the *Church*, so in like manner I would say the Articles are received, not in the sense of their framers, but (as far as the wording will admit, or any ambiguity requires it) in the one Catholic sense.'

The new ceremonial began modestly about 1837 and 1838, with little signs like the wearing of a scarf embroidered at the ends with crosses. In truth the movement for more elaborate ritual was a far wider movement than that of the Tractarians. Cambridge, as the original centre of that group of church-restorers and decorators and designers known as the Cambridge Camden Society, was till 1845 more important than Oxford in the matter. It was another part of that almost universal turning from the head towards the heart. Its roots lay in the desire to turn the churches into houses of prayer and devotion, where people would let their hearts go outward and upward in worship, instead of preaching-houses where their minds would be argued into an assent to creeds or to moral duties. 'The desire that all things done in church should be done decently could not stay confined to the architecture. It must affect also the appurtenances and ornaments, the methods of conducting service. The restorers, influenced by the Romantic revival, looked to the medieval centuries to guide them. They were rebuilding chancels, favouring pointed arches, advocating frescoes instead of whitewashed walls. Inevitably, and without any leap of transition, they looked to antiquarian precedent to teach them how to restore the dignity of worship.' As sanctity undervalued was now swinging towards sanctity in haste, so dilapidated altars, dirty cloths and hangings and surplices were now swinging towards decorated altars, clean cloths and surplices, and ornamented hangings. This was a movement far wider than the Tractarian; the leaders thought these novelties to be then undesirable and improper, and advised their disciples against them. Yet there was something in the thought of the Oxford Movement which cohered easily with this revival, came in part to dominate and guide it, and finally was itself part dominated and transformed by it, as the elaboration of ways of worship, running ahead of any justification in Anglican doctrine, refused to be halted but forced the Anglicans to reconsider their doctrine.

One side of Tractarian theology 'called the Church of England to revive the ancient ways. The ancient and undivided Church must be the model, not only in doctrine, but in liturgy and devotion. In appealing to antiquity they examined the Book of Common Prayer with microscopes and found that the rubrics of the Prayer Book, understood in their historical context, commanded daily worship, frequent celebrations, and more ornaments and vestures than were commonly to be found in English parish churches.'[8] Had not the old high church tradition itself favoured a particular reverence for visible and external devotion? And now, with the Reformers on one side, and with the alleged aridities of Latitudinarianism believed to be repellent, antiquity and romantic aesthetics were both moving to give content to the nature of that reverence for visible and external devotion. 'We', wrote Oakeley, 'are for carrying out the symbolical principle in our own Church to the utmost extent which is consistent with the duty of obedience to the rubric',[9] and he amplified this dictum by suggesting that every church should be furnished with a prominent cross (not a crucifix); stained glass in the windows; penitential ornaments for the altar in Lent and rich hangings for a festival; flowers and two candlesticks upon the altar (but lighting them 'might give offence in these days and we do not advise it, though inclined to regard it as strictly Anglican'); bowing to the altar; facing east when consecrating the Holy Communion. 'If to anyone some of these suggestions should seem trivial, let us remind that care about minutiae is the peculiar mark of an intense and reverent affection. Nobler task there can be none for a rational being than that of providing, with the most punctilious exactness, for the due celebrating of the Creator's honour; nor any worthier dedication of the offerings of nature and the devices of art, all alike His gift, than in the seemly adorning of His earthly dwelling place. At the same time we desire nothing less than that

[8] *The Founding of Cuddesdon*, p. 55.
[9] *British Critic* (January–April 1840), p. 270.

matters like these should be taken up without constant reference to 'weightier' things; that were indeed to begin at the wrong end; nay, we would go farther, and say that there is something quite revolting in the idea of dealing with the subject of External Religion as a matter of mere taste.'

Such was Oakeley's view. Dr Pusey would have expressed the warning more strongly. He disapproved of Oakeley's article. He believed that there was no time for anything else at present but re-asserting Catholic truth, and that to devote energy or thought or controversy to the externals of worship (so that the externals of worship were reverent) was to divert the attention from what mattered. And he believed that the unadorned simplicity of the Church was fitting in its penitential plainness, representing humble sorrow at the divided and unsaintly condition of Christendom. Keble and Newman were no more concerned with ritual than Pusey. But it will be evident how easily and naturally the doctrine of faith and the doctrine of authority, the desire to avoid shallowness in worship and to seek the awe and the mystery of religious experience, cohered with the less guarded desires of younger men to experiment in liturgy and ecclesiastical art. The revival of ceremonial began with a few antiquarians. It was taken thence into parishes where the incumbent might have neither the knowledge nor the restraint of the academic liturgiologists, and was simply concerned with the pastoral effect upon his congregation.

On this doctrine of faith, the borderland between the way of prayer and the way of belief is not always easy to determine. Therefore the mode of worshipping might begin to affect the credal propositions believed to be true. The Tractarians condemned the 'Romish' doctrine that saints might be invoked in prayer. Was the 'Saint X, pray for us', found in some liturgies judged in that condemnation? In Tract 90 Newman argued this to be an open question, and it remained an open question for a long time among the descendants of the Oxford Movement. But if personal devotion in pursuit of enrichment adapts liturgical formulas where the 'pray for us' is used and assumed, then the question whether the Church of England condemns it begins no longer to be open.

THE INFLUENCE OF THE MOVEMENT

The Oxford Movement changed the external face, and the internal spirit, of English religious life. But these changes were primarily religious, and only afterwards theological. They succeeded, far beyond the expectations of many, in transforming the atmosphere of English worship, in deepening the content of English prayer, in lifting English eyes, not only to their own insular tradition, but to the treasures of the Catholic centuries, whether ancient or modern.

They failed, beyond their own expectation and trust, in affecting the religious belief of Englishmen except so far as the new modes of worship helped to create an acceptance, or toleration, of more patristic or medieval modes of theological expression. In so far as the Oxford Movement was affirming a particular doctrine of authority, or a particular interpretation of the nature of dogma, or particular doctrines like baptismal regeneration to the exclusion from English religion of other interpretations of regeneration, the Movement failed. Dr Pusey's devotions for prayers during the day are still used and valued within the Church of England. His belief in an ancient and undivided Church that was infallible, or his particular mode of expressing a 'branch' theory of the Church, now seem to be obsolete.

It might be reasonably argued that within the Church of England itself its doctrinal, as opposed to its religious consequences, were too significant to be described as failure. The proposed 1928 Prayer Book of the Church of England represented, as is the way of liturgies, the prevailing theology of many instructed Anglicans. There are other influences entering into that Prayer Book; but the influence of the descendants of the Oxford Movement is stronger than any other in dictating or suggesting theological changes from the legal Prayer Book of 1662. The authors of the 1928 book were no longer frightened of the associations of certain words feared by the Reformers and restored by the Tractarians. They were ready to suggest the idea of Eucharistic sacrifice; to use a stronger language from the Fathers about the gift of the Holy Spirit in confirmation, to introduce a commemoration of the main Greek Fathers into their calendar, to strengthen the language which commemorates the faithful departed. And yet, despite such signal exceptions, the doctrinal consequences of the Movement were less momentous than its devotional. Indeed, one of the reasons for a certain untidiness or anarchy which seemed, in the years before and after 1900, to be creeping into the Catholic Movement within the Church of England was this distinction – the devotional 'power' was still increasing at the moment that the doctrine of authority was weakening.

For it was not the withdrawal of Newman, or Ward, or Manning, or Robert Wilberforce, that was responsible for this comparative failure in doctrine. Those withdrawals, and especially that of Newman, who, despite his dialectic, his touch of irrationality, his wish to believe in ecclesiastical miracles of high improbability, and his later Ultramontanism, was a natural leader as well as subtle thinker, weakened the force of the Movement and confirmed the suspicions which it had so inevitably aroused. But the Movement was meeting needs of the heart; it was only delayed by withdrawals which would have completed the destruction of any teaching which was superficial and nowhere touched the deeper chords of the soul. The failure in doctrinal influence was not caused because the teachers lost faith in their own teaching. It was caused by the appearance of altogether new stars in the firmament of Christian theology – the new science, Darwin, the new history, the Biblical critics. Intellectually, the teaching of the Oxford Movement upon authority was beginning to be an anachronism within a quarter of a century from its birth. Pusey believed that the monster which he termed 'rationalism' was always due to a failure in morals. Such a view, if ever tenable, had become obviously untenable by 1870.

To settle the thorny questions arising for the theologians from the new study of the Bible, to make terms with the new notion of revelation being forced upon sensible Christian thinkers, was an impossible task for the first disciples of the Tractarians. They had been plunged into the last ditch, and it needed a generation before any of them could lift their feet out and begin again. Liddon, ever faithful to Dr Pusey, devoted his later life to the maintenance of the Tractarian dogmatic against the rising tide; and since Liddon possessed an abler theological mind than anyone in the Movement except Newman and J. B. Mozley, this comparative waste is a measure of the temporary, intellectual, weakness of the successors of the Tractarians.

When the second and third generation came to be reconciled with the new notions of revelation, in Gore and Scott Holland and R. C. Moberly (especially in the volume of essays entitled *Lux mundi*, published in 1889), their intellectual endeavours again became fertile. They had abandoned most of the positions characteristic of Dr Pusey upon the authority of the Church. They had accepted a far looser idea of Biblical inspiration. They had rejected the belief that the ancient and undivided Church was inerrant. But in this sweeping revolution they sought to preserve what they believed to be of essential value in the position which Newman, Keble and Pusey had taken up. Though they no longer believed the Bible to be in the old sense inspired, they still looked to find the Word of God in the Bible. Though they no longer believed the ancient and undivided Church to be inerrant, they still believed the ancient and undivided Church to be authoritative. Though they could not accept Keble's statement of the doctrine of tradition, they nevertheless believed it necessary to Christian faith to see the New Testament as a document or documents addressed from faith to faith, the faith of the early Christians. And because they held a more traditional idea of Church authority, they were less easily frightened by the revolution of thought about the Bible. They provided for the liberal movement in England a ballast which helped it not to be swept along by the excesses of evolutionary theology and philosophy. Though they no longer believed dogma to be infallible, they still cared mightily for dogma.

Though their thought upon faith and its relation to conscience is still considerable despite the theological revolutions since their time, this is not because minds of the present day could wholeheartedly assent to it as it stands. The philosophers of religion were at least not liable to the charge of shutting religious thought within a high walled garden, where Christians might believe as they liked while the world went on its heedless way; a garden wherein Christian faith was preserved and deepened, but which was invisible to the supposed wilderness outside the wall. The

Tractarians would have denied that their doctrine of faith had these consequences. It cannot be said that the denial would always have been justified; and yet it is not likely that any sound Christian thinking will again lose that integral connexion between faith and the conscience, that essential link between religious propositions and moral judgments, which is one contribution of the Oxford Movement to English thought. Nor is it likely that any sound Christian thinking, however Biblical or however philosophical, can afford to dispense in the long run with some attitude towards the early Church and its understanding of the Bible. The Bible is the book of a worshipping community, and that worshipping community can only understand itself in the light of its own history and continuity.

The inheritance of Keble's *Christian Year* was nearer to the heart of the Movement even than the inheritance of Bull, or Hammond, or Hooker. Nor is there a clear line of division between the theological poetry and the theological prose. With the sermons of Newman, or Pusey, or Isaac Williams, we are often in a realm of prose according to the print, but in a realm of poetry in spirit and expression.

In order to share in this poetry, it is necessary not to shrink from the romantics as though they were harlots, but to engage them with head and heart as true lovers. It is necessary, perhaps, to be capable of pleasure in Wordsworth, or parts of Wordsworth. I will confess that I can only understand, with a bare assent of the intellect, the influence exerted by *The Christian Year*. Keble has moments of grandeur, moments of deep sincerity and simplicity; but the moments of bathos, or of superficiality, bring you down again to the dust too soon after you have soared above it. To read *The Christian Year* feels like seeing an honest and moral play where the illusion is often being broken. I give this only as a reflexion of personal taste. Perhaps there are those who can still, like their forefathers, elevate *The Christian Year* to the level of *The Pilgrim's Progress* or *The Imitation of Christ*.

If Keble sometimes seems, paradoxically, unpoetic among the leaders, there is the Newman whose poetic gift, despite 'Lead, Kindly light' or *The Dream of Gerontius*, flowered most fully in his sermons. Pusey's sermons, though, like his letters, they can sometimes be too weighty and solid and therefore earthbound, at other times reach upwards into the clouds with a beauty of mystic apprehension. There is Isaac Williams, whose verse possesses in its moods a haunting note of inwardness, of a quality rare even among the romantics; it was a minor literary, as well as theological, injustice that doctrinal odium prevented his election to the Professorship of Poetry at Oxford. Perhaps Williams, more than any of the others, was a disciple and lover of George Herbert.

This poetic strand is as integral to the Movement as that study of antiquity which issued in the editions of the Fathers and the encouragement of patristic learning. It is as natural and integral to the Movement as the desire to make the churches numinous, to transform them from bare houses of preaching into temples evocative of prayer. It was as natural and integral because, like the desire to make the churches numinous, it was part of that symbolic and sacramental consciousness which formed the deepest link, perhaps the only true and valid link, between Romanticism and Catholicism. It is not an accident, I believe, that one of the intelligent offspring of the Movement, R. W. Church, was also a perceptive interpreter at once of Dante and of Robert Browning.

Chapter 2

THE LIMITATIONS OF KEBLE

James Anthony Froude coined the phrase. The word *limitations* is not precise. Froude meant that Keble was narrow-minded and prejudiced. Geoffrey Faber added another limitation: that Keble's opinions were fixed to eternity. There is still another in the charge that he was lazy.

It is not self-evident that Keble was as limited as Froude thought. The legend needs dismantling and turning into history.

Keble died in 1866. The prosecution rests its case, at least the case for the supreme penalty, on three posthumous witnesses: Froude (1881), Tom Mozley (1882), and Francis Newman (1891). It is not a coincidence that all three witnesses have in other matters an unhappy reputation for bias and inaccuracy. None of the three knew Keble other than by casual and rare meeting. Froude hated the Oxford Movement partly because he resented his elder brother Hurrell. Francis Newman hated the Oxford Movement partly because he resented his elder brother John Henry. Tom Mozley was a garrulous bird whose talons were gossip and facetiousness. While editing the *British Critic* from 1841 to 1843 he got right across Keble by making sin ridiculous when Keble knew that it must be made odious. Late reminiscences of ancient decaying embittered men are the source of the legend, later to be popularized by Geoffrey Faber. So the famous phrases are still quoted – 'There really was no getting on with Keble without entire agreement, that is submission' (Mozley); 'If you did not agree with him, there was something morally wrong with you' (Froude). Since no one is infinite, everyone has limitations. But at least we must examine Keble's limitations on better testimony than this chorus of carcass-pecking vultures. We must ask for the evidence of Keble's conduct, and of witnesses with more contemporary and personal acquaintance.

Consider first the standards by which stature is weighed. John Henry Newman charitably rendered Keble a disservice by hailing him as the true and primary author of the Oxford Movement. Since this movement was believed to have changed the face of English religion, its supposed author was instantly weighed against authors of other powerful religious movements, a Wesley, a Luther. A simple country curate, with no understanding of dissent and little of low churchmen, a writer of poetry touching but not of the first rank, neither theologian nor evangelist but a quiet stable pastor – his person was beautiful but unequal to the burden which Newman's modesty compelled him to carry. We expect the lion to roar, and finding him meek and placid we suffer a twinge of disappointment.

Keble was the author of no movement. Meeting him, Newman understood for the first time the religious and ethical power of the Catholic tradition within the Church of England. Keble set Newman to work; but only as the perception of a sublime picture drives the apprehender to start painting. Newman's praise of Keble made men think, how light a man to lift so heavy a burden. We must take Keble as himself, and not as a man unfitted to do what he is supposed to have done but never did.

They entrusted the official biography of Keble to his old friend Mr Justice Coleridge. It looked a sensible choice. As an undergraduate in Corpus Christi College, Coleridge lived below Keble's garret and formed a friendship of more than fifty years. He advised Keble on earthly matters; no small responsibility, for one of Keble's friends labelled him the most impractical of men,[1] and he was so absent-minded that he arrived at his wedding with a collar-bone broken when he fell from his horse in a brown study.[2] Coleridge tried vainly to stop the fatal publication of Hurrell Froude's journal and casual remarks among the *Remains*. For a time he organized the re-editions and copyright and finances of *The Christian Year*. He managed the fund which paid for the stained glass in Hursley church. He was Keble's legal adviser on the matters of Church and State about which Keble was moved to write. He received a steady flow of letters from Keble about all the leading events of the ecclesiastical day. He was a sane

[1] *Letters of Lord Blachford*, p. 34.
[2] Battiscombe, *John Keble* (1963), p. 169.

Tractarian and loyal Anglican, and sufficiently the opposite of Keble, in being a man of London and the world, to suggest a measure of detachment. He had all the virtues of a biographer except the two most momentous. A biographer ought to be able to write; and, however profound his affection for the subject, he must eschew the scruples of delicacy. Coleridge could write the English language simply, but could not write a book. And he was afflicted with a delicacy so sensitive as almost to disqualify him from the task which he undertook. He knew that Keble wrote many of his letters in the way of spiritual direction and he could not bring himself to ask the obvious correspondents if he might see their letters from Keble. He knew that Pusey and Newman possessed large numbers of letters from Keble. But he refused to apply to either source. His motive was 'delicacy'. 'The work', Coleridge said, 'no doubt suffers in consequence.' He was right. It is a narrowed portrait. Reserve is not the best virtue for a biographer.

No one should underestimate the difficulty of Coleridge's task, the difficulty of any biographer of Keble. Newman was once asked to portray Keble with his pen. He replied, 'How can I profess to paint the portrait of a man who will not sit?'[3] Keble provided no materials for a biographer.

It is impossible to say with conviction that Keble was dull. It is certain that (without so expressing it) he wanted to be dull. He consciously effaced himself. Keble not only eschewed popularity and fame. He was afraid of the impact of his personality. He preached boring sermons of set purpose, that his flock might not be touched by human magnetism but led beyond to a higher Person. There was nothing uninhibited, no *élan*, no earthly freedom, no release of human power. He had no desire to be someone. He was always high-buttoned, with a three-inch collar of self-distrust and a white tie of rare clerisy. Such a man could have few intimates. The life of grace could mean emancipation. To Keble it meant self-control.

The life of every country parson who tries to do his job is likely to be dull in the written record. To be vicar of Hursley near Winchester for thirty years is not to afford the handiest matter to

3   J. Keble, *Occasional Papers and Reviews* (1877), p. xiii.

biographers. But the suspicion of dullness arises from something more profound in the personality. It is something to do with Keble's father.

Geoffrey Faber, whose portrait of Keble is a caricature, said that his mind was passionately contented with the past and that his opinions were unalterable. There are so many obvious examples of Keble altering his opinions during his life (from the doctrine of the Real Presence downwards) that the second charge may be dismissed to the limbo of happy myths. But he was decisively a man of tradition, not of speculation. The Church and its ministers receive and expound the truth. They have no need to seek it. Newman once sent him a sermon for his criticism. Keble returned it with the comment, 'Don't be original' – which is good advice to some of Newman's sermons, but only Keble would have expressed it so baldly. Newman said with unconscious humour that he practised the restraint which he recommended to others.

The tone of conservatism is deepened by his respect for his father. There may be something in the adage that revolutionaries begin by rebelling against their parents. Keble avoided the least hint or whisper of a rebellion. He reverenced his father and never escaped his thrall. His marriage, his work, his ideas, his vocation, were conditioned by allegiance to his father. If he wanted to agree with a statement of doctrine he would say, 'That seems to me just what my father taught me.'[4] He wanted nothing so ardently as to stand in the ways of our fathers, or at least in the ways of his father.

It is said that Keble was lazy. This verdict, if true, would be so out of keeping with everything else that we know of Keble's character that it would alter the Coleridgian portrait drastically.

The verdict is based upon two pieces of evidence: (1) Keble was in the habit of deploring his own laziness. He called himself an idle lounging man and kept making resolutions about punctual and regular habits, blamed his own long habit of idleness and told Coleridge that by sad experience he found idleness to be the besetting sin of country parsons.[5] (2) More than once Keble lamented that he was so poor a correspondent, and to the end of

[4] Sir John Coleridge, *Life of the Rev. John Keble* (1869), p. 564.
[5] Coleridge, pp. 110, 131, 152, 114–15.

his days regretted that he failed to write a letter in time to reach the dying Hurrell Froude.[6]

To this evidence a little more might be brought. He was always irregular in his manner of work, sitting at a desk in a room from which no one was excluded and looking up from his books to join the casual conversation. In his later years his health declined. His wife, who was never strong, lay back upon her sofa in a courageous Victorian manner and demanded her husband's time and emotion. Moreover Richard Church, who reverenced Keble and would not whisper a public breath of criticism, once confessed to Lord Acton, when they met at Antibes in 1888, that Keble had no *go*.[7] But a diligent man might lack *go*. No one questions that Keble lacked *élan*, drive, vital force. No one doubts that, unlike Newman, he was incapable of leading a religious party. He was so timid of push or aggression that he gave an impression of placidity, so cabined in his father's spirit that he could not kick. But this is not the same thing as laziness. To convict him of that sin is to take at objective value the self-mortifications of an unusual penitent.

Imagine a country parson, in charge of two parish churches and a chapel in a schoolroom; with a sick wife needing constant attention and in the end a bath-chair; with a curate compelled by the bishop to be no more than a deacon for sixteen years; a country parson who reconstructed both churches and built the schoolroom chapel; who taught in his school for an hour every morning and more on Sundays; who visited the sick steadily, and kept his confirmation classes for six months; who conducted an exhausting correspondence in the guidance of souls outside the parish; who welcomed visits from penitents and endured visits from sightseers; who was so engaged in the national affairs of the Church that he often needed to run to Oxford or London to meet or protest; who nevertheless succeeded in publishing an edition of Hooker so excellent that it was used, with minor revision, a century later; in writing a two-volume life of Bishop Wilson, and printing a volume and more of sermons, and a translation of the Psalms, and two fat volumes in the Latin language on Homer and ancient literature; in translating St Irenaeus and in publishing at

---

[6] Battiscombe, p. 185.
[7] 26 March 1888: Acton MS. 4990/212.

least twenty-two pamphlets and several important articles; who completed all this literary and political activity while keeping his parishioners as his first call; and whose single excess was in self-depreciation. Imagine that such a parson told us how lazy he was – are we to take his penitence seriously?

The truth is, he was an exceptionally diligent person. As a man can seldom be a hero to his valet, a vicar can seldom be a hero to his curate. Whatever faults the vicar displays the curate must first see. If the vicar shows signs of indolence, the curate is the first to suffer and resent. If Keble was lazy, his curates would know before all others. We have direct evidence upon this precise matter from the most distinguished of Keble's curates at Hursley. In emphatic words one declared that Keble devoted himself to the study and practice of his calling with an earnestness and industry far beyond that of most men.[8] Keble was more than *diligent*; people used of him the word *laborious*. Another of his curates declared that he was a model which all country pastors would do well to set before themselves.[9] One wonders how many Anglican incumbents have caused two different curates thus to speak of them. And if the epithet *diligent* may have an ill sound, as of a scholar who collects a pile of information without knowing how to order it, the epithet may stand to describe Keble's intellectual life.

Keble was no theologian. Feeling himself incompetent for anything, he felt himself incompetent for theology. Of the most important and clearheaded volume written by an English philosopher of religion during Keble's life, he remarked only that he had not read it and did not expect to understand it.[10] The sermon on Tradition is partly unintelligible, and what is intelligible seems to be not quite what Keble meant. In Tract 89 he had the reasonable idea of defending the allegories of the Fathers by analogy with poetical imagery, but another mind would have seen that the detailed examples of this defence were fantasy. In *Eucharistic Adoration* he came nearest to being a theologian. But

---

[8] R. F. Wilson, preface to the third edition of *Letters of Spiritual Counsel and Guidance* (1875), p. xiv.

[9] J. F. Moor, *The Birthplace, Home Churches, and other places connected with the author of The Christian Year* (1867), p. 14. Cf. R. W. Church, *The Oxford Movement* (1891), p. 22, 'Idleness was not in his nature.'

[10] Coleridge, p. 445.

the power in the book is the devotional poetry hidden in the prose, not the theology. Of all the short ways of dealing with the Victorian Biblical critics, Keble's was the shortest. 'Most of the men', he said, 'who have difficulties on this subject were too wicked to be reasoned with.'[11]

By contrast the edition of Hooker is scholarly. Those who underrate Keble's mind imply loosely that Church and Paget did most of the work for the edition which we now use. A comparison of the Church/Paget edition with the editions of Keble shows that this is false. It is the work of a careful editor, an antiquarian rather than a historian, but a genuine critic of the first rank. The earlier half of the long introduction is excellent by any standard, and almost the only passage of Keble which approached the astonishing prowess of his undergraduate years. The *Life* of Bishop Wilson is not a biography but a learned accumulation. Only Keble would have written a biography in which he kept describing himself as the Compiler.

Certainly he had no belief in toleration. What one man believes to be narrow-minded another believes to be sane conviction. He led a public protest against a Lutheran godparent for Queen Victoria's child. He was among the leaders who protested against the election of Dr Hampden to the See of Hereford and the bill to legalize marriage with a deceased wife's sister. He broke communications with his old friend Thomas Arnold when he felt that Arnold's public behaviour became intolerable. You think that John Wesley is to be admired. You have experienced the good that he has done. You must not trust your personal experience. You must judge him by the standards of Catholic faith and order. You think Selwyn a great bishop. Yes, he is a great bishop. But 'he makes me *shiver* now and then with his Protestantisms'. What are these Protestantisms which blot Selwyn's linen? Why, he praises the Church Missionary Society, abuses Becket as a haughty prelate, and preached at Cuddesdon a sermon denouncing no one but the Roman Catholics.[12]

Narrow-mindedness in any age. But the age was an age of forcible conviction. If Keble was bigoted in protesting against a

[11] Coleridge, p. 582.
[12] Ibid., pp. 250, 408.

Lutheran godparent or Dr Hampden, he was bigoted in the company of a lot of people whom no one has yet criticized for being limited. They felt the breath of Robespierre upon their necks and knew their shrines to be tottering. Keble agreed with Hurrell Froude that this was no time to talk of good men in all parties. It was an age when scoundrels must be called scoundrels.

But you must agree with him or you were wicked? The evidence does not support the charge. He supported Gladstone as MP for Oxford University long after Gladstone became a Liberal. (Though for a short time he was severe, and started referring to him as Mr Gladstone instead of W.E.G.)[13] We constantly find him differing in opinion from friends who thereafter remain his friends. In the fury over Jowett's stipend as Professor of Greek, Keble was the one to moderate and propose a compromise. Coleridge's son criticized Charles I in a review and heard that Keble was displeased. Walking with Keble he asked if the report was true. Keble said it was true. The young Coleridge said that he was very sorry to displease him, but a man must form an honest opinion on the historical evidence, and he could not think that what he had written was at all too strong. Keble embarrassed Coleridge by saying humbly, 'it might be so; what was he to judge of other men? he was old, and things were now looked at very differently, he knew he had many things to unlearn, and to learn afresh; and that Coleridge must not mind what he had said, for in truth belief in the heroes of his youth had become part of him'.[14]

No one will utter the phrase *breadth of mind* about Keble. But we have to beware that the posthumous legend does not condition an understanding of the living person. Coleridge had a pastor who became a Roman Catholic. Could he continue to invite the pastor to dinner as of old? Keble replied that, though it was difficult, he personally would not invite him, partly because it would be scandalous in respect of the servants. Some infer from the story that Keble had a principle of never meeting an ex-Anglican who became a Roman Catholic. But the former pastor of the servants and the family was a unique case. To argue from it to a universal ban is ruled out by the evidence. On one occasion

[13] *Letters of Lord Blachford*, p. 158.
[14] Coleridge, p. 581.

Keble gave dinner to a Roman Catholic priest at Hursley vicarage. His name was Father Newman.

He was limited; who is not? He hardly travelled, he lived in and for his parishioners, his reading was all directed to that single end. Self-limitation of a kind is necessary to any work of substance. Mrs Battiscombe is perceptive, and suggests that thus he was lovable. Frankly disclosing the hedged experience and restricted vision, she argues fascinatingly that men loved him for his idiosyncrasies, for his very limitations, as well as for his sanctity (p. 354).

It is a hard saying. Men and women (provided that they were Anglican and well educated) came to love *The Christian Year*. When they met the author, they found his person to conform perfectly to his book of devotions: modest, quaint, unpretentious, quiet, even naive.[15] But a Coleridge, a Moberly, a Newman saw him with open eyes. They saw his intolerance and some at least thought it too fierce. But they allowed their reverence to brush a kindly shadow over the warts. They accepted the limitations and enjoyed the man in despite.

Yet as philosophers argue that without evil there would not be good, a nobility of character sometimes depends upon a limited vision. A child may have ideals the easier because he or she knows not the human compromises necessary to embody those ideals in act. Keble's nobility was partly of this kind. The most characteristic of all his sayings is the dictum at the time of the Gorham case,

If the Church of England were to fail, it should be found in my parish.

The stance is so squared and so real that it takes a moment to see how cloud-capped are the towers thus defended. The limitations were not only warts. They helped him to frame high and poetic aspirations.

---

[15] On 29 November 1851 the Methodist preacher at Southampton called on Keble. He went to Hursley to see R. Cromwell's grave and 'found' that Keble was rector. Keble took him into the study and they talked. 'He has a beautiful poetic countenance. His face is the symbol of his genius – mild, sweet, gentle, contemplative, and of marble whiteness. He is bashful to awkwardness. He was by far the more embarrassed . . . He was very cordial, and offered to serve me in any way in his power' (B. Gregory, *Aut. Recoll.*, p. 399).

Chapter 3

THE ECCLESIASTICAL COMMISSION

The public was always hazy about the work of the Ecclesiastical Commission. A Victorian ordination candidate, asked what religious sects had appeared during the nineteenth century, included in his list the Ecclesiastical Commissioners (Walsham How, *Lighter Moments*). A lady from South London, during the reign of George V, who paid the Commissioners rent and liked them as good landlords, thought that their title was the Elastical Commissionaires.

The historian of the Commissioners was Professor Geoffrey Best. Since the days when he wrote his book, he moved his interest to other fields, like the laws of war and of peace. Nevertheless the *Temporal Pillars* (Cambridge, 1964) is a fundamental contribution to Victorian social history as well as the history of the Church; so that a Victorian might lament the departure for other pastures. But no one is likely to deny that the history of nuclear armaments, or the theory of a just revolution, are to an objective eye subjects as important for us as the history of the Commissioners; so that we have to express only a very happy lament; rather as Mozart, when he wrote his penitential Kyrie Eleison, made his sackcloth and ashes into the most cheerful of garments.

The Ecclesiastical Commission was unique because of the nature of an event which happened three to four centuries before it existed: the English Reformation. That was a special kind of Reformation, both in thinking and in administration. The bit of it that concerns us is that almost everywhere else in Europe the Protestants could see very little use for bishops, or for deans and chapters. They might keep bishops for a time – in North Germany and in Scandinavia till now – but their utility was more a way of preserving old endowments than out of enthusiasm for

63

an apostolic office. I shall be stating it a bit crudely if I say that the Protestant countries did not need a body like the Commission because they removed the endowments at the Reformation and turned them into other uses, of which the best was education, and we draw a veil over the worst; just like the endowments of the ruined monasteries. They regarded deans and chapters as only another form of monastery, which was what they were; and therefore their endowments should be treated like the endowments of the dissolved monasteries. Then, during the eighteenth century, and in the French Revolution and its European aftermath, the Catholic countries of southern Europe did much the same. Bourbon kings could not turn their ramshackle states into modernity without taking a lot of Church money; and the French Revolution had no manner of use for churches and a desperate need for all the money it could get from anywhere; so despots and radicals alike took away the historic endowments of bishoprics and chapters and in their case also monasteries and made other arrangements – as the French government to this day maintains, and maintains badly, the old fabrics and as the Italian government, to the good fortune of the Pope, has the duty of paying for the upkeep of the historic churches of Rome.

Almost everywhere else in Europe, between 1520 and 1800, these historic endowments of the Church of the Middle Ages vanished, or at least were much diminished. It had to be confessed that these wide acreages of Church land were excessive in relation to the other needs of those societies.

They were not so excessive in England, because Henry VIII took the land of the monasteries and so England was not confronted with the difficulty of the Bourbon Catholic kings. But he cared about bishops. He even founded a few dioceses with money from monasteries. Bishops were inseparable from sees, that is from cathedrals; and cathedrals were inseparable from chapters. And so the chapters, monasteries though they might be – monastic in the full sense in many cases, secular clergy in the other cases but acting like monastic colleges – remained.

That is not to say that all the old endowments apart from the monastic lands remained for the purposes of the Church. Queen Elizabeth cared much about bishops, but she bullied some of them outrageously to part with the best endowments of their see before she would sanction their appointment. She kept the See of Ely vacant for eighteen years because she wanted the income, and that was only one example. She salaried some of her highest civil servants and agents abroad by making them deans or canons, but in that she only continued the habits of her medieval predecessors. Then civil war hit England, and the Parliament of the Commonwealth abolished first bishops and then deans and chapters; and so came into line with most of Protestant Europe. And because they – or rather not they but the Army – committed the folly as well as the crime of cutting off the head of the King, that ensured that the historic endowment would survive the eighteenth century as nowhere else in Europe, and made the Ecclesiastical Commission essential not only to England but to the Church of England. By the year 1830, we had a mass of historic endowments for a variety of Church offices which dated back in many cases to the Middle Ages and into which hardly anyone had ever attempted to introduce much rationality.

Sydney Smith was a delightful man and a good canon; corpulent, long-nosed, with a receding forehead; a large paunch and an air of joviality which was not put on. His attack upon the Ecclesiastical Commissioners is tremendous fun, but it was the sort of attack which does more to lower the reputation of the attacker than the attacked. Bits of it would not be regarded as acceptable writing nowadays; though we have all known stuff put out by clergymen in our own time which none of us regarded as acceptable. The then Archbishop of York (Vernon Harcourt), who comes out of Sydney Smith's letters as a sweet-natured but ineffective person (which was much what he was), did what some people today do with *Private Eye* – he refused to allow Sydney Smith's *Letters* into his house, but was happy to have Sydney Smith himself. Whether or not Sydney Smith was right in saying that the Commissioners did too much, even Sydney Smith freely admitted that somebody had got to do something about it.

If a committee is creating rationality, it has three difficulties. The first is that not everyone is agreed on what is rational. In fact, they are sure to disagree on what is rational. If you do nothing, you will offend no one except a few ardent spirits. If you make drastic changes, you will make mortal enemies of half the population. And the situation in 1830 was, the only impossible policy is to do nothing.

The second difficulty is that, since the human race greatly dislike drastic change in normal circumstances, they will only accept drastic change in an emergency. They have to be sure that there is a crisis before they accept what you propose. Therefore you have to try for rationality in conditions which are not the best. It is best if a committee can sit down and think things out without any pressure on it to come to this or that conclusion. But a crisis is always liable to produce action under pressure. The only thing that is to be said is that, but for the crisis, you would have got no action at all.

So – cries of destroy the Church of England – a reactionary body with masses of posts with no function but that of giving the sons of squires a decent income at a comfortable house in the country; the near-revolutionary ferment of Britain from 1830 to 1833, the last time, if we exclude Ireland, that Britain was anywhere near a revolution, was the crisis which made it certain that something must be done and something like the Commission must do it.

The third difficulty is more fundamental. The distribution of money is not and never can be rational, at least fully rational. Let us suppose that, in 1830, a widow in the City of Durham leaves money to the See of Durham. She happens to admire the bishop very much – that would not be very surprising, for he was an excellent person, van Mildert. No committee anywhere can stop her leaving her money to the See of Durham. She knows that the bishop would use it in the way she would like and she has a gratitude which she wants to express.

Yet, what she is doing is to give money to a person who, at current values, has half a million a year, except that out of his half-million he has to maintain a couple of castles and an unusually large administration. That is, benefactors are not rational, as the whole of a land sees rationality. What they see is a particular need – *this* cathedral roof, *this* parish stipend. And benefactors' wishes must be respected. They must be respected on moral grounds and on rational grounds. On moral grounds because you must not embezzle trusts. On rational grounds because, once the benefactors know that no one will respect their

wishes, there will be no more benefactors. This third difficulty
was the greatest difficulty to confront the Commissioners 150
years ago when they were made a corporation with the right to
hold property. Their business was to introduce some sense into
the world. That meant, crudely, they had to take money from
Durham, which had lots of money, and give it to the slums of
Manchester, which had nothing like enough money. But since
money is never enough for anything, Durham people could see
plenty of crying needs in the mining parishes of County Durham
– why should *our* money go to help Manchester? And the
Commission had the one crucial saving defence that most of the
benefactors were unknown and long dead or very long dead, and
everyone admits that benefactors ought not to be able to control
the use of their money in perpetuity, when after the change of
generations, the circumstances have changed.

Besides these three real difficulties, the Commissioners were
under a particular temptation. If you are formed to make things
rational, are you under a temptation to make them more rational
than things need to be? For example, does the pay of curates in the
diocese of Exeter need to be at precisely the same figure as the pay
of the curates in the diocese of Bath and Wells? Some cathedrals
had numerous residentiary canons; some cathedrals had only a
few residentiary canons. Whether they had many or few, they all
seemed to manage pretty well in those days. At a committee
meeting in London, the Commission decide that every cathedral
can manage comfortably with four residentiary canons, and they
will take away all the canonries in excess of the number four
except in those cathedrals with special responsibilities like
Oxford. But then they notice that Lincoln and St Paul's only
have three residentiaries. So Rationality says they must have four
like the others. But Lincoln and St Paul's got on well with three
residential canons, and what the Commission are crying for is
money for the slums of Manchester. That is: it is easy, or it was
easy in 1836, to muddle things up and imagine that to act logically
was the same thing as to bring less chaos to the Church.

Let us pause on the curates' pay, because it raised a very
fundamental question in 1836. The Commissioners see a lot of
endowments. They see a lot of very impoverished clergymen, the
Mr Quiverfuls of the Church, with pay at subsistence level and

numerous children. They realize that they could administer the endowments much more effectively by better management and produce more out of them than is produced at the moment. But then they make their calculation and realize (to their surprise) that this wealth is nothing like so wealthy after all; that if they divided it up among all the curates, they would put everyone's pay up by a very small sum, perhaps £10 or £20. Is it after all so rational that the end product of a great act of rationality in the Church is only to put up all the curates' pay by £10? Should we have achieved anything important, worth all the fuss, bother, envy, hatred, malice, uncharitableness, political infighting and Acts of Parliament and good people's time?

To this basic plan, there were two rival choices as a policy. In university policy at this moment, the government takes the view that you do worst if you spread not enough butter over all the slices of bread and best if you give selected institutions a bit of fat. In the 1830s, it could be said that the strongest institutions in the Church are the cathedrals. They have exercised a national influence for good as in no other Protestant Church. The large number of prebends attach to them a very wide circle of people. They really are what make the dioceses important. They are the people with the means to encourage scholarship and theological training. They can surround the bishop with the council of advisers which he needs. Instead of dismantling the cathedrals for the sake of the poor curates, we ought to be fostering what is strong. Admittedly the cathedrals, as we have them, must be brought more into harness with the parish system. But they are already in touch with the parishes through the system of prebends.

This plan of an alternative policy was asserted very loudly, because the members of the cathedral chapters were the most articulate clergymen in the Church of England. It had no chance of being adopted as a policy. Those who wished to answer the argument had the easiest of replies. The Bishop of London, Blomfield, who, after Sir Robert Peel as Prime Minister, was the man who really *organized* the Ecclesiastical Commission, put it in a very dramatic speech in the House of Lords which became famous and is famous in all histories of the Commission to this day – he only had to go for a walk in his diocese and he passed St

Paul's Cathedral and imagined Sydney Smith in his canonry, sitting comfortably and being humorous, and then he went a mile further to the north-east and met a vast mass of unchurched people and knew that he had no money to help with their care unless he turned to the cathedrals. That was not actually an answer to the defenders of the cathedrals. But it felt like an answer; it appealed strongly to all that was best of the pastoral sense which suddenly, and with a shock, realized how the new cities were outdistancing the old parish organization of the Church. To strengthen the cathedrals instead of weakening them would have been an oligarchic eighteenth-century method of dealing with rationality. They were entering the age of democracy. They ditched aristocrats in the State for the good of the poor, they ditched aristocrats in the Church for the good of the slums. Of course they did not think or intend to ditch the cathedrals. They thought they only stripped them of surplus fat.

But there was more than this in the atmosphere of that age, which now it is hard to realize. Because the sinecures of the Church of England – that is no work, some pay – were usually attached to cathedrals, the public reputation of cathedrals was lower – far lower than was just. Sir Robert Peel called them 'nests of sinecures'. Bishop Monk of Gloucester called them 'the ornamental parts of our system' (Best, pp. 332, 334). Sir Benjamin Hall said in Parliament 'I contend that deans and canons are useless officers.' Joseph Hume asked in Parliament, not rhetorically, 'What is the necessity of deans?' (Hansard 112, 1396). There was laughter in Parliament when an MP (Horsman) cited mockingly the following questions and answers from a Commission report:

Q. What are the duties attached to your office of dean?
A. The usual duties of a Cathedral dean.
Q. What are the duties attached to your office of sub-dean?
A. To act for the dean in his absence.
Q. What are your duties as chancellor?
A. The usual duties of a chancellor. (Hansard 98, 1073)

Or, again in Parliament (Horsman again): 'Wherever these venerable cathedral establishments are found to raise their heads, there the Church was always found to be weakest and there dissent would be found to be most active and most rife' (Hansard 98, 1065).

Therefore, for better or worse, that rival policy – to strengthen the cathedrals as centres of spiritual power – had no chance.

But there was another rival policy which did have a chance. It was proposed by government. Let us take the fat from the historic endowments; leave the Church as it is now; but take surplus property, manage it better, hand the greater surplus to the government and make the State, with that surplus, pay for the upkeep of parish churches when they are in need of repairs. This policy meant, do not put your money into more curates or new parishes. Put your money into a historic buildings fund. The Commission was within distance of becoming a historic buildings commission a hundred and fifty years before the time. The original suggestion was that it, as the agent now not so much of the Church but the State, should pay for the upkeep of existing naves of parish churches. The chancels were the duty of the rectors by law, and the cathedrals were thought to be able (as they still seem to be thought to be able, we hardly know why) to look after themselves. And how many vicars' hairs would have gone less grey in consequence, when their roofs fell in, one hardly likes to think.

This policy had for a moment a chance. It was a government proposal. And that government of Lord Melbourne had the power to carry it off if it liked. But the policy had basic objections.

The first was that the government which proposed it was Whig. So many threats had been uttered by Whigs about stealing the money of the Church that the Church of England in those years, unlike the Church of England now, was inclined to be very Tory in feeling. Of course there were many good Anglican Whigs, but I speak of general feeling. Anything proposed by a Whig government must be bad. Sydney Smith imagined a bear saying to the Church, 'Let me get my arms about you, I have not the smallest intention of squeezing you' (*Works*, 1859 edn, vol. 2, p. 283).

The second objection was that it would indeed mean a loss of money to the Church. In many parishes, the repairs to the nave were done by a church tax, like a local rate, the church rate.

Naturally this was hated by many dissenters. In the big towns it was impossible to enforce. The Whig government, which actually wanted to do good to the Church of England, thought that the Church would be much benefited if it no longer forced crowds of resentful non-Anglicans to pay a tax to maintain the Church of England, and peace and harmony would again prevail in the land. That was a good argument. But it made the cathedral endowments pay for a lot of church roofs which at the moment the State was paying for. To the Tory party as a whole, and to most leading churchmen, that seemed revolutionary. The Archbishop of Canterbury was a wise person. He had the merit that he looked and sounded like a pushover: everyone thought they could bend him to their wills. Inside he had quite a backbone of steel; the only person who knew that he was not a walkover was Sydney Smith, because he was at school with the future Archbishop, who had once knocked him over with a chessboard. This apparently malleable Archbishop would have absolutely nothing to do with this plan. If the Ecclesiastical Commission was going to function at all, it was going to function for the good of the parish system of England and Wales, or he was not going to have anything whatever to do with it.

So the Whig government withdrew its plan, in the face of Tory outcry and uncooperative archbishops and political difficulty in Parliament; and the hairs of vicars were going to go grey as their roofs fell in and their windows fell out; but the parish system of England and Wales was destined to be a far better thing in the end, not able, no doubt, to cope with the expansion of Victorian England and its cities, but much less unable to cope than the Church of Sydney Smith if it had been left to try to cope in the state that it was in when the Commissioners were founded.

So the Commission was founded: to make sense of the parish system of the Church of England and Wales. This was herculean work – to receive masses of property scattered about the country on varying tenures; to cope with empty canons' houses no longer needed because the canonries were suppressed; to adjust diocesan boundaries; to build bishops' houses where they had none; to abolish peculiars and alter the system of patronage; and very soon (after 1843) to found new parishes and build churches within their borders. In two respects it was unfitted to do the task. The

first was that it had very little money for some years. The second
was, what sort of a body is fit to do this enormous and complex
operation?

Bishop Blomfield of London was able and hard-working and
had fewer weaknesses than most men. Late in life he realized that
even he could not run the Diocese of London single-handed. But
at the time when the Commissioners were founded, he sometimes gave people the impression that he supposed himself able to
run, not merely the Diocese of London, but the Church of
England single-handed. And yet, if you make Blomfield run all
this, has he the time or expertise to cope with the leaseholds of the
prebends of Southwell Minster, where the prebendaries died
unusually early and therefore presented the Commission with the
first of its insoluble problems? And if you made an accountant,
who understood leaseholds, manage the Commission, what
would he know about the pastoral and spiritual needs of the
Church, which could affect even particular decisions on small
estates? To take a mass of chaotic medieval endowment and turn
it into a modern and sensible method of supporting the Church
was work demanding the technical expertise of surveyors, stock-
brokers, accountants, possessed less commonly by ministers in
holy orders. And yet, if you have to decide whether to found a
new parish in a new town area, or how to support a new church
in a vast underchurched slum, you needed to be expert in bishop's
work, or archdeacons's, or to have had pastoral experience in
urban parishes.

A meeting of Church Commissioners once took place, in the
Guard Room of Lambeth Palace, with Archbishop Fisher in the
chair. Present were, among others, a delectable bishop, Baddeley
of Blackburn. Lord Silsoe, a professional expert if ever there was
one, presented the annual accounts of the Church Commissioners. It was a time, not the only time, when the stipends of the
clergy were outrun by inflation. During that year, the profits on
investments were lucrative. New money. A demand came from
the clergy that every penny of this new money should be allotted
to stipends. And, brilliantly and forcefully, as those who remember him would expect, Lord Silsoe explained how, as for any
other institution, it was a necessity to put money back into the
business. Every time Lord Silsoe called the Church of England *the*

business, Bishop Baddeley jumped an inch or two in his chair. I remember thinking how this conflict of just interests was created by the nature of the task, part technical and part pastoral, which the reformers of the 1830s assigned to the Commissioners.

Therefore, to get the constitution right was difficult. The original Commission was thirteen people, five bishops and eight lay politicians, the politicians all churchmen. Naturally the canons, very articulate canons, said that this was Erastian; it was selected by the State; it was unrepresentative of the Church at large. This body must be seen to be a Church body. So, four years later, all the bishops were put into the Commission, with three deans (two of the deans, however, were also bishops). This worked worse than the Commission of thirteen. It worked appallingly. It was a mere front. The Church must be deluded into thinking that the bishops were reforming the Church. But they could do nothing of the kind. The body was too big. It was too inexpert. Some of them never came. One asked that he be not sent notice of meetings. The usual attendance was ten or eleven people, more bishops than laymen. The Secretary did not bother to send out agenda for the meetings and controlled what was done there. Almost nobody knew what was to be discussed before they arrived. They could not do any homework. Only where a case concerned a particular bishop could that bishop be got there to provide the local knowledge.

The time after 1845 was a terrible time for the Commission. It came within distance of being abolished, which in the long run would have been disaster.

I must now introduce a villain: a strange and honourable villain, Edward Horsman, MP for Cockermouth in Cumbria. He made a momentous contribution to the history of the Commission and so of England. The Commission of 1845 was vulnerable to attack. Horsman worked hard and collected every instrument, fact, inquiry, by which he might injure it at its most vulnerable points and then twist his dagger in the wounds. He made it go through hell.

It was hard to judge him. He was not, let us say, a rebellious Roman Catholic MP from Southern Ireland using attacks on the Church for political ends. He was an Anglican, though born in Scotland. No one knows to this day whether he was a sincere, radical churchman who cared deeply for the Church, or a violent anti-clerical masquerading as a faithful churchman. Disraeli called him 'the superior person' of the House of Commons. His hearers found him pompous-sounding and called his oratory bow-wow. He was animated, it was said, but the animation seemed like the liveliness of a riding-school or a rocking-horse (*Daily News*, cited *Guardian* (1876), 1, 1580). If he was an Anglican, it has to be said that he made the atmosphere of the House of Commons unpleasant, so that good men came to dread debates about the Commission because they foresaw how personalities would fly across the chamber. And yet, reading Horsman's speeches now, and not being able to experience the manner of the superior person, I am inclined, though only just, to award the benefit of the doubt and believe him to be a person who really did care with passion about the parish system of the Church of England.

It was very devastating. It was devastating for some individuals. It was revolutionary for the Commission. It was devastating for the bishops. With the aid of misstatements which were culpably careless if they were not unscrupulous, he sank Bishop Blomfield's reputation to zero; so that Blomfield's grandson said that his grandfather's last ten years were rather tragic. No one did more than Horsman to create that national mood which now makes the Barchester novels so amusing. No one did more than Horsman to postpone for a quarter of a century the formation of the needed extra dioceses. No one did more than Horsman to force constitutional revolution on the Commission.

He saw our system of national pastoral care as unparalleled in all Protestantism for its virtues; a truly national Church, blessed in her teaching. Again and again he pointed out to Parliament how poor clergy were suffering; and how the purpose of these historic endowments was the poor. 'It is for the poor that our established Church exists. The revenues of that Church are the heritage of the poor; and we in this House are their guardians and protectors' (Hansard 95, 1097). This Church, and these parishes, and these poor parsons ministering so selflessly, need bishops to care about them; men of a sacred function, and a higher spiritual order, and illuminated with a brighter knowledge, and inspired by a more uninterrupted communion with holy things, and engrossed by one intense and soul-absorbing principle (Hansard

110, 954). What were true bishops like? He reminded the House of Commons of the great bishops of the early Church – of Cyprian and Ambrose and Augustine, and of the great bishops of English history, Andrewes and Jewel and Bedell.

And now 'alas'. The Church has been plundered at different periods of our history: by our monarchs first – by nobles next – by our bishops in the last century – and in our own day by the Ecclesiastical Commissioners. When the inner cities are crying out, what are the Commissioners doing? They bought a palace for the Bishop of Gloucester and Bristol, lots of bedrooms. When this wonderful pastoral system is languishing, what are the Commissioners doing? Because they hand over Huntingdonshire from the diocese of Lincoln to the diocese of Ely, they eject the Bishop of Lincoln from his palace at Buckden, which they sell for partial demolition at a few hundred pounds, and then buy an enormous and expensive estate at Riseholme outside Lincoln. Who decides these things? The majority at the meetings of the Commission are always bishops. They are feathering their nests; plundering the Church. And they cannot be trusted. They now have to hand over to the Commissioners surplus income above what the Act of Parliament has laid down. Yet the Bishop of Durham is notoriously wealthier than before. Anyway, what are the bishops doing, sitting at a London committee on leaseholds when they ought to be at home caring for their flocks?

At various times, Horsman moved awkward motions: a vote of censure on the Commission; a motion that all bishops be ejected from the Commission; an inquiry into deans and chapters on the ground that they misused their revenues.

All this was important, it was searing, in this history. One difficulty was, there was hardly a voice to defend. The bishops needed defenders who were not bishops. Their natural defenders, the very articulate mouths of the Church, dwelt in cathedral closes; and in those circumstances a march of canons to defend the bishops was likely to consist of stragglers. Therefore the defence of the Commission rested upon a handful of laymen in the House of Commons; among whom I name with honour the young Mr Gladstone. The young Disraeli was no use: he loathed Bishop Blomfield. But the unexpected defender, who protected the

Commission far better than anyone else, was the Prime Minister, tiny Lord John Russell.

In other contexts Lord John Russell's attitudes to the Church of England were sometimes bigoted and crude (he was quite crude in his hostility to the disciples of the Oxford Movement). In our context he was everything that you could wish. He had been one of the original members of the Commission in 1836. He had not attended much. He greatly regretted the change of constitution in 1840 when all the bishops became Commissioners and so became reponsible for every mistake that was made, like buying a house with too many bedrooms for the Bishop of Gloucester and Bristol. Lord John Russell confessed a need for drastic change in the constitution. But he stoutly defended the Commission as a necessity and he defended the character and integrity of the bishops.

This was the more necessary because the Commission had other enemies besides the Horsmans and the Humes and Halls in Parliament; and besides the far more gentlemanly critics among the deans and chapters.

The first arose from disappointment. All this loose talk about the Church's vast wealth produced the feeling that the historic endowments of the Church of England were a gold mine. The entire parish system could be strengthened in a moment. Nothing could be more deluded. Partly because the government of 1843 also gave them the duty of founding a lot of new parish districts and building churches on them, the Commissioners could help no one for ten years after 1844. The Commission first came again into credit in 1856, twenty years after the foundation, and then the credit was £5,000. Its principal difficulty was the longevity of canons. The Commission depended for its money on people dying. Something about the atmosphere of cathedral closes must have been particularly healthy. And the legislation was humane, and suppressed not every canonry (above four) at death, but, after two suppressions at a cathedral, allowed a third canonry to survive for that time, so as to slow down the decline in cathedral posts, and correspondingly slow down the money of the Commission.

It was only by about 1870 that the Commission really began to fulfil the vast hopes with which it was founded. The last prebendary who had tenure under the old regime died in 1891. Very appropriately, he held the prebend of Wiveliscombe in Wells Cathedral (G. F. A. Best, *Temporal Pillars* (1964), p. 501).

Therefore, in the 1840s the Commissioners were given an enormous work to do and no money to do it. That did not endear them.

The other kind of enemy was necessary out of what they were founded to do. Central to their task was to make the administration of property efficient; that means, in modern terms, make people pay economic rents. The old endowments rattled along for centuries, managed by unbusinesslike parsons, who did not like offending their tenants. Now, a board in London was to get rid of the inefficiencies; and, with the inefficiencies, something of the good humour.

Most of the land was on lease. The most common form of lease was for seven years, with a guarantee that it would be renewed for another seven, or even a third seven years. Another very common form of lease was for life. The lessee bought himself or herself a life-tenure in the property. On his death the lease fell in to the owner, who got another large payment. So if (let us say) three lessees died in three years, the bishop or the canon got two large capital payments. If someone lived on and on, he deprived the bishop or the canon, and perhaps their successors, of any money at all.

That was a traditional and accepted way of gambling. But, if your concern was efficient administration, this was the worst possible method. To budget sensibly, you needed to know how much money would come in. On this historic method you could never know.

Therefore, from the first the Commissioners knew that one of their main tasks was to end these archaic forms of leasehold. And, in the end, nothing could do more to raise the revenues of the Church. But to change a long-accepted mode of tenure would run, all over the country, not only into vested interests of various kinds, but into feelings of resentment at injustice among lessees

Horsman in Parliament; bishops making mistakes; deans and chapters glum or murmuring; lessees resentful – and on top of it all, the Secretary of the Commission – into whose hands so much power fell while the bishops stayed away from meetings – was found to have defalcated with some of the Commission's money and was dismissed and emigrated to Australia – not at all quietly to avoid scandal; there was a Parliamentary paper to explain it. At that point, between about 1847 and 1863, the Ecclesiastical Commission was running well in the stakes for being the most unpopular institution of the country, outdistanced only by Cardinal Wiseman.

If the Commission was to survive, three things were essential.

The first was that the bishops must cease to be responsible for the management. If we put it in contemporary terms, we might put it like this: since any management of a lot of endowment is going to cause problems, some of them personal and difficult, it is essential that the critics, if something goes wrong, shall not be able to blame Lambeth Palace or the General Synod at Church House, but shall blame Number 1 Millbank. Clearly, in 1851 there needed to be a strong link between the managers and the bishops, just as today there needs to be a strong link between Number 1 Millbank and the General Synod. But the link must not be such that the churchmen are made responsible for the management. That meant, in 1850, that the management side of the Commission had to be jacked up. It could no longer do with a management which was merely the secretary to the bishops, like the defalcating Secretary. Hence, Lord John Russell created the three Estates Commissioners, who are still with us, largely in the same form to this day. Henceforth the management lay with these three, plus two members, one lay, chosen by the Commissioners from themselves. Bishop Blomfield was made one of the first two, but was now past his time of effectiveness. During the next century that seat was held by the Bishop of London far more often than not, for the obvious reason that its occupant needed to live in or near London.

The next essential for survival in 1850 was to fuse the funds of the Commission. They had money from bishops' endowments, the Episcopal Fund; and money from suppressed canonries, the Common Fund. To amalgamate these was probably a breach of ancient trusts. Some sensible men wanted to keep the funds separate to finance the new dioceses which were needed so greatly. But Horsman made the union of the funds essential for survival. That union might postpone for too long the making of new dioceses. But it stopped the mouths of those who accused the Commission of buying too many bedrooms for the bishop of Gloucester and Bristol while Mr Quiverful, the curate, could hardly feed his numerous brats. The flowing of bishops' endowments into parishes had become a necessity.

The third necessity was more a matter of feeling. The new Estates Committee had to recognize that efficiency is not everything. Good feeling in the locality is important pastorally. A trustee is bound to try for the market rent. A churchman who cares for the welfare of parishes may not be able, and may not wish, to enforce it all.

Suddenly the Commission was confronted by a problem which none of its founders expected. A board of trustees is conscious of the trust. It sees Mr Quiverful, the hard-pressed curate in the parish of suburban Barchester. Because it has Mr Quiverful in mind, it has to make the most of the rent or the dividends in any way that is legal and honourable. Tenant farmers sing an elegy of hardship, but the trustees are not out to help tenant farmers in trouble, and are legally bound to do all they can for Mr Quiverful. Yet there instantly came points where morality started to hit. A course which is legal, and is consistent with honour, is seen by a section of opinion, conscious perhaps of some desperate farmer's wife, to be less than the highest morality. This problem – that the trustees need to seem not just moral, but compassionate, as well as effective trustees – first hit the Commissioners during the 1840s over changes in leaseholds. But it stayed with them and was bound to stay. And it was rapidly recognized, in fact at once, that some element of flexibility in the trustees' duty was a necessity.

The world pays the Church a high compliment. It demands a unique standard. No one blames the University of London because its biggest benefaction came from Holloway's Pills, which chemists showed to be sham. No one blames Guy's Hospital because Thomas Guy made his money by speculating in the South Sea Bubble. The world pays a compliment to the Church in not following this rule.

The See of London had a Paddington estate. The See of Winchester had a Southwark estate. These estates passed to the Commission. By the 1880s they caused grossly irrelevant and grossly unjust criticism of the Commission for getting its money out of pubs and prostitutes. The nub lay deeper. If a slum leasehold in South London fell in – the legal duty of the Board is to maximize the revenue – tear the whole place down and build flats for the middle class; and the heart starts to beat, and compassion starts to pour, and the Church is seen to have a unique chance to do something for the impoverished of South London; and the pastoral care of the Commission rubs against its duty as trustee. What about Mr Quiverful? In this century, armaments shares, brewery shares, tobacco shares, and shares with South African links have been the problems of this sort to be much debated. Underneath, and with less public attention, the question of the use of property was always present. It is curious that no one anticipated this problem. The drafting of the great Act of 1840 betrays no consciousness of the difference that was being made. If Bishop Blomfield owned the Paddington estate, his duty was to all the inhabitants as well as the curates. If a board of trustees owned the Paddington estate, it was the curates whose interests it was founded to help; and no one could deny that the curates needed help badly.

Therefore, the best the managers could do included pastoral motives, which could make 'the best' mean not in all respects the best that is legally possible, but the best for the Church, taking that in its largest sense.

That wider view quickly widened the vision of the Commission. In Lambeth Palace library, it would be right to express gratitude for the law 29 & 30 Vic. c. 111. 7–8, which made the Commission, by then administering the Canterbury estates, liable for the upkeep of the library, one of the little handful of historic libraries which the nation possesses. Or take another example of wider view: pensions for clergy. The Commission was founded to abolish sinecures – no work, some pay; a pension is a form of sinecure – no work, some pay. Therefore the Commissioners doubted whether they would be acting legally if they helped to fund a pension scheme. Eventually, and nervously, very late, not till 1907, they argued that to pay some people to be idle is good for the cure of souls, and started a modest pension scheme. It needed the Church Assembly to exist before they could get a Measure, in 1921, which made sure that all this was legal.

I must now introduce a minor hero. The first of the First Estate Commissioners, paid and full time, was the third Earl of Chichester. He had no professional qualifications. He was a Guards officer who was an earl from the age of 22, and was put on to the Commission as one of its lay members as early as February 1841 – that is while the Whig Lord Melbourne was still Prime Minister. He was a devout Evangelical, who often presided at the meetings of the Evangelical societies at Exeter Hall, and became President of the Church Missionary Society, with which he was connected at least from the middle 1830s. He was consistently inaudible in the House of Lords; on two or three occasions Hansard is reduced to saying that the speech of the Earl of Chichester was inaudible, and on several more it begins the report of his speech by saying, 'The Earl of Chichester was understood to say ...'. He was a personal friend of Champneys, the Evangelical slum pastor, and of Bishop Crowther, the first black bishop. He had a high regard for Bishop Blomfield, which is a mark up to that controversial prelate. He was an expert on prisons and one of the earliest to care for juvenile offenders. He cared about open spaces for recreation, and hated cruelty to animals, especially dogs, though he insisted that tenants on Church estates should not be stopped from shooting rabbits. Most important of all, in that moment when the Commissioners were accused by Horsman of plundering the Church, and when the Secretary had just defalcated, he was well known for a kind of stiff or ramrod rectitude.

He stuck out the office of First Commissioner for twenty-eight years, and became known as the Father of the Board. The new pattern of management was established under the leadership of a person who cared not just about the money but about the pastoral welfare of parishes which money could aid. And, since his regime coincided with the real flowing in of the canonries' money and with the enfranchisement of the archaic leaseholds, suddenly the Commission was, after all, a fairy godmother to the Church, making viable many thousand parishes which were hardly viable when they started and which would have collapsed if they had not been helped. He had an impartial judgment and an accurate memory, and he happily stood up to abuse. When he finally retired in 1878, *The Times* called him the main instrument in the revolution in connexion with the distribution of Church property in England (*The Times*, 30 October 1878).[1].

Not long after he took office, one thing stood out unmistakably: the sanguine expectation that this was a gold mine was false, in this sense: about the middle of the fifties Chichester and others realized that, however valuable they made the historic endowments, they could never cope with the whole pastoral system of the Church as it ought to be, and that the Church must depend, and depend largely, on private donation and generosity. This was not a comfortable recognition for everyone, partly because the virtue of the old system was to make the parson independent of the parishioners and, therefore, not likely to be swayed by popular vote as might happen to the Congregationalist pastor; and partly because the purpose of the endowments was to reach out to the poor, who could not afford to contribute. If the Church said that it depended on contributions, that might mean that it became more middle class, while endowments were intended for the people unable to contribute. Nevertheless, Chichester and his men saw as early as anyone that the necessity lay upon them. From the late fifties of the last century they began to augment parishes where voluntary contributions were forthcoming. This was loudly criticized as making the Church more middle class. But Chichester kept an exceptive clause – that this did not apply when places of destitution were in question.

Chichester held his eye steadily on the interests of the whole Church. That was controversial. Should you give Durham money to Manchester? The Commissioners came under pressure, both from local interest and then from Acts of Parliament, which compelled them in various ways to take local needs into account in places from which they drew revenue as, for example, places from which they drew tithe. But Chichester's eye was always upon destitution. I have the impression that he never liked this pressure from local interests. It is the worst places which need help. The obligation to help local needs is a form of queue-jumping; a less needy parish gaining help before a more needy. The eye should be fixed upon the whole Church and not upon a particular county or city or diocese. The sharpest such conflict

---

[1] The Earl of Chichester's younger brother was J. T. Pelham, Bishop of Norwich, 1857–93.

came when someone produced a bill in Parliament to allot the stipend of one of the suppressed canonries of St George's, Windsor to put up the pay of the Military Knights of Windsor. Here was local interest with a vengeance. Chichester never used stronger language than in resisting this bill, as contrary to the Commission's purposes and to the Acts of Parliament which founded it. When I say that he never used stronger language, I do not mean that his language, even then, was other than quiet and restrained; unless, as is very possible, the Hansard reporter heard little of what he said. Chichester is a classic case to prove the law that in a controversial situation it is useful when nobody can hear what you say.

It will be worth giving one instance of what a relief it was to get controversy out of the responsibility of the bishops. A tenant at Godmanchester was vociferous, and, so far as can now be seen, very unreasonable about the renewal of his lease. He got a local peer, the Earl of Sandwich, to raise the matter in Parliament. It was no minor benefit to the Church that the Bishop of Ely need have no part in the wrangle and the duel could be fought between Sandwich and Chichester, who was capable of being inaudibly unbending to an army of earls.

The question is, did the Commission do what it set out to do? There may be those still who regret what happened to Barchester, which never was the same again. Sir Herbert Butterfield warned us not to assume about the past that a side which won was the best side. In the old world it had become almost a convention that the Bishop of Llandaff was also the Dean of St Paul's. On the face of it, and on the axioms whereby the Commission was founded, it was ridiculous. But, in fact, the then bijou See of Llandaff got far bigger men for much of the year than otherwise would have been possible, and probably St Paul's hardly suffered. The disadvantage was not the results of that particular case but the example which it gave to less satisfactory links. Sir Richard Kaye, the Dean of Lincoln, by his death (1809) vacated not only the deanery of Lincoln, but an archdeaconry, two prebends, and three rectories, making seven offices in all. For some clergymen it was a good time. And yet, if we complain about the Dean of Lincoln having seven jobs, we suddenly remember that a saint of the Church of England, now in our calendar, namely Lancelot

Andrewes, at one period of his life had seven jobs, and today we know country clergymen in something of the same situation. Still, 1836 was *not* a good time for the Quiverfuls or the Crawleys of Hogglestock. In the work of converting the Church of England from the Church of Barchester to an instrument capable of taking on the battle with the modern world, even if it lost the battle quite often, the Commissioners were a chief instrument.

As with all historic institutions, things sometimes went unpredictably. Founded to abolish pluralities, they found themselves in the twentieth century supporting, by necessity, more and more pluralistic clergymen. Founded to abolish sinecures, they found themselves in the twentieth century supporting more than 9,000 sinecures, which would have made Bishop Blomfield or the Earl of Chichester unable to sleep at nights; the difference being that to qualify for the 9,000 you needed to be a certain age, and to qualify for the sixty-odd it was best to be of certain families. Created to help the poor, they found themselves not only doing that, extensively, but also, and of necessity, in the same cause, propping up middle-class vicars. Founded to help the inner city, at least as a primary task, and in the end doing that extensively, they also did excellent work for the rural parishes, and probably propped up by indirect means more historic country churches than would have been achieved by the rival government scheme to make them a church repair commission. Changes of times alter what institutions have to do. I do not think any serious historian can look back and be other than grateful for what was done, even though he or she might regret moments of what happened or aspects of the institutional change. And the reason why I think that may be pointed by a quotation from a speech in Parliament from the most lacerating enemy the Commission ever had. Here is Edward Horsman, 1 August 1848 (col. 1077):

The Acts of Parliament (which founded the Commission's work) 'have been followed by results which their most sanguine supporters could not have anticipated; there was a new race of clergy; and the Church has been raised to a usefulness and a popularity unknown before. Society has been much benefited by these Acts; but they cannot work effectually or satisfactorily unless the machinery by which they were commanded and superintended is put in order'.

So if even Edward Horsman said that the Commission was a

very good thing, at least in potentiality, and if even Horsman with his bow-wow oratory said that the Commissioners' existence helped to create a new race of clergy, it must indeed have been a good thing, for compliments from one's enemy are the best of all compliments.

Chapter 4

'LEAD, KINDLY LIGHT'

THE PILLAR OF THE CLOUD.

LEAD, kindly light, amid the encircling gloom
  Lead Thou me on!
The night is dark, and I am far from home –
  Lead Thou me on!
Keep Thou my feet; I do not ask to see
The distant scene – one step enough for me.

I was not ever thus, nor pray'd that Thou
  Shouldst lead me on.
I loved to choose and see my path, but now
  Lead Thou me on!
I loved the garish day, and, spite of fears,
Pride ruled my will: remember not past years.

So long Thy power hath blest me, sure it still
  Will lead me on,
O'er moor and fen, o'er crag and torrent, till
  The night is gone;
And with the morn those angel faces smile
Which I have loved long since, and lost awhile.

At Sea   June 16, 1833

Afterwards a title was given to the poem or hymn: 'The Pillar of the Cloud'. Newman first gave it, perhaps more as a text or motto than a title, when he reprinted the poem in *Occasional Verses* (1868). It is a very inappropriate title. A pillar of cloud led the Israelites by day, a pillar of fire by night. The author of the hymn is in dusk. The original had no title but 'Faith'. The first table of contents described it correctly as 'Light in Darkness'. That table of contents placed it under the general heading of 'Faith'.

Newman had written verse from time to time since 1819. At the end of 1832 he began to write systematically. When in December 1832 he set off with the two Froudes for the Mediterranean, the leisure and the absence of books allowed him to try his hand at verses almost regularly; sometimes day after day. He already had a purpose beyond the expression of a poetic instinct. In that November he suggested to the editor of the *British Magazine*, Hugh James Rose, that he should print a series, under the name *Lyra apostolica*. The object would be to assert truths 'with greater freedom, and clearness, than in the *Christian Year*' of John Keble. He told his friend Rogers (1 December 1832) that stirring times bring out poets, and that he hoped by this poetry to create 'a quasi-political engine'.

By the time he got back to England he had quite a collection. It was enough to feed the *British Magazine* with verse till the end of 1836, with the help of friends, especially Keble. In the collected edition of *Lyra apostolica* there are 179 poems; 109 are by Newman and 46 by Keble. It was almost entirely a Newman–Keble collection, and Newman predominated.

In Rome, March 1833, he talked with Froude of the verses as having a purpose. To his friend Rogers he justified the time spent on versification: 'Ten thousand obvious ideas become impressive when put into metrical shape; and many of them we should not dare to utter except metrically, for thus the responsibility is (as it were) shoved off of oneself and one speaks *hos paidizon* (as if playfully), though serious. I am so convinced of the use of it, particularly in time of excitement, that I have begun to practise myself, which I never did before.' To his sister he called the verses 'my follies' (*The Letters and Diaries of John Henry Newman*, edited at the Birmingham Oratory, 3/236 and 132ff. – hereafter *LD*).

After being near death from fever in Sicily, he set off for England again from Palermo in June 1833. He sailed in an orange boat on 13 June. The *Apologia* does not quite say, but has been commonly understood as saying, that 'Lead, Kindly Light' was written as the ship lay becalmed in the straits of Bonifacio between Sardinia and Corsica. Newman's diary shows that he must have written it while the ship was becalmed before it entered the straits. For the poem is dated 16 June. The diary shows that they came in sight of Sardinia on 17 June and were through the straits on 22 June. A letter to Capes of August 1850 described it as written 'in the sun off Sardinia' and mentioned the cool translucent lazy wave. So the dusk of the poem was mental.

The editor of the *British Magazine* grew nervous of the political freedom of the verses which he was being asked to print as *Lyra apostolica*. This nervousness caused Newman further to express what he thought his verse intended to do. 'What is the *Lyra Apostolica* but a ballad? It was undertaken with a view of catching people when unguarded' (to Bowden, 17 November 1833, *LD*, 4/109: Bowden contributed six poems to *Lyra*; his muse was pedestrian; he was a very close friend of Newman). But when in 1836 Newman collected the verses in a single volume, the devotional idea predominated over the political, as was proved by the discussion over the format. Both Newman and the publisher wanted the volume to look like the *Christian Year* of Keble – same type, same size of page, same appearance. That is, they conceived it as a continuation of a devotional book, probably aimed at the same kind of reader (see *LD*, 5/334–5).

He continued to be very modest about his verse and intention. 'My object was *not* poetry but to bring out *ideas*. Thus my harshness, as you justly call it, (if nothing else) was part of a *theory*. I felt it absurd to set up for a poet' (to F. W. Faber, 1 February 1850, *LD*, 11/401).

Lyra apostolica came to three editions by 1838, and was evidently being used by a few hundred people as a devotional manual. Its authors were still anonymous, though now they were distinguished by Greek letters. Scott Holland would later call it 'the song book of English Catholicity, in its most militant and defiant mood' (in his introduction to the 1901 edition of *Lyra apostolica*).

Newman arranged that Samuel Wilberforce should review the book in the *British Critic*. This review appeared in the number for January 1837 (167ff.) and may have helped to make readers aware of the volume, but disappointed Newman. Wilberforce said that the disturbed times had led many members of the Church of England to study Catholic antiquity; and 'even as they have read, the spirit of poetry has come down upon them'. He said that the inspirations of *Lyra* had drawn from purer and holier fountains than those which nourished Methodist and Evangelical hymnody. He criticized the anonymous Newman for obscurity, and for something constrained and inharmonious. Miss Keble afterwards said to Isaac Williams, another contributor to *Lyra* (nine poems), as Williams recorded in his autobiography (written 1851, published 1893) that this criticism by Wilberforce was bad for Newman because it discouraged him from using his natural vein of poetry. We have no reason to think that Miss Keble knew much about Newman's feelings.

The Evangelical *Christian Observer* of 1837 (460ff.) reviewed *Lyra* as 'a chequered book'; with much sunlight and much shade; much admirable, much dangerous; the Church as primary, religion as subordinate. It talks of tradition, and the power of the priestly office, and prayers for the dead. The reviewer selected Delta (who was Newman) and said that he had more poetic tendency in his thought than poetic power. The reviewer said that the authors were ponderous and gloomy; that they trod the religious path painfully; and that every word was expressive of toil.

This was the first sign of what was to become the main attack upon 'Lead, Kindly Light'. It was sad. It had not the confidence of faith. It had not the sense of free grace. It was the soul struggling. The true Christian ought not to be in a world of gloom and twilight.

Earlier in life Newman wrote an essay on the nature of poetry (*Essays and Sketches*, 1 (1948), ed. C. F. Harrold, 55–82). Most of this meditation was nothing to do with the lyrics or semi-lyrics which he now attempted. But some of the phrases sound with an authentic ring – poetry 'provides a solace for the mind broken by the disappointments and sufferings of actual life; and becomes, moreover, the utterance of the inward emotions of a right moral feeling, seeking a purity and a truth which this world will not give'. 'With Christians, a poetical view of things is a duty – we are bid to colour all things with hues of faith, to see a divine meaning in every event . . .'

Some of the poetic influences can be discerned. Blake meant nothing, Byron nothing, Wordsworth (strangely) not a lot. Scott's poetry he loved, but it was of a different type from these lyrics. For this *lyra* we may think of three especial models in the general background of Newman's aesthetic sensibility: Crabbe, whom he often cited; Cowper, whom he knew well from his Evangelical days; and John Keble, for whom he felt at that time so profound an admiration. His own contributions to the *Lyra* have a truer vein of poetry than those which Keble contributed. In the 1901 edition of *Lyra* H. C. Beeching attributed the qualities of simplicity and directness partly to natural simplicity, partly to Newman's early study of Greek tragedy and its choruses; and Beeching was a sensitive and expert critic of English poetry.

The devotional poetry of *The Christian Year* by Keble began quickly to be incorporated into hymn books for the use of congregations. *Lyra apostolica*, though less used and less generally suitable, naturally came under similar consideration for use in hymnody. Surprisingly early someone saw, what Newman never dreamed of and for long afterwards refused to accept, that the three personal stanzas from the coast of Sardinia would make a singable hymn. As early as 1845 (!) Dr Horatius Bonar, a Scottish Presbyterian, put it into the *Bible Hymn Book*. So far as we yet know he did not bother to seek the permission of the author, whose name was still unknown to the public. And it is improbable that he sought any leave, because he altered the first line:

> Lead, Saviour, lead amid the encircling gloom.

And Dr Bonar was the first to realize that congregations would never have heard the word *garish* in the couplet

> I loved the garish day, and, spite of fears
> Pride ruled my will: remember not past years.

Congregations would not know the word, even though it came in Shakespeare's *Romeo and Juliet* and was the kind of word used by literary men when they were being literary. Dr Bonar changed it to

> I loved the glare of day,

which was not so good and did not have the nuance of the original. Dr Bonar's rewording was followed by a series of other attempts to cope with the word *garish*. (Julian traced several of these variants in his *Dictionary of Hymnology*, rev. edn (1907), 1/669.)

Here were two desires to amend the stanzas; first by making its beginning, and so its whole, more evidently Christian, and therefore by putting Lord or Saviour where stood the kindly light; and secondly by getting rid of the unknown word. The Americans found particular difficulty. Henry Ward Beecher's *Plymouth Collection* (1855) began

> Send, kindly light.

In 1860 an American book of the Protestant Episcopal Church, *Hymns for Church and Home*, coped with these two 'difficulties' in its own way. It began:

> Send Lord thy light amid the encircling gloom.

And it did better than Dr Bonar with *garish*, though not perfectly:

> I loved day's dazzling light.

But the Americans had a new difficulty. All the poem was personal, but the last stanza was the most personal. They wanted to Christianize Newman's portrait of the soul trudging over the moors and mountains and marsh:

> So long thy power hath blest me, sure it still
>   will lead me on
> O'er moor and fen, o'er crag and torrent, till
>   The night is gone.

The American Episcopalians produced the lowest bathos ever perpetrated upon this private poem in the effort to make it a congregational hymn:

> So long thy power hath bless'd me, surely still
>   'Twill lead me on
> Through dreary hours, through pain and sorrow, till
>   The night is gone.

So far as is known, no one asked Newman's permission for any of this piracy.

However, by now the identity of the author was clear. In 1853 Newman, as Rector of the University of Dublin, collected his own verses, including those in the *Lyra apostolica*, and published them at Dublin as *Verses on Religious Subjects*.

Anglican hymn books in England at first rejected it as unsuitable. They may also have been influenced by the controversial repute of the author, who had left their Church amid much publicity. Even the first two editions of *Hymns Ancient and Modern* (1860 and 1861), which was intended to be the Tractarian hymn book, and which soon conquered the Church of England, did not contain it. And yet when Newman wrote his religious autobiography during the first months of 1864, he described the circumstances in which the poem was written, and said

Then it was that I wrote the lines, *Lead kindly light*, which have since become well known.

If they were well known, they were not well known to everyone under that name, which so many books altered.

The Church hymn books objected to the poem because it could be sung by Unitarians. It was not theological enough for churchmen. The Unitarian *Hymns of the Spirit*, published that same year in Boston, Massachusetts, included 'Lead, Kindly Light', under that beginning; though the garish day was day's dazzling light and the moor and fen turned into dreary doubts. Hymn books, there was no doubt, could be a trial to a poet.

In 1870 one of the Evangelical collectors in the Church of England tried to remedy the situation.

Edward Henry Bickersteth was admired by many Victorians as a religious poet. In 1866 he published an epic poem, on the lines of Dante or Milton, describing a visit under guidance to the world of the spirits. It was entitled *Yesterday, Today and For Ever*. Princess Alexandra read parts of the poem to her husband the Prince of Wales in his near-mortal illness.

In 1870 Bickersteth published *The Hymnal Companion to the Book of Common Prayer*, which became the hymn book of the Evangelicals and more than the Evangelicals.

Naturally he wanted something more assured in faith than the stanzas which Newman wrote. He therefore added a fourth stanza:

> Meantime along the narrow rugged path
> Thyself hast trod
> Lead, Saviour, lead me home in childlike faith,
> Home to my God,
> To rest for ever after earthly strife
> In the calm light of everlasting life.

In the printing he added the stanza as though it was part of the same poem.

Four years later someone wrote to Newman to point out that a verse was added to his poem. On 17 June 1874 Newman wrote a humble letter to the publisher, Sampson Low and Co. ('I beg your pardon if this letter is grounded in any mistake'). He said that he did not doubt that he had given leave for the poem to be inserted into the collection, and readily, but an addition? 'It is not that the verse is not both in sentiment and in language graceful and good, but I think you will see at once how unwilling an author must be to subject himself to the inconvenience of that being ascribed to him which is not his own.'

The publishers passed this letter to Bickersteth, who explained to Newman that he had added a verse; that this verse was a great comfort in mortal illness to his daughter Alice Frances; and that he would add a note in the next edition to show that he had added a verse to Newman's poem. He told Newman that the verses as they stood did not make it a hymn, and therefore he added his verse; as if (he did not say this) he needed to Christianize Newman.

Newman's reply (20 June 1874) was a model of forbearance. He had every ground for severity.

I agree with you that these verses are not a hymn, nor are they suitable for singing, and it is this which at once surprises and gratifies me, and makes me thankful that, in spite of their having no claim to be used as a hymn, they have made their way into so many collections.

He thanked the bishop for sending him a beautiful memoir of his daughter. Never did Newman write a kinder letter.

Three days later Bickersteth sent Newman a copy of his poem *Yesterday, Today and for Ever* (8th edn, 1873). Newman acknowledged it with thanks on 11 July. The poem had 435 pages, of which 140 were cut by Newman or one of the other fathers of the Oratory at Birmingham (*LD*, 27/80, 88).

For Newman it was all very inconvenient. From all over the country, even from America, correspondents wrote to ask him whether the fourth stanza was his. In 1878 Bickersteth published a new edition in which he showed that the fourth stanza was by a different author from the first three. He did not get rid of the stanza altogether till after a protest by one of Newman's colleagues and in the 1890 edition, when he relegated the extra stanza to an appendix. Newman's letters of denial to correspondents grew steadily stronger. In March 1881 he allowed the editor of another collection to print it, but only on condition that it was printed unaltered. 'No one likes interpolations in what he has written' (*LD*, 29/351). To Talbot, the Warden of Keble College, he wryly pointed out that this business of interpolation was a crime which Protestants usually attributed to Catholics. That month he assigned the copyright in *Lyra apostolica* to Keble College. Talbot (11 April 1881) undertook that so long as the copyright existed the poems must be printed as written (*LD*, 29/359).

In extenuation of those who amended his poem, Newman was always one for amending his own poems. He was a great tinkerer with his texts in second or third editions. In 1868 he introduced the doctrine of purgatory into the poem 'Rest' in *Lyra apostolica*, with devastating bathos. He wisely removed it six years later. But he never touched 'Lead, Kindly Light'; unless we count a playing, not for the better, with the title of the poem.

The poem, in its original form, was now in *Hymns Ancient and Modern*, the hymn book of high churchmen, and in a corrupt but more obviously Christian form in the hymn book of Evangelical churchmen. It began to be so well known that it was used devotionally at death-beds. When Queen Victoria's son the Duke of Albany was dying, the Queen quoted all the last stanza, though not quite correctly (*LD*, 30/387). Perhaps the Queen had met the stanza in one of its 'corrupt' forms. In 1876 came the first of several renderings into Latin. Soon there were several translations into Welsh. It was the favourite hymn of the Archbishop of Canterbury, A. C. Tait (P. T. Marsh, *The Victorian Church in Decline*, 3n).

In the original text the poem was not suitable for funerals. It was an act of faith by someone near the start of a journey. The three stanzas had none of the feeling of a Nunc Dimittis. Bickersteth's fourth stanza made the poem into a hymn perfect for use at funerals, a very strong act of faith in life after death. As an act of faith for funerals it caught people's sentiment all over England. It grew so familiar as a hymn at funerals that it continued to be used at funerals even after the fourth stanza was no longer added. The angel faces of the last couplet, understood in

a particular way, were enough to keep people's love of it as a
hymn of departing. There were those who felt the loss of
Bickersteth's additional verse to be a religious loss (see *Notes and
Queries* (1880), 1, 480).

In January 1884 Newman's friend R. H. Hutton, the editor of
the *Spectator*, lectured to an audience of nearly 300 working men.
When he referred to 'Lead, Kindly Light', there was a 'perfect
thunder of applause' (*LD*, 30/294). The hymn had become
national. Newman himself must have been one of the minority of
Englishmen who never heard it sung (*Guardian* (1890), 1377). A
majority of hymn books still omitted it as unsuitable. Some said it
was too vague and weak a way to address God. But these books
were not the popular editions.

In 1879–80 the hymn was so well known that public discussion
arose over the meaning of the last lines:

> And with the morn those angel faces smile
> Which I have loved long since, and lost awhile.

When *Lyra apostolica* first appeared, William Greenhill went to
Newman's friend and colleague Charles Marriott and asked what
this meant. Marriott suggested that the couplet touched on the
idea that infants have a more intimate communion with the
unseen world; for Newman had talked of this sensitivity in the
little child in one of his parochial sermons (*PS*, 2/63–5):

There is in the infant soul in the first years of its regenerate state, a discernment
of the unseen world in the things that are seen and realization of what is
Soverign and Adorable . . . he has this one great gift, that he seems lately to
have come from God's Presence.

But when in 1879 Newman was asked what the couplet meant,
he refused to answer. He appealed to the doctrine of John Keble,
that poets are not bound to give a sense to what they have
written.

There must be a statute of limitations for writers of verse, or it would be quite
a tyranny if, in an art which is the expression not of truth, but of imagination
and sentiment, one were obliged to be ready for examination on the transient
states of mind which come upon one when homesick, or seasick, or in any
other way sensitive or excited. (*LD*, 29.11)

With Newman's permission Greenhill sent to the *Guardian* this
refusal to explain (printed 25 February 1880).

The wording of the refusal was remarkable. Somebody said that here for many years he had been valuing the verse as a true poetic expression of sincere religious feeling, and now the author tells him that it could be the mere result of depression caused by seasickness (see *Notes and Queries* (1880), 1, 232).

The refusal, and the wording of the refusal, left the field open to speculators. Was Newman running down his own poem because it was an Anglican poem and its author was not now an Anglican? Was this a man who now professed the doctrine of purgatory and must try to discredit non-Catholic words hardly compatible with a doctrine of purgatory (see *Notes and Queries* (1880), 2, 52)? Were the words to be suspect as the doubts of a man worrying whether to become a Roman Catholic? Did it make the poem suspect as a hymn, because it showed that its author had for the moment lost the qualities of faith and assurance? At Clevedon in Somerset they put their own interpretation into a stained glass window: an angel bears two babies to heaven, with Newman's couplet beneath, so that the meaning would be a hope in reunion with the departed. Other interpretations were proffered. Someone said *angel* in *angel faces* was only an adjective meaning good, and had nothing to do with angels. (Debate in *Notes and Queries* (3 April, 8 May, 12 June, 7 August, 1880), summarized Julian, 1/668). Though Newman refused to say, we must think Marriott's understanding to be correct.

We may take as an example of the objectors to 'Lead, Kindly Light' a booklet on *Our Church Hymnody* (1881) by the editor of the *Anglican Psalter Noted*, John Heywood. The words of hymns were becoming subjective, and too emotional. Such hymns dealt with the aspirations of a few individuals rather than the experience of Christians. Their use in a congregation therefore turns an act of devotion into a sham. 'Lead, Kindly Light' tells of a struggle which, it is to be hoped, few will have to undergo. Its proper use is by individuals, in particular circumstances of suffering. Used by a congregation, it becomes 'meaningless'.

As with all hymns a large part of the enchantment in congregational use was the tune. The tune came into the head of J. B. Dykes while he was walking in the Strand. When he got back to Durham he started writing it out, and published it in Barry's *Psalms and Hymns* (1867). Thence it was revised and taken into the appendix of the new edition of *Hymns Ancient and Modern* (1868). In 1886 two of the Oratorian fathers in Birmingham played over to Newman the tune by Dykes, which he had never heard before. 'He seemed rather surprised at its very quiet, hymn-like, quality' (E. Bellasis, *Cardinal Newman as Musician* (1892), 38).

The tune was the cause of as much argument as the words. During the time when the hymn was more usually the property of non-Anglicans, it was given various tunes, of which one survived into English hymn books, that by the Scot Charles Purday. Dykes's tune did not at first capture the field, though in 1874 he went to St Paul's Cathedral and heard it sung as the first hymn. It was abused as sentimental and even unworthy. People even talked of the 'licence' creeping into church music. Arthur Sullivan refused to have Dykes's tune for his *Church Hymns* of 1874 and composed his own, which has survived in some books. Robert Bridges could not bear Dykes's tune and composed his own for the *Yattendon Hymnal*. To this day some hymn books will only allow Dykes as an alternative tune.

But whether, as some said, the words were perfectly unsuitable to a mixed congregation, none of whom knew what they meant; or whether, as some said, the tune was sentimental and tasteless in the context, the union of Newman's words with Dykes's tune had captured the affection of the people of England.[1] For it had faith. That faith might be hesitant. But hesitant faith was what so many souls felt themselves to possess. When Newman was very ill during the year before he died, he asked the Oratorians that he might hear the hymn 'Eternal Years', a strong hymn by Faber on the assurance of hope and faith. They brought a harmonium to the passage between his two rooms. One father played, another sang, and a third knelt by his side saying words. Then Newman said:

Some people have liked my Lead, kindly light, and it is the voice of one in darkness asking for help from our Lord. But this (Eternal Years) is quite different; this is one with full light rejoicing in suffering with our Lord, so that mine compares unfavourably with it. This is what those who like Lead, kindly light have got to come to – they have to learn it. (Bellasis, *Cardinal Newman as Musician*, 38)

[1] Two exegetical commentaries on the hymn were published: J. S. Zelie, *The Book of the Kindly Light* (1910); Isaac Hartill, *Lead, Kindly Light: an Exposition* (1925). See also A. H. Jenkins, 'The Meaning of the Lyra Apostolica and the Genesis of "Lead, Kindly Light"', in *International Cardinal-Newman Studies*, XII (1988), 117ff.; and Gordon Wakefield, *Kindly Light* (1984).

Newman was wrong about himself and his hymn. It was the wrongness of his modesty. His poem had never been intended as a hymn, and to the end he thought it unsuitable as a hymn. He never regarded it as true poetry. Earlier critics said that it was sad. But when it was taken to the heart of the English people, it was found that a people's consciousness had more judgment than the critics.

Chapter 5

THE UNIVERSITY ON
MOUNT ZION

If ever a university got what its founders did not deserve, it was the dilapidated college which was founded at Dublin in 1854, and struggled for twenty-eight years till merged with the beginnings of something more viable. Some of the founders were playing politics more than education, and hardly wanted a real university. When they were courageous enough to appoint a genius as the head, they did what they could to hamper what he wanted to do; and on the face of it geniuses are not likely to make the best vice-chancellors. Even when they were well intentioned, they were clumsy, and sometimes they were downright mean. They had so little interest in academic freedom that they refused to allow their chosen head, who had more stature than any of them, to deliver a university address which he had prepared because they were afraid that its reasoning was imprudent, and prevented him putting Gibbon into his syllabus because they thought the *Decline and Fall* immoral.

Newman turned out to be much better as an administrator than anyone could have expected, even though he kept apologizing for incompetence. Despite the conditions under which he started, with little money, lukewarm backers, and an Irish antipathy to English influence, he collected a good team of professors and a few very interesting undergraduates. Many others could have done the office work better, but his name was more important to the survival of the institution than any amount of business capacity.

Not so much from his experience of a new university, as from his need to explain to a suspicious world what this new university ought to do, rose a classic of Victorian literature which every student of the philosophy of university education still cites. If he had had a real university to run, the *Idea of a University* could not

99

have been written with a straight face. The beauty of the book lies in its portrayal, amid some moving and sublime prose, of the ideal of a perfect mind, or of the perfectly educated man, towards which the university should encourage its young people to advance. He could not have written such paragraphs if he had run a new university for twenty years. The idealism was for the moment easy because the circumstances of his conversion removed him from old haunts; and though Oxford was still revered in his memory, and shadows from a more utopian Oxford fall across the pages of the essays, and the book could only have been written by an Oxford-trained mind of that age, he was as intellectually free of Oxford as he was devoid of information about any other university. He had read Gerdil and Huber and learned something about Louvain as a Catholic university. But he knew very little about any university but Oxford, and had no interest in the Scottish universities, which by example might have afforded him practical help. So *The Idea* attained its timeless quality: a university like that of Mount Zion, a Platonic idea of a university casting its shadow over every college of higher education from Saigon to Saskatchewan, as conceived in an original mind of subtlety and refinement, within the context of the long tradition of European culture.

The discourses were written, like the *Apologia*, against time. Therefore they are easy to misunderstand, and on occasion they contradict themselves. The commonest misunderstanding is the belief that Newman was not interested in 'research' as a function of universities. Since the end or aim was quality of mind, and not knowledge so far as it would be either useful or encyclopaedic, research was at first sight a by-product, perhaps inevitable but nevertheless secondary, from men who worked primarily with the young. He was perfectly open – it is the third sentence of his book – in saying that the object (i.e. the raison d'être) of a university is not 'scientific and philosophical discovery'. But this is easy to take too simply. He did all in his power to encourage the professors, whom he gathered, to undertake research, and founded a journal, *Atlantis*, where they might print their results.

But here was something particularly subtle from his Oxford past. In the Oxford of the 1830s the professor was in some respects the lowest form of academic life; the college tutor was everything. The professor was usually irrelevant to the studies of the young, and the professor of the recent past like Porson at Cambridge failed to lecture less because he abused the system than because no one came to hear. Newman believed that professors alone could make a university, but professors alone could not make a good university. He once wrote the Archbishop of Dublin an extraordinary letter, saying that as the professors would not for the time have anything to do with the government of the university, 'I have no personal interest in their appointment, and do not care who they are, so that they are good ones and creditable to the university.'

Newman has no patience with the notion that the essence of a university is an assembly of learned men, busy in acquiring knowledge, and allowing the young the privilege of watching. A research institute is likely to be the best place for research, but is not a university. The purpose of a university is to 'educate' young people.

To educate is not to make learned. The ideal product is not a walking encyclopaedia, not a professor of the chosen subject. It is a wise person. The ideal activity is to engender a *habit of mind* . . . *which lasts through life,* of which the attributes are *freedom, equitableness of mind, calmness, moderation, and wisdom.* To what wisdom consists, Newman tells us no more than his predecessors. How do you produce this quality of mind? Throw the branches of learning together in a common institution. Do not make the student learn all, lest you produce an arrogant fool. Make them study a special theme or themes. But they study the theme or themes in a context where others are studying different themes. Minds affect each other by mutual adjustment or respect.

Contrast a university which had no professors and no examinations, but brought together students for three or four years, with a university which had no residence or tutorial superintendence, and gave its degrees to any persons who passed an examination in a wide range of subjects; Newman, offered the choice, unhesitatingly preferred the first as the more successful in training, moulding, enlarging the mind. Why? Because the results have shown it: see whence heroes and statesmen and philosphers have sprung.

The reader is moved at the sublime prose in praise of the trained mind:

That perfection of the Intellect, which is the result of Education, and its *beau idéal*, to be imparted to individuals in their respective measures, is the clear, calm, accurate vision and comprehension of all things, as far as the finite mind can embrace them, each in its place, and with its own characteristics upon it. It is almost prophetic from its knowledge of history; it is almost heart-searching from its knowledge of human nature; it has almost supernatural charity from its freedom from littleness and prejudice; it has almost the repose of faith, because nothing can startle it; it has almost the beauty and harmony of heavenly contemplation, so intimate is it with the eternal order of things and the music of the spheres.

The reader is carried away, and for a moment he or she nearly believes – until he bumps into the historian who is nearly a prophet, and knows that the job of prophet is the only extra vocation from which an historian is barred. And then the reader begins to ask whether so profound a knowledge of human nature can be achieved by any number of books; and so looks outwards at his colleagues in the faculty and wonders whether all their ears are attuned to the music of the spheres; and then the illusion breaks, and the rhetoric is words, and we have caught an author deceiving us with magic; and the mind goes back to Newman sitting at high table in Oriel while Whately wolfed the food and banged out the syllogisms, or Keble saying wearily that these educated minds do nothing but criticize sermons, eat dinners, and jest at the eccentricity of dons.

Newman was in his age of self-conscious writing. The year when he delivered the *Discourses* was the year when he preached *The Second Spring* (31 July 1852), which is not only among his famous sermons but is the only one not to ring true to all its readers. Perhaps both these utterances owe something of their excess to the private suffering of mind under which he laboured, in fear of that moment of going to prison on a nauseating charge of libel (The Achilli trial was in June 1852). If we compare the prose of the Parochial Sermons in the thirties, or of the *Apologia* in 1864, we see that something is not quite right with the prose of 1852; some secret emotion or need unbalanced the author and diminished him from a good writer into a fine writer. A suffering man may be forgiven when the reality of his utterances is clouded.

But apart from the moment, there is error somewhere in the book, fundamental to its argument. It is the total separation of mental from ethical development. This chasm is powerfully stated in the most famous sentence of the book:

Quarry the granite rock with razors, or moor the vessel with a thread of silk; then may you hope with such keen and delicate instruments as human knowledge and human reason to contend against those giants, the passion and the pride of man.

Of course, a man may possess a cultivated intellect and delicate taste while simultaneously he is a sadist. But the book says more. Education never develops character.

It cannot be true. The experience of everyone who educates proves the contrary. And Newman knew it to be untrue. This disjunction between wisdom and ethical character is so extraordinary, especially in a Catholic theologian, that some critics have imagined two Newmans competing for the mastery, the convert versus the young Oxford logician fascinated by Hume. But the difficulty was not psychological. Character is the product of true religion – but not all highly educated men profess true religion. Therefore he will concede to the ideal of the educated man everything but the highest, which springs only from another source. Yet, whether he professes the disjunction or not, paragraphs in the essay are impossible to reconcile with the doctrine. The highest aim of education is wisdom; and in his deeper mind Newman knew that wisdom depends not only on knowledge and experience but upon a stability of judgment which is inseparable from moral being.

As St Paul sang a hymn to charity, Newman sang his hymn to the nature and beauty of the educated intelligence which is the goal of a university. It is these paragraphs of near poetry which gave the book its power to survive. That we seek to foster minds, not plied with mere knowledge but able to handle knowledge; that self-education is always more transforming than education by another; that a university depends less upon the personalities of individual teachers, however good, than upon the genius loci on which the teachers themselves depend; that the end of education is not to change the world materially, but human beings; that knowledge is always useful to society, but a university pursues it for its own sake and not because it is useful; that the educated judgment is a thing not only of prudence but of absolute quality – the dream had grandeur, and though in this perspective of time its dreamlike idealism is too evident, we shall forget it at our peril.

If ever a minister of education or vice-chancellor or academic theorist tells us that the object of a university is to be useful and nothing else, their pay should be stopped till they pass a written examination in Newman's book; and they shall not pass until they can give satisfactory explanations of some of its sayings, immortal in the history of education, such as these:

A university is an Alma Mater, knowing her children, one by one, not a foundry, or a mint, or a treadmill.

Knowledge is something more than a sort of passive reception of scraps and details.

Knowledge is a something and it does a something which never will issue from the most strenuous efforts of a set of teachers, with no mutual sympathies and no intercommunion, of a set of examiners with no opinions which they dare profess, and with no common principles, who are teaching or questioning a set of youths who do not know them, and do not know each other, on a large number of subjects, different in kind, and connected by no wide philosophy, three times a week, or three times a year, or once in three years, in chill lecture-rooms or on a pompous anniversary.

The common run of students ... leave their place of education simply dissipated and relaxed by the multiplicity of subjects, which they have never really mastered, and so shallow as not even to know their shallowness. How much better ... is it for the active and thoughtful intellect, to eschew the College and the University altogether, than to submit to a drudgery so ignoble, a mockery to contumelious.

Chapter 6

CHARLES KINGSLEY AT CAMBRIDGE[1]

In the midwinter of 1864 Kingsley, who was the Regius Professor of Modern History at Cambridge and therefore a natural person to review a work of history, reviewed a part of James Anthony Froude's *History of England* in *Macmillan's Magazine*; and in the course of the review – though it was nothing to do with the subject – accused Newman of not caring about the truth because (it seemed) he was a Roman Catholic priest. Newman asked mildly when he was supposed not to have cared about the truth. Kingsley pointed to a passage in one of Newman's sermons preached in 1843 – that is, while Newman was an Anglican. Newman protested; and Kingsley retorted that even while he was an Anglican he was a concealed Roman Catholic.

The quarrel developed into a war of pamphlets. They said strong things about each other. Kingsley accused Newman of not a little – credulity, silliness, absurdity, slavery to his own logic, the taking of perverse pleasure in eccentricities, and more. Kingsley was so worsted that he was constrained to apologize to Newman. But the apology was grudging and inadequate in its wording. Newman felt his whole life had been challenged, and the honesty of his time as the leader of the Oxford Movement. The result was the *Apologia pro vita sua,* a personal survey of Newman's part in the Oxford Movement; a book which put Newman back upon the national map of England from which he disappeared in 1845, and which put the Oxford Movement into the national consciousness as an historical event of importance, and which destroyed Kingsley's reputation – 'he appears', wrote

---

[1] Newman's portrait of Kingsley is as much a caricature, though more pardonable, as Kingsley's portrait of Newman is a caricature. Let us consider what Charles Kingsley was like; and why he delivered himself into the hand of one of the controversialists of the Victorian age, and so unwittingly started the real study of the Tractarians.

Newman, 'to be so constituted as to have no notion of what goes on in minds very different from his own, and moreover to be stone-blind to his ignorance'.

In May 1860 Lord Palmerston, who had tried at least two other names, appointed Kingsley Regius Professor of Modern History. We know of several people at Cambridge who were cross at the appointment, and can guess at more than we know. James Cumming, the Professor of Chemistry, was cross, and Professor Cumming was a goodnatured, kindly man. W. H. Thompson, the Professor of Greek, was cross, and he had the reputation of having the sanest academic judgment in the university. The Registrary, James Romilly, was by no means pleased.[2] Someone (though we have not yet found any such letter in the archives; it was perhaps the Master of St Catharine's) wrote to Lord Palmerston on the brilliance of the choice, while delicately suggesting the gamble in selecting a man so unknown in the realm of history. At Oxford Professor Arthur Stanley thought the choice excellent, and said so at Windsor.[3] But at present the evidence of vexation, in summer 1860, is rather more plentiful than the evidence of gratitude. It was rumoured that the Master of Trinity, when he heard of the appointment, said that the man was 'a howling idiot'.[4] Kingsley was well aware of these feelings. Even in his inaugural lecture, in saying what a pleasure it was to return to Cambridge, he told the univesity that he could not 'but be aware (it is best to be honest) that there exists a prejudice against me in the minds of better men than I am, on account of certain early writings of mine. That prejudice, I trust, with God's help, I shall be able to dissipate.'

Let us not fall into an anachronism and make erroneous judgment on why residents were troubled at the choice. Knowing the calamity that was to befall, historians and biographers have leapt to the conclusion that Kingsley was no good at history; and therefore we might be tempted to infer that this was the reason for vexation. We should be wrong. Universities take men as they find them. They do not instantly despise a man because he is

---

[2] Romilly's diary, 10 June 1860. See also Howson's evidence in *Life and Letters* (hereafter *LL*) II, 409.
[3] Dean Wellesley to Charles Kingsley, 17 December 1860, BM Add. MS 41,299/63.
[4] *London Review*, quoted *Camb. Indep. Press* (2 February 1867).

known to write novels. The experience of this century shows that highly respected dons may write in their spare time, and it does not matter whether the novels are good novels, middling novels, or even ghost stories provided that they are antiquarian. In 1860 anyone who had obtained a first class in classics, and professed himself willing to devote himself to modern history, was regarded by the university as at least qualified. Kingsley had gained a first class in classics, and dedicated himself solemnly to the study of history. The Master of Trinity, Dr Whewell, though he greatly disliked Kingsley's onslaught upon the university, sent him a generous letter of welcome; and in Kingsley's reply, which is preserved among the archives of Trinity College, he dedicated all his energies to the work of historical writing.[5]

They had wanted someone else. But they had not wanted him much. The only resident whose name was widely canvassed was Dr Woodham of Jesus College, an eccentric with a repute for vast learning, epicurean manners and hatred for heads of houses, who were unwilling to serve with him on committees. In one year he contributed more than a hundred articles to *The Times*, all in a vile handwriting, and willingly took up any subject the editor wanted, from war in Paraguay to the American elections.[6] W. H. Thompson, soon to be Master of Trinity, and famous not only for his judgment but for the barbs in his words, once wrote of Dr Woodham, in a sentence intended for the eyes of a prime minister, 'I would have called him "original", if I could point to anything of importance that he had originated.'[7] They tried his name on Lord Palmerston, but met blank refusal to consider him. When the Master of St Catharine's wrote to the private secretary

---

[5] Kingsley to Whewell, Eversley, 20 September 1860, Trinity College Add. MS, a. 207/163. In the Royal Archives are letters which show that one of the two previous men to be offered the chair was J. W. Blakesley, the vicar of Ware. Probably the other (if there was only one other) was Venables; not Edmund Venables the antiquary, as I once thought, but George Stovin Venables, like Woodham, formerly a Fellow of Jesus College and a frequent contributor to *The Times*. For these letters in the Royal Archives see *Theology*, LXXVIII, no. 655 (January 1975), 2–8; the whole number is devoted to Kingsley. For suggestions from Cambridge, we have in the Royal Archives only a letter from Henry Phillpot, the Master of St Catharine's, to Lord Palmerston of 24 March 1860, suggesting that none of the residents was specially qualified, and mentioning the possibilities, among non-residents, of Blakesley, Arthur Helps and 'Mr Johnson, Fellow of King's College, who is now living at Eton' – this, of course, is the poet Cory.
[6] A. T. Dasent, *Delane*, I, 28; II, 51, 244, 274.
[7] BL Add. MSS 4421/157: Thompson to Spedding, 10 July 1869, Karlsruhe.

of the Prince Consort, he was only able to mention non-residents. He did not even name Dr Woodham.

So the vexation against Kingsley consisted not in a feeling that he was unlearned, or that he was unqualified, or that someone resident should have had the post. It arose from what he had done and said. As he had pilloried his college, so he had pilloried his university before the public.

When he looked back, he knew that he had been unhappy at the university. But he felt himself to have been unhappy at home and at school. He once dated his happiness from 1841, during his last year at Magdalene. Not the three previous years, but the twenty-two previous years, he dismissed, 'spent in pain, in woe, and in vanitie'. No doubt he exaggerated. But before he even came to Cambridge he reacted fiercely against his home, or at least the religion of his home. Son of a dry and old-fashioned clergyman of the low church school, he was almost like the later Edmund Gosse or Somerset Maugham in fighting rules, sabbatarianism, primness, doctrines, and at last belief in God. He came to Cambridge a rebel against the principles of his home.[8] In retrospect he regarded the rebellion as not only doctrinal but moral – drink, horses, gambling, cards, prize-fighting. He talked about his experience of a 'doctrinal and moral somersault', which lasted several years.[9]

It appeared to him, in retrospect, that the society in which he found himself from 1838 was excellently fitted to encourage all this. Unlike him, the young men said that they believed in God and cheerfully accepted the Thirty-Nine Articles, but he observed that those professions made no difference to their way of life. As for drink, horses, gambling, cards, and prize-fighting, no group of young men could have assisted so congenially. In one mood he gives you the impression of being surrounded by Nyms and Bardolphs and Pistols, with a dark hint of a Mistress Quickly, yet somehow that these pot-mates nauseated his belly.

In passing we notice, first, that Kingsley was for three years a stalwart and unskilful member of the Magdalene College second boat, known as the Cannibals; and we know the number of bottles consumed at the Magdalene College bump supper for

[8] *LL.*, I, 48ff.
[9] Ibid., II, 108–9.

May 1842, just after he had gone: 54 of champagne, 12 of sherry, 12 of hock and 20 bowls of Punch; there is no record of the numbers attending, so we must hope that there were some guests.[10] Towards the end of Kingsley's time a professional Negro prize-fighter took up residence in the town and offered to give instruction in fisticuffs. On 25 April 1842 the Vice-Chancellor issued a draconian decree against members of the university who hired professional prize-fighters to teach them. But only two undergraduates can at present be proved to have profited from the Negro's skills, and one of these two was Charles Kingsley.[11]

For the first element in the bitterness was self-disgust; and more than self-disgust, disgust at the institution where such a self found itself at home. Afterwards he reacted violently against his sowing of oats and therefore against the University of Cambridge, so fair a field for the sowing.

It is clear that even while he was an undergraduate he reacted. It was not only that he started to work at his books, and surprised his tutors, and got his first class in classics. Like Wordsworth, he found an education at last. He came to value it but slowly. One would expect that a man could not get a first class in classics without falling in love with something of classical literature; and that is right, for Kingsley fell in love with Homer and the old Greek legends. More than a century later no one has excelled him as the story-teller of Greek legend; the simple beauty of the English language, the shining sense of glory at the myths of a Greek world, the perfect marriage between an English half-poetical prose and an old saga at the roots of European memory. But the odd thing is that he felt he owed little of this to the university. Like Wordsworth, he conceived his real education as apart from the studies of the university. Wordsworth came to love literature which was not part of the curriculum. Kingsley came to love literature which was part of the curriculum. But he felt as though he loved it although, and not because, it was part of the curriculum. He did not owe his Homer and his Heroes to Cambridge. About the classical syllabus he was prosaic, even materialistic. He loved a girl – perhaps she was above his station –

[10] Consumption, in *The Magdalene Boat Club 1828–1928* (1930), 9.
[11] Decree in CU MSS UP/14/647: *LL*, I, 47–8.

impecunious, he could never marry her without reasonable pay. He got his first in classics because he wanted to marry Fanny Grenfell and therefore wanted a good job. He was open about this.

Fifteen years later he told a pupil that 'Classics, as read at Cambridge, are noble training for the brain. They did me vast good ...'[12] Like all of us, he mellowed towards his place of education. This was not the impression he gave at the time.

If he thought little of the syllabus – and indeed it was still that narrow syllabus where men could do nothing but classics and mathematics – and thought less of most of the undergraduates, what of the dons? The Master of Magdalene, the Hon. George Neville-Grenville, was aristocratic but rather non-resident. The distinguished man among the fellows was Lodge, the University Librarian, but he had half-quarrelled with the society on whether he could be college tutor and University Librarian simultaneously, and went round wine-parties in the university airing his grievance. Young men in the college were rich; for when Lodge ceased to be tutor his pupils presented him with an elegant candelabrum costing 130 guineas, two figures from Westmacott supporting a branch ending in four tulips.[13] Judging by this munificent gift, some undergraduates of that generation liked some dons. But the gift, though offered before Kingsley came up, represents something about Cambridge which angered Kingsley. He knew that he was not in that sort of league, either in money or in class. He had a snobbery against them because he knew or fancied them to have a snobbery against him. And as for the dons, he looked back upon no one with respect. Men passed their examinations by hiring private coaches in the town. Nowhere in any Kingsley document appears gratitude to a don, until he came back as a don. When he ran into the Socialist stage of his life, and condemned the university because it inherited money to educate the poor and only allowed through its gates the extravagant, whom then it did not educate, he passed a sweeping condemnation upon dons. 'It is a system of humbug, from one end to the other. But the dons get their living by it, and their livings too, and their bishoprics now and then' (*Alton Locke,* chapter XIII). The

[12] Kingsley to John Martineau, Bideford, February 1855; Violet Martineau, *John Martineau*, p. 24.
[13] J. P. T. Bury (ed.), *Romilly's Diary*, 26 October 1838 and 6 January 1839; 29 April 1836.

colleges are monastic foundations with ancient rules trying to survive in a world which has repudiated all that the founders stood for. Why don't they change the names of the colleges, Trinity, Jesus, Christ's?

Because they are afraid to alter anything, for fear of bringing the whole rotten old house down about their ears. They say themselves that the slightest innovation will be a precedent for destroying the whole system, bit by bit. Why should they be afraid of that, if they did not know that the whole system would not bear canvassing an instant?

I have quoted enough to show that the undergraduate Kingsley was not in all respects pleased with the University of Cambridge; and the quotations which I have chosen are far from exhausting the subject. It can hardly surprise that when this wholesale assailant was bowed into the chair of modern history, Professor Cumming was cross, and Professor Thompson was cross, and the Registrary was cool, and the Master of Trinity was rumoured to have spoken furiously.

Here, then, was this unpredictable person – poet, Chartist, country parson, amateur scientist, historical novelist, social evangelist – suddenly made Professor of History at Cambridge. Such a crowd was expected to attend his inaugural lecture that his friends asked the Vice-Chancellor for the Senate House; and such his controversial fame that men feared for the grace giving him the Senate House lest someone utter a *non-placet*.[14]

The inaugural lecture was given in the Senate House, after a postponement, on 12 November 1860. Though Mrs Kingsley does not tell us so, the Registrary's diary (8 November 1860) shows that it was postponed because she broke her leg. The postponement was a relief to Kingsley, who like the rest of us needed more time for preparation than he was allowed, and who in addition had to preach at Windsor before the Queen just before.

Certainly the scene in the Senate House was the most unusual scene at any inaugural lecture of any professor in the history of the university – galleries crammed with undergraduates, front row with eight heads of houses, junior members cheering and mocking as though the occasion was for honorary degrees, vast

[14] Ibid., 8 November 1860.

ovation for Kingsley at the beginning and end, intent listening for
an hour and three-quarters, though his voice, which was a rough
and rasping voice, not very musical,[15] had not quite the range to
be audible throughout that building with its difficult acoustics;
reported in the newspapers as a triumph, and evidently a triumph
such as no professor, let alone a professor of history, had
achieved. No lectures, however, please all members of their
audience, and for contrast I quote the Registrary's opinion, which
he wrote in his diary after he got home, and which shows the
subjective nature of historical evidence:

The lecture lasted more than $1\frac{3}{4}$ hour!! It was not at all to my taste: and when
he meant to be pious he seemed to me to be merely solemn. He said that he
was aware that many persons thought ill of the tendency of his writings. The
lecture excited no applause except when he praised Professor Pryme[16] and
when he expressed a fear that he had trespassed too long on our attention. I did
not get home for dinner till past 4.

It is not easy, in historical study, to find witnesses who agree.
The Registrary had not liked Kingsley's appointment, and not so
many dons can manage to listen to a colleague for one-and-three-
quarter hours. But all the other evidence is of ovation.

Kingsley sent off a copy of the lecture, when it was printed
three weeks later, to various friends or patrons. As he sent one to
the Prince Consort, and one to the Dean of Windsor, we know
what Kingsley's friends in Windsor Castle thought about it.
Extracts from it were read aloud to the Prince Consort; and he
was reported to be 'very much taken with it', especially the part
about Luther, 'and the observations which his case exemplifies'.
Dean Wellesley of Windsor lent his copy to Arthur Stanley, who
thought it 'most interesting' and was likewise struck by the
Luther passage; though he wondered that Kingsley had made no
declaration of his future course of lectures. The Dean of Windsor
himself thought the lecture very judicious, and wrote how he did
not doubt 'but that you will conciliate and bring over many who
might have been prejudiced against your appointment at first'.[17]

[15] Ibid., 22 May 1861. See also 26 March 1861: 'Just as I had finished dinner came the Vice-
Chancellor and brought the address of condolence: – it had been written by Professor Kingsley,
but the Council (in a two hours sitting today) pared down a good deal of its redundance.'
[16] George Pryme, Professor of Political Economy, whose 'exact habits of thought' Kingsley
praised, and whose lectures he urged undergraduate historians to attend: see also *The Roman and
the Teuton* (1881 edn), pp. 326–7.
[17] Dean Wellesley to Charles Kingsley, 17 December 1860, BM Add. MSS 41,299/63.

The case of Luther, which attracted both the Prince Consort and Arthur Stanley, was central to the philosophy of history which Kingsley put forth in his inaugural lecture. Kingsley raised an early form of that question with which nowadays most schoolchildren have to grapple, the historian's difficulty between freewill and predestination. Luther changed the history of Europe. Would the history of Europe have changed in the same way if Luther had perished at birth? And if it would not, have we not at least to say that Luther was himself the product of an age, an environment, a heredity? But if he was simply the product of his age, why did not other Augustinian monks of a similar origin produce similar effects on history? It was important to Kingsley to declare his faith that men and women made a difference – whether by intelligence or by folly, goodness, or wickedness – they made a difference by their free choice. It was important because Buckle had lately put forward his theory of deterministic history, claiming that the historian was slowly bringing the behaviour of mankind under scientific laws. Kingsley believed in the progress of the human race, and declared his faith in that progress. But at bottom his lecture was a protest against deterministic history, and was widely regarded as a useful and necessary protest. People do matter; individuals choose. Yet Kingsley's protest was the more effective and acceptable because he recognized the value of the attempt to find laws of behaviour, recognized, even while he protested against the folly of explaining crusades only by economic conditions of unemployment in northern France, that material forces can have consequences for the human spirit, as with printing machines and the Reformation, or gunpowder and the rise of the masses, or that climate and soil may well influence the character of a people. Because the protest accepted what was right in the new historical insights with statistics and the environment, it was the more effective in its assertion that after all people matter.

Beneath this protest can be found a feeling in Kingsley which our generation will call historical scepticism but he would call sense of mystery. If history consists in collecting the numbers of suicides or illegitimate births, it is not mysterious and we do not need scepticism. But if it consists in explaining a society; and if, in explaining a society, you need to explain why some people behaved in the way they behaved – with such wisdom or such folly, such goodness or such vileness, such ardour or such indifference – we approach something inaccessible to the inquirer, the mystery that is every human being. Science was tempting history to look at men and women as things; and the historian was never to forget that he was dealing in people. We have to find out what we can, scientifically, carefully, impartially, looking at the evidence and not letting ourselves be misled by theories about the evidence. But when we have done all that we can, we shall know that we have come only a little of the way to understanding what has moved the human spirit and therefore society. This was the historical scepticism of Kingsley which he declared in his inaugural lecture and which may be found also in his courses of lectures. 'All harsh and hasty wholesale judgments are immoral' – that is a Kingsley epigram, and wholesale judgments are immoral, in his view, because they force human behaviour into preconceived theories of the evidence.

Like all historians, Kingsley was not able to live up to his own theory of history: especially in the matter of wholesale judgments.

In 1871 William Stubbs, who liked writing comic verse, produced one of the two famous and malicious epigrams which did most to lower Kingsley's reputation in the eyes of posterity:

> Froude informs the Scottish youth
> That parsons do not care for truth,
> The Reverend Canon Kingsley cries
> History is a pack of lies.
>
> What cause for judgments so malign?
> A brief reflexion solves the mystery
> Froude believes Kingsley a divine
> And Kingsley goes to Froude for history.

Kingsley was a friend of Froude. Nothing in his life was nobler than his helping of Froude when Froude was turned adrift by Oxford and in gravest personal trouble; and they married sisters. Mrs Kingsley believed[18] that Froude helped her husband; and there is a kinship in attitude to history, its drama, its portraiture, its readability and its giant pope being slain by stout English

[18] *LL*, II, 106.

hearts. But Kingsley's historical scepticism was formed on grounds which he did not owe to Froude and which had nothing to do with Froude. History, Kingsley told the university in his inaugural, is not 'irresistible', or 'inevitable'. If we are to use epithets, we should use epithets like 'crooked', 'wayward', 'mysterious', 'incalculable'.

Does our knowledge of moral nature enable any secure law of history to be ascertained? Kingsley thought that it could, and claimed the authority of his predecessor, Sir James Stephen. Moral behaviour in a society (not necessarily an individual) leads to prosperity, immoral behaviour to poverty. Or put it another way, as he put it: justice in a state is necessary for the progress of thought and science and therefore of humanity; injustice and tyranny cause the withering of thought and the weakness of society. This doctrine Kingsley claimed to get out of observation and inquiry. Some of his critics have claimed that it was only his form of a preconceived pattern of history to which the evidence must be made to conform.

Whatever he failed in, he was a triumph as a lecturer. Not only for his inaugural but for his normal courses. The undergraduates crowded him from small lecture room to larger lecture room.

History, though within the curriculum, was hardly known as a subject. In the circumstances of the early sixties, when the seeds of a historical tripos were being sown, popular lecturing put the subject on the map of the curriculum. More than popular lecturing was needed – an organizing power, and an ability so to command the respect of senior members that they would begin to regard the new subject as academically reputable. Kingsley had small organizing power, and was concerned only to interest undergraduates. As a student of history he had three qualities which were important to the success of this feat. First, he cared deeply about 'social life' in the sense of what people wore, or ate, or rode, or lived in, whether in the fifth or eleventh or sixteenth centuries; second, he had almost too strong a sense of continuity, so that he would electrify the audience by showing how some contemporary event of the 1860s was prepared and preshadowed by developments or decisions taken long centuries before; and third (contrary to what was later said quite often), he always went to the original authorities and tried to make his students go to the original authorities. These were considerable merits, and help to explain the success of a lecturer with a rasping voice. The librarians of the University Library said that after Kingsley's lectures undergraduates asked for books which no undergraduates had ever asked for before.

But to the need to interest young men, he sacrificed depth, and eventually the respect of colleagues who would have been pleased at smaller audiences and more profundity. W. H. Thompson, who came to respect Kingsley as a man, and admired the attractive power of his lectures, once criticized the lectures for their lack of *solidity*.[19] And when Kingsley committed the error of publishing courses of lectures (1864 and 1867) he laid himself open to the onslaught of men who did not think popular history to be in easy harmony with his office. Acton, who was not one of Kingsley's vicious assailants, and who believed more passionately than Kingsley that historians must make moral judgments, thought that the ethical earnestness in Kingsley's mind was such that it began to 'overpower' the 'scientific' side of the mind.[20] But it was not only the strength of his ethical views. Kingsley once told the undergraduates that an all-but-ideal preparation for a future king was to be captain of a band of outlaws.[21]

Despite the triumph of the inaugural, and the crowds of young men who came to his lectures, he carried a load: the existence of the novel *Alton Locke*, in which he ridiculed and abused the university. Perhaps Whewell, who now liked Kingsley and still disliked *Alton Locke*, suggested another edition. Perhaps the publisher required a reprint, and Kingsley in his new chair could not bear to print the old. He was conscious that some dons, and some undergraduates, resented *Alton Locke*, and still resented him because of *Alton Locke*.

In any case, a new edition of *Alton Locke* appeared in 1862. It was indeed a new edition. The two chapters on Cambridge University were rewritten. The undergraduates, who fifteen years before behaved like indecent brutes, became models of scholarship and good behaviour. They were now earnest, high-minded, and even sober. The dons are hardly mentioned at all;

---

[19] W. H. Thompson to Spedding, 10 July 1869; BL Add. MSS 44,421/157.
[20] *Chronicle* (13 July 1867).
[21] *David* (2nd edn, 1874), p. 2.

but that is a big change, because formerly the dons were accused of corrupt use of the endowments. He omitted all criticism of colleges for using sacred names though they were secular institutions. Even the aristocrats behaved more courteously to their inferiors. A few criticisms of the university survived. But a footnote added, 'It must be remembered that these impressions of and comments on the universities are not my own. They are simply what clever working men thought about them from 1845 to 1850 . . .' The emendations in the book may be illustrated by one very small word. The young hero of the book, the I, went down to the May races and, being careless on the towpath, was knocked into the river by a peer on a horse. He scrambled out. In the first edition he was shaking 'with rage and pain'. In the 1862 edition he was shaking 'with wet and pain'.

The pendulum had swung. Open-eyed Cambridge men thought that it swung too far, and smiled at Kingsley.[22]

But perhaps the university had changed. We know indeed that it had changed and still was changing, and men have written books to show how it changed. We need not doubt that the university was better adapted to its time in 1862 than in 1838. For one thing, you could now study, as part of the curriculum, modern history.

Kingsley had views on why it changed for the better. He attributed something to the Oxford Movement; and something to Dr Arnold and his ideas of education; and something to Frederick Denison Maurice and his social concern; and then general reasons, the country as a whole becoming more civilized, and the British upper class altering its ways and manners. He had no doubt that the university was vastly improved, and partly because England was improved.

Not only England had changed. Kingsley was no longer the brash young Chartist parson. People think that the world is full of the kind of people whom they meet as they go about their daily round. In 1839 Kingsley was drunken and idle, and therefore supposed that all the university was drunken and idle. In 1862 he was earnest and high-minded, and therefore supposed that all the university was earnest and high-minded. And in the meantime he

[22] E.g. J. S. Howson, in *LL*, ii, 409.

was different, and not only in moral ways. He was successful; a figure of Establishment; tutor to the Prince of Wales. And, it is clear, he was moved by the kindness with which the university, senior as well as junior, took him to itself when he returned as a professor. By the time he had been a professor for eighteen months, he thought that the university was above criticism.

Those first three years as a professor were the happiest of Kingsley's life. He still had health. He had reputation where formerly he had notoriety. For once in his life he felt secure, mellow. He accepted himself. This is important. Historian and biographer alike have read the disaster of 1864 back into 1860. It is anachronism.

In this happy mood he wrote, in spare time at Eversley and as a present for his youngest child, *The Water Babies*. It was published in instalments in *Macmillan's Magazine* during 1862, and between cloth covers in 1863.

One of Kingsley's deepest feelings of religion came through nature. As he walked in the fields he would be surrounded by a sense of 'meaning'; more than surrounded, he once used the word 'oppressed' to describe the sensation,[23] a sensation of awe, and of a harmony still hidden but just round the corners of the world, and of a fervour within, begotten of this mystic perception. Like William Wordsworth he could remember experiences of childhood when seen and unseen were not distinct. He would sit by a tiny stream and pulsate to the under-noise of myriads of insects and flowers, drinking in, he says 'all the forms of beauty which lie in the leaves and the pebbles, and mossy banks of damp tree roots, and all the lovely intricacies of nature which no one stoops to see' – whispering to him that in them lay a hint of the meaning of the world; and bringing back, as it were hovering over them all, 'the delicious sense of childhood'.

In the later fifties, encouraged by his wife, he turned towards a more academic study of English countryside and its history. He opened a correspondence with Philip Gosse, and Gosse's collection in the Brotherton Library at Leeds is one of the archives for

---

[23] *LL*, I, 77. For the Gosse material see Cambridge University Library Add. MSS 7027; Edmund Gosse, *Life of Philip Gosse* (1931), pp. 252, 280ff. For Kingsley's attitude to science see the article under that title by A. J. Meadows in *Theology*, LXXVIII (1975), 15–22. For the discomfort between the patriotic and Teutonic racial theory which he inherited and Darwinism, see Michael Banton, *Theology*, LXXVIII (1975), 22–30.

Kingsley's correspondence. In 1855 he published *Glaucus*, a study of the sea-shore. Now, in the sixties, at a time when Darwin's theory of evolution was controverted by most Cambridge scientists, led by old Professor Sedgwick, the Professor of Modern History became the best-known Darwinian in Cambridge, defending the master against his critics and gratified as by 1866 opinion veered right round towards the tenable nature of the theory put forward in *The Origin of Species*. Something in Darwin perfectly fitted his private awareness of developing meaning in developing nature. And the kind of evidence which Darwin loved to use, evidence of garden and hedgerow and nest and copse and stream, was just the evidence which ravished Kingsley, the amateur.

This insight into enchanted nature has never been more sensitively described than in the first chapter of *The Water Babies*. It is the only novel of Kingsley that is untouched by melancholy. It is not all of the highest quality; and a bit of it competes for the shame of being his worst writing because it is still too self-conscious, the moralizing too insistent; and though he could write magically for little children, and magically for adults, he succeeded only from time to time in the true art of the child's story-teller, writing simultaneously for child and adult. It is not the long words like *anastomosing*, which children do not mind. The shift in level is too patent too often. But embedded into a book which now you cannot read with pleasure all through are little nuggets of description, such as what it felt like to live at the bottom of a freshwater stream. To achieve this feat Kingsley needed his science, his sense of mystery and divinity underlying nature, and his painfully acquired experience in literary expression; and since no one else combined these qualities, the feat has never been repeated, though Kenneth Grahame achieved a related but different glory in *The Wind in the Willows*.

He could not resist, however, because he never could resist, side-blows all round his neighbourhood. Never has there been a successful children's book like this. This nursery story defended the establishment of the Church of England, denounced David Hume's philosophy about miracles, advocated the Darwinian theory of evolution, introduced for the first time into an English novel the newly found gorilla, and its discoverer Du Chaillu, denounced the tendency towards State education, recommended 'the good old Cambridge hours of breakfast at eight and dinner at five' in order to get more work done in the day, mocked professors of science who make over-dogmatic speeches at meetings of the British Association, ridiculed confidence tricksters in the medical profession, denounced tight stays for women and corporal punishment for schoolboys and ladies who wear shoes when swimming. Perhaps it is also against the use of climbing boys to sweep chimneys; and his interest might go back to a memory of his undergraduate days in Cambridge, for on 27 April 1840 a huge petition for a bill in Parliament to ban climbing boys was widely signed in Cambridge.[24]

Here, near the beginning, is the description of a spring in Yorkshire, which Grimes the sweep and Tom the climbing boy passed on their way to sweep the chimneys of Harthover Hall – derived from a memory of Malham Tarn and Gordale Scar, where Kingsley went on a visit to Yorkshire in July 1858:[25]

a real North country limestone fountain, like one of those in Sicily or Greece, where the old heathen fancied the nymphs sat cooling themselves the hot summer's day, whilst the shepherds peeped at them from behind the bushes. Out of a low cave of rock, at the foot of a limestone crag, the great fountain rose, quelling, and bubbling, and gurgling, so clear that you could not tell where the water ended and the air began; and ran away under the road, a stream large enough to turn a mill; among blue geranium, and golden globe-flower, and wild raspberry, and the bird-cherry with its tassels of snow.

And then Grimes stopped, and looked; and Tom looked too.

Tom was wondering whether anything lived in that dark cave, and came out at night to fly in the meadows. But Grimes was not wondering at all. Without a word, he got off his donkey, and clambered over the low road wall, and knelt down, and began dipping his ugly head in the spring – and very dirty he made it.

That passage shows Kingsley at his best, and not only because of the simplicity and appropriateness of the words used to tell the story. Nature is being regarded simultaneously by three pairs of eyes; the brutish old sweep who saw nothing but a means of getting cool, not clean; the child who found a mystery and beauty in what he saw, for was it a spirit or only a bat who might live in

[24] CU MSS, UP/14/84.
[25] *LL*, II, 58–9.

the limestone cave? – and the educated author, who knows the geology of the rocks and the names of the flowers, but whose mind takes him through the science of it, back to the poetic legends of old Europe, where fountains were haunted by divinity.

He had a conscious aim in writing the book – at least it was conscious after the book was written, for he explained it in a letter of 17 May 1863 to Frederick Denison Maurice, a letter now in the British Library.[26] He wanted to contrast the certainties of conscience with the uncertainties of scientific knowledge; to contrast the absolute commands if you look inside with the mysteries that lie all about you if you look outside.

Kingsley the parish priest of Eversley has nothing to do with Kingsley at Cambridge except this, that Eversley was the chief rival to being a don at Cambridge. There were some people, especially at the turn of this century, who saw Kingsley not as poet, or novelist, or social reformer, or professor of history, but as a pastor of a country parish, as famous as Hooker or George Herbert or Keble, so individual as to be unlike any of those, but in the authentic tradition of English village life. Gypsies were not to be denied peering from the edge of the crowd at his funeral. In the old tradition he cared about their bodies as well as their souls. He filled the church not just with educated visitors and tourists but with his own people. This is so easy for us all to picture that I do not need to dwell on it. I only mention one incident of extraordinary behaviour. Kegan Paul once went with him to a cottage where a man had fever in a room on the ground floor. The room had no windows, and stank. The moment Kingsley's nostrils met the odour he said no word but ran up the stairs to the room overhead, produced a large auger, and bored several holes in the floor or ceiling immediately above the sick man's bed. The other inhabitants of the cottage were astonished; but not so astonished as we may be that Kingsley happened to have on his person a large auger for drilling holes, and that he asked the leave of no one before he drilled them. One wonders whether the inhabitants blocked the holes again when he was gone.[27]

After 1863 he gave up his Cambridge house in St Peter's Terrace. In the biography his widow gave as the reason for this

[26] Add. MSS 41,297.
[27] LL, I, 227.

the impossible expense of running two establishments. In the British Library are the Macmillan papers, which show how much Kingsley earned in royalties from that publisher alone; and those papers weaken Fanny's story. There were two reasons, the more important of which she needed to conceal. They were reasons of health. She herself was always wretchedly ill in Cambridge. Simultaneously Charles Kingsley developed ill-health. No one was told publicly the nature of the affliction; but a private letter shows it to have been a liability to malarial infections and from a drawing made in one of his letters there may evidently have been added gout. Experience showed these diseases to be worse in Cambridge than in Eversley. His wife also kept hinting at brain fatigue, which she said[28] began in March 1863. And Kingsley confirms this in a letter to his wife from France in early summer 1864, when he says that he will return to her a different man – 'My brain is getting quite clear and well'.[29]

So they gave up the house in St Peter's Terrace, and Kingsley reverted to the habit of his predecessor, coming only to Cambridge to give his course of lectures and examine. Kingsley could still inspire young men with a course of lectures, and by personal interview in the weeks of the lectures. But however he might correspond with Henry Sidgwick and other interested parties,[30]

---

[28] Ibid., 192.

[29] *LL*, II, 203.

[30] See his letters to Sidgwick in the library of Trinity College on a course of lectures on the sixteenth century and the period covered by Motley. His lectures are ill recorded (for there were no lecture-lists, and individual professorial notices are lost), but they appear to have been: 1860–1: Early medieval Europe; 1861–2: The same (1861: The classes for the Prince of Wales and a selected company were: the constitutional history of England 1688–1832); 1862–3: The history of the United States; 1863–4: Invasion of the Teutonic races (turning into *The Roman and the Teuton*, published 1864); 1864–5: The Norman Conquest; 1865–6: The same (*Hereward* published 1866); 1866–7: The Congress of Vienna. The course published in 1867 as *The Ancien Régime* was given at the Royal Institution and not given as university lectures. It is a meditation on Tocqueville. 1867–8: Europe in the sixteenth century (he was much interested at the time in Motley's *Dutch Republic*); (Easter term) European science in the sixteenth century (published posthumously: the most original of his historical lectures); 1868–9: On certain philosophies of history (Comte, Bunsen, Carlyle, Maurice).

All his historical effort went into his lectures, which were intended to make later books (as in four cases, one posthumously, they did). The only historical book which we hear of him attempting is (1863–6, but the idea came earlier) a boys' history of England, of which we only know that it was intended to replace Mrs Markham for boys of 8–15, and was likely to be strongly Protestant in its emphasis: see BM Add. MSS 54911/103, among the Macmillan papers. His other commitments prevented it.

Kingsley's last service to the Cambridge history school was the choice of Seeley to succeed he could influence the building of a school of history in Cambridge no longer; which happened at that moment to need doing.

The enemies were gathering. And one reason why they were gathering is obvious. The young Kingsley offended everyone of the right. His friends and backers, therefore, were of the left; everyone who admired the Socialist champion, the assailant of dilapidated cathedrals, the critic of decadent universities, the thinker who refused to believe in hell. But his former friends were less than pleased with him. What had happened to *Alton Locke*, which had become a recantation? A man might be an ex-Socialist, but it was odd to find such a one on the Confederate

him. In the Lent Term of 1869 he was lecturing on Comte and counter-philosophies of history. During the term he finally decided to resign. He had lately read an article on John Milton by John Seeley, then Professor of Latin at University College (*Macmillan's Magazine*, XVII (1868), 299–311, on Milton's political opinions; *Macmillan's Magazine*, XIX (1869), 407–21, on Milton's poetry; republished by Seeley in *Lectures and Essays* (1870), vols. IV–V. The second article, originally printed in March 1869, is evidently the article which moved Kingsley). The article showed that Seeley was far from being a disciple of Comte in his philosophy of history. Kingsley then wrote to Seeley telling him that he was about to resign and suggesting that he (Seeley) succeed him. Seeley replied from London in March (42 Regent's Park Road, otherwise undated), with a letter in BL Add. MSS 41,299/142: 'one of the greatest compliments I have ever received in my life' – his private need to increase his stipend – asks for duties, number of lectures needed – is committed to editing Livy for the Oxford University Press – 'it is laborious work and would seriously interfere with my devoting myself as I could wish to Modern History'; – thinks the chance of being appointed small – Gladstone may think highly (he had very favourably reviewed *Ecce homo*), but he 'can have no reason to think that I have given any special attention to Modern History . . .' 'If I were he I would not be bound to a Cambridge man . . .' 'The truth is that though I have read discursively in Modern History and have really given a good deal of thought to Philosophies of History, I have not studied a single period of Modern History critically in the original authorities. Is there any chance of the chair being made one of Universal History? Gladstone, I suppose can do what he likes with it. If ancient history were included I should not feel so diffident.' 'No post I should like more if I were ready, but it would throw away my knowledge of Latin and ancient history which I have been polishing. You see how mixed my feelings are . . .'

In June, however, Gladstone offered the chair to James Spedding, who refused on 29 June (Spedding to Gladstone, Add. MSS 44421/71 – 'not the proper man' – 'it is too late in the day to begin a new education'. Gladstone then asked Spedding about Dr Woodham of Jesus, and about Charles Merivale. Spedding told Gladstone (Spedding to Gladstone, 6 July 1869, Add. MSS 44421/105) that Merivale would be excellent but would have a difficulty of residence; that several Cambridge men had spoken of Woodham, as the most learned, and that Woodham was a copious contributor to *The Times*; but that W. H. Thompson (now Master of Trinity) would be the best judge. Thompson gave Spedding for Gladstone a lukewarm commendation of Woodham (10 July, Add. MSS 44421/157). Gladstone offered the post to Merivale, who at once declined (Merivale to Gladstone, 12 August 1869, Add. MSS 44421/273). I find no sign in the Gladstone papers that he then offered to Woodham, but Woodham told Delane that he had had an offer. If there was one, it was perhaps an informal sounding. In September, therefore, Gladstone came at last to Kingsley's suggestion of Seeley, and on 25 September Seeley was appointed.

side in the American Civil War. Why did this former heretic seem to speak so ill of Bishop Colenso's attacks on the historicity of the book of Genesis? Kingsley was not winning the affections of the right, and was losing the affections of the left, who now regarded him as a renegade.[31] Promotion, said one of his disappointed critics in the newspapers, 'is proverbially injurious to a reformer, and it has been specially so with the Professor of Modern History'.

In January 1864 he published his review of Froude's *History, en passant* accusing Roman Catholic priests in general, and Newman in particular, of not caring for truth. Newman's reply turned Kingsley into a laughing stock for a good part of educated England. From that moment all the lean and hungry men started to put in their swords. In the novel *Hereward the Wake* comes a sentence, written during the autumn of 1864, which moves the reader if he knows the inner torments of the author: 'If a man once fall, or seem to fall, a hundred curs spring up to bark at him, who dared not open their mouths while he was on his feet.'[32]

No other Cambridge professor has ever been treated by the press with such brutality. If he committed a sin when he reviewed Newman, it was a sin for which he paid too ample a penalty. Yet he went on offending everyone – losing the friendship of the left, even of John Ludlow and Thomas Hughes, because of his attitudes to the American Civil War[33] and then to Governor Eyre, still losing the friendship of Conservatives because he advocated national non-denominational education. There is a case for believing that Cambridge, by making him mellow and happy, made possible the writing of *The Water Babies*. There is also a case for believing that Cambridge killed Kingsley.

[31] See report of London gossip in *Cambridge Independent Press* (5 December 1863).
[32] *Hereward the Wake* (1906 edn), p. 66. The *Apologia* had a very mixed reception: see V. F. Blehl, 'The Apologia: Reactions 1864–5', in *The Month* (1964), 267–7. Kingsley was really damaged, first by the scornful pamphlet before the *Apologia*, and then by his own reply to the pamphlet, which was the most lamentable thing Kingsley ever wrote and was (in part at least) lamentable because he wrote it in an incipient nervous breakdown. The controversy over the *Apologia* does not clearly make an exception to the rule that an author's reputation cannot really be lowered but by himself.
[33] *The Christian Examiner* (Boston, Massachusetts) printed extracts taken down by an unknown from Kingsley's university lectures on the history of the United States; and some of these extracts were reprinted in England and even in Cambridge, by *Cambridge Independent Press* (5 December 1863).

And yet, my favourite picture of him towards the evening of his life is at the Church Congress at Southampton in October 1870 — astonishing that he appeared at the Church Congress, a meeting heaped with ecclesiastics (and he had an excessive aversion to ecclesiastics); and not merely attending, but sandwiched as a speaker between the two most famous bishops of their day, each a spell-binding orator, whose unction could hold thousands for an hour at a time, Samuel Wilberforce and Magee of Peterborough. It was a working men's meeting, and the working men, cramming the hall with fustian jackets, were evidently not favourable to parsons. All the speakers were heckled, some vilely; even Wilberforce could hardly get a hearing, even Magee. But when Kingsley spoke, total silence and intentness. Out of the hundreds of clergymen gathered in Southampton that day, this man who never quite knew whether he was a radical or a Tory was the only clergyman whom dockers and stevedores wanted to hear.

Here is an Englishman more in need of a modern biography than most. He has been given five modern biographies, all of them useful in different ways; but a lot is still to do.[34] Here is a man full of colour, angles, sharp outlines; a man who said what he thought, and what he thought was always downright, at times too downright; no one ever gave himself away with more abandon. You will therefore expect everything to be open and easy to understand. But we are still surrounded with mystery. This is a most unusual family of intelligent people, and we still know little about its internal relations. During part of the time that Kingsley was Professor of History at Cambridge another famous novelist lived by the rectory at Eversley, his brother Henry. But Henry is not mentioned in the *Life and Letters* by Fanny Kingsley. Certainly that is odd.

Kingsley regarded his wife, Fanny Grenfell, as a saviour. She was an intelligent woman, with dark hair and shining eyes, and he felt that he owed her everything.

---

[34] The most important collection is in the Parrish collection in Princeton University Library: some 500 letters by Kingsley, of which 159 are to Sir William Cope and 101 to his wife, and some 75 letters to Kingsley. A number of these letters from Kingsley to Fanny were published by R. B. Martin, *Charles Kingsley's American Notes* (1958). My thanks to Mr Alexander D. Wainwright, curator of the Parrish collection.

In the British Library are certain drawings of a rather unpleasant character. Kingsley's sensuality with regard to his wife has long been known or suspected. His passion towards her, especially at the time of their engagement and in the early years of marriage, took unusual physical forms. In the biography by Susan Chitty which was published in January 1975, she documented this side of Kingsley's married life – a touch of obsession about nudity, sometimes connected with clean and pure water and baths, and (although he would never have dreamed of hurting anyone) a touch of obsession about violence. His wife was the person who preserved these papers as sacred. I mention this circumstance, partly because it looms large in a discussion of Kingsley and will loom larger, and partly because it helps to explain one of the mysteries about Kingsley.

Why was the anti-Catholicism so intense? This is not a Protestant of the Reformation; not a man who thinks the Pope anti-Christ; it is a man whom Protestants of *Rock* and *Record* attack as furiously as they attack Rome. This was a broad churchman, a man with an open mind in other respects, as his attitude to Darwin or to Socialism showed; a man who looked for truth in all men even when they were wrong. And Kingsley the broad churchman loathed Roman Catholicism. In the positive sense of the word he was not particularly Protestant. His Protestantism was negative, and that is unusual in so intelligent a man.

These new documents help. These obsessions of his, with nudity and violence, he sublimated into Catholic monkish asceticisms – hairshirts, talk of flagellation, drawings of naked women crucified. His wife, indeed, he had 'rescued' from becoming a nun; and the kind of activity which ordinary Christians thought morbid or even prurient he had used, at least notionally, to sublimate (or stimulate) the sexual obsession. Therefore, as he grew out of this temporary phase of life, he was filled, not only with self-disgust like the self-disgust at the potmates of undergraduate Cambridge, but with an overwhelming nausea against Catholic asceticism and every form of Catholicism that went with it. Therefore Susan Chitty, writing a one-sided biography about home and family and passion, has helped us to understand the element in Kingsley which weakened *Hypatia*, the novel about monks, and which at last brought him to self-destruction in the fight with Newman.[35]

Fanny Kingsley is commonly thought to be the classical proof that widows must not be allowed to write their dead husbands' biography. The more I meditate on Mrs Kingsley's life of Kingsley, the more doubtful of this verdict I become. Certainly she did not print everything; but she printed a lot, and so allowed us to see the colour of the man, bright and at times lurid, the collapses and the breakdowns. She edited letters, and the editing does not quite fit contemporary standards. If you compare the letters which she printed with the originals where they are available, you get surprises. She sometimes omitted passages without sign of omission, ran together as letters two letters which had nothing to do with each other, struck out the colourful personal phrase and left the informal religious sentiment; if Kingsley wrote 'poor old Luther', she turned it into 'Luther'. Kingsley was more colourful than the Kingsley of the widow's loving biography. But the Kingsley of the biography has colour enough for several men. She was honest; and perhaps her loyalty did not always see how scandalous were one or two of the sentiments which she printed, so giving a handle to the critics of posterity.

The silences of Mrs Kingsley need a little thought. In the *Life and Letters* she carefully mentioned all the main works of her husband in the text but two – which only appeared in the chronological list in an appendix. Were these two silences oversight? For the two volumes were very important in Kingsley's life. One of them was *The Ancien Régime*, which was an ultimate cause of his resignation of the professorship because not just 'the reviewers', but *The Times* knocked it about with contumely.[36] Was she silent on *The Ancien Régime* by accident

[35] It should be noticed, however, that he was capable of writing with true understanding of monks. The historical section on the monasteries as the bearers of civilization in the early Middle Ages is by far the best part of *The Roman and the Teuton*. Something in medieval monasticism continued to interest if not fascinate him, as is evident both from *The Hermits* and from *Hereward the Wake*, despite the hard sayings to be found in both those books.

[36] The Kingsleys suspected the author of the review of being Dr Woodham, and Fanny suspected that he was taking revenge because he wanted the chair. But the reviewer was not Dr Woodham. *The Times* archive shows that it was the Irish military historian William O'Connor Morris, and if Kingsley had known, he need hardly have taken it so seriously. For a less contemptuous but still very critical review, see Acton's review in the *Chronicle* (13 July 1867), reprinted in *Essays in Church and State* (1952), p. 411. A hostile review appeared in *Athenaeum*

or by reason of inner feeling? And then, *Hereward the Wake* – to posterity one of his two most successful novels, the most Cantabrigian of his novels, full of fens and brecklands and Cambridgeshire villages and Ely Cathedral and Madingley woods and the Fleam Dyke, the most interesting of all his books to a Cambridge man – yet she is silent about it; another big silence. For not only did she fail to mention it. She said that the autumn was filled with the preparing of university sermons for the Lent term. But unpublished private letters to Macmillan prove that the agony in the Kingsley household was the finishing of *Hereward the Wake*.[37]

To understand Kingsley you must take him as a whole. The students of the English novel put him in his place as a novelist; the student of English poetry sees him in the perspective of minor romantic poets; the historian looks with discomfort at some of the historical lectures; the theologian examines the preacher and Christian Socialist; the Catholic researcher puts the quarrel with Newman under a microscope; the lover of children's books sees the freshness of insight into the mind of a child. Because this was a many-sided man, it is not surprising that we have taken his sides apart. But if you read the works over a chronological period – whether they are novels, lectures, sermons, poetry, children's books, or private letters – you have a sense of surprise at the unity in the mind's development. And then, because this must be a platitude, since all sane minds are a unity, you are surprised that you are surprised, and ask yourself why.

This, we keep being told, is the most typical Victorian of them all.[38] You can see why men have thought this – the drive to

(10 August 1867), 174. For Fanny Kingsley's suspicion of Woodham in *The Times*, see the letter to F. D. Maurice printed in R. B. Martin, *The Dust of Combat* (1930), p. 267.

The silence on *Hereward* may be due to the fairly widespread surprise among reviewers that such a book could be written by a famous Anglican clergyman, and still greater surprise that it should be published in instalments by Norman McLeod in the periodical *Good Words*. See (e.g.) *Cambridge Independent Press* (7 April 1866); *Pall Mall Gazette* (2 January 1866), 27, 'we wonder what has been thought in the hundreds of manses and parsonages, and other peaceful and serious homes, into which *Good Words* finds its way, as month after month through the past year this story has come tearing and thundering along . . .'; *Cambridge Independent Press* (28 October 1865), 5; *Spectator* (7 April 1866), 387; contrast the praise of *Athenaeum* (14 April 1866), p. 493.

[37] Mrs Kingsley to Macmillan, BL Add. MSS 54912/53, 16 December 1864.

[38] 'Born in the same year as the Queen, Kingsley typifies the Victorian man as closely as she presents the Victorian woman', M. F. Thorp, *Life of Kingsley* (1937), p. 1; 'If there ever lived such a mythical figure as a typical Victorian, that man might be Kingsley' (R. B. Martin); etc.

bodily fitness, romanticism, enthusiasm, religion ardent but at times vague. But the verdict slanders both the Victorians as a whole, and Kingsley in particular. If anyone thinks that the ordinary run of Victorian middle-class Englishmen were like Kingsley, he has not begun to understand the Victorian age. Kingsley, of course, was a man of his time – a man of doubts and trials of faith, of moralisms and yet new freedoms, of patriotism and demonic energy. But he was typical of no one and nothing.

In 1857 (21 February) the *Saturday Review* printed a notice of Kingsley's *Two Years Ago*, and included this sentence:

We all know by this time what is the task that Mr Kingsley has made specially his own – it is that of spreading the knowledge and fostering the love of a muscular Christianity. His ideal is of a man who fears God and can walk a thousand miles in a thousand hours.

Two months later Tom Hughes published *Tom Brown's School-days*, full of the athletics of the Victorian school and the morality of physical endeavour. Fitzjames Stephen reviewed the book in the *Edinburgh Review* (January 1858). He pretended that Hughes's *Tom Brown* was symptom of a widespread ideal in education, as though the book was the product of a whole school of thought; and, he declared, the leader of this school of thought was Kingsley. The phrase was taken up; and by a twist its application was transferred. The label fitted Tom Brown, and his creator Tom Hughes. But Kingsley was saddled with the phrase. The press, the public, general conversation grinned at the idea of Kingsley the muscular Christian. Kingsley should have shrugged his shoulders, and smiled. He did not. He resented it fiercely.

It cannot be denied that something in the idea fitted Kingsley. The ecstasy of bodily effort in a crew on the river, that stands out in the description of undergraduate Cambridge in *Alton Locke*. And physical force, violence, courage, endurance, these are qualities on which he dwelt repeatedly, mostly in his novels but elsewhere too, even in the pulpit. The three novels by which he won a vast public were all novels of sound and fury, war and campaigning. *Hereward the Wake* gripped readers by murders; *Westward Ho!* by patriotic murders; *Hypatia* had nothing patriotic, but never was a distinguished novel more crammed with bangs and biffs, riots and bludgeons; you hardly find a page without blood on it even though the book is all about monks. Kingsley had gusto.

There was something more here than that fanatical concern for physical fitness found in many lesser men. It was almost as though he needed to keep proving to himself his own strength. He took such pride in his energy that we may think of it as obsessive. He must have been one of the few inhabitants of this frail flesh of ours who was pleased by the hope that in heaven we shall still be clothed with bodies.

If he had really been muscular like Tom Hughes, he would have cared for none of these things. On the contrary, he was a man whom the physical troubled, who worried over the physical, who did not take body for granted. We shall not fathom Kingsley unless we see that this is no giant pope-killer, but someone in need of compassion. Why should anyone mind being called a muscular Christian? Partly because he had a sense of the ludicrous contrast between the name and the reality – to be called this 'impertinent' name 'by men who little dream', he wrote to Maurice,[39] 'of the weakness of character, sickness of body, and misery of mind, by which I have bought what little I know of the human heart'. But the phrase was not uncomplimentary; and by 1868, perhaps to Kingsley's surprise, he found that he was supposed to have coined the phrase himself, to express the truth that sound mind requires sound body. 'Is it not curious', wrote a friend to his wife, 'that a phrase originally I suppose intended to annoy, is fast becoming a household word expressive only of what is wholesome and good?'

Did he like to be an outlaw, this figure of the establishment? Asked for his favourite character in history, he said 'David', and David was an outlaw. *Hereward the Wake*, his bloodiest, is in some ways his best novel, and for most of his life Hereward was an outlaw. 'By Thor's hammer', said Hereward (p. 104),

I have been an outlaw but five years now, and I find it so cheery a life, that I do not care if I am an outlaw for fifty more. The world is a fine place and a wide place; and it is a very little corner of it that I have seen yet . . .

Kingsley liked (in theory) to have every man's hand against him, to be dealing great blows all about him and standing up to great

[39] *LL*, II, 186.

blows in return. The trouble with his life was that he did not like it in practice. Nor did his wife.[40]

A later Master of Magdalene, Arthur Benson, looked across at the portrait of Kingsley in the college hall, and described what he saw:

this strong, sturdy, sanguine man, with his flashing eye, great aquiline features, and compressed lips; but he has been looking for something behind and above existence . . . He has enjoyed life, and enjoyed it fiercely; but something has held him back from joy, and fixed his gaze firmly on pain.[41]

He was odd, but that did not matter; what mattered was that he knew how odd he was. 'If you rejoice that you have born a man into the world', he wrote to his mother at the beginning of his fourth and last year as an undergraduate, 'remember that he is not one like common men – neither cleverer nor wiser, nor better than the multitude, but utterly different from them in heart and mind . . .'[42]

So he was a man apart, by nature; apart at school; apart as an undergraduate; an outlaw manqué through his adult life. Let no one think him a Goliath. Kegan Paul described seeing him at work writing a book. He could not write listlessly, or even steadily, as a routine. He had to work himself up. The words he was writing engaged the heart, became passion. Occasionally he was like a Victorian dervish: nothing much when the spirit was away, compelling and terrible and fascinating when the deity descended. To write he needed to feel like a swimmer in surf. And that was because his existence felt to himself like a sequence of waves. So he looked to others. The epithets which they naturally used were words like 'vehement', 'quick', 'eager',

[40] Henry Dunn to Mrs Kingsley, 7 November 1868; BL Add. MSS 41,299/137. Kingsley defined his entire attitude to 'muscular Christianity' in *David* (1865). For a modern treatment, Norman Vance, 'Kingsley's Christian Manliness', in *Theology*, LXXVIII (1975), 30–8, David Newsome, *Godliness and Good Learning* (1961), pp. 207ff., 235–6; W. E. Winn, 'Tom Brown's Schooldays and the Development of Muscular Christianity', in *Church History*, XXIX (1960). But for the way in which something in the idea was thought to fit not only Kingsley's novels but his sermons, see the opinion of J. S. Howson in *LL*, II, 409–10, for Howson disliked Kingsley in print because he preached a self-confident assertive Christianity and only lost the dislike when he came to know him. Kingsley was often angry at the charge; perhaps at his angriest when it was made in his friend Froude's *Fraser's Magazine*: see his fierce protest to Froude on 11 September 1863 in Add. MSS 41,298/138 – muscular Christianity 'a word and a notion which I abhor'.

[41] *The Leaves of the Tree* (1911), p. 230.

[42] *LL*, I, 57.

'impulsive', 'sudden'. Kegan Paul talked of his body 'fretted away by his fiery spirit'.

So this was not a strong man. Notice the word 'frantic' in the sentence, 'Unless I get frantic exercise of the body, my mind won't work.' This was a strong man manqué, racked with nervous tension, living his life from crisis of health to crisis of health, crisis of emotion to crisis of emotion, breaking down in tears before giving a course of lectures, setting his wife into agonies by his own agony of spirit. Kingsley was never at rest. His face was never still; it moved always. He could never sit long in a chair, but would suddenly dart up and hurry round the room. He cannot describe what is quiet. When he comes to the storm at sea, and the thunder of foam, and the planks of the ship breaking in pieces, and men crying out in fear of death, and rescuers urgent with their life-lines, he is a marvellous writer; you can feel the danger and tension of the moment in his prose. When he needed to describe peace, he could not. He set out to picture the still beauty of the fens near Cambridge; and the description leaps alive with geese squawking and bittern booming and duck springing up, nature as vehement and violent as a storm at sea. He was physically, emotionally, constitutionally incapable of understanding what it is to contemplate. I do not know what he could have made of Mary in the story of Martha and Mary in the Gospel. He had too vivid an imagination for a strong man. If he read in the newspapers of babies being hacked to death by the Indian sepoys, he felt it as though he was present.[43] In the spring he would be restless, peering out of the window for the first swallow, and once he had seen the first swallow of the year it seemed to soothe his troubled spirit. There was no calm. A friend said of him that he walked about like a man who had got the devil under, and that it was his bounden duty to keep him there. When he was tired, he would take up Carlyle's *French Revolution*, which makes events more like Niagara Falls than any other work of historical narrative.

Those who study the psychology of artistic temperaments may attach some weight to the stutter. It was a bad stutter. Strangers found it hard to bear; intimates did not mind it and might come

[43] LL, II 34.

to like it. It never afflicted him in public utterance. But he worried over it more than many men with stutters; practised speaking with a cork in his mouth, articulating in front of a looking glass, exercised with dumb-bells to help breathing.[44] Acquaintances who met his stammer called it 'a tremendous stammer', a 'great stammer', 'a painful stammer', a 'very unpleasant' stammer. A part of the force in all his utterance was physical, like a man *expelling* words from his mouth with muscular force. Sometimes he gave the impression of spitting out sentences. One wonders whether this physical need for force of speech had anything to do, psychologically, with that violence of utterance which led to calamity.

When he came to Cambridge to take his MA degree, the Registrary recorded in his diary (Romilly, 24 May 1860) that Kingsley was about the ugliest man he had ever seen. A more delicate narrator makes the same point by saying that the features were 'very marked', deep-set eyes, big nose, prominent side whiskers, large tight mouth in movement, face lined all over as if with care. A boy who went to see him late in his life saw the lines all over the skin of the face, and inferred to himself that this was a man 'who had not found life an easy business'.[45]

It is not a contradiction in terms to say that he was able but not clever. No hint of subtlety sullied his record. Sensitivity, yes; authentic appreciation, deeply; love of beauty, and a feeling for great words, and affection for genius, and penetration of a mass of scientific or historical detail. But not subtlety. It is impossible to imagine Kingsley ever engaging in an intrigue; of course you know that in Kingsley's case intrigue would end in fiasco. He had less sense of political wisdom than any man of his generation. Make him a cabinet minister and the government would fall within a fortnight. Make him a bishop and within six months the Church of England would be in schism. If you say of anyone else, he is *incapable of intrigue*, it would be a compliment. When you say it of Kingsley, you start to wonder whether something was missed in his make-up.

Then was he a simple man? – for some able men, especially when they are men of action, and occasionally even when they

44 *LL*, II, 262.
45 Benson, *Leaves of the Tree*, p. 245; Martineau, *John Martineau*, p. 5.

are philosophers, can be simple men. It is the particular difficulty and interest of Kingsley that he was not in the least simple. Direct, unsubtle, honest, frank, blunt, all these; tortuous or devious, never.

But unsophisticated, no; natural, only when he intended naturalness; innocent, not merely *no* but quite the opposite – who would have thought the good man to have so much blood in his fancy? If you go along with Kingsley until you begin to know him, you wonder whether this unsubtle man was not one of the most complicated souls you ever met.

Chapter 7

THE OXFORD MOVEMENT
AND ITS REMINISCENCERS

The name is much less accidental than the name Oxford Group for a modern religious movement, which appears to have gained its nickname because its leader toured South Africa with some Oxford undergraduates and a porter chalked the words Oxford Group on the luggage. The name 'Oxford Movement' was slower to develop. The first general name for the people was Tractites (1834), because they wrote tracts not liked by their critics. They called themselves Apostolicals, and the name came within a short distance of catching on. A later authority with a name for being untrustworthy alleged that at first they were sometimes known as Keble-ites, because Mr Keble of Oriel College, Professor of Poetry in the university, was one leader; but this is incredible: I have found the name nowhere else, if anyone ever called them Keble-ites, it cannot have happened before 1864, and after that must have been very donnish. Next (1836) they were called Malignants, in an emotional tirade by Dr Arnold of Rugby, also from Oriel College. Next year (1837) the same headmaster called them Newmanites, no doubt because Mr Newman of Oriel supplied a lot of the ideas. Then in 1838 they were Puseyites – indeed it is alleged that this name appeared in common parlance three or four years before, but we only seem to have written proof from 1838 – because Dr Pusey, formerly of Oriel, now a Canon of Christ Church and Professor of Hebrew, was an associate. Then they were Tractarians (1839), or Tractators (1842), or Newmanians, or Neomanians, Newmaniacs. Charlotte Elizabeth, in *The Christian Ladies' Magazine*, warned her young feminine readers to beware of 'the sleek, slim, Tractarian curate'. The normal phrase became the Tractarian Movement, and this lasted until the end of the seventies. If the phrase 'Oxford Movement' was used, the writer put it into inverted commas.

135

The first book to narrate its history called it drily 'The Theological Movement of 1833'. But already in 1841 we find the first use, controversially, of the phrase 'The Oxford Movement'. At first it was associated with a partial meaning; here is a religious movement going on with various centres, Mr Hugh James Rose, for example, in Cambridge or Dr Hook in Leeds, and the Oxford part of it is the Oxford Movement. But already in the later forties, we have the word *Oxfordism*, a body of doctrine or an attitude so that, in the end, even Mr Rose, though a very Cambridge man, could be said to be part of it.

In 1856 a vehement Roman Catholic called Browne, with the patronage of sixteen Irish bishops, wrote the first book called *A History of the Tractarian Movement*, which begins with the delightful sentence 'The progress of Christianity in England presents many curious features', continues in the same vein, and was dismissed by Newman with the single word *trashy*, which is an exact description. He used the phrase 'Oxford Movement' in the text, but only in inverted commas. Even in the middle eighties the phrase 'Oxford Movement' was as often as not put in inverted commas by journalists. By then it had lost its immediate link with the university; and about the same time (first instance known to me 1878) it began to be called the Catholic Revival by those who liked it, and afterwards the neo-Catholic Revival by those who disliked it.

I thought it would be a useful experiment to examine how the Movement would look to its participants when they grew old. The personal memoirs of the very old are sometimes boring and sometimes fascinating. They cannot so clearly remember recent events, but they see events of childhood almost as though they happened yesterday; they are quite clear on their youth and what they owed and how they became what they are; and as death gets nearer and powers fail they naturally are more interested in the past than the future.

It is well known that this has two aspects in psychology. The first and luckier is a mellowing; an oblivion of the past grievances, a sense of gratitude for what has been. And the second is the unlucky – a deepening of rancour, a sore place getting sorer as it is brooded over, a resentment which grows more resentful.

If a man was a young don in 1835 he was probably born about

1810. Therefore he would be seventy in about 1880 and 80 in about 1890. Consequently we should expect the Reminiscencers to appear in that decade of 1880–90; before 1880 they would mostly be living in the present and not in the past and after 1890 they would be mostly unable to reminisce. So I thought it would be worth trying this experiment about a much-studied religious movement and ask whether we can learn anything from looking at the personal reminiscences of participants when they had got to the reminiscing epoch of their lives.

I exclude three persons who fit neither my dates nor my category of elderly reminiscencer.

1. Newman's *Apologia pro vita sua* of 1864 was written in defence of his career and is not really a reminiscence in my sense. It served a different purpose – and gave its record of events with a totally different slant, with only enough reminiscence of the Oxford Movement to explain the development of his own mind.

2. The Esquire Bedell and Oxford coroner George Valentine Cox published *Recollections of Oxford*, first edition 1868, when he fits into my right age group for reminiscencing but not into the right age for being part of the Oxford Movement, since his undergraduate years were 1802–6. Everyone who reads Cox's annalistic quaintnesses will see at once that these are not in the least reminiscences of the Oxford Movement even though members of the Movement flit in and out of its pages. He was totally extraneous to everything it stood for.

3. William Tuckwell published *Reminiscences of Oxford* in 1901: a famous book about the Oxford Movement, but to be disregarded by us. Tuckwell had two foibles, and one of them was to pretend to be much older than he was. He was born in 1830. He wrote another book called *Pre Tractarian Oxford – Reminiscences –* but this is a Pickwickian use of the word *Reminiscences*, because during his pre-Tractarian years he was a baby of nought to two. What Tuckwell knew about were the fifties and sixties, and his portrait of Tractarian leaders is drawn from experiences in that later time; though quite often he likes to give the impression that it is much earlier.

Now, if we turn to the reminiscencers of the eighties, the authentic reminiscencers in my sense, we find at the outset a very striking thing – the people who resent it, or dislike it, or hate it, write their memoirs; the people who loved it and owed their soul to it and regarded it as the highest ideal of life they had ever known – are silent. Why is this?

(a) A sore place, getting sorer, causes you to write more than gratitude.

(b) The doctrine of *reserve*.

A very central doctrine of the Oxford Movement is the doctrine of reserve. Hide the self. Give excellent lectures on poetry if you can, but give them in Latin so that no one will be tempted to come for mere enjoyment. Preach in such a way as to make yourself small, not so as to make hearers think you a good preacher. Read prayers unemotionally, lest your personality intrude. Try not to have your portrait painted. Do not write an autobiography. Newman wrote half an autobiography, but then he had been libelled. We cannot imagine Keble or Pusey writing an autobiography.

Tractarian spirituality disliked what was flamboyant. It shrank from religion in the market-square. It was not fond of the seeking of publicity. It liked to hide from the gaze of men or women who could not understand. Religion was very sacred, too sacred to be cast among swine. They were quiet men. Stay away from too much traffic with the world and say your prayers. They heard of visiting American evangelists, and Primitive Methodist missioners, and could not think that their methods were the right way to promote truth. This reserve was continuous with much that was best in the English religious tradition, Hooker tending sheep in his field, George Herbert and his pastor, William Law and his retired prayerfulness at King Cliffe. But in the Oxford Movement it had a new edge: against worldliness, whether within world or Church. There was something puritanical, at times something hard, about the shrinking from the display of the self. But it fitted English ideas of courtesy.

But the difficulty was not only reserve. What happened on 9 October 1845 was to them tragedy. Newman, the leader, the man who stirred them to reform the Churches, who led them into making the Christian way of life more dedicated and its way of worship more reverent, left the Movement. So their memories as they looked back were not only confronted with gratitude for what had been. They met soreness and pain; if gratitude, then gratitude with sadness in it that the man to whom they owed so much should have left the cause.

The combination of these two things made it almost impossible to publish.

Copeland, Newman's curate, collected evidence over years with the aim of writing a history of the Movement. But he was never able to finish, never able to publish. And in this way the people who started to say what it was like in the Oxford Movement were not its heirs but its critics and renegades: A. P. Stanley, the biographer of Arnold; Archbishop Tait of Canterbury; James Anthony Froude, the younger brother of Hurrell Froude; J. W. Burgon, in *The Lives of Twelve Good Men*; and above all Mark Pattison, 1885, whose posthumously published memoirs were the bitterest ever written by an ex-Tractarian.

Tom Mozley wrote his *Reminiscences of Oriel College and the Oxford Movement* during 1881, finished it by November, and published it in the spring of 1882.

No one could have a better qualification: far better than Pattison, rather better even than Church. He was an undergraduate at Oriel, then fellow and intimate of Newman; he often dined with Newman, sometimes breakfasted with him of a morning, often walked with him of an afternoon; Newman felt an affectionate friendship for him; Mozley sat on the original committee which planned the *Tracts for the Times*, and helped to distribute those Tracts in Northamptonshire and Derbyshire, though he was accused of being a bit idle in the campaign; was strong on Newman's side in the battle against the Provost of Oriel; he assisted him at the sacrament; stood in as his curate; and sealed all this intimacy in July 1836 by marrying Newman's sister Harriet. Newman admired and honoured him at that moment beyond anyone else. 'I know no one of a higher and more generous mind – and unless it were throwing words away in these common place days to say so, of such heroic qualities – I mean I think him possessed of the most affectionate heart, and that he would do anything, neglect himself, and go through all perils for those who are possessed of it. Everyone who knows him at all must and does know this in a measure and though my words seem high flown, yet they are very true' (Dessain, *Letters and*

Diaries of John Henry Newman, ed. the Birmingham Oratory
(Oxford, 1961ff.), vol. 5, p. 324, to Henry Mozley). From
Newman, Tom Mozley took the editorship of the Tractarian
journal *The British Critic*.

And now came the cloud between these two intimates and
brothers-in-law. Mozley took Harriet on a visit to Normandy
and was bowled over by the worship in the Roman Catholic
churches which he entered. He found it far nearer to the ideals he
had learned from Newman than the prosy readings which he
associated with the Book of Common Prayer. He decided that he
must be a Roman Catholic. Newman hurried down to the Oriel
living of Cholderton to stop him, and persuaded him to undertake to make no move for two years. Harriet Mozley was
shocked by all this and broke off relations with her brother. The
parting of friends had begun.

Therefore from 1843 they could no longer be intimates, though
their hearts were not finally sundered for another four years. But
from 1833 to 1843 they held nothing back from each other.
Newman once said, as he looked over his old letters, that the
letters from him to Tom Mozley, and from Tom Mozley to him,
made the history of the movement to Rome and of his own
change (LD, 4, 23).

Tom Mozley became a writer of leaders for *The Times* In his
old age he claimed to have written 10,000 leaders. Experts in
the history of the press tell me that this is impossible, but it
could have been several thousands. That practised his pen but
hardly endeared him to Newman, for to be a reporter on any
newspaper, *The Times* or not, was regarded by middle-class
early Victorians, and not only by churchmen, as equal to a lapse
into the criminal classes. He seemed to have deserted his high
ideals, and taken up work unsuitable for a clergyman, and
secular in tone. And now, 1882, he published his reminiscences;
and like Pattison, an ex-disciple, with the acidity of an ex-
disciple. He wrote to Newman before the book was published to
say how he was sure that not a line in the book would pain
Newman (Mozley to Newman, 20 October 1881, LD, 30, 10–
11). Newman sent him back a friendly little warning against being
caustic.

The warning was needed.

When the book appeared, it was well received at the first flush of enthusiasm. Some good minds thought that he penetrated, as no one before him, the inwardness of the Oxford Movement. Pattison praised it to the skies, but then Mark Pattison wanted the Oxford Movement to be despised. 'It is the one book', wrote Pattison, 'to which, next to and as a corrective of, the *Apologia pro Vita Sua* the future historian of Tractarianism must resort.' And from Pattison the doctrine was taken up by the *Dictionary of National Biography* (s.v. T. M. Mozley) and so consecrated. One of Newman's sisters liked it very much. *The Times* liked it, but *The Times* is apt to like books written by its employees. Nearly everyone else thought it deplorable.

Newman was horrified. He read a few pages and could read no more. 'Chapter 2 has so knocked me down.' It was full of mistakes. 'All that you have said', he told Tom Mozley, 'is so uncalled for that I am almost stupefied.' He thought it cruel and untrue about his father. Mozley 'is a wild beast who rends one's hand when put up to defend one's face' (LD, 30, 94, 99). 'When a man aims at gossip', he told Pusey, 'he is obliged to dress up facts in order to make his story stand upright.' 'Very ill-natured', he called it to another friend. He resented it that some people seemed to read it with pleasure, and amusement, and even thought that they understood the Oxford Movement better in consequence. 'Wanton mistakes', he told Copeland (ibid., pp. 106, 114–15). After his first protest, he never wrote again to Tom Mozley, though characteristically he was very kind to Mozley's only child when, not two days before his death, she came to visit him at the Oratory.

Was all this fury justified? Mozley's eyesight was bad. He could not check anything. He had a mass of old letters but he could hardly read them. He wrote two volumes from memory. Inaccuracies sprouted on page after page. He never saw proofs. Longmans printed straight from his manuscript. Everything about the book shouted the epithets unscholarly and gossipy.

This was bad enough. Never did so many people write letters to the newspapers proving or claiming that this or that was untrue. But Newman had a special reason for hating the book. He could not bear the world to know two facts about his father: first that his bank had failed for a time to meet its creditors, and secondly that in consequence of this failure he became a brewer in Hampshire. He longed, absurdly longed, to keep these two items from the world because he wanted to protect his father's name. Once he left the instruction to any future biographer that he was not to mention either of these. And here Tom Mozley told all society. Whether or not the book was full of error, Newman was wounded.

Perhaps Newman could never bring himself to read more than a chapter or two of Mozley's book. But other Tractarian eyes read, and disliked what they found. Mozley seemed to trample on every ideal of the Movement. He gave trivial common room anecdote instead of seriousness of purpose, brash judgment instead of charity – 'Culling Eardley Smith was then at Oriel, very much the same ridiculous personage he always was, and a flagrant tuft-hunter' (1, 105). 'Theodore Williams was not only a very cantankerous but also a very ridiculous person in any religious reckoning' (1, 99). Hinds, later Bishop of Norwich, is called 'poor Hinds' – 'I think there was just a suspicion of craziness' (1, 271). 'Poor Reid' – 'after a not unsuitable marriage' he 'threw himself from a window at Venice into the canal' (1, 49). Professor Hampden 'stood before you like a milestone, and brayed at you like a jackass' (1, 380); W. G. Ward kept his Lenten fast by lying in bed till 11.0 a.m. with a large dish of mutton chops warming at his fire (1, 411). Mozley was almost as bad about colleges – the degradation of St Edmund Hall, the Fellows of Magdalen who desired no addition to their knowledge and ideas, for 'they were incapable of it' (1, 60); a former Fellow of Oriel who has an angry eye and a carbunculous complexion (1, 348).

No more quotations are needed, though more might be given, to show why Mozley's book was not seen as a good history of the Oxford Movement or a good history of anything else. It was brash. The Oxford Movement was everything that was not brash in religion: quiet, sacramental, concentrated.

Newman is the very core. He is everything, in Mozley's book. That is not easy to see, because Newman hated the book; and because his person is half hidden behind a cloud of gossip, and common room anecdotes, and malicious asides. But he is the core. When you read the book with clearer eye, you see why Newman's sister liked what she read.

Newman (according to Tom Mozley) was a genius, surrounded by yapping curs. Men said he was insincere. No one was more sincere. Men said he was a mere orator. Nothing could be more untrue: he minded about what he said and not how he said it. Mozley still remembered the gait, the rapid movement, the stooping head (1, 204). He had a restless energy, a pale face, lustrous eyes. He always wore a long tail coat, and it became the badge of his school. He was always busy, yet always found time for the man who needed him. He looked to encourage everything that was promising in his younger friends, and put his expectations of them high, sometimes too high. He had a faith in providence so strong that he applied it to the trivial circumstances and changes of life. He was interested in the varieties of human character and loved to study its diversity, and asked himself of this or that young man, what is he good for? what will he do best? He loved nature, trees and flowers, sky and cloud – Mozley says a strange thing of him: 'he carried his scenery with him' (1, 214).

So – hidden among the trivialities, and irrelevances, and sideswipes at worthies, some still living – the book had a hero; Mozley's own brother-in-law and long-parted friend.

The surviving leaders of the Oxford Movement found Mozley's book a degradation for the Movement. But only one of the leaders survived. Hurrell Froude died of consumption forty-six years before. John Keble died sixteen years before. Pusey remained, in his last two months of life; with the reputation of one who held the heirs of the Oxford Movement together through the terrible times of the forties and fifties.

Mozley's book began to obsess Pusey. He could think of nothing else. He returned to it again and again. He started destroying old letters, to stop this sort of thing happening again. Did it not show the dire need for a true history of the Oxford Movement, accurate, sympathetic, discriminating? A month before he died, he chose his man. Richard W. Church should do it; he could write history; he understood humanity; he had lived amid the events. He was the only living historian qualified to do the job.

In 1885 (or in 1884) Church began to write. Perhaps he wrote because the dying Pusey laid on him so solemn a charge. Perhaps he wrote because he too found Mozley's book trivial, and whatever else the Oxford Movement was, it was not trivial. In the unpublished papers we see a third reason. Mrs Hawkins asked him to edit her dead husband's papers. Church disliked Hawkins and had no such intention. But he read the papers. And he did not like what he found. There he saw the Oxford Movement seen from the other side; and it seemed to be misrepresented.

But he never finished. We remember how Newman's curate Copeland collected material and never finished. Church wrote essays and circulated them and polished them, but he never published them and he never even finished what he intended. Yet he was not a dithering author by nature. He was a man who all his life met deadlines punctually.

The ground began to be occupied. Other men printed their memoirs. And one of them disturbed Church a little. It was Dean Burgon's *Lives of Twelve Good Men*, published in 1888, just posthumously. It is a delightful book, and Church could not quite like all that he read therein.

Burgon was much less of a journalist, but he also was a gossiper and anecdotalist, more charming than Mozley and closer to the truth. His book pinpointed the fundamental difficulty of all this historical endeavour, the difficulty which made Church so uneasy as he drafted. Here was a religious movement and its leader deserted for reasons still unintelligible. The essence of the problem was the true place of Newman in what happened. For Church as for Tom Mozley, this was the only problem that counted.

Burgon had a short and easy way, throughout his life, with every doubt or difficulty which confronted him. Not in all the Victorian age was there another man who knew his mind so resolutely. To his difficulty over Newman, Burgon had a simple solution. The Oxford Movement was founded and led by a Cambridge man, Hugh James Rose – so far as it may be ascribed to any one man. It was like a great river, with its origins in many little streams and sources. But there was a single 'authoritative voice', a single 'commanding figure', 'conspicuous beyond the rest'. The Oxford Movement was not started by Newman; its course was influenced but not led by him; his disappearance in 1845 made small difference to its development. By what book will Newman be specially remembered? Perhaps, one might think, the *Parochial Sermons*; or the *Essay on Development*; or *The Idea of a University*; or the *Apologia*? None of these, said Burgon, but the *Arians of the Fourth Century*, an obscure, incomplete book of early life, showing more promise than performance (Burgon, *Lives*, p. 88). Burgon did not doubt Newman's sincerity or his truthfulness. But he doubted his loyalty (p. 163) and criticized his 'extravagances' (p. 136; see also p. 165). He allowed him to be a charming gentleman; to possess an exquisite felicity of style (p. 411); to preach fair sermons and to be the only preacher in Oxford who could keep Charles Marriott awake in a university sermon (p. 183); but he called his conversion by the name of *desertion* (p. 161), and quoted a fierce attack by Newman's successor at St Mary's in the phrase 'intense unconscious love of power' (p. 409).

The ground was being occupied, and in Church's eyes occupied wrong. Yet still he did not publish. He had a sacred charge from Dr Pusey to do the job. He saw everyone else doing the job badly. He must have known, what his friends saw, that he was the only Tractarian with a true historical training. And still he did not finish.

On 19 October 1888 the historian Lord Acton went for a walk in the grounds of Hawarden Castle, the home of Mr Gladstone. He walked with his host, and with Liddon, Dr Pusey's friend and biographer. They argued, should Church publish his essays on the Oxford Movement? Acton said that he was 'not against' the publishing. 'Not against' is not a phrase to portray enthusiasm. Certainly Acton was lukewarm. But Acton believed, and said then, that Church would not publish these papers so long as Newman was alive (Liddon's diary *ad diem*).

This is a true explanation. Biographers do not publish the lives of their subjects while that subject lives. Church was not writing a biography, he was writing a history. But for him this history was almost a single person. Church outlived Newman by less than four months.

Nearly everyone, except Lord Acton, who reads for the first time Richard Church's *The Oxford Movement* sees it as a classic of literature. It was published posthumously and edited and given finishing touches, by daughter and son-in-law. It has such English style, such penetrating and yet amused understanding of human beings, such poetic insight into the universe, such personal modesty and lack of ostentation on the part of the author, such a humane interpretation of the Anglican tradition in the context of the Catholic inheritance.

That it is a classic of literature no one can challenge. That it is a classic of *historical* literature, that is in question. Decades after the first reading hesitations and scruples crept in; and those hesitations and scruples affect the interpretation of the Oxford Movement.

Everyone knows of cases where a book is so important in forming opinion and yet is bad. *Eminent Victorians* is not just a bad book, it appals. Yet its non-historical quality is such that even now we can hardly understand Dr Arnold or Cardinal Manning aright because Lytton Strachey's portrait is stamped upon their faces as a magic indelible dye. Is it possible that this book by Church is the opposite of a bad book which blinds – namely a book so good that it blinds? Does Lytton Strachey take worldly masks and fit them upon characters that were in part though only in part otherworldly? Does Church take otherworldly masks and fit them on characters that were in part but only in part men of this world as well as of another? Is he the literary equivalent of the artist George Richmond, who painted the Victorians with a far-seeing refined spirituality in their faces; the aesthetic antidote to Lytton Strachey?

I am now going to ask in turn two questions about this classic history of the Oxford Movement, two questions which sound as though they must be contradictory and yet are not: first, why is the book so excellent? Second, why is it a failure?

Why is it excellent? Three reasons, in order: form, matter, range.

Church adopted a particular literary form: the essay. He was one of the best essayists in all the Victorian age, that great age of essay-writing. In those days intelligent journals could make good profits out of selling (what by modern standards would be) very few copies; and therefore catered for an élite public who would tolerate in one number an article of thirty, forty, or even at times a hundred pages; so that intelligent magazines drew writers out of the ordinary because they could shade their journalism into something more satisfying.

Church once explained why this mode of communication

attracted. The professional scholar writes for an enclosed world. He is shackled by sources, criticism of text, defence of argument, constraint on personal opinion, weight brought by striving towards completeness. The essayist says what he thinks. The reader wants to know about the man or matter of which the author writes, but is happier still to know what the author feels. He is free, bringing readers into his confidence, able to follow wherever taste or interest selects, careless that his pages may be ephemeral provided that he stirs others to read about his concern. He once talked of the need to throw off the *donnishness* of erudition (*Occ. Papers*, 1, 4). (The earliest instance of the word *donnishness* to mean a stiff pedantic manner is found a few years before in Newman.) Something about the idea of the word *essay* contrasted in Church's mind with the word *pedantry*: unbuttoned instead of stiff, human instead of arid, using knowledge instead of massing information, outgoing instead of jealous, loving knowledge with an affection that must wish to share its insight, bridging the chasm between an older society and our own by letting each be part of the other, men of former generations understood to be of the same blood and sinew and heart as ourselves, ourselves able to share their fears and hopes and emotions. He looked for breadth because he had a sense that narrowness was blind, because breadth could compare and so illuminate, because intense specialization grows stale and if the purpose is to understand humanity and society, freshness of mind is an indispensable quality in the inquirer – breadth of freedom or humanity contrasted in his mind with a cramped and servile assiduity.

So here is an essayist; who can write English prose as fair as Newman's; who is readable, because he eschewed of set purpose the foot-slogging of the professional historian; and who thinks it right to take the reader into his private confidence. From this aspect, at least, the Oxford Movement was fortunate to have its historian in a man who was no journalist, in any wrongful sense, but whose account is hard to put down.

The next reason for the quality of the interpretation is range. Some people took very simple views of the why of the Oxford Movement. They said dismissively, it was a part of the European right-wing reaction after the French Revolution; and its origin was in political theory. Or they said, it was the ecclesiastical reaction against the Reform Act and the new representative system in Britain; and its origins lay in politics, a war against the Irish Church Temporalities bill. Or they said, it was the recovery of old Arminian teaching in an age when the Evangelical revival made Calvinism so loud and so intrusive; and its origins lay in controversial theology, a counter to Calvinism. Or they said, it was only the religious side of the romantic revival, and we must set it with Wordsworth's poetry and Walter Scott's novels; a harking back to the past, a release to the imagination; and its origin lay in the new sensibility about history.

Political theory; politics; ecclesiastical reaction; anti-Calvinism; romantic imagination – all were contemporary diagnoses, and all had more than a breath of truth. But Church had the range to see that no contemporary diagnosis was sufficient. To understand this religious movement we must set it in a longer context. Its intellectual base lay in a tradition framed in Richard Hooker, or Lancelot Andrewes, or Jeremy Taylor, the English divinity of the seventeenth century; and beyond them to their roots, the hard and rigorous study of the Fathers during the age of the later Reformation. It was the recovery of perspective.

This was the second reason for Church's quality. He had range. He had written the best book on Lancelot Andrewes, the best book on Dante. He understood, not just the Victorian age, but the Christian centuries.

The third reason why the book is so good is the subject. It had nearly everything that a historical subject should have: unity of theme; limits of time, set close; fascinating and strange characters, from a vanished age; a sense of inspiration, and leaping vitality; a war; and a tragedy.

Men and women when they are different – and if they are in the past they are always different – do deeds which look to later generations bizarre; the easiest and the least understanding form of historical writing is veiled satire or veiled mockery. To refuse to despise is not to refuse to laugh. Human beings are what they are, and sometimes they are tragic and sometimes they are comic, but in either case they are often laughable. The quest for humanity has to rest upon a sense of the seriousness of the object, that is, an attributing of some sort of lasting value to the person or group which is being studied. It did not depend on the moral philosophers with the analysis of human nature in the abstract; even though an elementary knowledge of moral philosophy could not but be useful to the student of man. But in Church's eyes the student of humanity was always the student of living individuals; and he felt this study of the being in its various specimens to be stranger and more wonderful and more curious than the abstractions of humanity offered by students of will or of conscience or of aesthetics of beauty (*Occ. Papers*, 1, 7).

Nineteen chapters to a book on the Oxford Movement, and two of the chapters are on lesser men – Isaac Williams and Charles Marriott. Why? Can it be said that either contributed anything to the ideas or even the history of the Movement, except in so far as by Dr Pusey's folly Williams was beaten to succeed Keble in the professorship of poetry? We hear that Williams was a great cricketer – what is that to do with us? A convert of John Keble; a curate who abhorred mere display. We hear that Marriott could almost distress his hearers by his clumsiness to say what he meant, his long looks and blank silences; we hear how he wore a black veil over his college cap and that in his rooms you must make your way between layers of books.

The reason for these two chapters was not the weight of the two persons, but that Church had access to unpublished memoirs on both of them.

A part of the subject draws readers by its tragedy. The Movement could not hold its leader. Twenty years before Newman wrote an emotional book about his own desertion of the Movement and how that change happened. Church had no need to repeat an account of what happened. But throughout his book lurks a sense of tragedy. You would have expected the story of a man who found peace and happiness in a new Church to be the opposite of a calamity. Church found in it nothing but tragedy. This makes part of the failure of the book. It is also a constituent of its stature. It is a piece of history to engage the emotions, and that is not so common in the study of the past, wherein we watch frightfulness with mild indifference.

Now, what is wrong? Here is a man with every possible gift for writing the history of the Oxford Movement, and he failed. How could that be?

In the incomplete book, published by his daughter and son-in-law, is an historical obsession. This *thing* within the book may very likely have caused him hesitation before he printed. It is an onslaught upon the heads of Oxford colleges, taken corporately.

Everyone knows that the heads of colleges are not the most popular persons in a university. But this is no acidulated don. And he is not a disappointed man, with the motives of a Mark Pattison of Lincoln College for being sour. He is successful in the rightest sense of that double word. He is mellow, and comfortable, and kindly, and humorous, and wise, a Victorian gentleman.

The heads of Oxford colleges, he thought, that was what went wrong. They drove Newman out. They behaved with unexampled unwisdom; and worse than unwisdom, he tells us, they were childish, they failed, and failed deplorably, in justice and in charity; they were blind to the moral quality before them because they were incapable of seeing moral quality – 'There was that before them which it was to their discredit that they did not see' (p. 262). They were violent, and ignorant (p. 263), they wanted learning, they were scandalous in their imputations of dishonesty, they were 'inexpressibly childish' in sticking up notices at the gates of the schools or in college butteries. The whole affair was a 'continuous provocation of unfair and harsh dealing from persons who were scarcely entitled to be severe judges' (p. 270); all held up by Church to a contrast with the noblest motto ever possessed by a university, *Dominus illuminatio mea*. In short, two chapters at least of the book are not history but a philippic; an old man, whose bitterness was repressed in his middle years, coming out at last in the long perspective of the last years before death.

When men denounce with unmeasured fury the heads of the colleges, they mean, when you boil it down, the head of their own college. The Provost of Oriel was an intelligent man. Church confessed his stature. He was able and resolute. He was a man 'of rigid conscientiousness, and very genuine though undemonstrative piety, of great kindliness in private life' (p. 283). But he had not 'breadth' or 'knowledge proportionate to his intellectual power'. And that means, he was incapable of understanding what Newman and his friends stood for.

This is Church's view. Everyone is agreed that Hawkins was the weightiest enemy of the Oxford Movement in all Oxford. Hawkins is strange. Liddon thought him a very able theologian.

He could be a good talker at dinner. Everyone is agreed that he was a good man, a man of conscientiousness. But in Oriel he was nicknamed the East Wind. They said that he was *sharp*. Never did a man see so many trees and so little of the wood. He was exact about everything that was small. An undergraduate drank too much and fell off the roof in the night and died; and the Provost took a long time to arrive, and when he appeared his tie had been tied perfectly. He was a master of detail, and cold to get detail right. He could not see what all the details were for. (See Burgon, *Lives*, 225–9, 238.) 'He would have set a King right', said one of the bishops, 'if His Majesty had slipped in a date.' Therefore he had the highest dislike and disdain for the Oxford Movement, whether on its moral or its intellectual side. And so Church can sum it up in a fearful condemnation: 'In their dullness of apprehension and forethought, the authorities of the University let pass the great opportunity of their age' (p. 215).

A young man went up to Oxford as an undergraduate. The time was exciting in the university. He started attending the sermons at St Mary's given by a Fellow of Oriel College at 4.0 p.m. on Sundays. They were not well attended, because the delivery was not inspiring and the preacher held an ideal of sobriety which made him eschew the lesser arts that made words interesting. There in his pew at St Mary's the young Church was soon enchained by the moral force of the preacher, his insight into conscience, his *burning* (*Oxford Movement*, p. 113) faith in God and his counsels.

And then this religious leader, to whom he owed his soul, deserted the cause. Newman's leaving meant the exploding into laughter or contempt of some of the religious idealism to which Richard Church and others were now committed. And incidentally it caused agony to disciple after disciple – what were they supposed to do now? Join him in Rome, whose teaching they could not believe? Abandon the ideals which they had learned from his lips?

Some of Newman's disciples were like Mark Pattison, willing to blame Newman for their predicament. But not Church. He muted his disagreement and criticised him subtly amid the praise. Nevertheless, the obsession against the heads of colleges who drove out Newman had its roots here. He could not believe that

Newman went because he chose. He went because he was driven.
For Church the heads of colleges became a scapegoat, which bore
away the blame, and so rescued the integrity and honour of his
former leader, and enabled him to retain his own convictions.

To wait till your main subject is dead –

To see everyone else occupying the ground and occupying it
with error –

To doubt whether what you are doing is necessary, or even
right –

To wonder whether it can be the part of a wise man to expose
the folly or wickedness of heads of Oxford colleges whose
widows might still live –

To be a man of reserve, and reticence, and to hold this
reticence as a part of your spiritual and devotional ideal, and yet
to realize that if you write this book you cannot but be writing
autobiography –

Still, it is odd not to finish. And in my own mind there is no
doubt at all of the basic reason. To publish was too painful and
felt wrong. Talbot begged him not to leave it there; here was a
movement which changed the face of English religion, and yet he
left it at the moment of failure. He would not alter. He made no
attempt to add. That was what it was, failure.

The partial failure left a gap in historical writing which has
never yet been filled. We all drive young people away from
devoting their time to the Oxford Movement because too many
have made it an industry. But Church occupied the ground
without filling the gap. The earlier lives of Newman did little for
it. Liddon's life of Pusey added a mass of useful material but
much less historical understanding. In this century Swedes like
Brilioth or Härdelin tried to give its thought perspective from
outside Britain. For the centenary of 1933 much the most
important essay was Geoffrey Faber's *Oxford Apostles*, which
made it all very readable; but he thought a good deal too highly of
the reminiscencers Tom Mozley and William Tuckwell as
sources. We now are getting the full edition of Newman's
correspondence, and very valuable it is proving. Work is in
progress on Pusey's correspondence. We all have hopes that the
work on the history of Oxford University will give important
new perspectives.

But we shall never do without Church's book. It sprang out of the age of the reminiscencers; it was itself a kind of reminiscence by an old man, though that is concealed because it is written not by a man of common room gossip but by a historian; it is in part a failure because the memory of the man could not get over the rancour and the tragedy; and yet it remains a very influential piece of history.

Chapter 8

NEWMAN AND THE HISTORIANS

The historians were late getting at Newman. They only get at people when they are dead. Newman took a long time to die. He retreated from the world into a monastery in 1842. He lived for another forty-eight years; quiet, retired, prayerful, unpretentious, a bit scruffy. He appeared from behind the veil three times: once to libel, or rather not to libel but to be convicted of libelling, a very libelling ex-Dominican; once to defend himself, not in a law court, against a libel; and once to become a cardinal, the first cardinal whom the English people enjoyed having since they had had a Reformation. Historians like people who do things: who conquer Gaul, or fornicate on Capri, or evangelize the East, or are beheaded. They have not much to say about people who do nothing; and the class of people who do nothing consists, *inter alia*, of practically all dons, and practically all monks. Dons do nothing but sit at their desks and toy with paper. Monks do practically nothing but get on their knees and be silent or vocal before God. In two chunks of life, Newman was a professional academic, and after he resigned his academic posts he remained donnish in cast of mind, even though after the age of seventy he refused the offer of a professorship. And in all his life from 1842 to the end, if not before, he was a sort of monk. That left history with thin materials.

To this thinness of material comes a mighty exception. Newman was no diarist. He kept a little series of diaries, but the entries are usually one line long; and very external, and seldom useful to a historian – where he was, whom he met, who came to see him. For this laconic or jejune quality in the diaries he compensated by being one of the best of letter-writers; and as a letter-writer he had a quality even more important to the historian, in that he usually drafted the letter and kept the draft as his copy of what he sent. Therefore at his death he left in the Oratory at Birmingham a vast archive. The Oratorian Fathers inherited this collection and began systematically to extend its range. They bought letters at auction, begged letters, and soon were given letters; until the Library in the Hagley Road at Birmingham became an important archive of Victorian history.

Not quite everything was kept. Newman loved to look at his old letters and sort them. No one who has that habit can bear to keep quite everything. It is certain that Newman destroyed some letters. We do not know on what motives, but doubtless for the same motives as other sorters of collections, because the letters felt too private, or too misleading, or too unrepresentative, or too trivial. But if in doubt he preserved. For some letters which other men would surely have destroyed remained in the archive. There is a fearful series of letters concerning the quarrel between the Oratory at Birmingham and its daughter-house the Oratory at London, a *querelle de moines* if ever there was such; in cold print for the eye of posterity, the ice-cold charity of Christians when they make it plain that they forgive their enemies. Anyone who destroyed letters for the sake of clearing the record, framing the record, purifying the record, setting up history before it is written, would have burned those letters. Newman left them all. Perhaps he had the same motive as collectors of papers when they so constantly mislead future historians: namely, those who quarrel need to keep copies for future reference, those who are not quarrelling have no reason to keep a copy of what they said; and therefore the safes of institutions are full of tiffs and arguments, and the future historian will imagine that the life of that institution was marred by an endless querulousness. That well-known rule may have something to do with it. But not all. Newman preserved letters, even if they might ultimately be to his discredit. There was the record; it stood before God, if also it fell under the eyes of man, so be it; history would be the judge.

It has to be faced that vast collections of paper, though welcome to the historian, make his or her life more difficult. To write history is easier when your only sources are Livy and Polybius. And where you have a vast collection of trivial paper, you make historians waste even more than usual of their precious time. A lot of the letters of anyone must be judged trivial, or that person would not be a human being. And when the letters are those of a monk in his cell, they may concern profound matters of theology, or debatable points in the editing of a learned journal, or discussions on the progress of a monastery; but not so often will they hit the target of history, the nature of contemporary society and its processes of change.

With this doctrine – that the sources for Newman are bound to be trivial, not in the the least because Newman was trivial, but by the nature of his social and personal situation – there is a large compensation or counterweight. He wrote excellent letters. Except when quarrelling with Faber or Manning, he found it impossible to write tediously. He was a man who thought on paper. Personally he was often inarticulate; a man of long silences, of awkward moments, of such non-contribution to the conversation that people occasionally wondered, quite erroneously, whether he was offended. In good part this was due to a shyness that could be attractive; in part it was due to a moral fear of the tongue and its uncontrollability; but in part also, and this is what concerns us, it was due to the natural equipment, often found in able minds, that they only think systematically if they organize their thoughts on paper as they proceed, and do not like to express ideas unless they feel them to be organized systematically.

A man does his famous work before he is forty years old. He lives another fifty years afterwards. Towards the end of that period he has become part of history. People write books about the events, now long ago, but of which he was a main part. Yet in a curious way his very survival is an obstacle to the writing of good history.

This is a puzzle about historical writing which is something of a riddle and for which you may have various explanations, none of them fully satisfying. Why is it that the history of a person, written while that person is still alive, never fails to discontent? The reason cannot be lack of perspective, for half a century has elapsed, and we see in a real historical perspective other events which happened less than half a century ago. The obvious reason is, that so long as the man lives, his private papers are not open to the inquirer. This is a good part of the explanation, but not all the explanation. Another part is the antagonism between the personal attachment which is necessary to private rapport, and the detachment or neutrality of mind which is necessary to public analysis. The historian has a little in him of the anatomist or dissector. A surgeon who cuts someone up does not wish to feel the body to be an object of his private affections: he must treat it as a thing, simply as an intellectual or physical problem to solve. Charles Kingsley's widow wrote his life in two volumes; and the instance is generally taken as proving that a widow should never write the life of her husband. A private bond is too strong for it to be possible to win a public detachment. On the contrary, a historian frigid in heart towards his theme can hardly ever write good history. To penetrate a person or a situation, you have to be able to look with the sight of that person, or at the situation through the eyes of those who were tangled in its various toils. Rapport of some sort is almost always necessary to good historical writing, because without it there is hardly a chance of a more than superficial understanding.

There was another way in which Newman complicated the task of history by living to a great age. He lived long enough for the *media*, as I suppose I may call them, to get hold of him. The *media*, in our sense, were born into the world during the 1860s, with the abolition of the newspaper tax, the creation of modern newspapers, and the speedy development of a reading public by elementary or compulsory state education. Newman lived during about twenty-five years of modern media.

Media live by legends; or rather by labels, and a label is a sort of legend. The great mass of people, which is US, cannot do with an excess of complexity or subtlety. We have to be given a frame, or structure, of simplicity if we are to have any kind of context for what we read. A famous incident labels a figure. It may be quite untypical of that figure. Ever afterwards it is a placard hanging round his or her neck – 'This is Bishop John Robinson: he gave evidence for the defence in the *Lady Chatterley* case.' We, the public, need reminding who people are. This reminds us. The label helps. Yet the label creates a legend. We read all else we know of a character in the light of a label, which may record some moment or happening entirely untypical of the person round whose neck we see the label hanging.

The national newspapers of Newman's last two decades were nothing like so powerful, and therefore nothing like so label-making, as the radio or television media of the 1960s. But those newspapers got hold of him; and as must be the case, the way in which they got hold of him cluttered the historical problem.

Any label needs to have, first, a measure of truth, though of course not all the truth; second, drama; third, emotion; and fourth, controversy, in the simplest of terms. The label on which the educated public seized contained all four elements. It was the antagonism, or even enmity, between Newman and Manning.

Two Oxford men, two Anglican clergymen; both converted to the Roman Catholic Church during the wave of 1843–51; and then going their separate ways, the one to public affairs, hierarchy, power, the forefront of the Catholic fight, the purple, place, papal favour, and grandeur; the other to a monk's cell, retreating from the fight, solitary and unpretentious, a critic of hierarchy, oppressed by hierarchy, suspect to Rome, shabby in his cassock, as ungrand as possible; quiet meditator versus high ecclesiastic and politician. This label had all the merits. It was dramatic and emotional; it was all about controversy; it did a little in Protestant England to lower the esteem of the Roman Catholic Church; and no one could say that it was not true. Such a label in the media no one has any means of correcting or amending. All corrections or amendments are too subtle for our simple public minds, and look like triviality or pedantry. One thing, and one thing only, could be corrected. Newman could be given a cardinal's hat. Newman's hat had nothing to do with his theology; nothing to do with his books; nothing to do with his foundation of a religious house; nothing to do with his services to the Church; little to do with any desire to make him more useful to the operations of the Church. A papal promotion had become necessary as the only means of correcting one element in the label, namely the legend that Newman was against the Pope and the Pope was against Newman.

It is another well-known rule of history that the motives for an action have no relation to the consequences of that action. If the Pope stopped to consider Newman's theology, or imagined that the cardinal's hat would be taken as an imprimatur on his theology, he would have paused a little longer than he did. No intention existed to consecrate, for example, Newman's theory of development, or Newman's sense of history, or Newman's theory of faith, or Newman's anti-scholastic attitudes. Some people believed that if more people in the Curia had been able to read the English language, the cardinal's hat would hardly have been possible; and we know – indeed we could hardly be surprised – that some people in the Curia opposed the elevation probably on this ground. But the motives for an action have no relation to the consequences of the action. The hat could do nothing but good to the eventual influence of Newman's ways of thought.

Meanwhile the hat had another consequence not foreseen. It certainly killed any public idea that Newman was against the Pope or the Pope against Newman. It did nothing to quash the idea that Newman was against Manning and Manning against Newman.

The label of the media was canonized, very dramatically, when the official biography of Manning was published in 1896. It was an act of generosity on Manning's part to make Purcell his official biographer. He wanted to help Purcell financially, in return for services which Purcell had rendered. We need not here enter the enormous volume of controversy engendered by the publication of Purcell's life of Manning. It will be sufficient here only to notice that it canonized the antipathy between Newman and Manning; hierarch Manning versus anti-hierarch Newman, public Manning versus private Newman, archbishop versus monk, politician versus thinker, extremist versus moderate. And its publication worried the Oratorian fathers at Birmingham who had control of Newman's vast archive of unpublished papers and had the business of seeing that a proper and faithful and sympathetic and historical biography of Newman should be written. They appointed Wilfrid Ward, son of Newman's old disciple and then critic, to be the official biographer. In the prevailing situation, they would not leave him untrammelled. They bothered and fussed him at every turn. And although like any other author he resented the bother and the fuss, as an attempt to control or hamper the freedom of an historian, in this perspective of time we cannot wonder at the interference.

The name of Newman was, and is, precious to the Oratorians. He was their founder. Their reputation hung, in good measure, on his reputation. Their vocation rested, in good measure, on what was understood to be his vocation. Every religious community cares about its founder. They find among themselves high aspirations in prayer or service, and they look back with gratitude to a main cause of these matters. That sense of gratitude complicates the work of historians, in every case. It is enough to think of Martin Luther, or St Francis of Assisi, or St Benedict. We may put it this way and say, a movement to canonize a man or woman cannot be a help to true biography. Those who knew a founder in the community had affection for him and some of them, even those who could not know him, associate his name with their moral ideals. They have not the necessary detachment. They are like a widow seeking to write, or at least to control, the biography of her husband. Father George Tyrrell once suggested (1901) that the only way to get a biography of Newman written was to assassinate the Oratorian Father Neville who had charge of the papers and seize all the letters for Wilfrid Ward (Maisie Ward, *The Wilfrid Wards and the Transition* (1934), vol. 2, p. 336).

And now a new episode cluttered the historians and their work of understanding.

That process which is symbolically but misleadingly called 'Darwin' came into the mind of the Christian Churches with revolutionary force similar to the entry into the Christian mind of Greek intellectualism during the third and fourth centuries, or Aristotle during the thirteenth, or the Greek scholarship of the Renaissance, or the empirical philosophy of the seventeenth century. Every such process of intellectual adjustment demanded casualties, for reasons which are plain but need to be entered here. The worse casualties to the Church came from the impact of the Renaissance. 'Darwin', if I use the name only as a symbol, produced no trauma comparable to the division of the Church into Catholic and Protestant. But casualties it demanded. The adjustment which it forced was more radical than any change required by the sixteenth century.

No one had thought about the way in which a Church, with its stable ways of worship, and beloved formularies, and tradition of ideas to transmit, absorbs or rejects the newer cultural insights of a society; how, for example, it meets Platonism; needs to express itself, in a world where Platonism conditions all thinking, must adopt or adapt Platonic formulas if it is to be understood in contemporary society; and yet must reject whatever of Platonism is found to be antipathetic to its own Christian insights or inheritance. A new problem had to be faced. Here was the Church now in a society where Darwinian axioms became the property of every educated man and woman; where people, while having the haziest possible idea what the word *evolution* meant, were somehow persuaded that evolution, whatever it is, is true. A whole new range of ideas came into general culture. Churches must do what once they did with Platonism – express themselves in words that could be understood, adopt or adapt, and reject whatever was found after due meditation to be antipathetic to their own experience of truth or moral right.

When I say no one had thought about it, that needs modification. Two or three good minds of the Catholic schools of scholarship at Tübingen or Munich, early in the nineteenth century, had touched upon it. German Protestants of the nineteenth century spent so much time and effort arguing with Hegelian philosophy in one form or another, a philosophy where intellectual evolution was the key, that they could not help thinking about it; and in the decade after Newman's death (1890) it was prominent in the new German school of the history of religion. But no reputable Catholic theologian had done more than touch on it – with one exception. Forty-five years before, Newman wrote a book to which the very notions of the absorption or rejection of new ideas in a society were central. The name of Newman was going to become indispensable to an entire movement of Christian adaptation and adjustment. It took several decades before this happened.

Whose fault was the calamity of 1907 is still not settled, and perhaps it does not matter. The defenders of the Curia say that the abbé Alfred Loisy in Paris, in his free historical critique of the Bible, and the Jesuit George Tyrrell in England, in his free critique of the power structure of the Church, passed far beyond any point which the Church could tolerate and still be the Church. The defenders of the rights of radical thought say that a new Pope of simple piety and very conservative notions and a capacity for being shocked had no ability whatever to tolerate, let alone understand, the scholars as they worked at the Bible in a new world with more or less assured results of inquiry. Whatever the causes, the encyclical Pascendi, of 8 September 1907, was one of the disasters of Christendom in the twentieth century. It condemned all these intellectual developments, of which some were wrong, but more were fertile and tending towards the truth, threw Church authority on the side of obscurantism and created the image of a Church with a mind closed to ideas that mattered – a Church versus the soul of the modern world, instead of a Church as the soul of the modern world. In condemning such developments it used hard words, even abusive words. Whoever drafted it drafted it ill. As the Syllabus of Errors was the document forty-three years before which pledged the Church for the moment to political obscurantism, so Pascendi pledged the Church, for the moment, to intellectual obscurantism. Of course, intellectual ideas do not evolve in a vacuum, but proceed in a background of political and social evolution; and here was a case where the political predicament of the nineteenth century, which issued in the decisive anti-liberalism of all that century, helped to condition the intellectual anti-liberalism of the early twentieth century. We have to recognize that Garibaldi and the Italian nationalists had a part even in the background to Pascendi.

The Modernists whom Pascendi condemned did not recognize their theories in its large and hostile phrases. But some of them held that it condemned Newman. Trying to gain freedom for historical inquiry and non-scholastic attitudes in theology or philosophy, some of them appealed to Newman. Newman had cared about history. He saw that history forced the Church to restate its doctrines through the ages and was prepared to face the facts. He had a theory of faith which was not the theory of St Thomas Aquinas. And he was a cardinal and therefore a sort of approved authority. It was very intelligible that Loisy or Tyrrell or Houtin should think well of Newman and want to use him as a key to unlock liberty for their own minds. How much they did this varied according to their inclinations and whether they themselves had insight into Newman and his delicacies and subtleties of thought. But inevitably his name kept coming up. The Italian Modernist Buonaiuti (*Le Modernisme catholique* (French trans., 1927), p. 130) wrote that 'of all the countries in Europe, Britain was the only one where the Modernist movement, so far as its essential ideas were concerned, had a prede-cessor'. Paul Sabatier, who was a famous French Protestant but who had a rare understanding of some forms of Catholicism, not merely regarded Newman as a predecessor of the Modernists. He was confident that the Church, going the way which it was going with Pascendi, would soon have to condemn Newman himself (*Les Modernistes*, pp. 43–8; cf. J. Rivière, *Le Modernisme dans l'église* (1929), p. 83).

All this movement which culminated in Pascendi, and in the heresy-hunt which followed, was sufficient to scare many good minds away from Newman. On 4 November 1907 the Superior of the Oratory, Father John Norris, the man in charge of the papers which Wilfrid Ward needed, published a letter in *The Times* making an extraordinary avowal. 'After information which I have today received from the highest authority, I am authorized to affirm that "the authentic doctrine and mind of the Catholic teaching of Newman are not touched by the Encyclical, but that the theories of many who wrongly seek to take refuge in the shadow of a great name are clearly censured".' If the Superior of the Oratory had to publish in a Protestant newspaper such a statement, and such a carefully phrased statement, then the reputation of Newman was in dire trouble. Nothing could be more calculated than this to rouse Britain to the suspicion that all was not well with Newman. And it requires very little imagina-tion to conceive the effect on the Oratorian fathers in Birm-ingham as they still fussed Wilfrid Ward, their official author, in his preparation of the biography. On the one hand they must want to get Newman right, that is, Newman as he was in his authentic self and not as the Modernists claimed him to be. On the other hand it had to be confessed that within Newman were attitudes towards free inquiry in theology and philosophy which might be reputably Catholic but which it was not tactful to put forward too forcibly at that time. The Oratorians went on fussing Wilfrid Ward.

In 1905, while Ward still worked away, Henri Bremond published a psychological study of Newman. As he was a writer of grace and distinction, this study was widely read in France and England. Wilfrid Ward disliked it very much. Ward had come to feel, at least a little, as biographers tend to feel when they have charge of all the unpublished papers, that he and he alone really understood Newman. He had no sympathy whatever with this approach of psychological history. To him Bremond neglected most of the Newman that mattered, which was the theologian and the thinker, and concentrated on speculation about the person, his nature, and his piety. 'It is a very impertinent book', he wrote. 'Such an account of a great man, deducing far more than there are real premisses to warrant, can only be justified by a very reverent attitude and a real mastery of the character. The book shows neither' (Ward, *The Wilfrid Wards*, 2, 172). He reviewed Bremond's book in an exceptionally hostile review in the *Dublin Review* (141 (1907), 1ff.), and showed that he thought Bremond to have turned a giant into a pygmy. 'M. Bremond has taken as a model for his work a smaller man cut out of the real Newman – and a good deal altered and damaged in the cutting. He has dressed him partly in French clothes and partly in raiment supplied by his own exuberant fancy. I am bound to add that he has constructed so lively a marionette that at moments one thinks he is a real human being.' You can hardly say worse than that about anyone's attempt at a biographical study.

It was an ungenerous review. Ward had read a lot of letters which Bremond had no chance of reading. It is always difficult for Frenchmen to get inside Englishmen or vice versa (yet it has often been done), and perhaps there was a touch of French atmosphere in the way Bremond approached Newman. The Oratorians shared Wilfrid Ward's opinion of his book. One of them, Father Tristram, who was a sober scholar but very loyal to his founder, called Bremond's book 'a brilliant fantasy'.[1]

Wilfrid Ward's life of Newman appeared at last in 1912, when its author had four years to live. It was excellently done – very surprisingly, after all the pressure which Ward suffered. It was excellent for three reasons: first, the author hid himself, and wove the letters together, standing back and not obtruding his own judgment; secondly, his selection of the material was coherent and even more, was fair-minded – none of the pressure succeeded in diverting him from the path which he felt to be right; thirdly he was a moderate man who saw the strength in Catholic

---

[1] *Newman Centenary Essays* (1945), p. 241.

liberalism and yet was a strong servant of the papacy, and therefore had a rapport with Newman's own mind; and fourthly, he happened to be using material which is exceedingly interesting. It now became clear, what till that moment was not quite clear, that Newman was a writer of excellent letters, many of which bore printing and reading by posterity.

It was important, Ward's life. The Modernist controversy put Newman at the bottom of his influence among Roman Catholics. 'Newman is too original, too personal a thinker to be followed with safety', said a famous French theologian de Grandmaison (cited in *The Rediscovery of Newman*, ed. J. Coulson and A. M. Allchin (1967), p. 169). Some years before that a German Catholic periodical had said, 'It is a pity that this unusual man could not sufficiently overcome himself to be rid of the last remainders of his Protestant past' (ibid., p. 177).

The revival of the modern years has been well documented, though still only partially. The French school of Catholic history between the World Wars needed freedom of historical inquiry and especially freedom of historical inquiry into dogma, and used Newman's theory of development to justify their theory. Reviving Catholic scholarship in Germany under the Weimar Republic grew interested in much the same way. The concern about the relation between the revelation of God and history was central to the problems of modern Christian thinking. Since 1945 the revival of German historical scholarship had much the same effect as the earlier French revival. And when with the death of Pius XII the years of the 'Prisoner in the Vatican' were over at last, and the Church turned to go outwards to the world instead of defending itself against the world, there was Newman ready for use. We must not exaggerate this availability. It is an illusion to think that Newman's ideas were very powerful in influencing what was done by the Second Vatican Council.

But the most important thing that happened to historical studies of Newman happened during the last thirty years. The Oratory at Birmingham produced at last a scholar worthy of the task which awaited them all.

Stephen Dessain came of a Belgian family. He tried his vocation as a Carthusian. It would not do for him, yet he always seemed to retain a touch of the secret stillness which was associated with the Carthusian hermitage. He came into the Oratory at Birmingham. There he dedicated himself to Newman and Newman's letters. He formed the plan – an extraordinary plan when the volume, weight, expense, and time are considered – of publishing all Newman's letters. He started to edit them. He proved to be a scholar of the first rank and an editor of genius. It was natural that he could not complete the plan. He died appropriately, at the altar during a service in commemoration of Newman, when the job was two-thirds done. It was continued by successors. The first volume (numbered no. 11, because it began with the first year of Newman's Catholic life) appeared in 1961. The thirty-seventh volume (numbered no. 6) appeared in 1984. The lovable Father Dessain created one of the new monuments of Victorian studies, comparable to the Gladstone diaries or the Dickens letters.

Therefore we are at a new age in the development of the subject. First we have freedom, not worried about Modernism; if Newman was used by the Modernists, who cares? And secondly, thanks to a rare person with infinite care and great industry, we now have almost all the materials needed. The results are not going to turn Wilfrid Ward's biography, or even Bremond's, on their heads. We are going to see a more balanced Newman. His stature is not going to be smaller despite the fullness of know-ledge. That will not mean that he is sure to be far less of a mystery.

Chapter 9

HENRI BREMOND AND NEWMAN

Henri Bremond's love of Newman was one of the by-products of the French anti-clerical legislation of the later nineteenth century – one of several by-products to benefit England. As a Jesuit he was expelled from France at the age of twenty-seven and was forced to live eleven years of his life in England. Since it was the Jesuit rule that Jesuits should learn the language of the country where they worked, he threw himself into English literature of every description, from good poetry to bad novels. Naturally he discovered the religious writing of Victorian England. He got interested in the more famous poets like Browning and Matthew Arnold, and the better novelists like George Eliot. He grew interested in the Church of England and the Church history of Victorian England. And, though not quickly, it began to be Newman who commanded his chief interest: not just Newman the Catholic convert, but also Newman the Anglican, Newman the preacher in the University of Oxford, Newman the troubled soul, Newman the autobiographer, Newman the religious heart solitary before his Maker. He became fascinated; partly by Newman the person, but partly also by the possibility and the difficulty of analysing other people's religious feelings. It was the attempt to analyse Newman's religious experience which helped to turn Bremond to his life's work, the analysis of the development of religious emotion and experience during a classical age of France.

It has been said that every historian is a concealed autobiographer; that his or her interests and approaches to history are conditioned by something in his or her personal life. If this is true at all of historians, it is likely to be true of historians of religion. For to grapple with religion at all, even when it is the religion of the past, becomes a sort of engagement. To understand it requires a mental apprehension or sympathy which affects more of the mind than the rational processes.

Whether or not this is true of a lot of people, it was true of Bremond. He was a troubled soul himself. The trouble in his own heart led him straight to his interest in the most troubled of Victorian religious souls and gave Newman his attraction.

At first he was not very serious. He thought of writing novels and was under fire from the rector of his North Wales college for being too flippant in what he put out. The rector thought that a Jesuit ought not to write anything that could not at once be seen to edify. Even when Bremond started to write, he did not attempt anything weighty. As late as 1898, when he was thirty-three, he was still thinking about writing novels. He put out a little study of Sir Thomas More. Even at the age of thirty-five, in 1900, when he passed into the crisis of his personality and his vocation, his friend Maud Petre tried to get him to sublimate his internal turmoil by writing a novel. In a way, the study of Newman, though not in the least a novel, was a better and higher form of sublimation, or way through a personal crisis. When he was working towards it his mind was not in repose. He was impassioned by the Modernist controversy in the Roman Catholic Church. He then realized that he had grown totally out of sympathy with his religious order, and was miserable as a member of it, and that he must get out and go to be a secular priest. And meanwhile he was doing rather strange things – writing all sorts of articles in liberal magazines under various pseudonyms.

If there was an engagement of the heart with Newman, it was in part engagement with a religious soul of the past who did not for a time know quite where he stood. This interest was not simply a biographical one. Newman did not just interest him because he was a famous Catholic of recent history. Newman interested him as a strange, subtle, sensitive, complicated example of a complicated thing: of religious feeling, especially when it is in turmoil. It was Newman who made him realize that what he really wanted to study and understand was *le sentiment religieux*.

His first idea was to get Newman better known in France. He wanted to get the whole Oxford Movement better known in France. His method of doing this was by anthologies; three volumes of selections from Newman were published, from 1903 onwards. Bremond was forty before he put out his first real book.

But before the anthologies, there came a series of studies with the later title of *Inquiétudes* (*Disquiets*). He first published them in the Jesuit journal *Etudes*, between 1894 and 1896. He was then one of the journal's editorial board with particular care for literature, and permission if he liked to specialize in English literature. The *Inquiétudes* include studies of various Victorian churchmen, of whom several were Anglican clergymen and two of whom remained Anglican, while three became Roman Catholic: William George Ward, Sydney Smith, Pusey, Manning, and Newman. They are not profound studies. They are more like ephemeral book reviews. They are not important to the study of the persons or subjects which they treat. But they are important for the development of Bremond's cult of Newman. Later on in life he looked back and was modest about his serious study of Newman that was to come; he thought that then, when he tried to present Newman in totality, he was in 'the age of illusions' and perhaps attempted something that was too hard for him; and he commended these *Inquiétudes*, partly because they were shot through with Newman's spirit, and partly because their fragmentary nature made them less ambitious (*Inquiétudes*, vol. 1, p. viii). No objective reader of the *Inquiétudes* compared with the Newman can suppose for an instant that the *Inquiétudes* have something important to say which the Newman has not. They may have the virtue of being more hesitant. They also have the vice of being more superficial.

These *Inquiétudes* have two themes or motifs which helped Bremond with his personal predicament. The first was a very conventional distinction between the faith that is mere assent to truths or to dogmas, a faith in which only the head is engaged, and the faith which is real, a faith which experiences truth, a faith in which the being of man is engaged. He cited the famous text of St Ambrose so beloved of Newman: 'Non in dialectica complacuit Domino salvum facere populum suum' ('It is not by argument that God was pleased to save his people'). The second motif was less conventional; at least in the way in which Bremond framed it. *Inquiétude* is the way to truth. It is a good. It is indispensable.

Without it, you are a mere dogmatist; or you are a mere unthinking respectable member of the middle class in a pew. And he quoted another famous phrase of Newman: 'To be at ease is to be unsafe' (From *Parochial Sermons*, 1, sermon IV, 56). When he reprinted the articles he put this quotation and that of St Ambrose on the title page, as though they were the motifs of the little collection.

These selected eminent Victorians gave him examples of just what he wanted to prove. If ever there were two dogmatists they were William George Ward and Manning. Ward treated dogmas as though they were mathematical truths. Manning treated dogmas as though you loyally accept what the Pope says and get on with your job. Sydney Smith was a good man who did what he could to get justice for Roman Catholics. But he was a comfortable canon of a cathedral, and the idea that he should ever doubt much could hardly enter his mind. He might be disturbed about the behaviour of the Bishop of London, but he could never be disturbed about God. In Bremond's context he was a well-dressed example of middle-class respectable unthinking faith in its cushioned pew.

Now Pusey was different. Bremond's portrait of Pusey was sympathetic. Here is a person with *Inquiétudes* of a sort; more than *inquiétudes*, deep disturbances. Bremond was the first to seize upon the extraordinary side of Pusey's marriage as disclosed so frankly by Liddon in the enormous biography.

He could not understand himself when he wrote tenderly of Pusey. He knew that he disliked Pusey. He first met Pusey's writing when he read his *Eirenicon* of 1865, which was supposed to be an olive branch to Catholic reunion and which Bremond found a sour, even sulky (*maussade*) piece of Protestant controversy. That set him against Pusey. He visited Pusey House in Oxford and looked at the doctor's bust and portrait and decided that this was the face of a man who wanted to be amiable but actually was cold, and shut up, and stubborn. He read Pusey's sermons and found them heavy and decided that not a line in them could draw him like one sentence of Newman's sermons. Here was a puritan, with a Bible held tight under his arm. He wanted Pusey to be human and found him not human enough. It seemed to him astonishing that his idol Newman could have had an affection for such a person. He went round asking people who had known Newman to find out whether this could possibly be true. The Anglicans said that Pusey was a saint. Bremond smiled at such a panegyric. In reality, he believed, the man was dry, authoritarian, and obstinate. Such a man could not be thought to have a true Christian piety.

But then he came to Liddon's unreadable life of Pusey. It was so detailed that somehow it enabled the reader to be at home in Pusey's house and family; to see him when he prayed and when he wept; to watch him by the beds where his children and his wife died. And the arid portrait vanished. Liddon's excess of detail enabled the most sensitive French student of the Oxford Movement, who had no natural sympathy whatever for Pusey, to get rid of the caricature which he had formed in his mind and to see that after all this was not just a puritan.

Yet caricatures usually have a part-truth. A Roman Catholic must think that Pusey had a shut mind. If so, why was the mind shut? The theory that he was arid, or was not a man of true piety, vanished. Bremond came to the equally improbable theory that inside Pusey was a secret weakness of mind (*Inquiétudes*, 1, 47–8). He was 'immobile in his stall at Christ Church'. The immobility of Bossuet, the immobility of the Gospel, of the Church, of the Catholic tradition, this is immobility; and yet for the young Bremond the immobility of Pusey is a word of abuse. Pusey (according to this view) was held above the *inquiétudes* by an immobility of faith which is not unlike Manning's. The Fathers of the Church have spoken; let us get on with the job. Bremond showed a horror (not too strong a word) of this 'immobility'. Blessed are the discontented – blessed are they that suffer in their minds – blessed are they that endure turmoil – for it is they who shall find the kingdom of God. The best Christians have open minds. They look for the truth. They listen to other people, who might be prophets of God. It cannot be right to have a mind so shut that no argument, no influence, no evidence can affect its attitudes. Pusey's mind is a sort of *inertia*. It is paralysing to the mind, not fertile for the mind. And, said Bremond, where we find this inertia of the immobile mind, it is 'almost always' due to 'a mysterious and incurable sickness of the intelligence' (*Inquiétudes*, 1, 48–9). Tell a man like this to open his eyes. He opens them. And in opening them turns his back upon the light. Pusey, he says, had as little logic in his mind as it was possible to have. For years he could look at a necessary logical deduction without making the inference which stared him in the face. And Bremond talked of the marvellous grace of being able to recognize that one is wrong and to allow it to be possible that other people see more clearly than one does oneself.

Therefore of the six Victorian minds in *Inquiétudes*, it is only Newman in whom Bremond found what he wanted to find. And that immediately prompts the historian to ask a question about both Bremond and Newman. Because he wanted to find disquiet of heart in Newman, and needed to find it for his own personal. life, did he find more disquiet than was in reality to be found in the Newman of history? Did the engagement with Newman, as one part of the study of Newman, lead him to draw into a higher relief, and even out of perspective, something that was undoubtedly there in Newman's many-cornered history but which ought not to be exaggerated?

In 1899 was published the first volume of Paul Thureau-Dangin's *La Renaissance catholique en Angleterre au XIXe siècle*. This first volume was entitled *Newman and the Oxford Movement*. It was a good book. It did for the French what Bremond hoped to do, and what he perhaps but only perhaps would have done better. It stopped Bremond doing it. It helped him in his own study of the theme, by organizing a lot of information. But it was not his kind of history. He wanted to penetrate (so far as it could be done with evidence) minds, faith, even psychology. And he thought that the defect of Thureau-Dangin's book was the external detail. You did not get to know Newman because he was covered up by information (Bremond to Ward, 23 July 1899; Emile Goichot, *Bremond*, p. 41). To show the Oxford Movement as a sort of English Port-Royal might now be impossible for him. But it was all the more necessary to try to understand Newman and to get the French to understand Newman. And he still thought, early in 1901, of writing a big history of *le sentiment religieux* in England during the nineteenth century. Even at the end of 1907 he was thinking of writing a history of English religious liberalism – which he defined as an attitude of mind almost free from accepting dogma but yet retaining something of Christianity (Goichot, p. 46: note of 23 December 1907).

At this point Bremond ran into his personal trouble. That trouble of mind was connected intimately with the Modernist controversy. It made Newman even more urgent to him. It simultaneously made it more difficult for him to write about Newman. In defence against the Modernists the Church closed its ranks; that is, it was going for authority, condemnation; and to Bremond this began to be like the shutting of the mind. It was the immobility of a Pusey who could not face new ideas. For him Newman was the Anglican and Catholic prophet of an open mind; of the Church's mind as moving in history; of its infinite receptivity to new culture and new ideas. And Bremond had discovered the friendship and the philosophy of Maurice Blondel, in whose work he found the ideas which he found foreshadowed in Newman. To represent Newman as Bremond wished to represent him was to show him to be counter to the way the Church then moved. He could hurt Newman's reputation as well as his own. One of the volumes which he now published was of texts on faith, *La Psychologie de la foi*. It was soon in trouble at Rome with the Congregation of the Index. For months unpleasant rumours circulated in Paris about Bremond's alleged heresies. It was difficult for the Congregation of the Index. They thought that the book was riddled by doctrinal error or imprudence or ambiguity. But since the book was in Newman's language it was hard to condemn. They contented themselves by telling Cardinal Richard, the Archbishop of Paris, to administer a severe rebuke to Bremond, to ban a new edition, and to get what copies they could out of circulation. The Cardinal of Paris did what he could to protect Bremond.

The fact was, Bremond was writing the first full study of Newman's mind just at the time when it was dangerous for a Catholic priest like him to write about Newman. Quite unnecessarily, he made it more dangerous. George Tyrrell, like him an ex-Jesuit, offered to read the proofs of his English translation. Tyrrell was already on the edge of excommunication for his Modernism. To the book, *The Mystery of Newman* (1907), Bremond allowed Tyrrell to write a preface. That practically

assured the more conservative Catholic world that this was a
dangerous book. It also ensured that that conservative Catholic
world would not weigh the book fairly as a study of Newman's
mind. And Tyrrell's judgments could not please all the admirers
of Newman. He said in his preface that it would be better if
Newman had not accepted the cardinal's hat; that Newman was a
profound egotist; that Newman's reply to Kingsley in the
Apologia, and his various satires on Anglicanism, were marked by
lack of generosity, dignity, and fairness; that the merit of
Bremond's book was to show the spiritual greatness of the man
amid his negative qualities as well as his virtues. This preface by
Tyrrell was an error of judgment by Bremond. Occasionally
someone would quote one of the more extreme utterances of
Tyrrell in it as though its author were Bremond.

Now it must be said, and it was immediately said after its
publication, that Bremond's book is a strange book, in one
respect. Bremond's second sentence describes its strangeness. 'The
study of Newman's doctrine is relegated to a sort of appendix at
the end of the volume, which I should like to have made still
shorter.' But Newman is a theologian. He thinks about God. He
teaches the faith. His doctrine is his public work. It is connected,
must be connected, with his inner personality. 'This', went on
Bremond 'is not because I take no interest in that doctrine, but
because I should fear to deprive it of its true character, if I were to
detach it from the moral and religious experiences which it strives
to express.' And he was aware that what he was about to publish
would shock or at least would disconcert some of Newman's
disciples. He warned them not to judge hastily. But if they are
disconcerted, he wrote, 'I can do nothing in the matter. We must
take Newman just as he is, with his sceptical intelligence and
profoundly believing soul . . .' (preface, dated Paris, December
1905).

Now, when we consider how it is that Bremond came to help
us about Newman, and how he came to mislead us somewhat
about Newman, we need to remember, first the conditions under
which he worked; and secondly the attitude of mind or heart
which led him to be so very interested in Newman. When these
two things were put together they pushed his work in a particular
direction which was unique, and therefore fertile of future

inquiry, and had simultaneously the potentiality of getting New-man out of focus.

First the conditions. He did not know Dessain's collection of Newman's letters, which started publication only in the early 1960s. He visited the Oratory at Birmingham, but the Oratorian fathers absolutely refused to let him see their letters and caused him to denounce them publicly as tenacious bunglers ('la tenace maladresse', French, p. 51); and those who have had the benefit of that collection, and the privilege of knowing its first editor, can hardly imagine how anyone before that edition can be said to have known Newman as he ought to be known. Nor did he even have an adequate biography at his disposal. There ought by then to have been a biography, but we have seen that the Oratorian fathers were so nervous that Wilfrid Ward could not produce it. Bremond thought they hurt Newman by this conduct; that their refusal to produce Newman's letters led everyone to suspect that they contained revelations of his 'persecution' by Rome or such angry or improper letters as would be unfitting for a religious leader and the founder of a religious house. What Bremond had was Newman's autobiography, so far as it was an autobiography. He had the unpleasant attack by Abbott, which took the form of a biography but of which the main purpose was to hold up to scorn the more tortuous side of Newman's mind –'pitiless book', Bremond called it, the most irritating of all the cases for the prosecution, who treats Newman like an old title-deed, and by the time he has finished the life of Newman resembles a very old printed volume gnawed by generations of insects (French, p. 76); but nevertheless Bremond believed that it could not be neglected totally. He had the first volume of Thureau-Dangin's work on the Catholic Renaissance in England. He had Tom Mozley's *Reminiscences*; and he saw it for what it was; his verdict upon it could hardly be bettered – 'this very disagreeable book. What a style, and what gossip! The *mémoires* of Port-Royal, written by a reporter of the Matin!' (Bremond, *Mystery*, p. 74n; this was a comment which he thought better of, for he removed it from the French edition of 1933. Yet once at least he cited Tom Mozley as though the citation were important when in fact it was a wild opinion by Tom Mozley). He had the still nastier and more uncomprehending study by Newman's brother Frank. And he

had R. W. Church's study of Newman in his book on the
Oxford Movement and his Occasional Papers. And Church
understood Newman, especially the earlier Newman, as well as
anyone could do.

All these dealt mainly with the Anglican Newman. And it was
the Anglican judgment on Newman which Bremond chiefly
valued – in the French edition he specially mentioned not only
Church but Hort and Lake and the Catholic layman Aubrey de
Vere.

Bremond thought very little of all this material. He thought
that practically everything so far written on Newman was bad.
He said that the books swarmed with misunderstandings (Bremond, p. 10, French, p. xix). They contained little but stupid
caricatures, or vague apotheoses. From this sweeping consignment
of books to the dustbin, he made one exception: R. W. Church –
in whom, he said, Newman found his Sainte-Beuve – who knew
him well, both as a disciple and a friend, and who 'loves his
model too much to disfigure under the pretence of embellishing
it' ('aime trop son modèle pour le défigurer sous prétexte de
l'embellir'). And he had absurdities to ridicule – Lord Acton
comparing Newman to Rosmini, or Barry comparing Newman
to Savonarola, or Abbott comparing Newman to Hamlet.

But by far his best evidence was Newman's own writings. He
had few enough of the letters: the two-volume Anglican collection edited by Anne Mozley. But his base was of course
Newman's writing. For Newman's writing was always personal,
and not only in the *Apologia*.

The materials at Bremond's disposal, therefore, so far as they
were reliable, pushed him towards the earlier half of Newman's
life. That meant, this was a Catholic writer interpreting a
Catholic mind chiefly by means of its Anglican past.

But what was especially important and interesting about
Bremond was that he did not mind this situation. He had come to
his cult of Newman through religious inquietude, through his
desire to interpret his own inquietudes. Probably there was no
part of Newman's life in which disquiet was wholly absent; he
was born by constitution to endure melancholy from time to
time. But if the need is to study him when he was in his extreme
state of religious perturbation, naturally the inquirer focussed on

the years immediately before he changed his denomination, with such doubt, and pain, and anxiety over his friends. If Bremond's sources took him more to the Tractarian Newman than to the Oratorian, his personal interest in the nature of religious disquiet made the years from 1839 to 1845 the centre of his interest; and even earlier, for the question at once arose, what sort of a religious mind was this that in 1838 was so convinced of the truth of Anglican doctrine and had a programme for reform of the Church to present with power, and three years later lost confidence in his doctrines, his convictions, and his programme of reform? To understand the Catholic Newman, Bremond had to understand Newman's psychology of faith. And he could only do that by studying Newman at the height of his power, the Newman of the thirties, the Newman who after all was a Protestant clergyman.

Bremond put this in a way which is now shocking to hardly anyone, but which must have shocked quite a number of his contemporaries: 'The first conversion of Newman is of infinitely more importance than the last' (p. 14; cf. p. 183 of the conversion at 15: 'this was the most important date of his life').

The psychology of anyone's faith; the psychology of anyone's anything – historians shrink from it but cannot always avoid it if they wish to understand. Bremond started by saying that he had embarked upon shedding what light he could shed upon a mystery; and that the effort could only end in half-light; and that the inquirer must be content, sometimes, with discovering contradiction while he knows that his subject must be a unity. And he went right into a chief contradiction in Newman's personality: on one side, strictness of principles and strength of conviction and sureness of continuity; on the other side, openness of mind; readiness to listen and absorb; power of discussing with another ideas or principles and then, so to speak, trying them out in his own mind. The one side made a mind of immobility; the other side made a mind of movement. The one side gave force, and toughness, and a controversialist, and an assailant, and even a mocker. The other side made the friend, and an understanding pastor, and the respecter of persons whom he trusted, and the reverer of tender good men, a Keble or a Philip Neri; a sign of an underlying humility of character, hard to reconcile with the embattled character who devastated Dr Hampden, or Dr Godfrey Faussett, or Achilli, or Charles Kingsley. The one side was tender and affectionate, the other side solitary and stiff.

The contrast did not trouble Bremond. He was prepared to use about Newman such phrases as 'the fits of passion', 'des beaux accès de passion' (French p. 58), which give their force to and which sometimes make an aberration in his controversial literature.

There are moments, both while Newman is an Anglican and while he is a Roman Catholic, when he gives every sign of enjoying religious polemic. Parts of the famous *Lectures on the Prophetical Office of the Church* of 1837, which was his statement of the theory of the *via media* not only in the Tractarian Movement but in modern Anglicanism, could have been written by an anti-papal controversialist of the seventeenth century; and the author shows signs of enjoying the demolition in which he engages. It seemed to be not only a duty to truth to annihilate the pretensions of the Church of Rome but a pleasant duty. Bremond thought the book to be lamentable. He was as fierce as possible about it. 'Je ne me rappelle pas avoir rien lu de plus suavement perfide, de plus spécieux, ni, au fond, de plus violent contre nous' ('I do not remember ever reading anything more suavely treacherous, more specious, or at bottom, more violent, against us'). In the least satisfactory of all Newman's phases as an author, the time from 1846 to 1853, he shows signs of enjoying the demolition of the Church of England in which he engaged. It was not only a duty to truth, it was a pleasant duty. Bremond wrote: 'Il y aurait donc plusieurs pages de Newman que l'admiration la plus pieuse voudrait pouvoir effacer de son oeuvre.' He wrote that he 'est trop souvent injuste et sans pitié pour son adversaire'. It is remarkable that this early psychologist of religion who was Bremond did not bring before himself the theory that Newman could only have written with such violence because already even in 1837, his subconscious had a doubt about it all which needed shouting down.

And yet Bremond shared the view of the Anglican Professor Hort, that somehow these polemical passages, which for a time seemed to be dominant, were not 'the real Newman'. How can you possibly say that they are not the real Newman when so many lie bleeding by the roadside as he passes? Not 'the real Newman'? Everyone who enters into Newman's development is persuaded, somehow or other, that this paradox has truth. It is the shallow part of him that wields the bludgeon, even when at times he deceives you into thinking that the bludgeon is a rapier or a surgeon's knife. The deeper part of him is incompatible with all this banging about.[1] The deeper part of him is tender, even to error; and looks to find what truth can be discovered and fostered among those whom he thinks to be in error.

And the next contrast was as odd. Newman changed from being an Anglican to being a Roman Catholic. He never regretted the change. He felt that he came home. Of this there can be no question; and the Dessain letters, which Bremond did not have, settle it finally. Then – why are the six volumes of Anglican sermons on a higher plane, as Christian and even Catholic utterances, than the two volumes and more of sermons from his Catholic period? This comparison has been denied. But it has only been denied by people without an objective judgment, who a priori were sure that the sermons of a man who was a Catholic must be better as sermons than the sermons of a man who was a Protestant. This is not to say that the Catholic sermons are not on occasion fine. But Bremond had no doubt that it was the earlier sermons which were on a higher level. And many people have followed this opinion; most persuasively of all, that Oratorian editor of editors, Stephen Dessain. This is far from the same as saying that all the works of the Catholic period are on a lower level than those of the Protestant period. Certainly Bremond did not think so; for when he asked himself what was the highest effort of Newman's genius, he answered that it was the poem *The Dream of Gerontius* (Bremond, p. 4).

After his delirium on the travels in Sicily in 1833, Newman wrote a private note on the sensations about himself which this time of danger produced.

What was he like, Newman asked himself. Hollow. Then he amended that – nearly hollow; that is with little love, and little self-denial. This is self-abasement. But everything else about the self-examination was positive. He felt that Keble was the origina-

---

[1] Bremond (French, p. 59) was struck by the phrase in *The Life and Letters of F. J. A. Hort*, 1, p. 231.

tor, and he the exponent; that his system of ideas was based upon one or two true axioms from which everything else followed; that he had 'considerable mental capacity' for drawing out principles into their conclusions; and had the 'refinement to admire them', and then the power of the rhetorician to expound them; that he had no great love of the world and its honour or riches, and 'some firmness and natural dignity of character'; and was also a man with 'some faith', the phrase implying not a lot of faith. He came to the conclusion that he was at once distinguished and mediocre. It is surprisingly realistic for a mood of self-abasement; it is not far short of being self-satisfied, this mood of a young Anglican priest looking back on danger.

The lack of pomp was a strand in Newman's character which was part of his attraction for Bremond. He knew he was not pompous. Perhaps his self-examination prided itself on being so; not a guru (though to many young people in the Oxford of the thirties he was a guru); not to be deferred to; unvenerable. It might even have made a difficulty for his life, when he had to be the leader of a religious movement, and later the superior of a religious house, and then head of a university, that he was so little on a pedestal by nature; and after all, in spite of Tyrrell, who perceived the incongruity, there was something to be said for Newman becoming a cardinal because then he was forced up on to a pedestal and no one need bother any more with the self-contradiction of a leader who never looked like a leader.

Who cut whom? Newman's *Apologia* says that Whately cut him from 1834. The letters show that it was he who broke the link with Whately. Is it necessary for a friendship to fall apart because opinions have started to differ? Such an idea is out of keeping with the philosophy of life of the twentieth century. The early Victorian age, and even later, had a feeling that to be seen to be friendly with a person of the wrong principles was to compromise the right principles. Naturally that caused suffering to the person who felt it a duty to throw over a friendship and anger in the person whose friendship was thus repudiated. Newman and Keble and Pusey all shared this view. It was a rare moment when the three of them met together in Hursley vicarage so many years after Newman became a Roman Catholic. Whately's friendship with Newman was especially close at one time, for it included the necessary donnish stimulation to Newman's critical intellect. By 1833 Newman felt bound to repudiate the friendship. The reason was not or not only that he could not be seen to be a friend of a person whose opinions he now thought to be destructive of the truth. It was more fundamental. One must not, in the absolute, associate with such a person. Whately was hurt and told Newman that at the last, before such a sundering, it was the bounden duty of a friend to meet and discuss the differences and remonstrate about what were believed to be errors.

For Bremond was convinced that Newman was essentially a solitary; just himself, the individual soul before his God. 'The attractive and winning goodness of one of the most self-absorbed men that has ever been known', 'la bonté attirante et conquérante d'un des hommes les plus personels que l'on ait jamais connu' (French, p. 314). To define this solitariness or alleged solitariness he took the word *autocentrisme*. This word was risky. The English translator turned it, because he could hardly do anything else, into the word 'self-centredness'; and in English to say that a man is self-centred is a damaging accusation, equal to saying that he is selfish. That was not what Bremond meant. For he also said, 'the solitary of Edgbaston is a lover of souls', 'le solitaire aime les âmes'. He intended to say that Newman was much interested in his state of mind and mental processes and condition of soul – which can be denied by no one. But he had also in the word an additional tang – love of solitariness. He confessed that Newman had a few friendships of the heart – Hurrell Froude till he died, R. W. Church and Frederic Rogers until he left them by changing his denomination, Ambrose St John from early in their time together until St John's death (he could have added John William Bowden from early in the Oxford days to Bowden's death in 1844). But Bremond observed, or thought that he observed, a desire of Newman to represent himself in his solitude. In his Anglican sermons, he thought, he came back, again and again, to the soul in its isolation before its Maker; to a mind which goes about in company which he thinks will never be able to understand him, and to which he can never explain himself; to a heart which has affections and desires which yet seem to have no objective (outside God) which can satisfy it; to the conscience which has to guide itself, and take its own decisions, and can rely on no external direction and no other person to help it in its troubles; to the conscience which finds itself in opposition to the wishes or commands of those to whom the soul owes reverence and obedience. There are moments when he could 's'exalter' (French, p. 460), exult in the feeling of solitude. It was the feeling of the old hermit: the further from men, the nearer to God. Bremond put it in a phrase which now sounds damning but was not originally intended to damn: Newman 'se résigne a ne pas vivre pour autrui' (French, p. 46), 'he is resigned to not living for others'. In the sense of the hermit soul in quest of eternity, that could have some truth.

And Bremond wondered too whether the affection for little details of the past was not the characteristic of a solitary mind: how the seeing of old sights was to him like seeing the ghosts of friends; the snapdragon under the walls of his college rooms; and what his father said when he won a scholarship at Oxford; the blue cloak which covered him in his delirium at Castro Giovanni and which he kept by his bed.

One of Bremond's subtle insights was the perception of the connexion between Newman's meditation on the past and his spirituality. He took the narratives of the illness, just mentioned, at Castro Giovanni in Sicily; how Newman went at it again and again, in letters, in memoranda, in the *Apologia*. What interested Bremond was the feeling which Newman gives his readers that all this was somehow 'une histoire sacrée', 'a sacred history' (French, p. 297). He meditated over his past like any secular autobiographer; but it is the hand of God, He chose the place, and directed, and preserved; and the subject of the narrative seems to see in the most trivial moments little signs of a divine hand, little hints that the circumstance was intended to convey a message.

Into this context Bremond put the change of life which concerned him specially: the conversion from Anglicanism to Roman Catholicism. By 1843 Newman was sure that the Church of Rome was the true Church, because it was the truer representative of the Church of the Fathers. He still had the problem which the Essay on Development needed to settle. But he had no doubt where his religious affection now lay, and no doubt what his ultimate destination must surely be. Anglicans keep up the rumour that he will shortly be gone; Catholics expect it daily and are vexed that he delays. He gives out a mood of being on the brink, utters dark warnings to intimates. And then he does not go. Bremond had a charming simile. 'He talks and acts like a traveller who, with his luggage packed, is waiting for the next boat. And yet weeks, months, years go by, and he does not leave.'

What is the explanation? Is the problem intellectual – we must still settle the nature of the development of doctrine? Is the problem loyalty – whatever the truth about Churches, how is it possible to desert the Church of one's childhood and one's mother, the Church of one's conversion, the Church of Pusey and Keble and of such intimate friends and pupils as Rogers and Church? Is the problem a surviving sense of repulsion – this Church of Rome is not only the Church of the Fathers but the Church of contemporary demagogues like O'Connell? One of these, or all three of these, would be most people's explanation. But none of them is Bremond's. He rejected the idea that it was due to a last intellectual problem, or to a heart not yet totally committed. Bremond has an odd explanation which is not an explanation, and which at first the reader rejects; but on reflexion he finds that it has something persuasive in it. The reason for the delay, said Bremond, is simply that he 'waits for the wind', 'attend le vent' (French, p. 298) 'consulte les présages', 'takes the omens, looks up to heaven for signs'. And Bremond's evidence for this is powerful. It is Newman's behaviour at the coffin of his friend Bowden in London. Bremond is confident that he can tell us what went on in Newman's mind as he knelt by the coffin. 'We can determine with sufficient exactness', he says loftily, 'the thoughts, desires, and the prayers which pressed upon each other at that time in his inmost soul'; this is Bremond at his most airy. But the point is fine despite the airiness. Newman said afterwards that while he knelt he was looking for light to his mind as to what he ought to do, for he had expected that Bowden's last illness would have brought this light. And he sobbed over the coffin because Bowden went away from the world without settling his mind for him; 'left me still dark as to what the way of truth was'.

Bremond confessed that Newman could write beautifully about friendship. But he was so convinced about his doctrine of the solitary that he could not quite believe that it corresponded to

Newman's feelings of the heart. Newman must have written beautifully about friendship not because he understood friendship but because the man could write beautifully about anything. He is a sorcerer, 'cet homme est un magicien. Sa plume embellit, transforme tout ce qu'elle touche ...' The prose of Newman never lies, and yet you can say that it is always telling lies. He writes beautifully about the friendship of the Oratory in Birmingham, Philip Neri's sons, my dearest brothers of this house; and how the friendship of Ambrose St John reached back into Oxford days, and so was a symbol of all those earlier friendships which at the university were his 'daily solace and relief ... thorough friends' who 'showed me true attachment in times long past'. For Bremond to dismiss this passage, it is enough that he knows how the common room at the Oratory, just like or even more than the common room at Oriel, was awkward in conversation because no one, least of all Newman, could think of anything to say.

The passage on friendship at the end of the *Apologia* is strange. No one can deny that it is strange. Most writers would shrink from so personal and emotional an exhibition of their most private feelings. It can hardly have pleased Ambrose St John, whatever he afterwards said to Newman, to appear in capital letters at the end of a famous book as a literary example of friendship of the soul. Bremond sees this strangeness and infers that it is not quite sincere; not unreal, not false, but at least the magician gave it a spell. Since to the objective eye the prose has an element of the ridiculous or the overwritten, it stinks to Bremond of rhetoric. He calls it hyperbole (French, p. 40). But a very different view is possible of the passage. Newman needed to tell the world that he was happy. He had already written a couple of hundred pages of self-revelation. He was not at that moment shrinking from self-revelation. He was a very emotional man. The friendship is the climax not because it is magic or because he thought it beautiful, but because it happened to express his feelings of affection about the house of prayer and pastoral care where he found a home and a family. That is a much more natural interpretation of the passage. Bremond will not have it because he has a doctrine of the solitary, and Newman had to fit that doctrine.

Yet there was something true which every observer of Newman could assent to. He did feel up against other people. He did feel that he did not get the sympathy that he might. He did feel that the world was against him, and that he had few enough to whom he could turn for help. But then the world usually was against him. It is the fate of reformers that the world is against them. Newman had a thin skin. He was easily hurt.

He was conscious of enemies. He left the Church of England partly because so many Anglican leaders attacked him. Yet in 1875 he told the world, astonishingly, that he suffered still more trials during his Roman Catholic life than during his Anglican life. In neither of his Churches did he think the management perfect. In both he preferred that the bishops or the Curia should go about their business in another way. He seemed to sit quiet and remote in a retreat, an Oxford college, or a house of prayer in the Midlands. It was nothing like so quiet as it looked. The silence spoke loudly. The management of both Churches regarded him as dangerous. He was too big to leave alone in his solitude.

We thus find some curious incongruities in Bremond's view of Newman. Newman wrote marvellously about friendship, but this was not the real Newman. Newman was a fierce controversialist; but this was not the real Newman.

The Protestants said that Newman was a sophist; that he believed what he wanted to believe and took no notice of objections; that he suppressed difficulties if they disturbed his doctrine – etc., and worse. The agnostic scientist Huxley said about Newman that he, Huxley, could extract from Newman's books a little manual of scepticism. Bremond played with such an idea as though it bore some relation to reality. At one point he said of Newman, 'if he were not of the most robust faith, he would be the most formidable of the professors of scepticism' (p. 13).

But Bremond knew it to be nonsense; or true only in the sense that anyone can deform someone's principles if they try hard and select what they want. Bremond had a very simple reply. 'Newman affirms, without a shadow of hesitation, that man is made for truth, for certitude. But, according to him, the faculty which has the truth as its immediate object is not the pure reason but the noetic faculty – in other words, the moral sense' (p. 64n).

Even that positive phrase would be thought not positive enough by most of the best students of Newman's mind. But Bremond saw how Newman regarded himself as an ethical thinker and a theologian rather than a philosopher; how in the realm of religious truth he always believed the pure processes of the intelligence (separate from the conscience and the perceptions of the whole man) to be unreliable, and even to turn thinking into a game; how he always or at least usually preferred to show probabilities rather than to look for certainty; how strong a sense he had of the provisional; how he moved in shadowy woods, among views, and doubts, and light amid the uncertain gloom.

There was a paragraph of Bremond on the leading principles of Newman's mind, principles which always nourished his emotion and 'quickened' the life of his intelligence. What on this view were these principles? A handful of recollections of childhood; the clear vision of God present in the conscience; the idea of the Church of the Fathers; Oxford, or rather a special sort of Oxford, 'un Oxford très particulier' (French, p. 74), which is crossed by the shadows of Plato and later of St Philip Neri, the founder of the Oratory; the kingdom of Christ on earth, the angels and the saints and the souls to whom God has given rest; the vision of the soul at the moment when it leaves the world and goes before its Maker.

With these as his guide he approached truth with an imaginative insight. And this always, according to Bremond, made him prefer the painting of an intellectual picture to the scientific analysis of a logical idea. Bremond took the most important work of theology which Newman ever wrote, if importance is to be judged by subsequent influence: the Essay on Development. It is 'a series of splendid frescoes'. If you need scientific analysis, can you be satisfied with frescoes?

Now take this epigram on Newman. 'It is an odd thing, *chose bizarre*, that among his equals Newman's mind is the most detached, the least inquiring mind which the last century has known'; *l'esprit le plus détaché, le moins avide – avide* need not quite mean the least inquiring; or at least it need only mean the mind which is content for the time being to rest content in agnosticism or the provisional about a problem which it cannot yet solve. If it were taken to mean least inquiring, nothing could be more false. Did not this scholar research into the nature of tradition among the early Christian Fathers, and the course of the Arian controversy, and the nature of the doctrine of reserve in primitive Christianity? Did he not spend a long life thinking and meditating, always with a personal originality, on the nature of faith? Did he not spend three years thinking with seminal originality about the contradiction between the Christian sense of an unchanging Gospel and the dictate of history that the expression of ideas is changing all the time? Was he not the earliest English Catholic to face fairly the enormous looming question on the inspiration of the Bible?

Yet Bremond's next page has another epigram not far off it; and although we are learning to suspect Bremond's epigrams, we are pulled up sharp by the force of its truth. 'The author of the Essay on Development would never have written the history of dogmas, still less the history of a dogma.' That epigram will command the assent of every student of Newman. And suddenly there is a real mystery about Newman, and if we could solve it we should have gone a long way in understanding what made his intelligence tick. Here is a man with the mind of a true historian – at least the person best capable of judging that matter, Lord Acton, thought so, with whatever qualifications. And this man has a sense of the movement of doctrines in history. Anyone else with his interests and equipment must want to write a history of doctrines as they developed, a *Dogmengeschichte*, or if that is slightly anachronistic, at least a book like Johann Adam Möhler's *Symbolik*, a general study of doctrine in the Catholic Church within a historical perspective. Newman showed no signs whatever of having a plan for such a work. Bremond's epigram is absolutely convincing. The idea that Newman should have considered such a plan is impossible. Why?

I should make some sort of an answer by a very simple reply: diffidence. Who am I to write learned books? That is the kind of work I must leave to others. I only write, either to satisfy myself – on whether doctrine changes in history, or on the nature of faith; or to persuade other people to accept the Church, whether it be the Anglican Church in the earlier stages or the Roman Church in the later. My vocation is not the quest of the historian, because I doubt whether I have that kind of gift. This diffidence, which sprang out of a personal modesty as well as a doubt about the value of intellectual constructions of tidy systems, has a striking proof which Bremond noticed with amazement; and then failed to draw the true deduction.

The Essay on Development was undertaken to satisfy Newman's mind. His heart now accepted that he ought to be a Roman Catholic; his head told him that the Roman Catholic Church of today was so different from the Church of the Fathers that it would be a crime against the intellect to join its ranks. Could the difference be explained in a way to satisfy himself?

He did not finish the book. Suddenly in early October 1845 he knew that he was sufficiently satisfied, that his vocation told him that it was time to move. What did he do? He did not bother to finish the book. He did not even bother to finish the page. The argument stops dead, and ends in asterisks. Bremond (p. 76) regarded this as a tangible proof of his contempt for *science*, objective inquiry. 'Newman, a first-class dialectician, endowed with an understanding, subtle, quick, penetrating, illuminates and renews all that he touches; but he does not seem possessed with the desire for knowledge' (il ne semble pas possédé du desire de connaître' (80, French, p. 93).

Yet a more compassionate view is possible. He had no contempt whatever for the inquiry. It mattered to him at that moment as much as anything could matter. He did not say, this is true for me, I do not care whether it is true for others. He did care whether it was true for others. He cared very much. The subsequent troubles of the book in the Roman Curia, the subsequent bombardment of the book by an American convert, and Newman's perturbations, proved that he minded very much whether it was true for others. He still minded very much, more than thirty years later, when one would not expect that it would matter any longer. Then he even took the trouble to complain about a Jesuit reviewer publishing articles against it. But what he thought he had proved was a general principle, not a fundamental explanation of a lot of historical information; into which his diffidence wrongly thought that he was incapable of inquiring. He believed that such a fundamental inquiry, such a *Dogmengeschichte*, must be left to others. And certainly what mattered to him was that he satisfied himself. Bremond had one of his poetic phrases: 'On the unfinished house which he took two years to build, a flower of prayer blossomed' ('Sur l'édifice inachevé qu'il a mis deux ans à construire, s'épanouit une fleur de prière (French, p. 89)).

Was it right then for Acton and others to suppose that Newman had the gift of the historian if he had wanted to use it? Was it really true that what he wanted out of history was not so much objective truth as the moral example which would help him? Was he in the stage of pre-modern history, where the purpose of history is to provide good and bad examples from the past? Newman lived with the early Christian Fathers. He much preferred reading them to reading modern divines, with whom he hardly bothered. But did he live with the Fathers as they were or with them as he wanted them to be? When he took the Church of the Fathers, did he take what edified and gloss over what was painful? Bremond said, 'Before taking them for masters, he wished to have them as friends' ('Avant de les prendre pour maîtres, il veut les avoir pour amis' (French, p. 90). No one knew better than Bremond himself, when later he was a mature historian of ideas, that you cannot understand a figure of the past unless you try to get inside his or her mentality. It is also true that it is more difficult for good men and women to write history because they like the human race and are hardly willing to believe that mortals are capable of the foulness which happens and therefore do not see things with a detached eye. Nevertheless, of the two faults or excesses, failure of understanding, which is in part a failure of sympathy, is the more disqualifying for sound judgment of the past. Newman's quality for understanding the past lay partly in scholarship, partly in true sympathy for the subject which concerned him; and partly because he understood how the private sources are often of more weight than the public documents.

It is a bad thing for a historian to waste time writing novels. Nothing will reconcile us to Newman writing two of them, *Loss and Gain* and *Callista*. Even Bremond, who liked parts of *Callista*, admitted that one chapter of it at least was the work of a very amateur novelist, 'un romancier bien novice' (French, p. 248). But *Callista* is easier to be reconciled with than *Loss and Gain*. For it is a sign of the historical mind. The novel is about the daily life of an imaginary Christian group in the earliest times. Whether any real Christian group was ever like this is a question about any historical novel. Newman was not a good novelist and put edifying speeches into the mouths of his characters. But the attempt to portray early Christian life by means of a historical novel was a sign of the author's concern with the social and religious life of ordinary men and women; which certainly was a modern historical instinct.

Let us again confess that with Newman, and probably with every religious person, the life of the pure intellect is not the highest activity of man. To blame him for not thinking that it is is the same as to blame him for having a moral concern. Let us again remember the diffidence. That prosecuting attorney Abbott accused him of taking up subjects and never bothering to master them. You write about Athanasius and yet you are not in the slightest degree interested in getting at the authentic Greek text – and he replies, I have neither the intellectual equipment nor the library to check the text of Athanasius; I must do the best I can with the best text that is available to me, and I hope that it will be useful to some other people.

Yet what he attempted to do was certainly history. No sane critic of Newman doubts that he had a historical gift. Whatever Kingsley said about him, Newman did want truth; and part of the truth, for him one of the weighty parts of the truth, is what happened long ago. Bremond talked of the historical curiosity which was always active in him, 'curiosité historique toujours éveillée' (French, p. 254). When he was an Anglican he wrote the series of essays about the early Church which was bound up together in 1840 as *The Church of the Fathers*. When he was a Roman Catholic he went on with such essays and bound them up together as *Historical Sketches*. Because such essays were at once overtaken by other essayists or students of the early Christian age, by German research, and by Lightfoot and by Harnack, people ceased to read these essays by Newman and remembered him for other and more controversial writings. But to read them is to know that this was where his affections lived. They were friends to him, the Fathers, like Hurrell Froude or John Bowden or Ambrose St John. That is a sign of historical power. He could use them to prove points – to stir the Church of England out of its comfortable complacency, or to show how the Church of Rome could defend what seemed to be an innovation. He was not the critic of a new world of inquiry. He was still a man of the older historical training. But he did not only use information to prove points which he wanted to prove.

Bremond admired Sainte-Beuve as one of the greatest of French essayists. Yet he can say that Newman's historical portraits of early Christians like Theodoret or Chrysostom were the equal of Sainte-Beuve and that if Sainte-Beuve had read them he would confess that equality. Bremond expressed his admiration for Newman's historical power here with an outburst of eloquence. I have not the command of words to describe the serenity, breadth, proportion, sure historical sense, affectionate irony, and unique charm of these pure masterpieces: 'la serenité, l'ampleur, les proportions harmonieuses, l'infaillibilité de sens historique, l'ironie affectueuse, le charme unique' (French, p. 121); the hidden revolutionary force underneath the understatements; the quiet style.

The book which made the chief weapon for the prosecution, who wished to show that this was an anti-historian, was the book, written while he was an Anglican, on *Ecclesiastical Miracles*. Even Bremond preferred to expunge this little book from the works of Newman (French, p. 109) and only wanted to keep it for the light which its amazing nature shed on Newman's mind.

God works in the world. Therefore we expect his interventions. We shall not a priori rule miracle out of possibility. Since all Christians are agreed upon that, they cannot treat the miracles said to be wrought by the saints in church history with an a priori dismissal. Belief in them depends on evidence. But the Christian who accepts the probability of miracle will treat the evidence with more openness of mind than the non-Christian who rejects the possibility of miracle. So far, fine; all are agreed. But then Newman started to apply the argument. And the argument disturbed everyone. The miracles which he thought he could prove in church history certainly did not rest upon solid evidence. This is spiritual reading, not an attempt at history; it is a devotional exercise, a stirring up to prayer. But even as a spiritual reading, that essay is not attractive reading to anyone with historical instincts.

Then Bremond turned the condemnation on its head. In his opinion Newman took no pleasure in recording these stories of marvels and in discussing them. 'In truth he forces himself to believe them; it is painful to him to believe them. His faith does not rest on miracles; he struggles to stretch it out to include them and though the stretching succeeds, it only just succeeds' (French, p. 114; 'Au vrai, il s'efforce, et péniblement de les croire. Sa foi à lui ne repose pas sur les miracles, elle tache de s'étendre jusqu'à eux et elle n'y arrive pas sans peine').

In such a book is he trying to do any good to anyone, or is he still writing to satisfy himself? It must be the second. He is a Tractarian leader; his work is to bring back the Church to the age of the Fathers. The more he goes into the age of the Fathers, the more complicated he finds this work to be. And one of the complexities is the credulity of the Christians in that age. It is a worry to him. All the miracles which he treated as examples were miracles of the age of the Fathers. He bothered with no later miracle, no contemporary miracle. He wrote the essay because he needed to reassure himself. God has chosen to reveal himself by miracles – whether we like it or not we have to try to feel at home with them; and so he struggles, and twists, and turns, and does his best, and comes out not quite with a certainty but with a sort of hope that everything will be all right. And in this way the age of the Fathers is vindicated from credulity; and as we ought to share their outlook in all we can, so we ought to share their outlook in this openness of mind to the direct intervention of God in our lives. The inadequacy of this essay, on which such abuse has been heaped, was a sign of discomfort. His mind needed to be persuaded; but his faith did not rest there. For thirty years of his Catholic life Newman could have gone to visit Lourdes. It never occurred to him. 'For the needs of his personal inner life he neither expects nor desires any kind of miracle', 'il n'escompte ni ne désire aucune espèce de miracle' (French, p. 116). 'The silent voice', 'l'imperceptible voix', which he hears speaking deep in his conscience, is enough.

Yet near the end of 1843, there was announced a series under Newman's editorship called the Lives of the English Saints. The saints were medieval, and Newman chose the authors. The series started with the life of the Cistercian Stephen Harding, which was translated by his friend and co-monk Dalgairns, and which Newman thought safe because it had 'hardly, if at all, any miracle in it' (Meriol Trevor, *Newman*, vol. I, *The Pillar of the Cloud*, p. 311). The series instantly ran into trouble, and Newman thought it better to give up the editorship. Newman wrote to Hope, 'Church history is made up of three elements – miracles, monkery, and Popery. If any sympathetic feeling is expressed on behalf of the persons and events of church history, it is a feeling in favour of miracles, or monkery, or Popery, one or all.' But his attitude to these saints was more laconic, and had not the expansiveness and affection with which he turned to the big men of the earliest Christian age. Those were his friends; and after he was a Roman Catholic he came to think of the best of them as his intercessors. The only saint after the age of the Fathers who became a friend was Philip Neri, the founder of the Oratory. In 1864 Newman wrote a private commendation of his soul to God in view of his possible end (*Meditations and Devotions*, p. 608; Br 256); and the saints whose intercessions he supplicated, outside the New Testament, were Philip Neri; St Henry because of his personal name (but which St Henry? One would like it to be Henry of Uppsala, the Englishman who evangelized Finland and was martyred there); Athanasius, so much of whom he translated; Gregory Nazianzene; John Chrysostom; St Ambrose; Pope Gregory the Great; and Pope Leo the Great. It is curious and striking how Newman never had any feeling of friendship with the greatest of the Fathers, St Augustine.

When Biblical criticism of the Old Testament became accepted among many late Victorian Christians, the Evangelical tradition in England found it very hard to accept. They retained a faith in the literal historical truth of all parts of the Old Testament. They then tried to use this in devotion, by talking about the need for the sacrifice of the intellect, of the mind taking up its cross. And Bremond (French, p. 116) was willing to think of Newman doing this to his mind in the same way: 'un nouveau sacrifice intellectual, . . . ces humiliations et macérations de l'esprit qui lui sont devenues si chères'. But Newman never thought of the sacrifice of the intellect, the cross of the intellect, in Evangelical language. He thought always of the inadequacy of the intellect to probe the mysteries of God; which is a different idea.

But he republished the essay on ecclesiastical miracles. Twenty-seven years later, when he did *not* need to satisfy himself, he republished it. Did the mature man who allowed criticism its just part in religious life really think that the essay was still valuable? Or was it due to a sort of resigned honour, a part of republishing all his works – this was what I was like when I was a high church Anglican; you must take me for what I was and I wish to conceal nothing, even if it is damning?

The imagination is a poetic instrument. But like the imagination of poets, it is an instrument of a living intuition of profound realities (French, p. 97). 'Out of the dust of old books a vision has appeared to me – the Church of the Fathers; hands have been stretched out to make signs to me, voices have called me. Call it an impression if you will, but a luminous, a convincing impression. Then, by dint of contemplating these ghosts from the past, it seemed to me that they were not dead; or rather, their bright light spread itself over the men and the things of today' (86, French, p. 98).

Therefore there is nothing inconsistent, and nothing deceiving, still less the least thing that is crooked as the prosecutor implied, in this mind which is so many-sided. His intelligence can devastate some of the conventional arguments for the existence of God, but no one was ever more certain of the direct experience of God. He did good work on the study of the early Church and did not think it very important, not important enough to make it a life's work. He can tell you that his impressions of what the early Christians were like is such and such, and then withdraw and leave it to others to determine whether his opinion is correct; but meanwhile he has had to act on what he found because that is moral necessity.

The portrait of Newman at prayer in Bremond is one of the most sensitive of all his insights. It starts with the sense of mystery in nature; and then with the perception that nature is a sacrament of the invisible world. This meant that in his poetic utterances the world is peopled with the angels and the spirits, so that a true human being is at home with angels and archangels as with his friends and his family. Here is a sense, the possession of which ought to make a mystic. Yet there is very little of the mystic about Newman. He distrusts the mystical. He likes plain and sober ways, the liturgical offices, the quiet prayers that he is used to. He does not find prayer easy or ecstatic; he thinks it a duty to be regularly performed. It needs the formulas of the Church, not to restrict us but to form the background and to give an attitude, and clothe our private thoughts in the thoughts of the Church and of the communion of the saints. The forms should be short; not impassioned, but calm. Like all the Tractarians he thought extempore prayer likely to be dangerous or impoverished. He wants private prayer to be liturgically based, or liturgical in its tone. When he was an Anglican he loved the *Preces privatae* of Lancelot Andrewes and translated them from the Greek for one of the Tracts for the Times. He continued to use them when he was a Roman Catholic. The affection for them made the best side of the Oxford Movement's revival of Catholic ways of prayer.

Then are we to be disappointed? Here is a person who could lead people up to the heights, and he only tells them to say their prayers? 'His prayer has no wings, his piety no fire' – that saying of Bremond is not quite true. But then he says, Newman was less devout than religious; and it may be said, in a certain sense, that some of his friends who remained Anglicans, Keble or Pusey for example, would have derived more profit than he from the riches of Catholicism (p. 325). Here is speculation. Yet the reader who knows both Newman and Pusey pauses; and is forced to think; and to ask, whether in so provocative a statement there is a grain of truth.

Let us list what may be misleading in Bremond's analysis of Newman's mind. (1) He believed in the new methods of modern psychology, and the belief that such methods afforded insight into the minds and motives and temperaments of historical personages where evidence was available; and Newman afforded plentiful evidence because nearly all his writing was in some manner autobiographical. (2) Bremond was engaged with the person of Newman because he was unsettled with the Society of Jesus and even for a moment with the Catholic Church, and saw Newman as the prophet of an open-minded Church in contradiction to the Church of his day, which was closing its mind in reaction to Modernism. (3) He had a certain literary rather than historical quality in his own way of writing, which Father Louis Bouyer condemned as verbal arabesques, and which at times gives the modern reader pause, but which makes a part of the enchantment of his book. (4) Of necessity he wrote before much of the Catholic evidence was published, at a time when the Oratorian fathers at Birmingham were too nervous to allow Wilfrid Ward to publish the biography, and long before Stephen Dessain got down to giving us the letters. (5) Because he was looking for *le sentiment religieux* of Newman, he largely neglected the more formal parts of Newman's doctrines as a theologian, relegating them all to a relatively short appendix; and so opened himself to the charge that he treated the private person at the expense of the public man.

All these five disadvantages were also weaknesses. But they were not only weaknesses. Even the verbal arabesques were not only flowers and ornament. They quite often make the meditation of a sensitive mind; and that they are sometimes put into poetry does nothing to diminish their sensitivity.

It sounds paradoxical to say that it was an advantage as well as a weakness to write before the modern and best evidence was published. But let us look at this in another light, thus:

In those days Newman was a divided personality. He was an Anglican Newman. Then he was a Catholic Newman. These were not the same person. People wrote about him as a Protestant and a Tractarian, or they wrote about him as a Catholic. That continued to be true after Wilfrid Ward's biography was at last published. Newman helped the division because he divided his own life thus in the *Apologia*; which, however, was the first document to show that the division, if rigid, was false.

Bremond was in search of the man's *sentiment religieux*; and in *le sentiment religieux* what were important to Bremond personally were the inquietudes. Therefore he could not understand the Catholic Newman without understanding the Protestant Newman; more, he needed to interpret the Catholic Newman by means of the Protestant Newman. If he were looking for mental turmoil he must go to the years 1841 to 1845, when Newman struggled to find the truth and discover what his conscience was telling him to do; and he could not understand the predicament of 1841 to 1845 unless he went to the Newman of Oxford in the thirties, the Newman of the parochial sermons, and of the lectures on justification, and on the prophetical office of the

Church. That means to say, Bremond was the first Catholic mind
to try to understand the Anglican Newman with a total sympathy; and that also meant that he was the first Catholic mind to
treat the whole of Newman, Protestant or Catholic, as a unity.

These were considerable virtues. Because he could not achieve
what he set out to achieve, the book was in certain respects a
failure. The verbal arabesques could mislead the reader as well as
lead him deeper towards the centre of Newman's being. Psychological speculation, as so often with psycho-history, was too often
mingled with real evidence in a way which is uncomfortable
when it is analysed. But among so much meditation there are
insights. Bremond saw – no one had seen it before him – the
importance to Newman's spirituality of meditation upon the
past; the importance to his spirituality of what Bremond called
'waiting for the wind', that is, being attentive to events and the
way that they lead, looking for signs, hesitant until the conscience
is sure.

Chapter 10

THE ESTABLISHED CHURCH
UNDER ATTACK

The influence of moral ideals upon a person is not something which the person himself or herself can chart or fathom, still less his or her friends, still less the analyst dependent on written sources. *A fortiori* the influence of the same ideals upon a large group of persons, or a nation, can only be given illustrations. George Lansbury attributed his Socialist principles to his upbringing in the Church of England. It is difficult to doubt that in some respect or other Christianity contributed to Lansbury's Socialism, but we are not able to define in what respect, or distinguish such an influence from the influence of (let us say) a Marxist like Hyndman, even if we have some evidence that the moral element in his nature was the strongest of the forces that made him a politician. Dr Barnardo believed that he was under the direct leading of God in the work that he did for waifs and that without God he would never have done it. It cannot be doubted that the Christian drive of the Victorians included a drive to save and to better the poor and sick. Christianity was integral to the ideals and the work of countless reformers, from Florence Nightingale or Sister Dora or Josephine Butler or Dora Greenwell to Quintin Hogg and Samuel Barnett and W. E. Gladstone. We cannot of course tell how far they were Christians because they were good people and how far they were good people because they were Christians. But certainly it was in part the second of these. For some of them set out to 'convert', and in the process found themselves rescuing from disease or starvation or prostitution or illiteracy, until the rescuing became much more their work than the converting. The career of the Salvation Army, which began as a preaching revival and turned into a force among tramps and drunks, is typical of much social endeavour during that age. 'I know no Liberalism', Arthur Stanton was wont to say, 'except

198

that which I have sucked in from the breasts of the gospel';[1] and we are not able to speculate how far he was right in his self-examination, and how much he owed to schoolmasters or to an admiration for Gladstone.

The Church of England was under attack, first, because it was one of the Churches and all Churches were under attack throughout the reign of Queen Victoria. But the attacks at the end of the reign looked different from the attacks at the beginning.

In 1837 the Churches were attacked by the pamphleteers of the working men, heirs of Tom Paine and the political programme of the French Revolution. These pamphleteers were sometimes blasphemers and for the most part ignorant, fanatical, and easy to disregard. Authority did not always disregard them. When Sir Robert Peel was Prime Minister the Archbishop of Canterbury (8 January 1842) wrote to him about the problem of atheist pamphleteers, and Peel gave little hope of action by the government, for the government would only sell the pamphlets if it prosecuted.[2] But many of these working-class pamphlets the government was able to treat almost as it treated obscenities. The pamphlets had no sort of influence on any of the citizens who were educated and on few of those who possessed a vote.

A lot of the attacks on the Churches towards the end of the reign came from the ideological and social descendants of the working-class pamphleteers. Modern research tends to show more continuity in the tradition than might have been predicted. But in the nineties the working-class pamphleteers had the vote, and far more education was accessible to the writers, and thanks to national education an incomparably larger public of working men was capable of reading what they wrote. The Churches believed in education and always strove to improve it. But just occasionally their less wise members lamented that advancing education merely made it possible for the uneducated to read anti-Christian books.

Therefore the attack of working-class culture upon the Churches, though in essence the same attack early or late, was more powerful in 1890 than in 1840. For it was with better

[1] G. W. E. Russell, *Arthur Stanton*, p. 43.
[2] Peel Papers, British Library Add. MSS 40499, 144, 146.

weapons and could reach the furthest village in the land. It was far from being treatable as pornography now. Part of it was serious argument and a little of it was sober inquiry, and some of it might be bought on a bookstall at the station.

And yet the working man was not deeply moved by these activities. Most observers agreed that the Churches and the parsons puzzled him or passed him by, but did not anger him. He sometimes had an obscure feeling that the church worker was an unconscious agent of the Conservative Party or even of the police, and he often supposed that ministers, like other members of the leisured classes, did no work that could be called work. But usually he was indifferent and not hostile. Observers noticed that he was apathetic to nearly every other interest that was not connected with his daily bread. In the midst of his apathy he felt inarticulately that the world was unjust to him and that these kind parsons were mysteriously associated with the injustice.

For by the last decades of the century the pamphleteers, failing to persuade the masses to resent either Christianity or its official representatives, succeeded in injecting into the consciousness of the poor a powerful idea: the preachers contribute to injustice by the promise of future rewards. *Suffer here and you shall be crowned hereafter* – resignation into the hands of God was central to the Christian ethic. Are we to be content with our lot when that lot is inflicted upon us by the robbery sanctioned under the laws of property? 'We want', Karl Marx's daughter said in the refreshment room of the British Museum, 'to make them [the masses] disregard the mythical next world and live for this world, and insist on having what will make it pleasant to them.'[3] The working man was told that the doctrine of the future life was not only a doubtful truth but a dangerous lie, a way of keeping him down. In the East London of the nineties he began to use the contemptuous phrase (in its origin without the affection with which it became used in the slang of the twentieth century) 'sky pilot' to describe a Christian minister. Down into the villages went 'secularist' lecturers who stood on the green and told the people of the untruths of Christianity and of the social ills fostered by the Churches. A secularist shoemaker settled in a

---

[3] Beatrice Webb, *My Apprenticeship*, pp. 258–9.

village and offered lectures on Sunday and converted at least one mother to the belief that she had been wrong to take her children to be baptized in church.

And yet the country, even at the end of the Queen's reign, was still in many respects a deeply Christian country. Nothing is more remarkable than the religiousness of the early leaders of the Labour movement when they wanted to capture the political allegiance of working men. The early writings and speeches of Keir Hardie or Ramsay MacDonald or Philip Snowden or George Lansbury not merely show that the religious and moral ideal was integral to their own conception of Socialism, and that they had little use for the cruder doctrines of 'opium of the people'. They tend to show that a religiousness of mood and language was politically desirable; that is, that they would be more likely to be heard by the audience which they sought, if they dissociated Socialism from its continental atmosphere of class warfare and revolution and associated it with Christian ideas of fraternity and care for the poor. That did not mean to say that they did not attack the Churches. Their attack upon the Churches was often bitter and extreme. But, like some of the early Chartists, they were more likely to attack the Churches because they were unrepresentative of Christianity than because they represented it. They assailed the Christians because they failed to follow Christ, not because they sought to follow him. They sometimes sought to show that in modern society the programme of Socialism was a necessary outcome of Christian ideals.

Keir Hardie's family deserted the Church when he was young because they associated (Presbyterian) churchmen with middle-class and hypocritical and unjust conduct. In later days Hardie would preach in Methodist pulpits or in Labour churches, or associate himself with the theosophists or the Pleasant Sunday Afternoon. When the TUC met at Norwich in 1894 many of them walked in the close at sunset; and, as they heard Psalm 23 sung by the worshippers inside the cathedral, it was Hardie who led them all off, Christians and agnostics, to join in the song – 'not so much in any devotional spirit as out of deference to the influence of the place'.[4] He once puzzled a mass audience of

---

[4] *Life*, p. 98.

continental Socialists in the square at Lille by telling them, 'I myself have found in the Christianity of Christ the inspiration which first of all drove me into the movement and has carried me on in it.'[5]

But he could be bitterer than anyone else about the hired professors of Christianity. His Christmas message in the *Labour Leader* for 1897 was unparalleled for bitterness among Christmas messages.

Although many more people did not go to church or chapel than in the early Victorian age, it must never be forgotten that many more people did go to church or chapel than in the early Victorian age. The country was far more populous. Thus we have the curious paradox, which may now be regarded as proven statistically, that the Churches had a wonderful sense of expansion and well-being during years when they were failing to keep pace with the growth of population. To understand this is necessary to the understanding of Victorian 'secularization'. The statistics prove that during the last twenty years of the century the Churches were losing significantly, if to 'lose' is equivalent to a failure to expand by the same percentage as the population of the country was expanding. On this basis of percentages modern books have criticized the Victorian Churches for their 'failure'. But the Victorian Churches themselves had no such notions. They saw a great task in front of them, in the rapid urbanization of England and Wales, and made extraordinary endeavour to meet the need, and felt modestly rewarded. They might see country congregations declining, but they could see town congregations growing larger or (more commonly) subdividing in remarkable ways. What they cared for was their obvious growth. The increase of Christian worshippers was more evident to them than the increase in the total numbers of the people.

The sense of expanding numbers was often accompanied, during the eighties and nineties, by another feeling, that of increasing influence in the State. The phrase 'the nonconformist conscience' was originally a phrase of abuse during the affair of Parnell's fall, and was adopted by the Methodist minister Hugh Price Hughes as a term of compliment. The phrase stood for an

[5] *Life*, p. 303.

obvious truth: that the political power of nonconformity, between 1867 and 1905, was a force to be reckoned with. This political power must not be understood merely as one of the forces behind the electoral successes of the Liberal Party. Its existence helped to condition public attitudes to moral issues, such as temperance, or prostitution, or Sunday observance, or Bulgarian massacres, or concentration camps in South Africa, or oppression in the Congo. It brought the conscience of the middle classes to bear upon national questions, sometimes in an emotional way, but seldom in a way which politicians could afford to disregard. Not all its manifestations, when based upon an ill-informed emotion, were equally moral. But 'the nonconformist conscience' was neither exclusively nor even generally nonconformist. It was one aspect of a force which Bernard Shaw would later pillory as 'middle-class morality', but which on its better side displayed and developed the influence of the Churches in the public life of the nation. Archbishop Benson of Canterbury declared in 1893 that everyone saw how the influence of the Churches had increased during the last twenty years. Far more children were being taught the Christian religion in 1890 than in 1850. It was true that the universities of Oxford and Cambridge and Durham, and King's College, London, were prised apart from the Church of England by a series of Acts of Parliament between 1854 and 1899. But most people able to make comparisons believed that Oxford and Cambridge universities were more encouraging to the religion of their undergraduates in 1890 than twenty-five years before. Two of the three Prime Ministers of the last twenty years of the reign (Gladstone and Salisbury) were far more Christian than the first Prime Minister of the reign. At the highest level of political life we cannot easily find that the attacks upon Christianity diminished the influence of the established Church or of any other Church.

In the realm of ideas we find far more uncertainty.

If Christianity included a belief that the world was 6,000 years old and not more, or that Jonah was swallowed by a whale, then Christianity was proved untrue, and its influence must diminish and vanish as society progressively realized its falsehood. And since some people believed that the geologists or Darwin or Colenso had 'disproved the Bible', those people also believed that the philosophy which alone justified the Churches was obsolescent.

But not many intelligent people did believe this. They perceived that Christianity had other content besides various pieces of historical information with which it was hitherto often associated. It is not at all easy to find a Victorian who 'lost his faith' because he discovered that Genesis chapter 1 was not literally true. One highly intelligent Victorian, Leslie Stephen, is sometimes represented as losing his faith because he could no longer believe in a universal flood. He did this during the sixties, when for thirty years most educated men had ceased to believe in a universal flood. It is impossible to suppose, despite Stephen's biographer, that he took orders in the Church of England with a total and unquestioning faith in a universal flood. From Stephen's own descriptions we sense a more subtle attitude. It was less a question of intellectual dissent than of moral repudiation. Here was he, a clergyman who did not believe in stories in the Bible, placed by his Church in a situation where the liturgy compelled him to read such stories as though they were true. He could do it no longer. He could not assume, as his successors could assume, that the congregation would not for one moment suppose him to take the story of Noah to be history.

But if it is not easy to point to individuals in intellectual difficulty over particulars, it is easy to illustrate the general unsettlement of ideas arising from new knowledge. Victorian doubt should be judged less by the leaders of the argument than by schoolboys who heard vaguely that Darwin proved the Bible not to be true. And the difficulty was not made easier, either by the aggressiveness of a few scientists like Huxley and Tyndall, or by the obscurantism of some clergymen, from Cardinal Manning downwards, who asserted the incompatibility between Christianity and doctrines of evolution.

How far this general unsettlement weakened the Churches it is not at all easy to determine, or to see what evidence would enable us to make a precise estimate. The statistics of London and of Lancashire, two of the few places where we have fairly reliable statistics, show that in the last fifteen or twenty years of the century the number of worshippers ceased to rise, not merely per cent of the population, but absolutely, and began to fall. We have a little, too haphazard, evidence that the persons sometimes known as 'nothingarians' – adherents of no denomination – began to rise in the same period. It is necessary to remember that this may be more the result of social conditions than of intellectual, and yet difficult to imagine it as altogether unconnected with the militancy of a Huxley, the liberal divinity of a Matthew Arnold, the rumours about Colenso – or, above all, with the circumstance that no open-eyed individual of 1890 could read the Bible with the same attitude as it was read by most people fifty years before.

What on present evidence looks probable is that changes in social conditions were more important than new knowledge in changing religious practice. There have been preliminary attempts to distinguish between the effects of related but cognate developments, like urbanization and industrialization.

We may provisionally distinguish:

1 Change of habitat; certainly important in breaking habits of churchgoing; and more people than ever before in English history were changing their place of dwelling.
2 Change of habitat to a place where the individual was lost in a crowd and his individuality less evident, and his neglect of custom unperceived.
3 Change in manner of work, from work associated with a rural economy to work associated with an urban economy – and there is as yet no reliable evidence that this was important, though this is not to say that it was not.
4 Change in relationship to the employer, from one of personal service to one of contract. Some Victorian observers, concerned about the declining churchgoing of the rural labourer after the agricultural troubles of the seventies, were inclined to diagnose this change as important. In crude terms, the farmer's employee used to go to church because the farmer went and he stood in a personal relation to the farmer. Few men working in a mill thought of going to church because the mill-owner set him an example. On present information, however, we are not able adequately to test whether this contemporary feeling was justified. Some of those who lamented the fall in the churchgoing of the rural labourer were inclined to adopt hazy and utopian pictures of the villages before the troubles of agriculture afflicted them. A little evidence has been produced that villages where the property was parcelled out in freeholds were less likely to produce numerous worshippers than villages where the squire owned all the property and the inhabitants (or most of them) were his tenants. If further investigation confirms this, it would be a striking pointer towards the Victorian belief that the squire's example and influence were very important to the moral and religious behaviour of the village; and that the decline of the squire, in the

general decline of agriculture and the landowning interest, was of consequence for the welfare of the established Church in the country districts.

Here, then, we have two great facts troubling the Churches: a general shaking and revision of all accepted ideas by an extraordinary influx of new knowledge, scientific and historical; and a vast movement of population, creating new ways of life and uprooting the landmarks of centuries. The Churches, which by the nature of their liturgical function could not adjust their thought or their practice rapidly, must nevertheless seek to adjust themselves as rapidly as possible; and the time-lag between the necessity of adjustment and the possibility of successful adjustment naturally contributed to the problems which they encountered. But in some areas they responded remarkably. The building of new churches and chapels to meet the new urban populations was a generous feat. The acceptance of evolutionary theory into Christian thought, and the adoption of the historical methods of Biblical criticism, were accompanied by pains, but were substantially completed over thirty years.

We have seen that of these two great facts upsetting the Churches, the intellectual and the social, such evidence as exists points on the whole to the social as the more important of the two. This may be partly because a social influence is easier for the historians to test than an intellectual influence. But little signs point to it. In the nineties the country churchgoers were disturbed by Sunday golfers coming down from London and getting out of the train with their golf clubs just as the worshippers were on their way to church. Why? Was it merely that the development of trains and of golf-clubs made easy a way of Sabbath-breaking which was hardly possible before, and neither urbanization nor intelligence had anything to do with it? Was it simply that the Sunday trains suddenly juxtaposed the incomparable customs of town and country? Or had the customs of the town changed, either because it was a larger town than it used to be, or because being larger it inevitably contained more people who did not accept any duty of churchgoing? Or had the duty of churchgoing weakened in the town because newspapers and books and conversation made known ideas which challenged the basis on which the duty of churchgoing rested? Or was it nothing but a mysterious and irrational change of social custom, like the increase of hair on men's faces after the Crimean War, or like the death of the belief that clergymen should not go to theatres?

We hear of men who hesitated to take orders in the Church of England, or to accept a pastorate in one of the Free Churches – among the latter, William Hale White (Mark Rutherford) is preeminent. Victorian critics were inclined to declare that 'many men' were deterred from taking orders by their inability to profess what the Church insisted that they profess. Of course men had always been deterred from taking orders by this inability. It is easier to find general assertions that more men found it difficult during the second half of the reign of Queen Victoria than to find instances of men who found it difficult and told men why. These assertions are particularly common during the earlier sixties, when men argued over Colenso and the historical truth of the Old Testament, and during the nineties, when they argued over miracle. Mrs Humphry Ward constructed one of the most famous of Victorian novels, *Robert Elsmere*, about a clergyman who must resign his parish because he could no longer believe and teach what he was expected to believe and teach. The individual loss of faith perhaps most momentous in its consequences, that of Leslie Stephen, dated from the earlier sixties. The future statesman C. F. G. Masterman would have liked to take orders in the nineties, and yet found an obstruction in his mind, arising from the difficulties of historical knowledge. Though we cannot find many instances, we do find a few to illustrate the general assertion that in the sixties and nineties intellectual travail prevented some from taking orders who on every other ground, *ex hypothesi*, would have wished to do so.

However, the statistics of those taking orders do not confirm at all points this view of the matter. It is true that the numbers, which rose unsteadily, reached their maximum in 1886 and then turned downwards; and they thus far confirm the supposition that the intellectual troubles of the nineties had their effect. But if this turn downwards rested solely upon the intellectual argument, we should expect an even more remarkable turn downwards during the sixties, when the intellectual argument was much more exciting and caused far more turmoil among Christians. On the contrary, the number of persons ordained during the sixties continued (on the whole) to rise; and an examination of the quality of the candidates does not suggest that the rise of the sixties was achieved by opening the doors to candidates not qualified intellectually. The percentage of graduates (confessed to be an imperfect test of intellectual qualifications) remained sufficiently stable. When therefore we are told that 'men do not take orders nowadays because they are compelled to profess what they cannot believe', we need to make quite sure that the assertion is not made by a liberal who wishes the Church to adjust itself more rapidly to modern knowledge as he (the liberal) conceives that it ought to adjust itself, and that the fall in numbers is not the cause of the assertion rather than the other way round.

When, therefore, the fall in ordinands was at last observed, we must also take into consideration some of the following: the level of tithe; the expansion and respectability of professions like teaching and the civil service; the decline of the landed interest, of which many country parsons were formerly part; the extent to which bishops and other pastors talked publicly about the poverty of the clergy, in order to raise additional money for their support; the changing nature of the work, as so much of it became suburban and as the parishioners became less immobile. I do not say that these reasons, or any of them, account better for the turn downwards of ordinands than the intellectual unsettlement. But we need much more evidence before we can determine whether a social cause (like the level of stipend) was less important than an intellectual cause – such as, you must identify yourself with a Church which is regarded by some intellectuals as teaching what is not true.

Let us try to state another 'social' cause, and see whether it takes us anywhere. 'The Churches were less central to the activities of the state in 1901 than in 1837.' Putting a point to this proposition, we ask whether clergymen and ministers at the end of the reign were doing work more peripheral to society than similar ministers at the beginning of the reign – without wishing to define precisely what could be meant by 'peripheral to society'.

The preacher Robertson of Brighton once wrote this:

By the change of times the pulpit has lost its place. It does only part of that whole which used to be done by it alone. Once it was newspaper, schoolmaster, theological treatise, a stimulant to good works, historical lecture, metaphysics, etc., all in one. Now these are partitioned out to different officers, and the pulpit is no more the pulpit of three centuries back, than the authority of a master of a household is that of Abraham, who was soldier, butcher, sacrificer, shepherd, and emir in one person.[6]

As is evident from the last sentence, Robertson was not contrasting the present time with the recent past but with the age of the Reformation. Yet the manner of the comparison suggests that he was aware of something beginning to happen in his own day. The country clergyman was once the only educated man in the village apart from the squire and perhaps a farmer or two. His parishioners learned their reading and their history as well as their religion and morals out of the Bible. What he said was instruction *de haut en bas*. The clerical handbooks of the earlier part of the reign assume that the pulpit is a place where the parish will gain knowledge and recommend the parson to take much time in preparing his sermon because it is so important to the parishioners. The town parson at the end of the reign was one educated man among many. His words were the words of an equal, to be weighed and discussed. He must convince more by reasoning than by authority. Rather than communicating to men a truth which they were supposed to accept passively, he must lead them onward to search out the truth for themselves.

The symbol of this was the creation of a national system of education and the consequent diminution of the clergyman's part in the total scheme of education. Many parish priests continued to take an important part in the religious education of the country. But, even where the schools were Church schools in a formal sense, they were almost always receiving taxpayers' money for their support, and they were no longer the parson's private and personal school in quite the way in which they started. More momentous than the grants of government money was the consequent development of the profession of teachers. In the days of Dr Arnold it had not been quite 'respectable' to be a teacher unless one was also a clergyman. It was not a profession which a 'gentleman' considered entering. After 1870 the lingering remains of this feeling rapidly disappeared. Though many clergymen were

6 Brooke, *Life of F. W. Robertson* (new edn. 1873), vol. II, p. 54.

still schoolmasters, the profession lost its particular link with the clergy as education in England broadened out and became lay.

The people of England, as their rate of literacy rose, were able to support, and be further educated by, an expanding number of newspapers, a few national but most of them either local or in some way vocational. The best of these provincial newspapers, like the *Manchester Guardian* or the *Birmingham Daily Post*, were of the highest quality in journalism, and treated religion with sympathy and understanding. At the opposite extreme were sheets intended to propagate some perhaps fierce brand of dogma, theistic or otherwise. There is little doubt that the expansion of the press made the people of England sit a little more detachedly to religious commitment. It is not quite clear why that should be so, nor is it easy to find evidence to illustrate such a growth in detachment. In a manner the press was situated like the government. It was dealing with a mixed population, which corporately could apprehend only simple issues. An editor from Birmingham, who was a staunch member of a Church, urged the Church of England to face the fact that the newspapers could not but be neutral among the Churches nowadays. This relative neutrality in newspapers of wide circulation did not mean that specially religious newspapers were wanting. The expansion of the press included an enormous proliferation of religious newspapers or magazines intended for the parish, the town, the congregations, or the ministers. Parish magazines date from the sixties. But, though several attempts were made to found a 'national' newspaper of a specially religious kind, no such attempt succeeded.

A similar move away from the central control of society was the rapid decline, especially after 1872, in the number of clerical magistrates. At the end of the century there were still a few clerical magistrates, but the number diminished through the reign. The axiom that something of incongruity rested upon the clerical magistrate became so commonly held that there was a little jolt of surprise when a modern scholar (Dr Kitson Clark) pointed out how natural and how public-spirited was the link between clergyman and magistrate during the earlier part of the Victorian age. Later Victorian clergymen themselves felt something inappropriate, as though the office must be a barrier to those social encounters with the poor, the delinquent, and the ordinary folk which were seen to be their special work.

In this sense the Christian minister again became a little less engaged with the government of society. But it would be erroneous to see in this change of custom any part of the process that might be called 'secularization'. The clergymen became a little less involved in the governmental structure of the country, but no less involved with the people of the country.

In just the same way the incumbent was formerly chairman of the vestry and therefore *ex officio* the chairman of the local government of the village. In towns his official place in local government vanished much earlier. In the country it nominally remained until 1894, or nearly all the reign. For in 1894 the Local Government Act separated the secular government from the vestry and left the incumbent and his churchwardens with no *ex officio* status upon the new parish council — though of course they might be elected to it. Some people said at the time that this Act was a subtle way of disestablishing the Church of England. This view of the Act was absurdly exaggerated. For the incumbent, if he was a good man, continued to play a very important part in village affairs, after as before. And long before 1894 the powers of the vestry had been whittled away almost to vanishing. The real government of the village lay with various authorities created at various times, from county councils to highway boards. The vestry, as a secular body, had become an anachronism, and the Act of 1894 was tardy in recognizing the need for something new.

It is not easy, then, to establish that Christian ministers were any less central to the activities of the society, except in two main respects, both of which had far-reaching consequences:

1. Clergymen in villages were inevitably more central to the life of their society than clergymen in towns – but at the beginning of the reign England was largely a rural society, and at the end of the reign England was largely an urban society. In a big town Christian ministers often played a big part in public life, sometimes a leading part. But they might be ministers of any denomination, and the part which they played often rested more upon their personal qualities than their office.

2. By the end of the reign Christian ministers were no longer the chief agents in promoting and maintaining the schools to educate the mass of the English population. Nor were the ancient universities, as formerly, linked constitutionally with the Church of England. Education, like history and science, established its independent rights apart from the Churches; though the overwhelming majority of the country believed that any education worth the name must include religious education.

Now try this proposition: Christian ministers were less influential in the society of 1901 than in the society of 1837; meaning by society, Society.

The Anglican clergyman of 1837 was very influential with the upper class because he was so often himself a member of the upper class, the squire's younger brother, the peer's younger son. It was a vocation of public spirit which a young man might undertake. Fifty years later such younger sons usually went into other professions, army or civil service or even business. The most remarkable illustration of this is the different attitude of the squire and the Church towards private patronage, illustrated in the two parliamentary reports of 1874 and 1880 on the question, which yet show enough conservatism to make it clear that many members of the upper class still valued this mode of 'placing' their sons in work which both befitted their station and benefited local society.

This is so easy to caricature – and a number of Victorians, from Anthony Trollope downwards, were quick to caricature it – that we shall be in danger of smiling and underestimating the importance of the change in the trend towards 'secularization'. Canon Stanhope in *Barchester Towers* certainly did less to maintain the influence of the Church of England than the poorest curate in the County of Barset. And yet good men during the sixties and seventies – men like Professor Stubbs or Bishop Samuel Wilberforce – for no merely external reasons regretted that the idea of a *clergyman* was slowly being prised away from its almost necessary connexion with the idea of a *gentleman*; merely because the town parishes needed far more clergymen than the leisured classes were able or willing to supply. They could not point to any particular evidence, except the datum of much experience (though far from all experience, as the quite contrary evidence of the less independent chapels proves) that the uneducated were helped more by an educated minister than by one uneducated. They had a sense that the link between the Church and the leisured classes was being weakened and that this must diminish the general influence of the Church in society. If, however, good men held this opinion, there were other good men who held quite the opposite. Hurrell Froude called the opinion the 'gentleman-heresy' and had many successors who were equally contemptuous. This view of Froude won the argument because events were upon its side; and by the nineties it seemed to be an opinion held only by nostalgic conservatives. Before we dismiss it, we should remember that to the end of his life Cardinal Manning longed for Roman Catholic priests, so many of whom were Irish, to acquire the standing in society which came naturally to the Anglican clergymen. He thought that his priests were shut up in the sacristy and could never come out to influence ordinary life until their place in English society was more assured.

Chapter 11

THE YOUNG LIDDON

Liddon was born in 1829. His mother was a devout Evangelical. His aunt, his father's sister, who was also his godmother, was a devout Evangelical and important to him for the first twenty-nine years of his life. Liddon was therefore another case of the Evangelical-to-Tractarian transformation by difference of generation, and by difference of circumstances in the new generation, like Pusey, and Newman, and two Wilberforces, and many another.

In several such cases the change meant a temporary alienation from home and parents. Liddon, still looking young but already sounding old to his friends, went up to Christ Church, Oxford at the age of eighteen, in the year after Newman became a Roman Catholic. In one corner of Tom Quad he found the notorious Dr Pusey in the house of the Professor of Hebrew. After about a year Liddon was the young disciple; almost the acolyte; constantly at Pusey's house. Since Pusey, whatever his strangeness, was other-worldly, and ascetic, and generous with his money and time; and since he was a learned man, with a great library, and a rare fund of knowledge in Oriental Studies, the young Liddon, only nineteen, gained a reverence and an affection for Pusey which he never lost.

Pusey was far from being everyone's natural idol. He was the son of an elderly ultra-Tory and domineering martinet, and his childhood and youth left him with a sorer faculty for feeling guilty than is the affliction of most men or women. He fell in love with a girl called Maria Barker and was kept away from her by her father's order for several years. When at last he married her he had eleven years of happiness, which were idyllic, except that their little baby Katherine died. But it was an odd household, even while she was alive. Mrs Pusey was the first wife ever to be a reliable research assistant to an English professor. She had small interest in religion when she married him and was so dedicated in religion when she died that it was natural that her daughter Lucy showed signs of wanting to be a nun. Mrs Pusey died of tuberculosis in 1839, and all the natural light went out of Pusey's life and left only the supernatural; so that he was grave, too grave; the memory of her death remained with him and kept coming into his mind; he refused to use the spacious drawing-room where she was the hostess; he sublimated his grief by too long hours of work; Liddon could see that he loved his children passionately but saw also that the strictness of the nursery was overstrained; even when he was on holiday with his children he still said seven services in the house during the day. He was liable to long silences, for he was a man of many words with the pen, and of too many words in the pulpit, and of few words out of the pulpit. His whole day was spent at his desk unless he went out to lecture or to the library, or interviewed someone who came to consult him. He sat reading, drafting, writing – books, articles, letters. He did not take exercise except the little walks to cathedral or library, and on holiday. He was short in stature, and old-fashioned in dress (swallow-tailed coat like Keble), but the appearance was striking because of his skull-cap, which did not always look as though it fitted. He was very Evangelical in his piety and deeply Catholic at the same time. A visitor found something profoundly sad in him; something naturally mournful in the voice, but also within the soul. As he moved about the house he could every now and then be heard to mutter some sudden staccato prayer to his Maker.

In that year 1846 the name of Pusey stank in the Church. At least half the Church, and more than half the university, regarded him as a heretic and the leader of heretics. The worst of this was over confession.

From 1838 Pusey began to be asked to hear confessions and guide souls. Among a small but growing circle he was much valued as a confessor. He started regularly to make his own confession. Three or four times a year he went over to Hursley to see Keble for the purpose. Since he was afflicted by so terrible a sense of sin from the circumstances of his childhood, he found the practice of confession and absolution to be an overwhelming relief and a powerful help to him in his spiritual life. He saw that the Protestant Churches neglected something important to souls by letting this way of penitence fall into disuse. He became, not exactly an evangelist of confession as a help to the soul, because the world *evangelist* does not quite fit the professor sitting at his desk among the Hebrew and Arabic texts. But he told the world in no uncertain terms what he thought about confession.

It was no worldly advantage to a young undergraduate to be despised as Pusey's disciple. Pusey was almost ostracized in college and university at that time. Even to be seen waiting at Pusey's door was a black mark. The youth might be suspected by his tutor of waiting his turn to make his confession. Pusey was a bad influence, they thought. Young undergraduates near the end of their first year ought to be kept away from him.

To define what Liddon found to revere in a person who was too austere for most of the young and more of the elderly, would be a matter of guesswork. Undergraduates may be attracted to a don who is suspended by the Vice-Chancellor and a court of doctors from preaching for two years. An undergraduate with guts may want to rise to the defence of someone whom he sees as the under-dog. The magnet was not likely to be the ultra-gravitas, for Liddon had an astringent sense of humour and a ready wit. Nor was it likely to be the searing sense of sin, except in the form that it appeared as an excess of meekness, humility, and self-abasement; virtues which can be repellent if insincere, which they usually are, but magnetic if they are seen to be genuine and of the heart. We do not know enough to define how it happened. But before long Liddon looked upon Pusey as his father in religion; and as something of a father in the flesh. That is very much, but even that is not enough. He looked back upon Pusey as a very dear friend, a beloved friend, *amicus dilectissimus*.

Liddon's own practices soon gave rise to comment and led to his being hauled in front of his tutor. He used to say the office of Compline in his rooms. The undergraduates were wont to tell mocking stories about the number of candles which he lit. He kept the services of the Roman Breviary, and was eager about the new Gothic architecture. He wondered whether to take a vow of celibacy, but decided to postpone the decision. Perhaps his mother's death in February 1849, while he was still on the undergraduate course, did nothing to diminish his earnestness.

Whether he spent too much time with Pusey, or on Pusey's devotional matters, or on theology under the impetus of Pusey, his course of study did not go as he hoped. In 1850, at the age of 21, he took classical honours and was placed in the second class. Many young people would be very content with this achievement. Liddon was not. He regarded it as proof that he was never intended for the academic life which he had half-begun to expect for himself. The memory of this failure to get into the top class affected important decisions taken later in his life. He was quite naive, it seems, about the infallibility of examiners.

Pusey did not absorb his life. Through Pusey he was brought into a distinguished and distinctive company of young dons who had been Newman's disciples and who at that time were feeling bereft and at sea by reason of Newman's departure. Richard Meux Benson, the future founder of the monastery at Cowley; R. W. Church, close friend of Newman, reverer of him, and at last critic of him; Charles Marriott, quaint and amusing, who worked with Newman as a Fellow of Oriel College; and especially the Observer, that is the director of the Radcliffe Observatory, Manuel Johnson, who had an interest not only in stars but in illuminated manuscripts – they made a Tractarian coterie in Oxford which was not quite Puseyite, because they were in no way dominated by Pusey, but was resolute in defence of Pusey. Now that Newman had gone, the group did not look to Pusey as a leader because by nature Pusey was not a leader. They might look towards John Keble in Hampshire, but he could hardly be even the figure-head of a group at Oxford. At Manuel Johnson's house Newman said a goodbye to all his Anglican friends.

Liddon took to dining with the Observer nearly every Sunday evening. He was in the thick of the Tractarian group. Some of them one would expect to be there, but Liddon made no mention of them: James Mozley, powerful Tractarian critic of Newman; his brother Tom Mozley, who had married Newman's sister and had by now more or less deserted the party; Mark Pattison, still at this moment a Tractarian, but with a bitterness against Newman and beginning to react against the Oxford Movement. Liddon was much the youngest. He was only twenty-one; Church was thirty-five and Marriott thirty-nine.

He intended to be ordained, but he could not be ordained at twenty-one. What was he to do for two years? Most such people went to a parish and worked as a layman in return for keep, preferably with a parish priest who knew some theology and could be a teacher of the faith as well as of pastoral method; or they earned money by becoming tutor to some late teenager of wealthy family who was either backward or on the Grand Tour or both; or they stayed in Oxford with what money they could muster and learned some theology from the university. He tried a bit of the last. He competed for university prizes in theology, and with partial success.

The years 1850-1 were a time of strain to the surviving Tractarians. In the Gorham case a secular court which was also the highest ecclesiastical court, the Judicial Committee of the Privy Council, held that to be a rector or vicar a clergyman need not believe the traditional doctrine of regeneration in baptism. It looked bad that a secular court told the Church what to believe (as it seemed). It also looked bad that it should tell them to believe something contrary to what the Prayer Book said. Manning became a Roman Catholic, and so did young friends of Liddon. He must have experienced perturbation of mind. The diaries for 1851-2 are lost. It is possible that he destroyed them later because he did not like his own expressions of emotion. But Liddon's early letters (now at Keble College) show former undergraduate Tractarian friends pressing him emotionally to become a Roman Catholic; and show Liddon replying that Dr Pusey did not move.

Liddon did keep diaries of the foreign tours on which he now went. He went to Scotland to examine Presbyterianism and did not like its outer signs. Then he went as a tutor to the continent. He was moved by high mass in Bruges, though he would have cut some of its elaboration. He was not impressed by the Swiss Reformed. He despised the only two sermons which he heard in Switzerland. He argued with Catholics on whether if a man is to be a Catholic he must accept the supremacy of the Pope. In 1852 he tutored a boy in Scotland and then went by himself to Italy.

What followed appears to the modern reader so scandalous that a little explanation is needed of the mood or feeling of that time. This was September 1852. Looked at from Rome, the Oxford Movement appeared a marvellous gift to the Roman

Catholic Church. Seven years before, its leader submitted. Now the Gorham Case sent over more. These were not likely to be exceptions. Dr Pusey was forbidden to preach by his bishop. How much longer could he stay an Anglican? Was it not likely, as Newman claimed just at this time, that the entire Oxford Movement must by its inherent logic end in the Roman Catholic Church?

All the Catholic world outside England, and part of it in England, expected that the coming of Pusey was only a matter of time. They said to each other that he had a true sympathy of the heart for Rome. They said that he waited because he only had a last doubt or two to settle. They were sure that he would come in the end. They were confident that when he came he would bring with him a big fraction of the Church of England. Such was the portrait in Rome of the stature, the influence, the mood, and the intention of Pusey. Even as late as 1879 Robert Louis Stevenson went with his abominable donkey Modestine to the Trappist house of our Lady of the Snows near the Cevennes, and there met a monk who prayed for the conversion of Dr Pusey every day, night and morning; a habit which he formed in his seminary with six young Irishmen who in those days kept him informed of the ecclesiastical state of England. 'I thought', said the monk to Stevenson, 'that he [Pusey] was very near the truth, and he will reach it yet. There is so much virtue in prayer.'

Therefore, when a young Oxford graduate, who was reported to be very close to Dr Pusey, appeared in Rome, it was axiomatic among the Romans that it would not take much to make out of him a proselyte.

Liddon carried with him to Rome a letter of introduction to Monsignor George Talbot. Who gave him this letter is not known. If the introducer was an Anglican, he was irresponsible. Talbot was an ex-Anglican clergyman who became a Roman Catholic five years before. He was already a papal chamberlain. We know a good deal about Monsignor Talbot fifteen years later, and by then he was not an advertisement for the priesthood of a Church. It is not impossible that Liddon, at that moment, was almost ripe to become a Roman Catholic; and if so, it was fortunate for the Anglicans that the priest set to make the proselyte was George Talbot.

In Rome Talbot gave him luncheon and put him in the way of several permits to see sights. Liddon found him 'excessively polite'. He perceived that he wished to convert him. Nevertheless he did not shrink from the meetings ahead. Clearly the young man was fascinated by what Talbot might say, and thought it a duty to hear. In the Vatican on 29 September 1852 Talbot tried to prove to his Anglican ordinand that Anglican orders were invalid. Liddon only noted that the arguments which led up to this proof were 'curious'. Talbot then took Liddon into his little chapel and begged him to become a Roman Catholic. Liddon saw that this was not an argument to his intelligence but an appeal to emotion and imagination. The invitations mounted; Talbot offered to find him rooms inside the Vatican (!), and invited him to dine next day, and gave him various books on the Anglican–Roman controversy, and said that they should have an audience with the Pope. Politeness – luncheon – permits – appeal to emotion in front of an altar – offer of lodging inside the Vatican – dinner – private audience with Pius IX – nothing could have been laid on thicker. None of it was in the least suitable to the subject of these experiments. The converts of stature – a Newman, or a Manning – convinced themselves. The methods of Monsignor Talbot were suitable for young persons susceptible to flattery. No doubt he did not perceive that Liddon at the age of twenty-three had stature.

At the audience with the Pope next day, Liddon genuflected in a wrong place as well as the right and kissed the Pope's toe without any apparent qualm. He also gave the Pope some little objects to be blessed. He felt it a wonderful day in his life. The Pope spoke in French and hoped that he would pursue his studies with constant prayer, and hoped that he would be led into the truth.

Three more times Talbot gave him lunch. On the last time, 11 October, as Liddon was about to leave Rome, Talbot went with him to the door, and begged him 'with much importunity instantly to take the step'. Liddon felt that now his vanity was being appealed to. Then Talbot committed a final blasphemy. He reminded Liddon of 'that sorrowful look which our Blessed Lord cast on the young man who did not give up all to follow him'.

'You are that young man.' He refused to say goodbye, and 'disappeared'.

Liddon's mind was in a turmoil, but it was not the kind of turmoil which Monsignor Talbot wished. 'Never do I recollect having felt so much affected by a few words. They quite suspended my power of thought; they left me with ideas on *the* question in hopeless confusion. They did not illumine and direct by a *coup de main*; they only gave me a quite terrible feeling of the distance which exists in spirit between the Church of Rome and other bodies.'

Yet he had no desire at all to leave Rome, and was sad that he must go. Next morning early he went to Talbot's mass and took breakfast with him and gave him a note 'to close the controversy; he was very melancholy, but quite touchingly gentlemanly about it'.[1]

Nevertheless, letters out of the Vatican pursued him to England. The letters tried to persuade him that his loyalty to Anglicanism was not based on principle but rested only on a private attachment to Dr Pusey.

Two months later, that December 1852, Liddon was ordained to be a deacon in the Church of England, to serve as the curate of Wantage. So far as is at present known, no further communication ever passed between himself and Monsignor Talbot.

Two months later he had to give up his curacy for reasons of health. When he was ordained priest in 1853, he already knew that he could never after all be a parish priest.

Until the nineteenth century the theological nurseries of the Church of England were the Universities of Oxford and Cambridge. As soon as Anglican leaders came to believe that the ancient universities were failing in this traditional duty, they perforce founded colleges for ordinands. A single date illustrates the change. The year 1854 was the year when Parliament passed the Act which altered the constitution and government of the University of Oxford and the colleges therein. It was the year when Bishop Wilberforce of Oxford founded Cuddesdon College.

[1] For the Liddon–Talbot encounter, see J. O. Johnston, *The Life and Letters of H. P. Liddon* (1904).

Until about 1850–60, and sometimes much later (we know a case in the 1940s – Dr Headlam, Bishop of Gloucester), the bishops assumed that a candidate with a university education was adequately prepared for ordination. Most undergraduates came from families where the exercises of Christian worship and the duties of Christian morality were respectfully or devoutly or in token performed. The young man could not take a degree at either university without professing himself a member of the Church of England. While he lived at the university he was expected and compelled to attend the services of the chapel. The head of his college was normally in orders; so were many of the fellows. Even in 1840 something like half the population of the two universities expected to take orders. The purpose of the university bore an imperfect but recognizable resemblance to the purpose of a modern theological college. Where a candidate was sanctioned and recommended by a university, the bishops might be forgiven for assuming that he was sufficiently prepared for ordination. Most of the eminent religious leaders of the nineteenth century were trained under this ancient system; and the nineteenth century did not lack eminent religious leaders.

The years from 1800 saw an intermittent attack upon the universities as schools for ordinands. The most vociferous critics were not churchmen but reformers like the Utilitarians, who denounced the universities as closets of superstition and reaction. The general outcry certainly persuaded churchmen to examine the fortress which they must defend. But other, and Christian, influences were leading them to the conviction that the religious training of the universities needed reform.

The Evangelicals steadily raised the ideal expected of the Christian pastor. For many years they proclaimed standards of earnestness which still won them the epithet 'methodistical', but which slowly leavened the popular notion of the Christian minister. The universities produced gentlemen of general education whose profession alone distinguished them in habits and tone from the gentle laity. The Evangelicals were demanding that the Christian minister should know his commission to be of God; that he was called to a labour which separated him from the standards of the world; that in the preaching of the Word and the ministry of the sacraments he acted as the instrument of God's eternal purpose; that he should accept his awful responsibility for the cure of souls and know that he must render account for them in the day of judgment.

In the face of language like this the prevalent idea of the educated parson in each parish began to seem meagre. Inside the university the activities of a Charles Simeon contained an implicit criticism of the normal religious education. Outside the university some Evangelicals refused to regard an academic course as the ideal preparation for certain kinds of evangelistic work. In 1809 the CMS accepted for training an intelligent shoe-maker named Thomas Norton. The committee decided to send him to the university. But Thomas Scott (the Biblical commentator) urged them that the life of an undergraduate was 'not favourable to the cultivation of the missionary spirit and of missionary habits of life': the committee sent him to Scott instead of the university. The Tractarians adopted and reinforced the earnestness of the Evangelicals. In the 1830s and 1840s Tractarian writers were claiming that the universities, though offering a general education desirable for the Christian minister, were not offering any training in the essential background of ministerial life – theology and the devout life.

This is the age when the 'clerical layman' became an object of public humour. In 1855 Anthony Trollope published the first of the Barchester series, *The Warden; Barchester Towers* appeared in 1857; George Eliot's *Scenes from Clerical Life* in 1858. It was the age when stories of the diminishing race of squire-parsons were popular material for the witty speech or the weekly article; the age when round the clubs ran the complaint of the retired merchant that, out hunting and thrown at a jump, he lay helpless in the hedge while seven parsons rode over him, disregarding his clamour for help. The reformers disliked whatever gave ground for the sneer that the clergy formed 'the port-wine faction'. At one end of the scale they were troubled at the old curate who rested between services at the Three Fishes and in his shirt-sleeves refreshed himself with bread and cheese and a tankard of ale. They lamented when an ordinand appeared the day after his ordination in 'a coloured waistcoat and a single tie'. At the other end of the scale they were setting a new standard which inevitably separated men from the normal habits of lay life. The decade when Cuddesdon was founded was not only the age of Trollope; it was the age of Charlotte Yonge and the best of the Victorian morality-novels (*The Heir of Redclyffe* was published in 1853).

How the hopes of the religious reformers were shifting from the universities to the theological colleges is shown in two letters of John Keble:

What sad accounts I hear of the Germanization and secularization of Oxford. I should think it would be very soon necessary for people who wish their sons to have a fair chance for being Christians to send them to some other place; and for Bishops to resort ordinarily to the Theological Colleges ...

Or again:

Oxford I fear is too far gone (in the Germanizing way) – unless Cuddesden[2] prove able to stop the decay: certainly there seems a great blessing on that place.

The earliest attempts to provide postgraduate training for ordinands were the two diocesan colleges of Chichester (1839, refounded 1846) and Wells (1840). The opportunity to create these colleges arose because cathedral chapters were in the melting-pot. Dr Pusey, in a pamphlet of his pre-Tractarian days (1833), argued that the proper use of the cathedral chapters should be the provision of theological training: and the argument exerted wide influence. The foundation of a chair of Ecclesiastical History and a chair of Moral and Pastoral Theology, attached to canonries at Christ Church, and the unfulfilled intention to found a similar chair of Biblical Criticism, issued from the same movement of ideas which helped to create the colleges at Wells and Chichester. At Chichester, though the bishop opposed the Oxford Movement, Tractarian influence was marked from the first. The Tractarians, in reviving the ideals of primitive antiquity, were recalling the ancient method of training (or what they supposed to be the ancient method) – the bishop surrounded by his ordinands and supervising their instruction. Archdeacon Manning was the chief link between Chichester and Oxford; and he and his friends secured as the first principal Charles Marriott, Fellow of Oriel, friend and (up to a point) disciple of Newman.

[2] In the early years many authorities, including the Post Office, spelt the name of the place 'Cuddesden': and the earliest advertisements for the college appear with that form. But there was no unanimity, and eventually the *o* captured the field.

Neither of these colleges was the direct offspring of the Oxford Movement. But from their earliest years the Tractarian ideas began to penetrate them.

Samuel Wilberforce was consecrated to the see of Oxford on 30 November 1845. Among his notes of January 1846, written immediately after his consecration, is a list of agenda; second on this list is 'a diocesan training college for clergy to be founded at Cuddesdon'. Through the early years of his episcopate he worked towards this goal. In his charge of 1851 he publicly declared that 'I shall never feel that our diocese is furnished with that which is essential for its welfare, until it is provided with such an instrument of welfare' as a diocesan training college. In the same year he decided that the time to go forward had come. He selected his future principal: a young man among his chaplains, Alfred Pott.

The bishop did not expect that the post of principal would be as responsible as it proved to be. He supposed that he himself could supply the wisdom and the experience. The early history of Cuddesdon can be understood only in the context of the bishop's belief that he could effectively supervise the running of the college. Filled with the ancient picture of the bishop surrounded by his ordinands and in person preparing them for ordination, he did not realize that the duties of a primitive bishop, who had no railway, were less onerous than the duties of a modern bishop, who had a railway. Moved by this illusion, he wanted to build the college within the grounds of Cuddesdon Palace and was only prevented from doing so by the opposition of his clergy, who perceived that to make the college too 'episcopal' might tie it to the apron-strings and opinions of future bishops. The change of plan meant delay: he needed to acquire the land across the road. But early in 1853 all was ready. Wilberforce prepared to lay the foundation-stone.

Wells and Chichester were founded in cathedral closes. In each close the bishop of the diocese lived. The Bishop of Oxford's cathedral was Christ Church: and the nature of the collegiate foundation meant that the chapter of Christ Church was (if possible) even more independent of the bishop than most cathedral chapters are. The universities still regarded themselves as training ordinands. Wilberforce was the bishop of a university diocese. A theological college founded in his diocese trespassed upon the preserves of the university more obviously than any previous foundation. It is significant that no theological college was founded in Oxford or in Cambridge until 1876, by which time the university had accepted the fact that it was no longer primarily Anglican in tone. Cuddesdon, it was true, was not in Oxford. But it was very near Oxford. And the fellows of Oxford colleges suspected its purpose. In speech after speech in the first ten years of the life of Cuddesdon College, its advocates were careful to explain that they were in no way attempting to infringe the rights of Oxford University. Wilberforce knew that he was founding a college against the wishes of many authorities in his university.

The second difficulty was the growing suspicion among the public that the theological colleges fostered Tractarian ideas. In the origins of theological colleges there was little that was specifically Tractarian. But during the years 1850 and 1851, stirred by the papal creation of diocesan sees in England and by the controversies over the Gorham case, the English became abnormally sensitive about doctrine or ritual or conduct wherein they might sniff the odours of Roman Catholicism. They listened with less indifference than usual to anti-ecclesiastical agitators.

In 1852-3 an attempt to found a theological college stimulated excited laymen into riots. The Bishop and clergy of Lichfield proposed to follow Wells and Chichester in creating a diocesan seminary. The proposal roused churchmen and dissenters in Staffordshire to fury. The streets of Lichfield were placarded with anti-theological college notices. 'Are the students to be expected', asked an impassioned orator at Stoke-on-Trent, 'are they to be expected – as at Wells and Chichester – to fast on Fridays?' A publication appeared entitled *The Tractarian Tendency of Diocesan Theological Colleges*; and it warned against the possibly sinister purpose of the college planned and 'now rising' at Cuddesdon. The malcontents succeeded in postponing the college at Lichfield until 1857.

Butler of Wantage recommended one of his curates to be vice-principal of Cuddesdon – Liddon. Since Liddon left Wantage, he spent his time between Oxford, Wantage, continental travel, and another temporary curacy. He was plainly not strong enough for regular parish work. In December 1853, when Liddon was staying at Cuddesdon Palace before his ordination to the priesthood, Wilberforce suggested to him that he might become the first Vice-Principal of Cuddesdon.

Liddon was not a man to conceal what he believed. He told the bishop his theological standpoint. On 28 December 1853 he wrote to Wilberforce accepting the post. Wilberforce meanwhile thought again and withdrew his offer.

Throughout the next six months Wilberforce and Liddon and Butler maintained a triangular and intermittent series of negotiations. The difficulty was obvious. Liddon was *the* disciple of Dr Pusey. Wilberforce distrusted Dr Pusey. He believed that Oxford rightly suspended Pusey for his sermon on the Eucharist in 1843. He distrusted Pusey's public advocacy of the sacrament of penance. He privately inhibited Pusey from preaching in the diocese of Oxford. He believed that Pusey was 'fostering the spirit of party' in the Church of England. He disliked Pusey's efforts to adapt Roman books of devotion for Anglican minds, and publicly attacked these efforts in his charge to the diocese of 1851. In May 1852, after prolonged intercession from mutual friends and exhaustive explanations by Pusey, he withdrew the inhibition. But distrust remained. To appoint Liddon, he feared, might introduce the spirit of party into his college. It might turn the college, he thought, into 'a mere collection of young men under Dr Pusey's direction'. And he had to face the question of discretion. He had no desire that public opinion should associate Cuddesdon with the Tractarian party. Liddon was known, not only as Pusey's disciple, but for what were called 'ritualistic frivolities' during his undergraduate days. It required conviction in the bishop to appoint Liddon against these considerations of diplomacy and public interest.

By the summer of 1854, after Liddon carefully explained that while he must insist for himself on using the sacrament of penance, he would not recommend confession *indiscriminately* to the students, the appointment was confirmed. The bishop insisted only that Liddon should cease to consult Pusey and should go for spiritual advice to John Keble instead; for Wilberforce always admired and trusted Keble. Pusey welcomed the condition – Liddon, he wrote on 19 June, was changing 'brass for gold'.

Keble, who always disliked the distinction in Wilberforce's mind
between the influence of himself and the influence of Pusey,
wished at first to refuse: but after exacting conditions from the
bishop, he accepted, and at the beginning of August 1854 Liddon
was officially appointed.

Liddon rather than Pott dominated training. The principal
lived outside the college; he had duties as vicar of the parish; on 5
July 1855 he married a wife (the bishop married them), and soon
a young family began to come. The college had no bursar: and the
management of its secular affairs absorbed his time. Above all he
began to suffer illness, and was forced to miss the Lent and Trinity
terms of 1857 while Liddon directed the college. Nor do we
know of any marked disagreement between principal and vice-
principal upon this question. We shall not, therefore, be wrong in
thinking that Liddon's ideal for the priesthood was substantially
the ideal which Cuddesdon taught its students in the years from
1854 to 1859. The content of this ideal may be found partly in a
few letters of Liddon which have survived, partly in an article on
'The Priest in his Inner Life' which he published in the *Ecclesiastic
and Theologian* during 1856-7.

Pusey had taught him not to be afraid of foreign, Catholic,
models if he found them good. There existed a famous Catholic
model of how to run a college for training future clergy. During
the middle years of the seventeenth-century, the training of
Catholic priests in France, unless they were well-to-do and
intelligent and were trained at a university, was lamentable;
sometimes it was lamentable even if they were all those things.
An alliance of French priests, from Bérulle's Oratory and then
from Vincent de Paul's Lazarists, inspired by the Oratorian
Charles de Condren and Vincent's disciple Jean Jacques Olier,
founded a series of seminaries which were much imitated through
Catholic Europe. Olier was the founder and head of the Paris
seminary of Saint-Sulpice.

Whether through Pusey or his own inquiries, Liddon knew
something of all these French reformers of nearly two centuries
before. He admired them as people. He valued their devotional
language. He liked the spirit which they engendered in their
charges.

They portrayed an ideal of the priest as the representative of

Christ to his people. They were more concerned with piety than with academic theology – the university could do the academic theology. They did not want to make their colleges into monasteries, but they kept the monastic hours of prayer, and quiet times, and monthly sacraments, and monthly confessions. Their methods of instruction were so elementary as to be intolerable – either slow dictation of lecture notes, or slow delivery of a lecture which the students memorized and then repeated. They found it more important for the student to learn of the sacraments, and how to preach, and how to conduct services, and how to advise consciences, than for him to appropriate a lot of dogmatic theology or church history; though they did try to give a very elementary grounding in Scripture and the creed and the Fathers of the Church. Naturally the manner varied from house to house according to the competence or diversity of the staff. But in the ideal of the Sulpician the college was a friendly community where teacher shared a common life with taught and was a friend among friends. The colleges were not places of games, which hardly interested the French. But the students had theatre, and plenty of time off, and adequate food and drink. Some in the outside world of France imagined the colleges to be prisons where young men endured unimaginable mortifications. That was not what they were like inside.

Among the practices of piety, though not at first, came meditation upon the Scriptures. At much the same period as the Sulpicians, a French author and a German author printed meditations for each day. The Frenchman was Avrillon, whom Pusey introduced to English readers as a help to keeping Lent. (This publication did more than anything else to alarm Wilberforce about Pusey's state of mind). The German was Nicolas Avancini, who taught at Vienna, and published meditations on the Gospel for each day of the year. Liddon valued these meditations.

The way of life at Cuddesdon during the 1850s was not very unlike the way of life at Saint-Sulpice during the seventeenth century – more like in ideal than in practice.

The Church of England, Liddon argued, had not left her priests without direction. The rubric which ordered Anglican clergy to say morning and evening prayer daily was a binding rubric. Though the Tractarians tried to underline this view, it could not be said that by 1856 many of the clergy obeyed the rubric. Liddon drafted the first form of that *Litany of the Holy Ghost* which in a revised form passed into many books of prayer. Into his draft he incorporated a petition 'that we may remember to say daily the morning and evening service, either privately or openly'. Wilberforce held that the clause was inappropriate (he was right) and asked for its removal. Liddon was very sorry, and argued strongly to the contrary. If it were argued that the priest might more profitably spend the required time in prayers likely to elicit emotion towards the person of our Lord, Liddon replied that 'obedience is a surer test of love than emotion'. In reciting the office the priest is acting as a priest, representing the people of God before His throne; 'he may be in his chamber, and they at their several occupations, but in the Communion of Saints, he is acting with them and for them'. 'The priest is never without a congregation, though it be far away, and have chosen an earlier or later hour than his own, or none at all; like St Paul, he is separated from it, in person only, not in spirit and reality.' This, he taught his ordinands, was the reason for the faithful discharge of the rubric. By this provision the priest was enabled to fulfil his duty to God and his people less inadequately. In his worship he needed not to rely on his individual choice of prayer and praise, but to use the words of Scripture which the Church selected for him. In worshipping with the office he became a man of the Bible, and he absorbed the truths of Scripture and the mind of the Church upon them. The office became a channel through which the truths of Scripture passed into his life and his preaching.

While Liddon helped to rehabilitate the rubric about Mattins and Evensong, he contributed more than anyone to the revival of the minor (monastic) offices (Terce, Sext, None, at the third hour (9.0 a.m.), sixth hour (12 noon) and ninth hour (3.0 p.m.). He believed in the devotional power of the minor offices, and worked to accustom his pupils to them. He thought that Mattins and Evensong contained so many elements of the medieval offices of Mattins, Lauds, and Vespers that to use these might be held to savour of disloyalty to the system of the Church of England. But this hardly applied to Prime and Compline, which only just overlapped with the offices in the Book of Common Prayer; and it did not apply at all to Terce, Sext, and None. From the moment of his arrival he sought to secure that the students should have opportunities for daily worship outside the two set offices. He could hardly expect the bishop to sanction Terce, Sext, None, and Compline at once.

Liddon's second hinge of the disciplined spiritual life was meditation. The Church of England, in prescribing the offices to its clergy, implicitly demanded other spiritual exercises as a regular part of the clerical life. To use the offices without a background of Scriptural devotion might lead to formalism. For the discharge of the duty of reciting the offices, 'a devotional and collected temper is required, which must be developed by other expedients'. It must be developed by meditation upon the Scriptures. England was a Bible-reading country: everyone took meditation for granted. But Liddon believed that most people suffered from hazy notions of its meaning and methods. Too many regarded it as an occupation for times when a man could find nothing else to do; on the contrary, the exercise demands all the effort of the soul, moral and intellectual. He therefore taught his men to survey their materials for meditation the night before and to come to it in the early morning when their bodies were refreshed and their minds undistracted. It was not an intellectual study of Scripture or a mere resolution, but an act of worship issuing in resolution. It must be made not at the desk but on the knees. After preparatory prayers of penitence and faith, the soul should come trustfully to the Bible, to put aside human reason and to listen to the Word that is spoken. The priest should seek to picture the incident on which he meditates, to clothe and enliven it by reverent imagination. Then the understanding should work upon the picture, dividing it into its component parts until it can select one element which evokes response from the will. Here the intellect 'retires', its function ended. 'The point upon which it has fixed as cardinal is transferred to the will.' The whole being seeks to absorb the moral truth which the intellect has selected, and so passes to resolution, always a concrete and practical resolution. Liddon taught that thus the priest would be led, on the one side to effective self-examination, and on the other to ejaculatory prayer, whereby recollectedness might become a quality of his pastoral life.

During his first term he gave the men *Rules for Meditating* and a scheme of subjects for meditation for three weeks. No time for meditation was allotted on the time-table (until 1875). In the Lent term of 1855 the men were recommended to read *Daily Steps towards Heaven* (an Anglican adaptation of Avancini). Liddon himself rose early. He taught that 'at least' the priest should rise at six in summer and seven in winter.

In all his language, from the notices on the board to the meditations for August–September 1858 which have survived in manuscript, Liddon conveys the feeling of urgency. 'To delay is possibly to be stranded for ever.' His manuscript meditations, which he habitually lent to students, ended with verses of the *Dies irae* and the contemplation of death and judgment. 'The penalty is eternal . . . Add years to years, ages to ages, count the leaves of a forest or the sand on the shore of the ocean – and you are as far as ever from achieving the idea of eternity.'

Sunday 2 December 1855. Preached at 7 o'clock service in Church for 55 minutes on the Second Advent of Jesus Christ. How terribly my sermon will rise up against myself in the day of judgement.

Liddon shared with Pusey the feeling of awful responsibility laid upon man by the gift of an immortal soul, by the gift of time to work for God and prepare for eternity. This weight of responsibility, he taught, was increased in priests and ordinands by their vocation. Inasmuch as a clergyman can only sin with a soul and body consecrated to God, his sins add the sin of sacrilege to their own intrinsic evil. He can 'lower the tone and aim of hundreds of souls', can put 'the earnest out of heart and reassure the libertine and the careless'. Representing his people in intercession before God, he can destroy the power of his prayer. He reminded his hearers of Chrysostom's opinion that of all callings the priesthood 'involved the largest proportion of its members in eternal ruin'.

For individual influence Liddon relied on walking with the men during the afternoons. To such purpose did he walk that one writer on early Cuddesdon could mention 'walks with the Vice-Principal' among the devotional and educative forces at the college.

Liddon's diary shows that during these walks he pressed earnestness upon his companions, and used various openings to that end. He would converse on the book *The Imitation of Christ*, or try, if he could, to discuss motives for taking holy orders, or at times to talk about private prayer, and to insist on the necessity of a prayerful habit. Sometimes he would find himself hearing about the unsatisfactory behaviour of the companion's clergyman at home. Sometimes he defended the Fathers of the early Church as the best guides to the interpretation of the Bible.

The atmosphere of Pusey's devotion, and in part of Sulpician devotion, was thus brought into the corporate feeling of the new college. For Liddon personally it was strengthened by a new relation to Pusey. Since the Bishop of Oxford banned him from going to consult Pusey on questions about the life of the soul, he begged Pusey to write for him a little book of private prayers for his personal use. Liddon took this collection and used it every day in his own devotions for the rest of his life. We have these prayers because after Pusey died Liddon published them (with the addition of a small amount of extra matter) as a little book, *Private Prayers of Dr Pusey* (1883), in the hope that they would be useful to others. They were useful, because the little book went through several editions. But they are not prayers which anyone could use habitually. They are markedly personal to Pusey's cast of mind.

In the Anglican scene of 1856 this air of Avancini, or Avrillon, or Father Olier, or Saint-Sulpice, looked strange. There was danger.

The bishop began with the notion that he could exercise effectual supervision. In opening the college he told the congregation that here he might see and pray with and help his ordinands 'day by day'. In his suggestions for students he talked of constant access to himself. He possessed a special stall in the college chapel; the members of the college used his private chapel for Mattins every day and for the Sunday Sacrament. But a bishop who was refounding Convocation as an effective debating assembly; who took seriously his duties as a debater in the House of Lords; who was in demand everywhere as a public speaker; who cared for the confirmations, the institutions, the consecrations of churches, in a very large diocese – he could not be at isolated Cuddesdon sufficiently often to make this supervision a fact. In 1857 he spent eighty-five days of the whole year at Cuddesdon. It is nevertheless surprising to see from the extant letters how amidst the pressure of business he found time to think of the ordinands at his college.

Wilberforce appointed two young men as principal and vice-principal because he saw them rather in the light of his examining chaplains than as heads of a college, rather as assistants to himself than as the officers of an institution which possessed an independent status apart from himself. His busy life compelled him to allow the officers, or one of them, to run the college on the lines they (or he) wished, subject to his *jus liturgicum* and his general approval. When he selected them he placed confidence in them, and left to them the administration of detail, sometimes assuming in them, as Pott said, 'a capacity greater than they really possessed, and deferring very often to their counsel when they would far rather be guided by his'.

With the bishop's supervision remote, and with Pott ill in 1856, and absent for much of 1857, Liddon became the acting principal of the college. Liddon knew what he wanted and what he believed. It was impossible that the students should not perceive disagreement beween their vice-principal and their bishop. A difference in the manner of celebrating the Eucharist was important. Wilberforce (until 1869) celebrated at the north end of the altar in his own chapel. In the college chapel Liddon adopted the eastward position. Some of Wilberforce's visitors were disturbed when they saw the decorations of the chapel, which they regarded as 'gaudy', and complained about a cross on the altar, and coloured frescoes on the walls.

The 1850s were a transitional era in the revival of ceremonial. The original impetus came from scholars and antiquarians, cautious and prudent men, versed in the principles of archaeology and liturgy. (The term *ritualist* was not in origin a term of abuse, but was equivalent to what we should now call a *liturgiologist*.) During the fifties it was evident that the leadership of the revival was passing from the academic theorists to the pastors in the parishes. From being the moderate programme of a few divines in the universities, the revival became part of the wider quest to make the services of the Church of England warm, popular, attractive, and vehicles of worship for simple people. When the leadership passed from the academic to the pastor, the pace quickened. The pastors were not wanting to revive the exact forms of ancient ceremonial, they wanted to convert their parishes. Some of them did not always perceive the import of what they were doing. But the movement was part of a wider movement and can be judged only against a wider background. During the early nineteenth century the stream of worship – among all sections of the Church of England – overflowed the confining banks of the 1662 Prayer Book. In 1861 the first edition of *Hymns Ancient and Modern* summarized the trend of the age. In that famous book, as its title suggested, was to be found a broader apprehension of the possibilities of hymnody for the Church of England, a lifting of the eyes from the familiar paths to the treasures of the Christian centuries, Catholic or Protestant. What was happening in hymnody must happen also in private devotions. Pusey and others, including Liddon, adapted continental prayers or meditations for English use. The same overflowing of the banks must affect the appurtenances of the liturgy.

Responsible churchmen knew that ceremonial or ornaments were of secondary moment in the Church. Nevertheless, many responsible churchmen thought that the movement to richer ceremonial should be encouraged. They could not assert *simpliciter* that a stole or a candlestick were 'things indifferent'. For they believed that in many churches the order of service was often irreverent; that the worship was often shallow, barren, or conventional; that worship might be deepened by external aids; that in a sacramental world a man must be led to worship with his body as well as his soul. They admitted that no doctrinal principle compelled the use of a cross on the altar; that the sole guide was the law of charity and edification. But edification demanded decency and order; and decency and order demanded dignity in externals. They allowed that externals were as nothing compared to the truths of the Gospel, but they could not deduce from this admission the proposition that externals were unimportant. John Keble's attitude may be taken as typical of the attitude of the best men in the Oxford Movement. In December 1855 he wrote that the question whether a cross should be upon the altar was nothing compared to doctrinal truth:

though I must own, I do expect, that when these outward signs of Truth are suppressed, the Truth itself which they symbolise will be openly persecuted, and probably forbidden to be taught in the Established Church.

Liddon shared these views. He wanted enrichment and worked for it. He was vexed when the prudence of the bishop or the principal restrained him. He wanted colour and life on principles of worship. He hated barrenness and irreverence and casualness in worship. But he did not encourage exceptional behaviour at services. He distrusted what he called 'Hyperaestheticism' wherever he found it among his students. Not all the students shared these opinions.

It was clear that by 1857 the college did the work for which the bishop designed it. Applications by vicars for curates from Cuddesdon were more than double the number which Cuddesdon was able to supply. In the Michaelmas term of 1857 the college was full, with twenty-one men. The bishop talked of appealing for money for an exhibition fund to help candidates with small means. The suspicions of the University of Oxford began to fade. To the annual festival in June 1857 came the two proctors, three heads of houses, and numbers of the country gentry, while the Vice-Chancellor sent an apology that he could not be there – 'So you see', wrote Liddon to his sister, 'we are making way in Oxford.' Wilberforce expressed his contentment to the diocese in his autumn charge of that year. The college was full and the demand was greater than they could meet, and now they must begin to think about expanding the accommodation and adding to the buildings.

When Wilberforce spoke, he already had the first inkling that it would not be expansion but contraction.

Rumours about the college gathered momentum. Some form of attack was inevitable. The very phrase 'diocesan seminary', which the bishop and others did not refrain from using, caused people to sniff the air for the scent of cassocks and ceremonial. Oxford dons and country clergymen murmured that the staff conducted the services in the college chapel with usages unfamiliar in the parish churches of the diocese. And when visitors poked about the college, they were surprised by the decorations of the chapel. It was partly that the altar had a frontal; still more it was the mural decorations. Amateur artists who paint saintly figures sometimes achieve lurid results; and the colour used by the student (one of the Porter family) who painted the murals in Cuddesdon chapel does not seem to have been delicate. The vicar of Sonning said that he liked the altar himself, but thought it 'very like another part of the vineyard'. Lord Dungannon appeared, thought Liddon, 'to wince' at the chapel. In October 1856 a group of visitors made 'a series of very vulgar remarks about popery' when they entered the chapel. Not all the visitors shared this suspicion. On the evening of 27 May 1857 Dr Pusey drove out from Oxford with the Bishop of Brechin (Forbes), refused to take tea with Liddon (Wilberforce did not like him to see Liddon), but was 'much pleased' when he was shown the chapel. In the beginning of the Lent term, however, in that year, the bishop enforced changes which Liddon disliked. It was a grief to Liddon that the chapel should begin to look bare.

In September 1857 there appeared a professional controversialist. For Tractarian historiography Charles Pourtales Golightly has always possessed the qualities of Mephistopheles. He was a loyal, sturdy, contentious Anglican who, since the time that he was Newman's curate, believed himself called to the task of resisting every kind of innovation in the Church of England. An impenetrable skin, which he attributed to his education at Eton amid the floggings of Dr Keate and the blows of his fellows, fortified him for a work demanding herculean resolution in an age of change. Affectionate and generous, he laboured under the illusion that sharp public controversy need not loosen the ties of private friendship. Wilberforce once called him 'the snake-in-the-grass', and a vexed periodical referred to him as the modern Titus Oates. Neither of these comparisons did justice to the simplicity of his character. Though he was a faithful pastor of his little parish, his mission forced him to appear before the public as a busybody. A memorable leading article once urged him to return to his parish and shepherd it – 'if he has a parish to look after, however small, we should earnestly recommend him to confine himself a little more closely to the strict line of his duty'. Golightly went on his way, a man of one idea, uninhibited by the doubts or hesitations which beset the intellectual. R. W. Church, who knew him well, regarded him as indefatigable, candid, well-meaning, and absurd. Liddon thought him an eccentric. By 1857 his pen was respectably prolific in tracts and letters to the press. In the days of Dr Pusey's big fight with his bishop, Golightly was the bishop's gadfly. He was well tutored in stratagems of war, the more formidable because he was unaware that he was a strategist.

He visited Cuddesdon for the annual festival of 1855 and did not like what he saw. During the next two years his growing suspicion of the college was fed by rumour. On 18 September 1857 he remonstrated with the bishop in a private letter. He wanted the bishop to know, he said, that the senior members of the university, and the nobility and gentry of the diocese, distrusted the bishop on account of the system pursued at the college. The bishop, he knew, abhorred Romish doctrine: the practices of Cuddesdon suggested by contrast that the bishop welcomed Romish rites and ceremonies. Golightly said he believed that men had come to Cuddesdon and there acquired 'Romish leanings'; and he explained to the bishop his particular suspicion of Liddon.

Golightly and Wilberforce exchanged views on Liddon. They did not coincide. Wilberforce said that Liddon was 'eminently endued with the power of leading men to earnest devoted piety ... I have rarely met with any man living who had equal gifts for stirring up a young man's heart into flame.' There, for the moment, the exchange rested. Golightly was not satisfied.

In winter a contributor to the *Quarterly Review*, Canon Whitwell Elwin, visited Cuddesdon inquisitively, put his head inside the door, chatted with a servant, and found his suspicions confirmed. In the January number (1858) of the *Quarterly Review* he opened a damaging attack upon theological colleges.

The writer claimed that as practical training for the pastoral ministry the theological colleges have failed and must fail. 'The chaplains and directors cannot take their disciples with them in a round of pastoral visits like surgical pupils at a clinical lecture.' You cannot practise pastoral work: 'the poor do not choose to be practised on experimentally'. If this be admitted, the only possible training which can be given is a special theological training. The best place for the study of theology is without question the university. The theological courses at the universities need reform. If they were reformed, we should not need theological colleges. To segregate the training of the clergy from all other training is to breed professionalism and exclusiveness. It has 'hitherto been the boast of our country that the clergy and laity, educated together, and separated by no mutual jealousy, have reciprocally exercised a beneficial influence on the formation of each other's character'. The young man, 'a sound Protestant perhaps in all essential points', acquires a rigid view that makes him identify discretion with compromise. He has, 'like a plant in a hot-house, been overstimulated by a forcing system of training'.

Theological colleges, in fact, breed party feeling; remote from pastoral cares, which demand discretion, they tend naturally to extravagance. And the circumstances of our age turn this trend to extravagance in the direction of the high church party.

The writer illustrated his point from Cuddesdon. Here we find an altar with flowers and lights, adorned with lace; rinsings in a piscina; genuflections; a service book 'concocted from the seven canonical hours of the Romish Church'. For some students theological colleges might be useful: but these colleges must command the public confidence, and Cuddesdon does not. 'That theological colleges should become the established door to entrance to the ministry would be the most disastrous blow the Church of England could receive.'

In the Oxford diocese Pott was hurt, and depressed, by this powerful article. It set a spark to the suspicions with which many dons and clergy regarded Wilberforce's foundation. 'It is evident', wrote Liddon in his diary, 'that this article in the *Quarterly Review* is doing us great harm.' Golightly seized the opportunity. On 28 January he issued a pamphlet to the clergy and laity of the diocese of Oxford, containing the relevant extracts from the *Quarterly Review* and a letter in which he alleged that the tendency of the college teaching was 'to sow broadcast the seeds of Romish perversion in the counties of Oxford, Berks and Bucks', and that he had remonstrated with the bishop 'in private but in vain'. The principal asked that the bishop would issue a commission to the three archdeacons of the diocese to examine the charges.

The archdeacons were appointed; and sat for four hours at the college on 6 February 1858. In a week they reported. They cleared the college of every one of Golightly's imputations. But their report did not content Liddon ('Less favourable than I expected'). It did suggest that the appurtenances of liturgy were not fully Anglican.

The attacks of the next eighteen months fell mostly upon Bishop Wilberforce as the person ultimately responsible. The bishop ran a college. That college was accused (1) of being a seminary; (2) of having its chapel colourful; (3) of having a prayer book that contained other prayers besides those of the Book of Common Prayer.

Wilberforce could either back Liddon or sack Liddon. To back Liddon would do his college, the Church and himself far more good – if he could back him successfully. That was what he wanted to do. And if the charges had remained only the three above, he would have succeeded, since nothing was wrong.

But this resolute policy became impossible when first one and then another of Liddon's pupils became a Roman Catholic. Then the charge was suddenly more shocking. 'This Anglican college, run by a famous bishop, has a close disciple of Dr Pusey on its staff, and he encourages young men to be Roman Catholic.'

Another incident, which had nothing to do with the controversy, affected what was to happen to Liddon.

John William Beale was a butler with a wife in Northamptonshire and was also the lover of a cook named Charlotte Pugsley at a gentleman's house near Bath. Liddon knew Beale when he was a butler in Bristol. In September 1857 Beale and Charlotte went walking in the woods near Bristol. On the following day a gamekeeper found her body among the undergrowth in a gorge, with a bullet through the head and her throat cut. When at last the body was identified, the search of Beale's room in Northamptonshire produced Charlotte's luggage, two pistols, and bullets of the same sort as the killer-bullet. Beale lied to the police about some lesser matters; and so the jury was quick to convict him. He was due for public hanging in January 1858.

Liddon not only knew Beale, and was at Taunton when the execution was to take place, but was the nephew of the surgeon to the gaol. Liddon saw Beale several times in his cell, and went through the Passion with him, and tried to bring him to confession, and called on him every day, and gave him the sacrament, which he received with much devotion. Liddon preached what was known as 'the condemned sermon' and took as his text Ecclesiastes 12.7, 'Then shall the dust return to the earth as it was; and the spirit shall return unto God who gave it.' He went out with Beale to the scaffold, where a crowd of 8,000–10,000 people were waiting. Beale expressed his gratitude for the kindness of Liddon and the chaplain to the gaol. Liddon noticed that he seemed to die without any severe struggle. Then he went to comfort Beale's widow, who was sure that her husband was guilty.

Someone at Bath with a wen in the neck applied for leave to touch the body because it would be a cure for the wen.

This connexion between Liddon, and Christ Church, and Cuddesdon, and a condemned murderer got national notice (*Times*, 13 January 1858). Naturally it deepened devotion to Liddon among the young men at Cuddesdon. Naturally it did nothing to diminish the suspicions of stout Protestants about a priest who was willing to communicate the sacrament of forgiveness to a brutal killer.

On 13 February 1858 Wilberforce resolved that the chapel walls be whitewashed and that Barff the chaplain must go. Liddon was told that Barff must go because he was so stiff and rigid. The *Record* (6 October 1858) thought that Barff had to go because of his 'extreme views' and because his brother and sister had become Roman Catholics. Liddon was very sorry at the sacking of Barff. He paid out money to help Barff furnish his new and distant vicarage.

Into Barff's place as chaplain Wilberforce appointed the curate of neighbouring Wheatley, Edward King. He was sane and normal and Wilberforce saw that now his college must avoid all surprising eccentricities.

Wilberforce had no way of saving his own reputation, or that of his college, with half England except by sacking Liddon also. But by now Liddon was quite a national figure in the Church. To sack him would hurt Wilberforce's reputation, and that of his college, with the other half of England. Therefore the bishop capered about. He advised Liddon to shave off his side-whiskers.

The altar-frontal was no longer changed in Advent or Lent. The painted murals of the saints and apostles were blotted out. The reredos which Street designed was removed. Flowers were no longer placed on the ledge behind the altar. Liddon was engaged upon the ungrateful task of revising his office-book. Right into the autumn the bishop worried Liddon about the length of his surplice, and his intentions of prayer at the sacrament, and the way he heard confession; and that when he celebrated the sacraments he wore on his arm a maniple.

In November, despite refusals by Wilberforce to accept resignation, Pott resigned the office of principal. Liddon was alarmed at what the bishop might do in choosing a new principal.

Liddon had good reason to fear that the bishop, in choosing Pott's successor, could not help being influenced by diplomacy. The friends of the bishop – his chaplains and eminent clergy – asked·themselves, what appointment will do most to right the bishop with the laity and the diocese? The group was strengthened by the conviction that it was useless to appoint anyone to the college unless it were a man under whose rule the college would survive. And if policy were to dictate the selection, Cuddesdon would receive a principal with whom Liddon might find it impossible to work.

The quest for a principal hovered over various names, all of which made Liddon uneasy. Actually, after what had happened, there was no one who could possibly be principal in anything but name if Liddon was there. Liddon was the son of a sea-captain and not born to be anyone's lieutenant. Meyrick? – inconvenient; rambling good-hearted Protestant. Burgon, the Dean of Oriel? – impossible; trenchant and amusing egoist. Robert Milman? – rough; but he understood the Oxford Movement, and Liddon wanted the bishop to appoint him. Swinny? – good man, but did he understand Catholicism? Wilberforce decided to offer it to Burgon, and if he refused, to Swinny. Liddon offered to work with Burgon, but it was an offer painful to make. Luckily Burgon refused. Part of his reason for refusing was that he would not accept the job unless Liddon were ejected, because he knew that they could not work together. Another reason for refusing was the stipend. He would not come unless it were made £500 a year. This demand Liddon thought disgraceful – until he discovered that Burgon needed the money to support his sister, and then he was penitent.

So Wilberforce appointed Swinny, who in Liddon's eyes had

the two demerits of being (a) a Cambridge man, and (b) a moderate. Swinny said that he was very sorry if any changes which he made should force Liddon to leave, but 'the feelings of religious evangelicals ought to be respected'. Liddon's comment on Swinny was that 'moderate opinions are not a fair and tolerable representation of the Revelation of God'.

In the autumn an ex-student was discovered to have become a Roman Catholic. Early in December 1858 one of the existing students, by name Francis Burnand, decided to become a Roman Catholic. He never liked Liddon, and Liddon always distrusted him. Later in life he was to be famous as the editor of *Punch*. This event made Wilberforce think that after all Liddon must be an influence for turning Anglican ordinands into Roman Catholics. He accused him to his face of spending most of his time reading Roman Catholic books. 'I told him that he was mistaken.'[3] Wilberforce criticized the content of one of his sermons. He complained that Liddon had not obeyed his rules about ritual.

The situation was beyond the point of being impossible for Liddon. Yet John Keble, whom he visited at Hursley (19 December 1858) pressed him to do his best work at Cuddesdon, and to give up all unnecessary ceremonial, and to 'submit to any alteration of the devotional system of the college'. On the way back he called on Butler in Wantage and received much the same advice – 'make the most of the position – difficult and trying as it has undoubtedly become'.

Keble and Butler and Robert Milman and probably Pusey – Liddon never knew about Pusey because he was not allowed by Wilberforce to ask him – believed that the issue of the Oxford Movement lay in raising the ideals of the clergy; that Cuddesdon was the chosen instrument to make this ideal practical; and that Liddon was the person inside Cuddesdon who had a chance of making the ideal come alive. Therefore they were agreed that Liddon must stay. This was tough doctrine. They were agreed that Liddon must stay even if it were almost impossible for him, in conscience, to stay. And Edward King, the new chaplain, who

---

[3] Liddon made a list of what he had read during eleven months of 1858. It is an interesting list. Some of the early Fathers; quite a lot of Anglican divinity of the seventeenth century; two German commentaries on the Old Testament; Mansel; F. W. Newman; Gibbon's *Decline and Fall*; Kingsley's sermons; Lancelot Andrewes, *Preces privatae*. The only Roman Catholic author in the list was the French Jesuit Surin (1600–65): the work, his spiritual letters.

was a personal comfort to Liddon, was discovered by Liddon to think that he could hardly stay.

Liddon had already endured a bishop telling him to shave off his whiskers. He had already endured a bishop accusing him of spending his time reading Roman Catholic books. For the sake of obeying Keble's order to stay, he now had to endure worse.

Wilberforce at last was bored with his college. It gave him nothing but trouble, bad publicity, and embarrassment. He found himself accused of insincerity because he said one thing and his college did another; and the reproach of insincerity, because it so long stuck to his name in legend, was a charge to which he was sensitive. It now bothered him that some of the ordinands were so *peculiar*. Why should they wear 'neckcloths of peculiar construction, coats of peculiar cut, whiskers of peculiar dimensions'? He observed what he took to be a sort of high church gait – perhaps Newman's famous glide but more probably mere imitation of Liddon by young men who admired him. He listened to a strange way of reading lessons. He decided that some of them were an effeminate lot – without vigour or virility – 'they come out too much cut out by a machine'. Then, when he went into the students' rooms, he was alarmed by the number of pictures of the Blessed Virgin (which he had asked should disappear) and by the crosses on the chimney-pieces, and when he went into chapel he observed a sort of apparent raptness which he took to be ostentation. He found all this 'a heavy affliction'. He was bored with his college, and the way its affairs were conducted. It could not be denied that under the last principal and in the present interregnum Liddon was the conductor. Such sentiments were very unpersuasive to Liddon. He was the last person to think that muscular Christianity, 'boisterousness' as he thought of it, was a leading quality for a priest.

Liddon was shattered by the new rules with which the bishop and the new principal crowded him. Wilberforce stopped him hearing the confessions of the students. He tried to stop him teaching the Real Presence as the Anglican doctrine of the Eucharist. Liddon replied that he could not honestly consent not to teach what seemed to be part of revealed truth. Then Wilberforce said he must not hear the confessions of any former students. This shattered Liddon, because it was something which the bishop had no right whatever to demand. He found it 'a terrible letter'.

He sent in his resignation to the bishop. He found that Butler and Edward King agreed that he was right. On 29 January 1859 informally, on 5 February formally, Wilberforce accepted the resignation. Two days later Liddon caused a sensation among the students by announcing that he was going.

What was he to do next, this able and learned and devout young Tractarian, this closest disciple of Dr Pusey, who in physique was evidently not strong enough to be curate in an English parish, and in personality was too strong to be anywhere else? Swinny told him to take a long holiday. Someone was foolish enough to suggest that he go to India as a missionary (it was the year of the Indian Mutiny). Lancing College, lately founded, offered him the chaplaincy. His friend Benson told him not to accept. 'I feel regularly stranded. My first great attempt at work in life has failed. This no doubt is good for my character.'

Butler had the best idea. Liddon was a Student of Christ Church and thereby had rights in the University of Oxford and a small stipend. Why not settle in Oxford, and study, and do what pastoral ministry he could? The decision was clinched by Dr Pusey. Liddon already had a lot of Hebrew and a little Syriac. Pusey wanted him in Oxford to develop his study of Oriental languages and so help with the commentary on the Bible which Pusey edited. He offered him lodgings in his own house in the corner of Tom Quad. But then the Principal of St Edmund Hall, Dr Barrow, offered him the divinity lectureship at the college; and later, with it, the office of vice-principal. Liddon was nervous about accepting. He remembered his second class as an undergraduate and doubted whether he could teach the classics. By the end of March 1859 his rooms at St Edmund Hall were being measured for book shelves. His pupils presented him with a testimonial, seventy-three volumes of theology. On 26 April 1859 a waggon was needed to transport his books to St Edmund Hall.

That day happened to be a bad day for Cuddesdon: probably its worst day ever. Another student had become a Roman Catholic, and on that day returned to try to persuade still others to become Roman Catholics. He had to be ejected by force.

Liddon had things still to do for the college which now he was not allowed to serve. He persuaded students not to leave because he left. He persuaded his former students not to withdraw their support from the college. He accepted invitations to help Wilberforce in the diocese. His funeral sermon on Wilberforce was to be generous. After Edward King succeeded Swinny as Principal of Cuddesdon, he recovered his own hopes for the college. But when years later he drafted the life of Pusey, the critique of Wilberforce was devastating. In his huge four-volume life of Pusey, he excluded every mention of Cuddesdon, except as a palace for the Bishop of Oxford.

And meanwhile, he thought that in Oxford he had work to do. Dr Pusey imagined that he was coming to Oxford to be an academic. He knew perfectly well that his vocation in life was religious rather than academic. 'I think', he wrote to his sister, 'it would be possible to turn St Edmund Hall into a little Christian Fortress in the midst of the Rationalism and Indifferentism which lay modern Oxford waste.'

In this not realistic plan, he did not altogether succeed. But the plan was adapted to circumstances. The fulfilment of this fortress-mentality came eight years later, in the most famous course of Bampton Lectures ever given in Oxford. This was the course of lectures about the truth of the Bible and the Incarnation, *The Divinity of Our Lord Jesus Christ*. These lectures hurled the old faith at the heads of dons and undergraduates and at the world; with learning, force, devastation of the follies of opponents, and no power to persuade waverers. They turned Liddon overnight into one of the leaders of Victorian religion, a place he kept till his death. Some people thought then and later that Liddon's Bamptons recovered for the Oxford Movement the intellectual force in English religious ideas that it partly lost when Newman ended his career in the Church of England.

Chapter 12

THE CHOICE OF BISHOPS

In Lutheran Europe, and Zwinglian Europe, the Reformation imposed control of Churches by the State; for freedom, prosperity, and the reform of ecclesiastical corruption were believed to lie, and at that date usually did lie, with the power of princes or city councils. In Calvinist Europe the theory was very different but might issue (as with the Palatinate, or for most of the time in Scotland or in Holland) in much the same result. England was not at all unique in subjecting the Church to the sovereign State. It was only unique in having a more traditional polity in the Church that was subjected to the sovereign State. Throughout the reign of Queen Victoria this subjection hardly altered, though most of the environment or context altered.

Before the Reformation the sovereign appointed bishops. The Pope's approval was needed, but was mostly nominal. The Reformation abolished the Pope and left not even a nominal check. The State could only choose priests, already selected by bishops. The State did very well; to choose Cranmer, or Latimer, or Andrewes, or even Laud, showed that big men were there to choose and that the State was not frightened of choosing big men. The Reformation sovereigns milked the Church by keeping sees vacant, not by making corrupt appointments.

Queen Victoria, therefore, chose all the bishops consecrated or translated in her reign.

When I say *she chose*, the constitutional convention had grown that the sovereign could only act on the advice of his or her ministers. No one knew quite how far this rule extended. The only sanction seemed to be, the Prime Minister can threaten to resign if the Queen fails to do what he wants, and if he resigns on a weighty issue, he will leave the Queen the most unpopular person in the country and create a movement towards a republic. But it was obvious that this could only apply to weighty matters of policy. If Lord John Russell said that he advised the Queen to nominate X for the see of St Asaph, and then the Queen said that she would not accept the advice because X was an ignoramus, and then Lord John Russell resigned on such a triviality, the Prime Minister would look silly in the eyes of the nation. He would look very silly if X was an ignoramus, and rather silly even if X was not, or not very.

This was not at first perceived; the Queen did not perceive it herself in her earlier years. She knew little enough about the Church, and bore and brought up her children. Prince Albert gave a deal of advice on ecclesiastical appointments, but coming from Coburg he found it hard to understand the Church of England and harder to know about the people from whom the State must choose its bishops. For the Crown to exercise an influence on the choice of bishops, its occupant must know a lot. The Prime Minister might not know a lot, but he had all the staff he needed to take private advice. At first the Queen was in no such situation. The Prime Minister was far more likely than she to know whether X was an ignoramus or a good divine.

Therefore the earlier Prime Ministers of the reign were very decisive: Melbourne, Peel, Russell, Palmerston. So far at least as bishops were concerned, the Queen did what they wanted. She protested to Lord Aberdeen that he nominated a Tractarian without telling her. This was Liddon's friend Walter Kerr Hamilton, who was a vicar of St Peter's-in-the-East in Oxford while Newman was vicar of St Mary's and fell under the influence of his neighbour and was made Bishop of Salisbury in 1854 after Professor J. J. Blunt of Cambridge had refused the see. The Queen told the Prime Minister that she considered 'Puseyite tendencies' to be fatal to the Church. Aberdeen was gently firm with her. He told her that Hamilton was moderate – actually he was quiet and gentle rather than moderate. There was talk of questioning the appointment in Parliament, but that was unconstitutional and nothing came of the idea.

Nevertheless, even though the Queen was less powerful in nearly everything than the King of Prussia, she had one great advantage. England never took to a Minister for Cults or for Church Affairs. There never existed before the second quarter of the twentieth century a high civil servant one of whose principal duties was the selection and appointment of leaders in the Church. England never had an Altenstein. If the Queen was ignorant about clergymen to select, some Prime Ministers were equally ignorant if not more ignorant. Palmerston pretended to know nothing about these matters. He knew more than he pretended, but what he knew was not much. Disraeli knew very little, and also pretended to know less than he did, and was amused at the incongruity of his situation, the son of a converted Jew choosing Christian leaders; but he could not doubt the rightness of the system, and was at times to use it to his own political ends. It was with Gladstone that the Queen first met a Prime Minister who knew as much about the Church and churchmen as any layman of the established Church. He was a devout high Anglican, was personally engaged in almost every ecclesiastical controversy of her reign, and cared very much about the kind of man who should hold high office in the Church.

The Queen began to exercise a real influence on Church appointments with the arrival into office of Disraeli. First, she was near to coming out of her retirement as a widow and began again to take an interest in government. Secondly, she had in Disraeli a Prime Minister who wanted to be charming to her, knew how to gain her good will and use her influence in weightier matters, and was perfectly ready to give way to her on anything he thought less important; and he was so constituted that there were quite a number of things in the world which he thought less important; and the precise choice of bishops was one of those things. The spectacular sign of the Queen's new power was shown in 1868 when Tait became Archbishop of Canterbury. Disraeli did not want Tait. He strongly pressed another name on the Queen. He wanted several before Tait. None of the possibilities was a Tractarian. Disraeli pressed the New Testament scholar C. J. Ellicott, a good man and a learned divine but with a weak-sounding manner and probably not strong. Disraeli argued to the Queen that Tait was 'obscure in purpose, fitful and inconsistent in action, and evidently, though earnest and conscientious, a prey to constantly conflicting convictions. There is in his idiosyncrasy a strange fund of enthusiasm, a quality which should never be possessed by an Archbishop of Canterbury, or a

Prime Minister of England. But what Mr Disraeli deems the most dangerous feature in the Bishop's character is the peculiar influence which Neology has upon his mind; not one of elevation and cheerfulness, but one which, while it fascinates, disheartens him, and which is likely to involve him in terrible and perhaps fatal embarrassments.' It is hard to imagine a more negative letter from a Prime Minister about someone whom he had the responsibility of recommending. After such a letter it is extraordinary that Tait became archbishop. Either Disraeli did not want anyone else very much, or his advisers told him that Tait would be adequate. The choice is a sign of real power, prerogative power, in the Queen. It also boded ill for the Tractarians.

Gladstone cared far more than Disraeli, and was much tougher with the Queen. He also worried much more about doing the best thing. The Queen suspected Gladstone's advice on all subjects. Since he was a Tractarian layman and she thought Tractarianism destructive of the Church of England, she was likely to think his suggestions for bishops lamentable. He needed to be well-armoured in his approaches to her.

The change began, quite dramatically, not with the choice of a bishop, but in the chapter of St Paul's Cathedral; which mattered less to the Queen. In 1869 Gladstone nominated Liddon to be a canon of St Paul's and so brought again a leading Tractarian into a post of ecclesiastical influence in the capital. The choice could be defended on the grounds that the duty was to preach and that this man of the Oxford Movement was known to be a preacher of excellence. He was also by now a distinguished personality in his own right. Then in the very next year Gladstone had to select a new Dean of St Paul's. He brought in, from an obscure country rectory in the West Country, Richard Church. The appointment was not so odd as it looked, for Deans of St Paul's were expected to be able to wield a pen, and Church had already won acclaim as an essayist on history and literature, who could write English prose. Nevertheless, within two years to appoint to the chapter of St Paul's the intimate of Dr Pusey and one of the intimates of Newman made a dramatic change in the exercise of the patronage of the Crown.

All this had a weighty consequence in the Victorian establishment. The Queen could not affect or influence an informed

Prime Minister without being herself informed. She had a private secretary, but she had no extended civil service at her disposal. What she had was the Dean of Windsor, who was the nearest thing to a private chaplain that she possessed. At the beginning of her reign the Dean of Windsor was useless for these purposes, a dinosaur from the eighteenth century out of touch with men or events in the new reign.[1] But in 1854 Gerald Wellesley became Dean of Windsor. He was the nephew of the great Duke of Wellington and therefore had an aura of prestige; and, equally important, he had his uncle's laconic common sense. Almost at once he started to use his position close to the Crown to get more idealism, and less political interest, into the system of choosing bishops. He did not like Lord Palmerston's methods, and began the process by which the sovereign tried to turn the exercise of patronage rather into a way of benefiting the Church than a way of bolstering a Prime Minister or fostering his political party.[2]

The development of representative government during Queen Victoria's reign encouraged the coherence of political parties. In Parliament whips started to wield more power. The number of independent members of the House of Commons declined. The Church did not suffer much if a Whig Prime Minister chose Whig bishops and a Tory Prime Minister chose Tory bishops, because the parties sufficiently alternated in power and it was good for the Church that both the main parties in the State should be represented among its leaders. But as the press developed from a local press into a national, and the fourth Estate began its work in public opinion, the Church suffered by being seen to be a political instrument. That Lord Palmerston chose a Whig for a bishop might be very good personally if, as always, the man were a good man. But it was not good in public esteem if it happened unvaryingly. The Church came to look like a political agent of government. And by the middle of the reign of Queen Victoria this idea was abhorrent to a lot of Englishmen. The nineteenth century had experienced a religious revival. Basic to that revival

---

[1] This dean was the Honourable Lewis Hobart, the fourth son of the Earl of Buckinghamshire. He was one of the old-fashioned pluralists. In 1845, as well as being Dean of Windsor, he was dean of the collegiate church at Wolverhampton; vicar of Wantage in Berkshire, rector of Haseley, Oxfordshire and vicar of Nocton, Lincolnshire.

[2] For Gerald Wellesley's part, see especially Monypenny and Buckle, *Life and Letters of Benjamin Disraeli, Earl of Beaconsfield*, vol. 5, pp. 58ff.

was the ideal of making the Church and its clergy less worldly. Political appointments to bishoprics cried aloud that the world took over the otherworldly society for its own very worldly aims.

Consciously Dean Wellesley began the process of trying to free the patronage system from the political swings and roundabouts. The choice of Tait for the See of Canterbury in 1868 was a stage in his endeavour, for Tait was not quite of Disraeli's politics. Once Tait was archbishop, Wellesley's endeavours became easier. Tait lost several children in an epidemic of scarlet fever, and the compassionate Queen felt very close in heart to someone who suffered so terrible a tragedy in the home. For the first time an Archbishop of Canterbury began to be a routine part of the system of choosing bishops. The Prime Minister would suggest a name; the Queen would ask the Dean of Windsor; if the Dean had scruples, she would tell the Prime Minister that she doubted, and would demand to know what the archbishop thought of the selection. In this way the sovereign's power brought to bear upon the Prime Minister the opinions of two men, the Archbishop of Canterbury and the Dean of Windsor, who both wanted to keep politics out of the system. By means of the sovereign's personal power, the Church began to exert a not insignificant influence in the choice of its own leaders.

Dean Wellesley died in 1882. That was a bad year for him to die, because Archbishop Tait died a few months later, and Wellesley's absence produced less than the best appointment to the See of Canterbury. The dying Tait wanted Browne of Winchester, who would have made a better archbishop but was already seventy-two years old and had not strong health. If Tait could not have Browne he preferred Benson to any other, Benson then being the first bishop of the newly founded See of Truro. Benson was no Tractarian but he sometimes sounded as though he were. Dean R. W. Church of St Paul's, whose judgment Gladstone preferred to that of any other ecclesiastic, and whom even Gladstone thought of as a possible archbishop at this moment, wanted Benson, no doubt in part on party grounds, but not only on such grounds. 'He is quiet, and he is enthusiastic, and he is conciliatory, and he is firm.' The Queen wanted Browne. Wellesley before he died wanted Browne. Most other bishops wanted Browne. Gladstone won. Benson became Arch-bishop of Canterbury. The two Tractarians in the system of appointment defeated everyone else because the Prime Minister was one of them and because he trusted Richard Church.

The Queen's idea, actually, was better. Benson had not been in all respects a good headmaster, and was a classical scholar, but knew little theology. The things in his favour were that he looked like an archbishop and that he was only fifty-three and full of energy and organizing power. It is not unimportant that arch-bishops should look like archbishops. It is desirable that they should have energy and organizing power. But it is most desirable that they should have judgment. The willingness of Archbishop Benson to try Bishop Edward King on ridiculous charges over petty matters of ritual afterwards remained a permanent stain on his reputation.

Harold Browne was a theologian with a fair mind. He had, it is true, published an exposition of the Thirty-Nine Articles which was useful to ordinands, and any one who did that was sure to be accused of heresy by somebody. Though his health was not good he lasted another seven years before needing to resign the See of Winchester. If it is desirable for an archbishop to have experience of the parishes of the Church of England, Browne had far more of it than Benson. It was an even argument. But it is not certain that the two Tractarians were right in their selection.

At once the Queen quarrelled with Gladstone over the choice of a new Dean of Windsor to succeed Wellesley. Without asking the Prime Minister she invited a canon of Winchester, George Henry Connor. She had known him in the Isle of Wight at Osborne and liked him and made him one of her chaplains. She never saw any reason to regret the choice, except that he had neither the knowledge of men, nor the knowledge of the Church, nor the judgment, to be able to do for her what Dean Wellesley had done: to resist Prime Ministers when they were likely to appoint a less than satisfactory bishop.

But what was the constitution? Had the Queen the power to appoint a Dean of Windsor without taking the advice of the Prime Minister? Either view was possible in the constitutional tradition. Gladstone was indignant. And perhaps he was the more indignant because the choice had few merits except that the

Queen's principal chaplain ought to be someone whom she trusts in religion and likes as a person. Gladstone objected to the Queen by-passing what he regarded as his constitutional right. Henceforth Deans of Windsor were and are appointed nominally on the advice of the Prime Minister, but the Queen got and gets the person whom she wants.

Connor died after only a few months (Dean 10 October 1882; died 1 May 1883). The Queen selected Randall Davidson. He had no distinction in his previous career but was the intimate friend of Archbishop Tait's son, and four years before had married Archbishop Tait's daughter and only surviving child after the epidemic and the death of the son. It was a sure way to the Queen's heart, especially when he was able to report to her the circumstances of Archbishop Tait's death-bed. That made him a marked man in her eyes. Even before he was Dean of Windsor she consulted him about whether Harold Browne or Benson should be archbishop and found that he thought Harold Browne's health not up to the work ahead. Through his marriage to Miss Tait and his chaplaincy of Tait he already had a wide knowledge of the bishops of the Church of England.

But Davidson was only thirty-five years old. Gladstone said he was too young to be Dean of Windsor. It was a big argument, but the Queen got her way. And Benson, the new archbishop, was satisfied that young though he might be, Davidson would be able to perform the function of being an unconstitutional adviser (as Lord Palmerston had called the office) about the arguments over the choice of bishops.

The choice was excellent. He not only had experience, but a wise head. The system set up by Wellesley and Tait continued almost as though it was never interrupted, the more easily because two of the prime ministers till the end of the reign, Gladstone and Salisbury, were devout Anglicans. Since both the Archbishops of Canterbury after Tait were not very effective in these matters – Benson because he was a vacillator, a courtier, and a man of complexities in the psyche, Frederick Temple because he was so ancient as to have little knowledge of the coming men in the Church – the Queen's personal brake upon the Prime Minister grew even more important. Frequently she would veto the Prime Minister's first choice, and Lord Salisbury at least cheerfully or sadly accepted the veto. She would still demand to know what the archbishop thought, but really it was her opinion rather than the archbishop's which counted; and her opinion was more formed, and better formed, by a Dean of Windsor with youth on his side and broad sympathies among a wide variety of church-men. The appointments were good. At the top they were marked by that excess of caution which was to be Davidson's chief problem all his life. Temple became Archbishop of Canterbury, at the age of seventy-six; and it is true, with archbishops as with popes, that if a man is elected at the age of seventy-six, the explanation can only be that some more exciting person needs to be excluded. Still, if they were sometimes cautious, they were partly learned and partly pastoral.

And some of them, at least a few, were Tractarians. At last they had reached the bishoprics not just as exceptional, like Walter Kerr Hamilton of Salisbury, but as a normal share in the patronage of the Crown. The earliest was Woodford to the See of Ely in 1873. But then, when Benson was archbishop, and Richard Church was still Dean of St Paul's, and the fair-minded Davidson was Dean of Windsor, and the leaders of both political parties were dedicated laymen, several more came into sees: the historian Stubbs to Chester in 1884, to Oxford in 1889; John Wordsworth to Salisbury in 1885; Edward King to Lincoln in the same year; in 1890 – as a climax – after the Queen had frustrated earlier attempts to get Liddon offered a see, Liddon was offered the see of St Albans, but refused as he had refused earlier soundings. In the Queen's eyes it was rather like making Dr Pusey a bishop. And then, though Richard Church died in 1890, there came another – Talbot, formerly friend and colleague of Liddon and King, to St Albans in 1895. They were not in many sees; and none of them was as yet in one of the five leading sees. But their numbers were sufficient. The movement could be seen to be an accepted and continuing part of the life and leadership of the Church of England.

—⊃ *Chapter 13* ⊂—

EDWARD KING

I EDUCATION

King was born on 29 December 1829. He was the third child and second son of Walker King, Archdeacon of Rochester and rector of Stone near Dartford in Kent. On the walls of Stone church may still be seen memorials to members of King's family. He was educated privately by his father's curate, and then at Oriel College, Oxford from 1848 to 1851. He learned Italian, and became a lover of Dante's poetry; acquired a permanent interest in botany, and always remained at heart a lover of the country-side; and became an excellent horseman.

His mother, Anne Heberden, was a charming, beautiful, and Christian woman, and from her Edward derived both religion and an enchanting courtesy. He went up to Oxford already religious in outlook, carefully attending the services of his college chapel. One of the college exercises was to attend university or other sermons and summarize them for a tutor's inspection. A notebook of the undergraduate King, full of such summaries, is in the Lincolnshire archives.[1] One of his tutors commented, 'Fair. Your sentences are very long and straggling.' It was a lesson which he learned, for no one could talk more directly and simply. His health was delicate, and he read for a pass degree. Never in his life was he tempted to put an excessive value on examinations as a test of education. He became a much more educated man, in the broad sense, than many with better records in examinations.

His undergraduate years coincided with a time of crisis in the Church of England. One of the Fellows of his College, the poet Clough, was just then agonizing himself out of Christianity; another, H. J. Coleridge, was agonizing himself out of the Church

[1] Misc. dep. 46. 5.

of England. The pulpits and common rooms of Oxford were not silent on the subjects which disturbed men's minds – the authority of the Church, its relations with the State, limits of doctrine. We find no traces of these disturbances in King. One of the secrets of his later power was the naturalness of his faith. Faith was nothing strange in the world. The love of God was never fanatical or irrational. It was man's true home. King had no experience of conversion. It is doubtful whether a soul who experienced such turmoil of mind could have conveyed the sense which King always conveyed of a perfect harmony between nature and grace.

Charles Marriott was the Dean of Oriel during King's first two years. His dusty floor was heaped with books and papers in disorder, his clothes were shabby, his rooms looked, said a friend,[2] like the ruins of a sacked and plundered library. He was a childlike and wholly delightful scholar. King came to know him well, and would often quote from Marriott, or say 'If I have any good in me, I owe it to Charles Marriott.'[3]

We do not quite know in what King's debt consisted. King was brought up a high churchman, in the sense which almost identified a high churchman with a strong member of the Tory party. Marriott was a high churchman after the new sort, Newman's disciples. But he was an unusual kind of high churchman. In those years after they lost Newman, the high churchmen were unpopular, and their leaders could hardly help a posture of defence. They sometimes adopted the mentality of guards in a fortress. One of their greatest hymns sang of the hosts of Midian prowling and prowling around the holy place. But Marriott was hardly touched by this mentality. His faith was always hopeful. And this same optimism, and extraordinary hopefulness even in adverse circumstances, came to mark King.

Perhaps King meant something else when he talked of his debt to Marriott. In King's first year at Oxford Marriott published a plain little book called *Hints on Private Devotion*. It is not at all an important book. But it contains a sober grave devotion of mind, elevated by a sense of the unseen world, and of a hidden music praising God all about us. Perhaps the debt lay in such a type or quality of devotion.

[2] J. W. Burgon, *The Lives of Twelve Good Men*, vol. I, p. 342.
[3] Ibid., p. 372.

Another don at Oriel in those years said of King, 'He is such an one as the best and holiest were when they were young.'[4]

2 CUDDESDON

When he left Oxford he travelled to see Palestine, and after a spell as tutor to the sons of Lord Lothian he was ordained by Bishop Wilberforce of Oxford to be curate at Wheatley, six miles east of Oxford, on 11 June 1854. After four years as curate Bishop Wilberforce made him chaplain at Cuddesdon; he had lately built the college opposite the gates of his palace. King was chaplain of Cuddesdon for five years, and was then (1863) made its principal. For fifteen years his work consisted in training men who had graduated at a university and were now preparing to be ordained.

In those years the Church of England had very few theological colleges, and such as it had were suspect to many good men. Clergymen received a good general education but little special training for the work. King was trained by no one in particular when he took holy orders. The incumbent was conceived as an educated gentleman in the parish. Find an educated gentleman and put him in the parish – that was all that was necessary.

The movements of society changed these ideas rapidly. The notion of the educated gentleman in the parish could easily be satirized. It was sometimes caricatured by novelists. It looked more suitable to a rustic and feudal age. England was becoming a country of cities and industry. They were years also when educated minds were troubled, partly over science and partly over the Bible. The Church needed clergy who were better equipped by special training for their task. And the universities, just then at the beginning of their voyage into the modern age, were less and less suited to supply what was needed. Theological colleges had become necessary. But they were unpopular. They were suspected of breeding partisans, and of making men remote from the world with which they would have to do. Cuddesdon was bitterly attacked in the press during King's early years there as chaplain.

From 1863 to 1873 King established the college in the eyes of

[4] J. W. Burgon to Samuel Wilberforce, 6 March 1854, Wilberforce Papers.

the Church of England, and with it the system of postgraduate training which it represented.

To the indifferent world he established it because he was a sensible man without fuss. To those who knew its inward life, there was much more to find. Cuddesdon, high on its hill, is a smiling village with a beautiful church. Those who wrote reminiscences of the college in King's time seemed to feel as though the natural beauty which surrounded them was somehow reflected in the moral character of their principal. They talked of him as happy, alive, sympathetic, delicate; and all these qualities were in some mysterious manner holy as well as natural. He was an English gentleman in an age when the natural home of the English gentleman was the deep countryside. He was a country vicar (the principal was also vicar of the parish) in an age when country incumbents were still the accepted norm of ministry in England. And they associated him with their first penetration of the depth and poetry in religion. The language which some of them used is extraordinary. Robert Milman visited Cuddesdon and said, 'It was like a breath from the garden of Eden before the door was shut.'

The Lincolnshire archives possess a little group of letters from former students during the years when he was chaplain.[5]

When he became principal in 1863 he was aged thirty-three, and still immature. During the sixties the growth of his personality was marked. He always retained what he called a suffering sense of diffidence. But as he grew in knowledge and responsibility, it ceased to hamper. By 1871 to 1873 he became one of the famous preachers and conductors of retreats. In the *Dictionary of National Biography* the statement appears that King was no orator. The author, G. W. E. Russell, must have judged King by the standard of his last and declining years. There is a mass of evidence to prove the contrary, during the seventies. A country clergyman who persuaded King to conduct a retreat thought the addresses 'marvellous' in their searching of conscience and knowledge of human nature. He also thought them exceedingly clever and thoughtful.[6]

He ran his little college – usually there were only twenty

---

[5] King dep. 2.
[6] *Memoir of Walsham How*, p. 96.

students – as a cheerful kind of democracy. His favourite text from the Bible was 'Thy gentleness hath made me great.' George Richmond painted a portrait of King which afterwards King gave to Cuddesdon College and which now hangs in the college dining hall. It is a superlative portrait, and most men outside Lincoln imagine that this was how King looked. It is the portrait of a strong man. King's friends did not altogether like this portrait. They thought it not gentle enough for the reality. But Richmond saw something true. 'God', said King once, 'has not given me a *chin* for nothing.'[7] Those who go to Pusey House and read in the archives the letters of Miss Frances Heurtley will find there a letter from King (16 November 1883) which must be one of the most severe letters ever addressed by a pastor to a soul asking for advice.

3 OXFORD PROFESSORSHIP

In February 1873 the Prime Minister, Mr Gladstone, offered King the professorship of Moral and Pastoral Theology at Oxford. To this chair a canonry at Christ Church was attached.

The offer did not lack critics.

King by this time was well known; not famous, but well known among those whose opinions counted in the Church. He made a much-discussed speech at the Church Congress in Leeds during the autumn of the previous year. And one of his Cuddesdon pupils was Stephen Gladstone, son of the Prime Minister. When those within the high counsels of state realized that King was a possible professor, they were perturbed, and tried to stop the appointment. King was well known as a high churchman, and those who were afraid of high churchmen, including Archbishop Tait of Canterbury, represented to the Prime Minister that he would be undesirable as a professor. Moreover, though universities are hardly interested in whether one of their professors has a pass degree, they are interested in having professors engaged in academic study and hard reading, perhaps even in writing. Even the high church leaders at Oxford would have preferred another professor.[8] 'I shall be very sorry', wrote the Archbishop of

7 Randolph and Townroe, *The Mind and Work of Edward King* (1918), p. 8.
8 Cf. BL Add. MSS 44237, 72 and 76.

Canterbury, 'if the appointment you mention takes place, for I fear it will greatly shake public confidence in the theological school at Oxford.'[9]

Gladstone knew his aim. He had just passed a measure which, at least in large part, prised the universities away from their traditional connexion with the Church of England. Some accused him of making the universities non-Christian. Some accused him of making it impossible for the universities any longer to train the clergy of the established Church. Gladstone wanted to encourage the universities, in despite, to continue their work in training clergymen. If he could take a man of proved excellence in such work, and put him at the heart of a great university, he would give Oxford a chance of fulfilling its old duty.

The announcement was greeted with surprise. In the House of Commons an MP asked rudely for King's qualifications for the professorship. Gladstone replied gently. 'It was a more personal charge than the other professors of divinity, and the gentleman appointed . . . should be possessed of strong sympathies and of the power of exercising a healthy and beneficial influence over character; and from his experience, of some duration, he believed Mr King . . . possessed those qualifications not only . . . in an ordinary but in an eminent degree.'[10] At Oxford a truculent don published a pamphlet against all the high churchmen in the neighbourhood, and expressed the 'greatest distrust' of the new professor.[11] When King moved with his mother into the canon's house at Christ Church (the house was in Tom Quad, on the east side next to the cathedral) prankish undergraduates hung a surplice upon the lamp-post outside.[12]

King entered the controversial time of his life. All his days so far had been quiet, calm, retired. He was not rigid, or viewy, or embattled. He was Protestant, in the sense of thinking the Church of Rome to be in error. He believed that the high churchmen were right to encourage and deepen the understanding of the sacraments, thought that many would be helped in their spiritual life by using the permission for confession provided in the Prayer

[9] Tait to Gladstone, 24 February 1873, Tait papers at Lambeth: copy in Lincolnshire Archives, Misc. Don. Eccl. 4. 10.
[10] Hansard, 3rd series, 215, 402.
[11] W. E. Jelf, *Quousque? How far? How long?* (1873).
[12] Randolph-Townroe, p. 65.

Book, and wanted a due and orderly reverence in external things. But he was so moderate that controversy should not have touched him.

He felt himself to be unsuitable for his professorship. He was more suitable than he looked. He was widely read among the moral theologians. His new colleague William Bright, the eminent church historian, regarded him as among the most intellectual persons whom he knew. His French and German and Italian were fluent. He wrote good English prose. He looked at every problem with independence and originality. Looking back he said that he was academically nothing when he arrived in Oxford.[13] The humility stood in the way of his academic, as distinct from his pastoral, influence. For all his reading he never quite regarded himself as a reading man. He could commit the classical fault of a non-academical preacher before an academic congregation, by heaping up dull dry quotations for the sake of learning. Occasionally he thought it his duty to try to sound philosophical, and all Oxford agreed that this would not do. '*I* should not choose the university to work in', he wrote, 'if I had my choice. I would rather be with the simplest agricultural poor, but it is not so arranged'.[14]

This sense, of not quite having what was needed, hampered him at Oxford. He never became a power among dons, nor did he ever exercise a wide influence on the university *as an institution*.

King started reading for a big book on moral theology. He read much in the writings of the early Fathers of the Church, and in the controversies of the Jesuits, and became especially interested in the ethical theories of Bishop Sailer, a German moral theologian of the beginning of the century. But the book was not written. Probably it never could have been written, even if he had been allowed longer than twelve years at Oxford. He was too interested in people. He had no defence against callers who wanted help. The longer he was at Oxford, the less time he found free of interruption. Undergraduates were the most frequent callers. But college servants consulted him, young dons, resident ladies, and he was prodigal of time for interviews. He was in

[13] *Love and Wisdom*, p. 134.
[14] *Spiritual Letters*, p. 54.

demand as a conductor of parish retreats and did not think it right to refuse. He was asked to hear many confessions, and all over England lived old pupils who pressed him for help, advice, judgment. He was a poor hand at saying no.

He lectured each term: one course on Hooker, one on the Ordinal, one on pastoral theology. Listeners were agreed that the best of his courses was that on pastoral theology, and best of all when he came to the subject of preaching. The notes for these pastoral lectures survived and have been published.[15] Even from the bare notes and headings the quality of the lectures can be discerned. He lectured in his own house, standing in the doorway between study and dining-room, and dressed in a cassock. The undergraduates were amused at the range of books which he recommended them to read in their study of moral theology. These ranged from the *Baptist Yearbook* to the *Ignatian Exercises*, from the *Catena* of Chinese Buddhism to the best sporting novels.[16]

His outside duties included the encouragement of missions in India, and in East and South Africa. Men came to consult him on names for colonial bishoprics, and he helped to found the Oxford Mission to Calcutta. He also helped to found St Stephen's House as a theological college in Oxford, and Lady Margaret Hall as a women's college despite stern opposition to such feminine education from eminent men among his colleagues. He encouraged the temperance movement among the college servants, though he was never himself a total abstainer, and was prominent in the White Cross League, which did what it could to save girls from being prostitutes. On the governing body of the college he needed to give his mind to the reconstruction of the belfry, or the reredos; to whether it was right to build an inn at Alverstoke station; to electing scholars and managing property, the price of breakfast, the patronage of benefices, to an occasional meeting of the governing body to discipline a troublesome undergraduate. Such matters were not King's happiest calling, and he did not find himself on many college committees. He did more for the great library than for any other college interest. He was also said to be

---

15 Eric Graham, *The Pastoral Lectures of Bishop King*.
16 *Guardian* (1885), 527.

the only one of the canons whom the boys of the choir school could understand and love.[17]

None of these various duties quite overcame his sense that it was strange for him to be a professor. 'I often feel so useless in Oxford', he wrote, 'that I am tempted to all sorts of naughty ideas.'[18]

It felt a strain to be in the Oxford of the seventies. It was the age of Victorian doubt. Was the Bible true? Was science the enemy of religion? All those whom King most admired, men like Pusey and Liddon and the other leaders of the high church movement, were dedicated to resisting the new ideas. Pusey and Liddon were more than a force in Oxford, they were a phalanx. But the new ideas advanced steadily in Oxford, because they happened to contain much truth. Liddon became pessimistic about the future of Oxford, more than hinting that parents might be well advised not to send their sons there.

Nothing in King's previous experience prepared him for the atmosphere in which he now found himself. Smart young sceptics were comparatively new in Oxford, and King had hardly met them. And yet he managed better than Liddon. Not that his faith was so serene as to be undisturbed by the spread of doubt or the influence of agnostics. On the contrary, he was perturbed. Probably he was more worried by it than Liddon, who felt it his vocation to attack it from the front. King believed that the right answer to the agnostic was not attack but better Christian life and worship. He moved with an air of serenity and hope impossible to Liddon. But inside he felt it to be a calamity. Atheism, he was sure, led to moral chaos. He watched the crime-rate rise and believed the rise to be connected with the failure of faith in society. With his peaceable sheltered background he found it disturbing that any day or any night he might find himself sitting at dinner next to a man who did not believe in the future life or the existence of God.[19] He had a sense of a 'wave of atheism' spreading through society. Throughout his time at Oxford he suffered from this sense of strain, and it was a relief of mind to him when he went to Lincoln. He read atheistic books as a matter

[17] A. P. C. Field's reminiscence to G. W. E. Russell, 13 April 1912, Misc. Don. Eccl. 4/13.
[18] King to Frances Heurtley, 5 July 1879, Pusey House MSS.
[19] King, *Duty and Conscience*, pp. 5–6, 10.

of duty and in order to help, but did not enjoy them. He read one atheistic book on his knees for fear of what was coming next.[20] He told the undergraduates of 1881, what no comparable teacher would have told them twenty years before or twenty years after, to beware of the temptation to despair of Christianity.[21]

The remedy, he thought, was not by writing clever books. It lay in helping the poor and visiting the sick. Honesty and love and purity are more convincing than the largest library. The Christian need not fear, God is on his throne. 'I would ask you, when you hear the word *agnostic*, to be quiet about it, and look round and see that it is only a passing trouble of the day. It does not really fit in with the needs of man's being.'[22] He did not think highly of apologies for Christianity. He would read them and lay them down discontented. He may not have known his contemporary Richard Holt Hutton, but would have agreed with his dictum, 'If I wished to doubt the possibility of a revelation, I should take a course of reading in defence of it.'[23]

At Oxford King was more a pastoral and religious force than an academic. But he would not have been so pastoral a force unless many saw through his self-depreciation and respected his mind. A learned colleague later said that King did more than anyone else to raise the reputation of professors as a religious power in Oxford.[24] Capable authorities believed that no one since Newman exercised such religious force among undergraduates and younger dons.[25] In the year that he left Oxford the undergraduates, rowdy as usual at the ceremonies in the Sheldonian, gave loud cheers at his name in the incongruous company of Lord Salisbury and Lord Randolph Churchill, while they gave Mr Gladstone a nearly unanimous groan.

Not everyone admired the force of high churchmen in Oxford. It was even rumoured that the great Master of Balliol, who probably never reconciled himself to King in Oxford, selected as his chaplain an advanced liberal divine who specially

[20] Ibid., p. 121.
[21] King, *Love and Wisdom*, p. 29.
[22] King, *Duty and Conscience*, p. 82: dated 1884; cf. 11, 59–60.
[23] Hogben, *Hutton of the Spectator* (1900), p. 105.
[24] John Wordsworth: *Chron. Convoc.* (1910), p. 101.
[25] F. W. Puller, *Guardian* (1910), 398; C. W. Furse, *Guardian* (1883), 799; E. S. Talbot, *Guardian* (1885), 187; Stephen Paget and J. M. C. Crum in *Life of F. Paget*, p. 96.

wanted to counter King's influence.[26] The wife of one of the
tutors at Brasenose College felt a sense of revolt against the
growing strength in the university of the 'orthodoxy' which she
identified with Christ Church.[27]

Gladstone sent him to Oxford to train ordinands, and many
besides ordinands crowded his lectures. But at the bottom of his
garden he found an old wash-house and early in 1876 he turned
this into an oratory, which he at once called Bethel. It had
coconut matting, a sacred picture on the end wall, and a
harmonium played by an undergraduate. Late on Friday evenings
he talked there in surplice and stole, meditating on Scripture, or
the seven deadly sins, or occasionally, to the regret of some
among his audience, Aristotle's *Ethics*. The chimney smoked and
emitted gusts through the room. At least one undergraduate
always associated his first glimpse of heaven with the fumes of a
smoking fire.[28] King began with a handful and ended with three
hundred men.

4 THE SEE OF LINCOLN

King's name was not rumoured for bishoprics. Though now a
well-known man, he was not well known in that way. Until very
recent years no prime minister in his senses would have nominated so stalwart a high churchman to a bishopric; partly because
many members of the public would have objected and partly
because Queen Victoria would have objected. King's name had
been discussed as a possible Scottish bishop several years before,
but it was evident that William Bright, who knew him well and
admired him, thought him far too gentle a man to be able to cope
with Scotsmen.[29]

Gladstone was determined to give all schools of opinion in the
Church of England a fair representation among the bishops. At
the beginning of 1885 he decided to nominate a high churchman
to one of the three bishoprics, London, Lincoln, and Exeter.
Among the high churchmen one stood out as obvious – Liddon,

[26] *Recollections of Dean Fremantle*, p. 110.
[27] J. P. Trevelyan, *Life of Mrs Humphry Ward* (1932), p. 32. See also the remarks of the Balliol man of 1879, in A. F. Hort, *Life of F. J. A. Hort* (1896), vol. II, pp. 276–7.
[28] *Guardian*, (1910), 333.
[29] Bright to Liddon, 1875, undated; Keble College MSS.

champion against unbelief, greatest preacher in England, leader of the high church movement since the death of Pusey. There had already been half-hearted attempts to get Liddon made a bishop, and they foundered on the opposition both of the Queen, who thought him an extremist, and of the previous Archbishop of Canterbury (Tait), who thought him rigid. Gladstone now wanted to nominate Liddon but had to get the Queen to agree and knew that the Queen would only agree if the Archbishop of Canterbury, now Benson, supported him. And Archbishop Benson was reluctant to support Liddon's name. It was Benson who first suggested an alternative high churchman if Liddon's name would not do, and so King, all unknown to himself, came into consideration for one of the vacant sees. But perhaps not Lincoln. He 'is a very living power in Oxford. His kindling power would be a little lost on Wiltshire Downs or Lincolnshire Wolds.'[30]

Gladstone persisted in trying to win the archbishop to support Liddon, and at last succeeded. But now the question arose whether Liddon would accept a bishopric. It would be absurd for the Prime Minister to risk controversy with Queen Victoria only to find afterwards that the controversy was futile because the subject of it was unwilling. Gladstone therefore adopted the device of unofficial sounding, and this device, it was later to prove, helped to ensure that Liddon would not be Bishop of Lincoln and that King would be.

On 22 January 1885 at a meeting at 10 Downing Street between Gladstone and the archbishop it was agreed to submit three names to the Queen: Temple (liberal) for the See of London, Bickersteth (Evangelical) for the See of Exeter, and Liddon (high church) for the See of Lincoln. But first, it was agreed, R. W. Church, the Dean of St Paul's, should sound Liddon to see if he were willing. If he refused, then King's name should go forward to the Queen. Church wrote Liddon a letter to Oxford, and telegraphed him to come to London. For an hour and a half Church tried to persuade him. Liddon's mind was in a turmoil, and he described the feeling afterwards as a great heartache. But he would not say yes. His reasons to the contrary did not seem

[30] Gladstone Papers, BL Add. MSS 44109, 113.

strong. He just could not decide that it would be right to let his name go forward to the Queen. He was miserable for the rest of the day.[31] Meanwhile Church reported to Gladstone that Liddon's mind was at present quite averse to the idea, and he had said that he did not see how he could say yes to a definite offer. That afternoon or evening Gladstone wrote to the Queen nominating Temple, Bickersteth, and King for the three vacant sees.

Queen Victoria was surprised, and relieved, to see the name of King. She had expected, and feared, the name of Liddon. As was her custom, she sent the names to the Dean of Windsor, Randall Davidson, for his advice. He told her that King would be a very decidedly better bishop than Liddon; that the high churchmen did need a representative; that King was nearly as prominent and popular as Liddon among high churchmen, but that he had a much greater power of getting on with all sorts and conditions of men; that he would counteract severe and gloomy views because he was so bright and cheery, and had a strangely winning power – 'a remarkable man in every way'.[32]

But the Dean of Windsor raised a little question, heavy with omen for King's future happiness. He went round to Downing Street to say how greatly he was pleased with the proposed bishops. But Lincoln was a diocese of low churchmen, and Exeter of high churchmen. Would it not be more sensible to send the low church bishop to the low church diocese and the high church bishop to the high church diocese, instead of vice versa as was proposed?[33]

Gladstone refused the dean's point. We do not know why. On 27 January 1885 the Queen approved the nominations. 'Thank goodness', wrote Gladstone's secretary, 'there is for the moment an end of episcopal appointments, which with Mr Gladstone's excess of conscientiousness give more trouble than almost anything else.'

On 31 January Liddon received from King an affectionate letter. King said that he had been offered the see of Lincoln; that he had accepted it; that he dared not refuse. 'I could not face the

[31] Liddon's diary, *ad diem*: Liddon House MSS.
[32] G. K. A. Bell, *Randall Davidson*, 3rd edn, vol. 1, p. 175.
[33] Hamilton's diary, 26 January 1885, BL Add. MSS 48639.

men here, if staying from my own choice, against God's will.'[34] Liddon did not sleep that night, and his laconic diary shows his turmoil of mind. The nominations were made public on 1 February. The high churchmen of England rejoiced that such a man could have been chosen.

Not everyone rejoiced. The *Record* (6 February) called it a great misfortune, and yet it was better than others who might have been chosen. *The English Churchman* (5 February) was not so friendly.

This happy, serene, popular, and harmless man now entered a world of unforeseen entanglements, which slowly gripped him, until for a time they almost destroyed his happiness.

Two parties were then reaching the climax of contention over the ritual uses of the Church of England. In varying degrees the high churchmen wanted to deepen reverence in church services and revive faithfully what the Prayer Book ordered, like vestments at the Holy Communion, or what the Prayer Book did not forbid but which was long disused in English services; and they had evidence that services with high ceremonial attracted the poor and helped some of the educated to say their prayers better. In varying degrees the low churchmen desired to resist this revival of old usages in church, fearing it as leading men towards the Church of Rome. Their leaders were afraid of popery being openly or surreptitiously introduced into their reformed and Protestant Church. But while low churchmen much disliked these innovations, as a whole they disapproved of the idea of prosecuting clergymen in the courts. Not so with a small group of their extremists. The Church Association was formed in 1865 to resist innovations in ritual. The high churchmen asked only for toleration and had no desire to prosecute low churchmen for their innovations; whereas this small group of low churchmen were determined to prosecute clergymen for irregularities in their mode of conducting services. They prosecuted clergymen for points of ritual. Several of these clergymen refused to take any notice of the courts and were therefore imprisoned for contempt of court. The bishops, who had the right to veto prosecutions,

---

[34] Liddon's diary, 31 January 1885, Liddon House.

were not prepared to face the damage to the Church done by such imprisonments, and therefore agreed, three years before King was chosen for Lincoln, to use their veto. Prosecutions almost ceased because the bishops refused to allow them.

The fanatics therefore turned against the bishops, because they had no other means of pursuing their objective. They prosecuted the Bishop of Oxford for using his veto against a prosecution, and failed. King was a famous high churchman, and while at Oxford publicly joined in a plea for toleration of the ritualists, and publicly declared that the policy of the Church Association was injuring Evangelical religion. By accepting a bishopric at this precise moment, when bishops were the target of prosecution, King stepped into a public role as principal enemy of a small group of fanatics.

At the end of March 1885 the council of the Church Association presented a memorial to Queen Victoria to complain of her choice of King on the ground that he held doctrines on the Lord's Supper and confession which disqualified him from the office of a bishop. They asked her to inquire into these allegations and stay all proceedings for his confirmation until she should be satisfied.

No one protested at King's confirmation at Bow Church (23 April 1885), though a protest was half-expected or feared. No one protested at the consecration (25 April, St Mark's Day) in St Paul's Cathedral, before a congregation of 2,000. By King's request Liddon preached the sermon. And the sermon was a manifesto.

Here we have a second reason for disaster besides the situation of the moment. High churchmen so rejoiced at King's appointment that some of them became provocative. And Liddon's sermon in St Paul's was one of the provocations. It showed why he was so much more powerful a preacher than King, and why he was less suitable for a bishopric. The sermon was one of the uncompromising high church sermons of the century. Many friends or disciples of King in that great congregation must have rejoiced that such a sermon could be delivered at the consecration of a bishop. But St Paul's Cathedral contained others besides the friends of King. The Archbishop was consecrating Bickersteth to Exeter in the same liturgy, and Bickersteth was an Evangelical and half the congregation was Evangelical. To preach such a sermon before so mixed a congregation was from one point of view a courageous act of prophecy and from another point of view a failure of tact. Archbishop Benson wrote in his diary later that day and called the sermon a 'manifesto'. The sense that King's bishopric had perils came over him.[35]

There was a third reason for the impending disaster: an absence of worldly wisdom in King himself. He had lived a sheltered life, had no idea of the pressures of public life, and did not well understand the need for compromise. He was at once notorious as a high church bishop, and in the prevailing atmosphere might perhaps have taken care not to look too high church. Oxford friends presented him with a mitre. Hitherto bishops had mitres on their spoons, their arms, their writing-paper, their carriage doors, their coffins. But never since the Reformation had a bishop of the Church of England worn a mitre upon his head. It seemed to King a proper and traditional vesture, and he accepted the gift, not wearing it in church unless he knew that it was acceptable. But he found that it was acceptable, for more than half the clergy wanted him to use it at confirmations during the first nine months of 1886.[36] That the custom was felt to be appropriate by many was proved thereafter, when the other bishops one by one needed to follow his example.[37] Such a thing did not matter to King. People wanted him to wear it, he saw no objection, and that was enough. In the following year enthusiasts gave him another mitre, so ornate that (we are told) the new mitre of the Archbishop of Cologne could not be compared with it.[38]

Lincoln was not a high church diocese, but it had churches with ritual. King, who saw no harm in these things and sometimes good, simply followed the custom of the churches where he went. When he visited the parish of Holy Trinity at Gainsborough in August 1885, he used the vestments which he found there, the first bishop since the Reformation to use vestments. He wore the mitre at services where he knew that it would be

---

[35] Benson's diary *ad diem*, Trinity College, Cambridge: cf. Boyd Carpenter's diary, *ad diem*, BL Add. MSS 46726.

[36] *Record* (1886), 1964.

[37] As early as 1893 six other bishops followed his example. The one with most consequence, leading to another protest, was Creighton of Peterborough.

[38] *Guardian* (1886), 1419.

welcome. When he went down to visit old Canon West at Wrawby, he wore his cope and mitre for the service. The photographer Smith, of Brigg, asked if he could photograph the clergy. They refused. Smith pleaded that on a boiling hot day he had carried his camera from Brigg, and they gave way.[39] The photograph appeared, of King looking dusky and glum, surrounded by clergymen looking high church. The photographer sold the negative to a shop in the Strand which was in the habit of displaying celebrities in its window; and so the Church Association got hold of the negative, and a pamphlet was issued, with the photograph as a frontispiece, and underneath a versicle about Priestcraft stalking through the land. The pamphlet was circulated to the parishes of the Lincoln diocese.[40] King publicly described himself as one who had 'been a little bespattered with printer's ink and lost something of the gloss of novelty'.[41]

Edward King therefore arrived to be Bishop of Lincoln under the gravest of burdens. In fact the least controversial of men, gentle, moderate, and eirenic, he was represented to the public as an extremist and a betrayer of the Church of England to the Church of Rome. The people of Lincolnshire were not on the whole high churchmen, and they suspected the man whose image was so misrepresented. The Archdeacon of Lincoln, John Kaye, even absented himself from the meeting of the dean and chapter to elect the new bishop. Nor did the dean turn up,[42] but he was old and ill. The archdeacon refrained from appearing in the procession at King's enthronement, and his absence did not go unobserved.[43] No good man could have started as bishop with worse publicity and with more of a handicap to overcome.

Unless, that is, the adage is true that it is better if men speak ill of you than if they do not speak of you at all. Lincolnshire was at least interested. When King went down to reopen Somerby Church near Brigg, on 17 June 1885, as one of his first engagements, such a crowd turned up that the restored church was too

[39] A. P. C. Field to G. W. E. Russell, 13 April 1912, Misc. Don. Eccl. 4/15.
[40] J. Hanchard, *A Sketch of the Life of Bishop King*. With portrait. A Manual for Churchmen (London, John Kensit, 1886).
[41] *Lincoln Dioc. Mag.* (1887), 8.
[42] Dean and Chapter minutes, 20 March 1885.
[43] Janet Courtney, *Recollected in Tranquillity*, p. 87. There is a charming portrait of Archdeacon Kaye in A. C. Benson, *The Trefoil* (1923), 127ff.

small, and he had to preach the sermon in the churchyard.[44] Everywhere that he went vast congregations came to hear him. They liked what they heard.

5 THE LINCOLN TRIAL

The prosecution of King was preceded by two other attempted prosecutions in Lincolnshire, each of which led towards the prosecution of the bishop.

In August 1886 a local solicitor attempted to prosecute the precentor of the cathedral, Canon Venables (a delectable man, known to the minor canons as Vedge) for ritual practices, and Archbishop Benson of Canterbury refused to permit the prosecution. That same autumn the churchwarden of Clee-cum-Cleethorpes, a solicitor named Read, prosecuted his rector, J. P. Benson, for various practices including the wearing of vestments. King vetoed the prosecution, and persuaded Benson to have Holy Communion with the old and simpler ritual once a month. Read was not content and appealed to the Archbishop of Canterbury, who refused to interfere. King's best advisers were beginning to worry. Dean Butler wrote, 'We in Lincoln are on a powder-barrel, which a very little more will explode.'[45] That autumn a speaker at the annual conference of the Church Association openly held up King as a lawbreaker and demanded his prosecution.[46]

On 4 December 1887 King went down to the church of St Peter-at-Gowts, half-way down the High Street from the minster, and celebrated the service as they were accustomed to have it. On the altar were lighted candles, he faced the east, he mixed water with wine in the chalice. Such customs were used in very many churches of England without harm or complaint. Mr Read, the churchwarden of Cleethorpes, joined with two labourers who were parishioners to lay complaint, and the Church Association undertook the prosecution. They petitioned the Archbishop of Canterbury to try the Bishop of Lincoln for his ritual offences. The Archbishop ought to have refused to hear

[44] *Guardian* (1885), 933.
[45] Bright to King, 31 January 1887, Bright's letters in Lincolnshire Archives, King dep. xvi, xvii.
[46] *Guardian* (1886), 1764.

the complaint, but for various complicated reasons he consented. On 21 November 1890 Archbishop Benson held substantially for King, and in the points where he went against him King at once and publicly promised obedience. On 2 August 1892 the Judicial Committee of the Privy Council, to which the Church Association appealed and before which King would not consent to plead, confirmed the Archbishop's judgment on every point but one.

These bald facts hide the agony of the time. For four years the bishop, and the diocese, and the Church of England, waited while the law was settled. It cannot be said to have been important to the English nation to determine by law whether or not a bishop was or was not wrong in refraining from ordering a clergyman to put out the candles before he consented to take a service. And this aspect of the matter was peculiarly distasteful to King and peculiarly distasteful to many Englishmen. King's reputation among the ignorant public, and some of the informed, even among one or two of the bishops, became the unjust reputation of a man who thought it of high religious importance whether the candles were lit or not. For a time it became the fashion to describe him as 'a narrow but well-meaning formalist'.[47]

But beneath this superficial and misleading view of the question lay two matters of high importance. Was a small and unrepresentative body of fanatics to repress by legal action a wider movement towards a more sympathetic understanding of that inheritance of the Church of England which was Catholic as well as Protestant? And secondly, the forces of the high church movement which rallied round King were powerful, and were determined that no action by a not very Christian State should interfere with the needs of Christian worship as they saw them. In the tension of the time a truculent Bishop of Lincoln could have split the Church of England into two. It was a mercy for the established Church that the new Bishop of Lincoln was a man without truculence.

Several people thought that the circumstances might prove to be a blessing in disguise. If these fanatical prosecutions were to cease, it was better that a bishop should be prosecuted than a

---

[47] *Guardian* (1889), 355.

priest; that that bishop should be prosecuted for some exceedingly moderate customs, more moderate (as was observed) than were practised in London churches attended by the Prime Minister and the Prince of Wales; and that the bishop who was prosecuted should be a man revered.

The Lincoln case had important consequences for the diocese of Lincoln.

On the one hand the diocese rallied round him. Good men of every school were bitterly ashamed that their bishop should be prosecuted in this way, and took him to their hearts and their prayers. Collections were made in many churches to help his legal expenses, and petitions in support of him were widely signed. Not everyone. Some parishes were uninterested; some clergymen disapproved; Archdeacon Kaye of Lincoln refused to sign any of the addresses in support. In addition King received the usual letters from eccentrics such as the one beginning 'To the *Arch-hypocrite*' and signed '*An Irritated Parent*'.[48] But far more than half the Lincoln diocese, far more than half the people of Lincolnshire whether they were members of the Church of England or not, came to regard him with affection, and with that sympathy bestowed by the public upon one who for no good reason is maltreated. And half the Lincolnshire clergy looked upon him with an awe or veneration which is the lot and the embarrassment of few, and which the enchantment of his private personality alone would not have gained. In this sense the Lincoln trial benefited his work in the diocese.

But in another sense the trial grievously affected his work, for it took a heavy toll from the man. During the time of strain he appeared to be serene, made calm and courteous statements, and never for a moment departed either from his natural gentleness or from what befitted a Christian bishop. More than one observer said that he was the only man in the diocese who did not seem to be troubled.[49] But inside the man this was not so. One of his closest friends said that the trial hung over him like a nightmare,[50] and the unpublished letters confirm this evidence. At the end of the case he wrote to one of them 'Personally too I am

[48] G. W. E. Russell, *Edward King*, 3rd edn (1912).
[49] e.g., J. Wylde, *Guardian* (1890), 1742.
[50] *Lincoln Diocesan Magazine* (1910), 57.

thankful that the strain of the last three years has been removed, as it was becoming almost too much for my strength.'[51]

His health deteriorated during the four years, and intimates attributed it partly to his inability to say no to requests and partly to the suffering of the case. During the summer of 1891 he suffered a severe attack of shingles, his right hand swelled up and had no power in it, and by the next year the muscles of his right hand were so affected that his handwriting was made permanently worse.

The reader of King's utterances has another impression: that in certain ways he was less effective in 1893 than in 1886. Later in his time as bishop he went down to the villages and preached very simple sermons such as a little child could understand, and the villagers loved him. But educated adults sometimes blamed his simplicity. Certainly we do not find after 1893, among the printed sermons, the kind of powerful sermon which once made him famous as a preacher at a university. The sermons, though as pure and sincere as ever, had not the earlier force. His addresses at the diocesan conferences tended to become a little less coherent, a little more in appeal to the heart and a little less in appeal to the reason. His first charge to his diocese was the best charge of his episcopate. Men thought of him now as a holy and delightful old man, but no longer as an intellectual. When he died the Archbishop of Canterbury went out of his way to correct a false impression, saying 'Nothing could be a greater mistake than to imagine that he was only a very good man.'[52] The archbishop could not have prepared his utterance, thus to talk of 'only a very good man'.

All this may have been nothing to do with the trial and its tension. His age was 59 when the trial started and 63 when it ended, and perhaps he was only growing older. But his friends hinted that the trial took something out of the man.

6 THE BISHOP

King was a diocesan bishop, in the sense that he devoted all his time and energy to his diocese. He attended Convocation but

---

[51] King to Bramley, 5 August 1892: Larken Papers, III, 59, Lincolnshire Archives.
[52] *Chron. Convoc.* (1910), 100.

rarely spoke, made no attempt to debate in Parliament, hardly ever went to Church Congresses or important public meetings, and seldom accepted invitations outside Lincolnshire. He had no desire to be a statesman, or to be a divine. He struggled on with his reading, but since he encouraged callers of every kind any morning, he reserved no time for serious study. The callers were frequent, partly because of his welcome, and partly because he moved the bishop's house from Riseholme, where his predecessors lived three miles out, to the old ruined bishop's palace on the edge of the hill to the south of the cathedral. Part of the ruin had been used during the eighteenth century as a kind of quarry to repair the cathedral.[53] Several advisers urged upon him the inconvenience of Riseholme (where, it so happened, his critic and archdeacon John Kaye was the incumbent). It was the age when men demanded that cathedrals be less isolated from the life of their dioceses, and part of their demand desired a bishop to live in or near his cathedral close. For a time King lived at Hilton House in Lincoln, while a house of the early eighteenth century was enlarged and restored and a new chapel, dedicated to St Hugh, built over the passage and butteries to the south of the great hall. He consecrated the chapel on 3 October 1888. Over the doorway of the house he had the words inscribed, *Pascite gregem*, 'Feed my sheep.' It was a big house, but it was not adapted comfortably, and he lived in it simply. People commented on his simple manner of life when they discovered that he would not keep a carriage.

Lincoln was a rural diocese and King, who had been curate and then incumbent of a country village, was always a countryman's bishop. By the end of his episcopate he had obtained a unique hold upon the affection of the villages. In a village church he felt at home; he was never happier than when confirming village children or meeting them afterwards, and believed in what he called their 'unapparent' qualities. There is a little evidence that virile Lincolnshire yeomen sometimes looked for a man externally tougher and were not drawn by the gentleness.[54] But the evidence of veneration in the villages is widespread, and may still

---

[53] Sir Francis Hill, *Georgian Lincoln* (Cambridge, 1966), p. 39.
[54] See for example *Lincolnshire Chronicle* (11 March 1910), 5.

be found surviving in unexpected places. He had a high sense of the value of village churches and their silent secret influence.

It was not an easy time to become bishop of a rural diocese. In the Midlands and East Anglia the agricultural troubles of the previous fifteen years left a heritage of acrimony between labourer and churches, from which some country parishes never quite recovered. Lincolnshire was not so grievously affected as some other counties, for dissent was already strong, and the tendency of the agricultural troubles was only to strengthen dissent further. King's comment on his first visitation returns was that the one overwhelming result was 'Dissent! Dissent! Dissent!'[55] Nonconformists could not be expected to approve of a bishop so notoriously high church, and they sometimes joined in regretting what King had done. One lady commented on his cope and mitre that he was 'a dear old gentleman but a wee bit too gay for a gospel minister'.[56] Moreover, King said what he thought and was not well qualified to make diplomatic utterances. The nonconformists were suspicious, and the suspicion was slow to fade. But King had a singular advantage in his dealings with Lincolnshire nonconformists. The majority of them were Methodists, whether Wesleyan or Primitive. Bishop Wordsworth, King's predecessor, at one time achieved a breach with the Methodists that was almost total. It so happened that King had acquired an admiration for John Wesley and his work, taught about him with sympathy, and persuaded the Anglicans to see what good he had done. In his first year as a bishop he lectured on Wesley, in his last year as bishop he used generous language in welcoming the Wesleyan Methodist Conference to the city, and when he died the Congregational Union, which happened to be meeting at Lincoln, passed a special resolution of sympathy with the Church of England in its loss.[57] He was not a controversial figure in the villages, for nonconformists came to hear him with the others.

The years from 1886 to 1910 are commonly regarded as years when village congregations across the nation were declining. The villages were slowly losing their people to the towns, and the

---

[55] King to Bramley, Larken Papers, III, 10, Lincolnshire Archives.
[56] Randolph–Townroe, p. 164.
[57] *Times* (16 March 1910).

habit of churchgoing was less of an obligation. Selected comparisons of the information on certain villages contained in King's first visitation returns of 1886 and his last visitation returns of 1907 (Lincolnshire Archives) show a fairly steady churchgoing and chapelgoing population. But we need much more local study of such a question before making firm judgments.

Depopulating villages were apt to depress the clergy, who saw their best young people move away. And the clergymen of 1886 were less universally countrymen than their predecessors, and some felt the isolation of remote places. The agricultural depression, by lowering tithe-values, lowered their stipends, and some of them were painfully poor. The rural parishes needed reorganizing, but the time for such reorganization was not yet, for it required legislation which at that time was impossible to get. Bishop Wordsworth had already done much for the poorer clergy, and King continued that work. What he could also do for the country clergy was to cheer them up. He had an unfailing optimism, had no belief in numbers, was perfectly content when he found himself talking to a tiny congregation, showed the clergy that their work was valuable despite its frustrations, and was tolerant (critics said, too tolerant) of failure. He understood the plight of the poor and became an officer of the Poor Clergy Relief Corporation, which privately assisted hard cases. Like other bishops he encouraged the country churches to stay open during the week, and persuaded more of them to have a weekly Holy Communion. He was much concerned about the many churches which still had no such custom, and about the 400 churches of the diocese which in 1892 were still locked from Sunday to Sunday.[58]

Two complaints were made against him. He was said, first, not to be a good administrator; and secondly he surrounded himself with advisers of his own opinions. One of his examining chaplains, Bright, wrote of the 'growlings' in the Lincoln diocese at the organization, with the remark that the bishop 'has not the same standard of order and method as common folks have'.[59] This complaint is not often to be found, and King was confessed to be an excellent chairman of the diocesan conference. There

[58] Charge of 1892; *Guardian* (1892), 1565.
[59] Bright to Liddon, 23 February 1888, Keble College MSS.

was certainly a muddle over the office and stipend of Walter Hicks, canon-missioner in the diocese after 1895, and Hicks was justified in protesting. But the muddle happened at the end of King's life, and perhaps Hicks did not make allowances for that last year.

Secondly, they complained that being a high churchman he surrounded himself with high churchmen. In 1886 King helped to found the *Diocesan Magazine* (it started for one number as the *Diocesan Gazette*) and kept a close interest in its proceedings, suggesting articles and reviews to the editor. The magazine reflected King's views, which were not then the views of a majority of clergy in the diocese. This impression was confirmed in June 1885, only three months after King's elevation, by the choice of a new Dean of Lincoln. The new dean was W. J. Butler, formerly vicar of Wantage and a famous adherent of the Oxford Movement. The moment that Butler arrived he began to transform the cathedral. The very minutes of the dean and chapter change their quality and their appearance from the first meeting at which he was in the chair. Here for the first time in Victorian history the bishop and the dean of the same cathedral were both prominent high churchmen. But Gladstone was far from intending this alliance. He wanted to offer the deanery to his son-in-law E. C. Wickham, whose opinions stood a long way from King's, and was dissuaded by his advisers, who thought that it would be a bad mark for his tottering government.[60] Then he offered it to a Cambridge professor, Westcott, who refused it, and then to an Oxford professor, Edwin Palmer, who also refused it. Butler, who brought Lincoln Minster into the modern world, was the fourth choice of the Prime Minister. Gladstone had not designed so strong a combination of high churchmen.

Whether designed or not, the changes at the minster affected King. He was often at the minster services, preached on the first of Butler's evening services crowded with working men, preached the first Three Hours devotion to be held there, and used it for many diocesan meetings, especially his retreats for the clergy. Archdeacon Kaye's opposition to what Dean Butler and a majority of the chapter wanted began to be recorded as notes of

[60] See Hamilton's diary, 20 April 1885, Add. MSS 48640. Wickham was afterwards Dean of Lincoln, 1894–1910.

dissent in the chapter minutes. When one of the four vanes of the tower would not budge, wits called it the archdeacon.[61]

King gave the doors to the restored arcade of the Chapter House. The lines over the doors record the gift:

> Aptavit valvas Edwardus episcopus istas
> Cui pateat patris caelica porta domus,
>
> (Bishop Edward put these doors here
> and may heaven's gate be open for him)

and in the tympanum are the words *Edwardus Episcopus*, and the date MDCCCXC, with the arms of the See of Lincoln impaling King's own arms.

It took the diocese a little time to realize that their bishop was after all so fair a churchman that he could favour men of other opinions. The realization came as he used his patronage with fairness; as he befriended the missionary College, founded at Burgh under his predecessor; and as he acted in a way which sometimes separated him from those who expected to find him an ally. One of these moments was in 1895, when there was talk by Lord Halifax of reunion with the Roman Catholic Church, and King declared a decided no. At the same time, and more important because on a fundamental question of ethics, he separated from almost the entire high church-party on the law of divorce. They said that marriage was so indissoluble that remarriage must in any circumstances be adultery. King was strong for the binding vow of marriage, but in his view, after much meditation and hesitation, there were at last overrriding considerations of pastoral care and charity. The charge of 1895, and the speech at Convocation in which he declared his opinion (7 July 1898) were two of the most influential utterances of his life. He later said that his views on the subject cost him many friends. Incidentally, this question caused a lessening of the gap which divided him from Archdeacon Kaye, a gap which before the end of King's life was closed altogether; so that his close friendship with Archdeacon Kaye was publicly remarked by an Evangelical newspaper.[62]

[61] Fowler, *E. L. Hicks*, p. 245.
[62] *Record* (1910), 238.

Outside the village and the cathedral his chief pastoral anxiety was Grimsby, then growing fast. He at once launched an appeal for church extension in Grimsby and it brought in little money, only about £1,250 in nearly two years; and perhaps the failure is a sign of the early suspicions of the diocese. He gave a large donation from his own purse to build an iron church in one district. In 1901 Grimsby was hit by violence among trawlermen who burned the offices of their employers, and King brought home to his diocese the needs of the town. This time his appeal was a success and raised £37,000, and during the last year of King's life a merchant caused him happiness by leaving a big bequest for Grimsby. It was felt right that one part of the memorial to King should be the completion of St Luke's Church at Grimsby.

Wherever he went he had a word for the working man. The porters on the railway were his special friends; the drivers of cabs; the women who sold flowers in the market-stalls; the children whom he confirmed; the young men whom he ordained. Once when he was ill, the porters at Grantham station came up to a passenger getting off a Lincoln train and asked, 'Have you any news of our bishop?'[63]

Bishop Wordsworth founded the theological college Scholae Cancellarii. As once the head of a theological college, and regarded as the father of theological colleges, King felt at home there and created a personal link, which Wordsworth had not attempted, between himself and the ordinands. He regularly attended the college chapel for the service when students were admitted and invited them to supper on Sundays at the palace. Randolph thought that the best utterances of his episcopate were private addresses to the ordinands. The only important speeches which he made in Convocation, apart from that on divorce, defended theological colleges against their critics and made suggestions for meeting their needs.

In the Church at large he devoted his main endeavours to the support of Church schools in elementary education. Hardly a diocesan conference passed without King talking about the education of the poor. But in the perspective of church history he

63 G. B. Hunt to the author, 10 April 1967.

was more important in the help which he gave to the biblical critics.

The question whether a man could be a good Christian and a good clergyman, even though he believed parts of the Old Testament to be legendary, came to the fore during the early years of his time at Lincoln. The debate divided the younger high churchmen from the old, Charles Gore versus Liddon. King's intellectual habits lay with the older men: he was a friend and admirer of Liddon. But when the battle was joined in 1889–92, over the book *Lux Mundi* which Gore edited, King carried much weight by appealing for sympathy for Gore, and by steadily retaining him on his staff; so that a conservative even collected a petition directed against encouragers of error among whom he included the Bishop of Lincoln.[64] The strong religious movement of that day entered the modern world of criticism with little difficulty, and in so doing owed a debt to King. This sympathy cost King pain. It must have divided bishop from dean, for Butler was strong for the conservative side. And King loved the Bible like any conservative Evangelical. He confessed that he was brought up to believe in the simple historical truth of the Book of Genesis, and that 'it still gave him a sort of pain when he heard such words used as "folklore", "legend" and so on, in relation to it'.[65]

King's influence was a personal influence over individuals, and therefore hidden in a way which the biographer can hardly touch. We have some of the letters which he wrote to advise souls, though there was one public protest against a suggestion that such letters be published, on the ground that they were too sacred. He wrote letters of consolation and strengthening and wisdom. These letters win no literary prizes. They are short, to the point, unadorned.

From the occasional reminiscence or disclosure in the diocese more of the influence can be detected. We hear of an occasional pastorate with public results, as in the condemned cell and on the way to the scaffold, with a young Grimsby fisherman who murdered his girl (1887). He took a special interest in all work to help the deaf and dumb. The people of whom we know most are

[64] *Guardian* (1893), 330.
[65] *Guardian* (1908), 1769.

those who afterwards became eminent enough to warrant biographies: Henry Scott Holland, canon of St Paul's and then Regius Professor of Divinity at Oxford; Bishop Winnington-Ingram of London; Bishop Talbot of Rochester and then of Winchester; G. W. E. Russell, the littérateur and Liberal Member of Parliament. Wilgress thought that of these friendships the most important to King was that with Talbot; and we know from Talbot's biography that he thought of King as 'a master in the spiritual life'.[66] He was seldom recognized as a power in the Church at large, which he had no wish to be. 'The Bishop of Lincoln', wrote one bishop to his daughter from Convocation, 'is sitting opposite to me, and has just dropped the ink all over his white robes in front, and looks very distraught in consequence.'[67]

But he was accorded a different kind of recognition. This was marked at the Lambeth Conference of 1897 (Archbishop Temple now presiding) when by request King delivered in St Mary's Lambeth, just outside the palace gates, the devotional addresses to the assembled bishops. Summaries of these addresses were published by one of the American bishops in a Philadephia newspaper. They contain all King's favourite themes, from the wisdom of Charles Marriott to the text 'Thy gentleness hath made me great.'[68]

Dean Butler died in 1894 and was succeeded by E. C. Wickham, whom Gladstone had wanted to appoint in 1885. Wickham was very different from Butler, no high churchman, a scholar to his fingertips, and an advanced Biblical critic. But he continued and extended the reforms which Butler began in the minster. We have a portrait from Dean Wickham's daughter as from one living in the close when King was old. There is a suggestion about it that he was becoming retired in his extreme old age, and that the diocese did not meet him so often:

The picture of the Bishop seen by most people I think was not so much connected with the cathedral but as the great father of the huge diocese and its countless little scattered parishes. And there was a sense of having a recognised

[66] Wilgress to Russell, 19 April 1912; Lincolnshire Archives, Misc. Don. Eccl., 4/14; Stephenson, *E. S. Talbot*, 116–17.
[67] L. Creighton, *Life and Letters of Mandell Creighton* (1904), vol. II, p. 135.
[68] *Guardian*, (1897), 1373–5.

saint secluded, with his shy nephew, among the romantic ruins of the Old Palace. When he emerged and for anyone who came in touch with him there was of course not only magnetism and inspiration but friendliness and humour.

> She brought some slum boys of her Bible class to a sacrament which King celebrated. He sent her a little note afterwards, which ended 'And such delightful grubby hands'.[69]

This suggestion of retirement is confirmed by the ill-health of his last years. He grew deafer, and could no longer hear what was said in debates. Some outsiders thought that he should have retired altogether (*Record* (10 March 1910)). In 1907, at the opening Communion before the diocesan conference, he collapsed and could not proceed. He was soon recovered, and conducted his spring confirmations each year. In 1909 he did something which caused old criticism to reappear – he was the solitary bishop to vote against Lloyd George's famous and controversial budget. The vote looked political, indeed to some Liberals of Lincoln was not intelligible, and one of the city council was said to have refused the bishop's annual invitation to dinner.[70] He voted against the bill although the Archbishop of Canterbury and many other bishops thought it a matter on which bishops should not take sides. But he was not the only bishop to take part, for the Archbishop of York and the Bishops of Birmingham (Gore), Chester, and St Asaph voted in favour of the bill; while the Bishop of Bristol spoke confusedly against, and the Bishop of Hereford spoke fiercely for, though these two did not stay to vote. So King was not, as is sometimes said, exceptional in the matter. Many voted against not because they were simply against the bill, but because they believed on constitutional grounds that so revolutionary a budget should not be introduced unless the government first received a mandate from the country.

King's last public engagement was a village confirmation at West Allington near Grantham. He fell gravely ill in February 1910, and after dictating messages of affection to his diocese and his friends, died on 10 March. In Convocation the Archbishop of

---

[69] C. M. L. Wickham to the author, 30 September 1967.
[70] *Lincolnshire Chronicle* (11 March 1910), 5. See also his vote at the vital debate of 30 November 1909.

Canterbury doubted whether any bishop or priest of the Church
of England for many years 'had a stronger, wider, or deeper hold
upon the best heart of England' than King. The Prime Minister,
Mr Asquith, in offering the see to King's close friend Talbot in
succession (but Talbot refused) called King 'a great, and in many
ways unique, personality'.[71]

It would be possible to quote many beautiful appreciations
from those who revered him. But on the principle that praise in
the mouth of an enemy is even more powerful than praise in the
mouth of a friend, here is the *Record*, which in the earlier years of
King's bishopric printed vitriolic articles against his conduct and
more than once denounced Gladstone for choosing him. The
editor first took a contemporary to task for heading its obituary
'A Great Bishop'. For he never rose to be a great leader, never
exerted influence in the councils of the Church, or anywhere but
his own diocese, for he was too gentle and retiring to force
himself to the front. He was content to be a pastor. 'He was a man
of deep spirituality of mind and life, a veritable Enoch, and his
daily walk and conversation were indeed an inspiration to all
who came into contact with him.'[72]

King made charming and inimitable speeches at a dinner or
luncheon. He could be unexpectedly trenchant, as when he said,
apropos of the churchwarden of Glentham, 'There ought to be
some diocesan building between a stable and an asylum in which
all two-legged asses should be put. It would have to be a large
one.'[73] He admired men of action more than politicians, and
thought General Gordon perhaps the greatest of his contemporaries, for to King empire meant cutting off the slave-dealers in their
stronghold. He was a perfect host, kept open house at luncheon,
and gave pleasure to the mayor and corporation by entertaining
them to dinner annually. Apart from the daily reading of the
Bible and weekly reading of Keble, he read poetry, and history,
and a few books on the philosophy of religion (or on distantly
related subjects like Darwin on earthworms), and as a matter of
duty a few good novels to broaden his understanding of human
beings. Of the poets he could not put up with Browning, and

[71] *Chron. Convoc.* (1910), 99; Stephenson, *E. S. Talbot*, p. 187.
[72] *Record* (11 March 1910).
[73] King to Bramley, 14 January 1893; Larken Papers, III, 65.

decided that he must be too old for the exercise. He liked Wordsworth's more philosophical reflexions, praised Tennyson, read Dante and Shakespeare regularly, thought Spenser noble for men but unsuitable for women, enjoyed Schiller but generally found that he was afterwards sad. He read Acton's Inaugural and Stubbs's *Lectures on Modern History*. Among theologians he awarded the palm to J. B. Mozley. He must have read Liddon's sermons, but no influence from them can be detected in his own sermons. He read occasional books of sermons, as by R. M. Benson, or Dean Church, or Archbishop Benson. He liked to look up the old books by his master Charles Marriott. His library was excellent. As he grew older, books of prayer seemed to express his theology better than books of formal divinity. He once told Wilgress that he 'would rather give to Dr Bright than to anyone a blank cheque to be filled in for his theology'; and he was thinking, not of the academic books of an eminent church historian, but of Bright's *Private Prayers for a Week*.[74]

His mien and his habit of mind suggested to observers that he lived in the consciousness of another world. He had a face which could properly be described as radiant, and people went away from him feeling the better for having seen him. Little things of nature gave him an intense pleasure, the scent of hay, children laughing, wild roses in a hedge. He felt in sympathy with them as if, thought Randolph, he was 'in league with the beasts of the field'.

When they met to discuss a memorial, a statue was suggested, and then it was said that he would not at all have liked a statue and would have wanted something done for somebody. But, said the Archbishop of Canterbury, if we only made statues of people who wanted statues, we should not make statues of the right people. It was therefore agreed that part of the memorial should be to complete St Luke's Church at Grimsby,[75] and that the other part should be a statue (they considered and ruled out a window) in Lincoln Minster. They entrusted it to Sir William Richmond, whose work did not proceed smoothly. The dean and chapter expected a figure recumbent on a tomb, like the

---

[74] Wilgress to Russell, 19 April 1912, Lincolnshire Archives, Misc. Don. Eccl. 4/14.
[75] Foundation stone laid by King's nephew Wilgress on 22 July 1911. Consecrated St Luke's Day, 1912.

memorial statue to Christopher Wordsworth and other bishops in the cathedral. Richmond produced a model of his statue supported upon four angels. The chapter disliked the model, partly because it was of action and not in repose, and partly because of the ugliness of the four angels. They rejected the model, and asked that the matter be referred back to the appeal committee.[76] After a long delay Richmond nevertheless persuaded them to a figure that is in action and not recumbent, and so created the famous statue of King, now in the south transept, in a posture as though about to confirm a child. It is larger than life, but King's friends thought it a striking likeness. It was formally presented to the dean and chapter at a ceremony on 22 September 1914. Upon it are the two texts of I John 4.7, 'Beloved let us love one another, for love is of God', and St Matthew 5.5, 'Blessed are the meek, for they shall inherit the earth.' The statue was dedicated on 22 September 1915, when the address was given by Randolph because the Archbishop of Canterbury was ill.

The two important portraits are (1) by George Richmond (1873) at Cuddesdon College, and (2) by W. W. Ouless, collected for in the diocese after 1897, nonconformists and Evangelicals subscribing (600 guineas), and now hanging in the Bishop's House, Lincoln.

At the church of All Hallows, Wold Newton, is a portrait of King by Ada Rothwell. Into the two buttresses of the bishop's chapel (now the chapel of the diocesan house) were built good little statues of St Hugh and King.

---

[76] Dean and Chapter Acts, pp. 191–3, 21 February 1911.

Chapter 14

A TRACTARIAN PASTORAL IDEAL

In the year 1932 was published a little volume in paperback, called *Pastoral Lectures of Bishop Edward King*. The publisher was A. R. Mowbray & Co., well known for its service in printing pastoral and devotional literature, especially in connexion with the old ideals of high churchmen.

Edward King died, a very old man but still Bishop of Lincoln, in 1910. He printed no pastoral lectures, and left no pastoral lectures among his papers. But before he was bishop, he was for thirteen years a professor at the University of Oxford.

We know that some people thought his lectures good. At lectures undergraduates take notes of what is said. An undergraduate of St John's College, by name George Ernest Frewer, was reading theology in a modestly undistinguished manner (he got a fourth class in the examination). He listened to the course which Edward King delivered at Christ Church, and made notes. These notes still existed in 1932. Frewer spent most of his working life as a country pastor, chiefly as the rector of Brede near Rye in East Sussex, and became a canon and prebendary of Chichester Cathedral. Finding these notes of old lectures, Frewer handed them to a friend, H. R. Scott, and told him to make what use he could of them, to help ordinands.

Scott consulted the Principal of Cuddesdon College. This was an obvious thing to do. Before King was professor at Oxford, he was himself Principal of Cuddesdon. He was the most famous of Cuddesdon principals at that moment. It was the reputation of his work in training ordinands at Cuddesdon which led the Prime Minister (Gladstone) and others to think him, for all his lack of higher academic experience, a proper choice for the pastoral professorship.

The manuscript was well placed at Cuddesdon for a second

reason. The Principal of Cuddesdon in 1932, when the manuscript arrived, was Eric Graham. As Edward King was a disciple
of the Oxford Movement in the nineteenth century, Eric Graham
was a true disciple of the Oxford Movement in the twentieth
century. For him high Anglicanism was the best way of worship.
He thought it the combining of Evangelical piety with the
numinous quality of the Catholic liturgies. It loved the Bible, that
is the Bible in the Church. Graham looked back with affection
upon John Keble and Edward King, and with only a little less
affection upon Pusey and Liddon. A fierce bishop once attacked
Graham for running at Cuddesdon a party college. Graham
denied it absolutely. But he said to the bishop, 'If you mean that
we endeavour to continue the tradition of the Tractarians, I
should immediately and proudly plead guilty.'[1] Graham had
something of Pusey's rigidity of principle. He thought divorce,
and remarriage of a divorced person, always wrong for a
Christian. He held all artificial methods of contraception to be
wrong. But it was not Pusey or Liddon who commanded his
chief admiration among the Tractarians. It was Edward King.
Why King more than Pusey or Liddon? Because he saw in King a
breadth, humanity, absence of rigidity.

Eric Graham was made Principal of Cuddesdon in 1929. His
portrait at the college portrays a prim person. The portrait is
misleading. He was shy. He had no small talk. He was very pious,
in an old-fashioned, masculine, English mode. He was not at all
prim. He was politically a Conservative, though no one would
have extracted this from anything he said. He had a satirical sense
of humour which deflated windbags as laconically as the brevities
of the Duke of Wellington. He was a very serious man, but
somehow managed not to be solemn. He was more likely to
attract respect than popularity, for he was not in the least hail-
fellow-well-met. To those who got to know him well he was
lovable. He was a Tractarian and an Anglo-Catholic and might
have been expected to propagate celibacy of the clergy. But he
had a warm-hearted wife and a lot of extrovert children whose
physical and vocal presence was welcome among ordinands
trying to look or feel holier than they were.

[1] Graham to Bishop Headlam, end of July 1940: R. Holtby, *Eric Graham* (Oxford, 1967), p. 53.

In his autobiography, *Some Day I'll Find You*, Harry Williams caricatured Graham as narrow-minded and absurd. But he was principled rather than narrow-minded, and he was not in the least absurd.

Graham received from H. R. Scott Canon Frewer's notes on Edward King's pastoral lectures. Frewer can hardly have expected Scott to make much of the notes. Other people's notes are not normally useful to anyone. Frewer nevertheless hoped that they might be published. To this end Graham gave advice and help.

For help was needed. To take down notes from someone's lectures is not an easy feat if the lecturer does not dictate slowly. From internal evidence these lectures were not dictated. But Frewer got down a coherent set of notes; no doubt not so coherent as what we now have in print, because Graham and Scott worked to bring them into order, in what Scott called 'the difficult task of revision'. But Frewer must have scrawled down on his paper what was sufficiently coherent. For otherwise the revisers could not have made sense of the lectures. And for the most part, they made sense. King did not dictate, but he must have delivered clear and well-ordered lectures.

At Scott's request, Graham provided an introduction. It described Edward King as a saint of the Church of England; as a man with a life of supernatural holiness and beauty, based 'firmly and explicitly on that full Catholic faith, which he always claimed as our rightful heritage'.

So the book was published by Mowbrays, who regarded this as public duty and did not expect to make their fortune by the sale. The binding was grey paper, quiet and unobtrusive and inexpensive but not mean or sordid. On the title page Scott printed this explanation.

Notes of Addresses and Lectures delivered by Dr King at Oxford in 1874 as Regius Professor of Pastoral Theology. They are now published in the hope that they may be found useful by ordinands and by those newly ordained.

Of these last two classes Graham evidently felt that the book would be more useful to the newly ordained. For henceforth he gave each Cuddesdon man, as he left the college to be ordained, an inscribed copy of Edward King's *Pastoral Lectures*. It is improbable that they all valued the gift, or even read the book.

But some of them did: though, being someone else's edition of someone else's notes of someone else's lectures, that might surprise.

The lectures must have been given in one of the years between 1874 and 1885: perhaps in more than one academic year; possibly in all those academic years. But the book as published is in four sections and the last section never made part of a lecture course to undergraduates, though the editors evidently thought that it did. It is separate. It is different in form and style. It makes up the notes of five addresses at a retreat. These addresses are not addressed to an audience of ordinands at a university. The retreat conductor addresses his hearers as *fellow-shepherds*. It is a retreat for clergy which he conducts. He assumes that they have a flock in their care, and that they need to have their faith in that flock renewed. He is also writing at a rather later date, when 'new responsibilities' are being given, evidently in part by Gladstone to the 'labouring classes', who are 'future rulers', so this must be not far off the time of the Reform Act of 1884. If it was a retreat given by Professor King and not by Bishop King, it must have been given to a Cuddesdon refresher course in 1884. But for a reason which follows this is impossible.

The retreat is evidently designed for mature priests; among them even aged priests in an epoch when hardly anyone retired, and then only if truly incapacitated. It is for priests whose energies are low (p. 78), and yet they must still try to work, who are conscious that their ability to preach is in decline, and yet they may still try to touch people by their perseverance in holy things; who cannot often go into cottage meeting or choir practice or school, because 'an old man should not be out on a night like this'; and yet can use their enforced seclusion, like some old hermit, to try to find the 'unveiled presence' of God; priests who must endure less frequent meeting with their parishioners but may still feel themselves close to them by sending messages or gifts and working through lay people; who have lost the idealism or the ambition of youth and whose temptations are the stronger because they are no longer protected from them by that idealism or earlier ambition; and especially the temptation of an excessive care over money; but not only money: Solomon and David fell late in their lives.

Therefore part 4 of this book, alleged in the preface to be lectures to undergraduates, consists of notes on a retreat for clergy. Can we from internal evidence date the retreat? It mentions a book of which a brief sketch appeared in 1886 and a new fuller version in 1888 – *Roman Catholic Claims*, by Charles Gore, who wrote it while he was Principal of Pusey House. He also wrote it while Edward King was Bishop of Lincoln.

Therefore this last part of the *Pastoral Lectures* was no part of the pastoral lectures as put forth in Oxford University by Professor King. Canon Frewer must have attended a retreat conducted by his old teacher when King moved to be a bishop. And this would explain why the entire tone of this last section is fitting to an audience of clergy, and would be strange if addressed to an audience of undergraduates, even if they were all ordinands.

While on this point of internal evidence, can we date the retreat any more precisely? Gore's book is the only book mentioned which was published after King stopped being a professor. Therefore the retreat was given not earlier than 1886, probably not earlier than 1889, and very probably not more than a year or so later than 1889.

Parts 1–3 have cited in them no books which were published after the time that King left Oxford. Nothing in the internal evidence contradicts the statement that these are indeed notes taken from King's pastoral lectures while he was a professor at Oxford. A book is cited that was published in 1876 (Ashwell on *The Holy Catholic Church*), and another published in 1883 (Bishop Cotterell's *Lectures*). Frewer matriculated in 1871 and graduated in 1874. King became professor in April 1873. Therefore by far the likeliest time for the delivery of the lectures is the academic year 1873/4. And 1874 is the year which the editors put upon the title page.

The next question is, can we assume that we have notes on *all* the lectures in King's course? That is, did the undergraduate Frewer attend without fail? Did he never miss for sickness, or idleness, or because family circumstances compelled him to go home? We cannot guarantee that we have a complete summary of what King said, or of all the subjects which he treated.

There is something improbable in the proposition that we have all. It is true that the notes of what we have are in general (as distinct from individual sentences) coherent and make a unity.

When King gave his lectures there existed a classic book on the subject which was commonly used. This was *The Parish Priest* (called in earlier editions *The Duties of the Parish Priest*) by J. J. Blunt, who was the Lady Margaret Professor of Divinity at Cambridge during the 1840s. This book was first published in 1852, and in a sixth edition just as King was about to become professor of the subject at Oxford. It was valued by those who cared about ordinands. King must expect some at least of his hearers to know the book.

Blunt's book, in its sixth edition, has 381 pages excluding the indexes. King's lectures, once the retreat is subtracted, have 65 pages; and each of King's pages has many fewer words than each of Blunt's pages. Each of King's pages has fewer than 200 words. An average page of Blunt has 350 words. King's annotator gave only one-ninth or less of what Blunt gave his readers.

In three places (at least) King summarized Blunt for the benefit of his hearers. The first passage is:

The Visitation of the Upper Classes
Notice that their world has not changed between 1845 and 1875. It is still possible for the pastor to take it for granted publicly that his flock is divided into classes. The problem is, that if you go into a house of a poor family you may go straight into a religious subject with hardly a moment of hesitation, because that is what they expect you to do. But if you come 'to the middle classes' [which King defined as 'farmers, tradesmen, etc.' p. 53] 'you can't talk religion with them'; the task of pastoral visiting is much more difficult; and you must find common ground to discuss, like the allotments; and you may find a chance to speak of a moral duty, like his duty towards 'his servants'. The common ground of conversation with 'the upper classes' may be made more churchy; if not religious, at least ecclesiastical.

King is reported as quoting Blunt inaccurately – 'It [the conversation with the upper classes] can't be definitely religious, but it should be ecclesiastically instructive.' And then King is represented as saying that:

e.g. we might try to remove the idea that the clergy are the Church. Try to make the laity realize the part they have in the matter.

Do they keep the Ember Seasons?

In the Ordination Service they may stop the ordination of an unworthy person; or after the *Si Quis.*

Again remove their false notions of what is *Roman.* And instruct them in missionary work. Be disinterested.

This is the undergraduate's summary of what was evidently a long passage of lecture by King: so short a summary as to make it partly unintelligible. But if we go to Blunt's book, we see that the whole passage is taken out of Blunt; and when we see the context, it all becomes very intelligible, even that apparently mad question 'Do they keep the Ember Seasons?' It is probable that King did not need to labour the point, as Blunt needed to labour it, that the clergy are not the Church. Blunt takes a lot of space to explain how wrong it is to say that someone is going into the Church when you mean that he is being ordained, and how wrong it is to say that some Act of Parliament is offensive to the Church when you mean that it is offensive to the clergy. No doubt such a doctrine still needed labouring a hundred years later. But it is very probable that the influence of the Church revival of the nineteenth century, and in part of the Oxford Movement, made ordinands, at least, fully aware that the baptized laity are the Church, and that they have as much part and duty in seeing that the Church does its work for God as have the clergy.

But the comparison between Blunt and King at this point produces alarm in the reader. *Do they keep the Ember Seasons?* The point, unintelligible in King, intelligible in Blunt, is that the laity have rights in the Church which they do not use and ought to use. The Church requires every young man who seeks orders to give notice publicly in the church where he dwells; and proclaims aloud (in the 'Si Quis') that if anyone knows cause or just impediment why he be not admitted to holy orders, he should now declare the same. Therefore (according to Blunt) the laity had no right to blame clergymen for being bad clergymen if they had the right to stop them becoming clergymen and failed to

exercise that right. Moreover, wrote Blunt in this wholly impractical argument, the Church makes everyone aware of the four
Ember Seasons in the year when men ought to be ordained, and
begs their prayers at those times for the ordinands. This is again to
remind the people that they have a say in the appointment of the
Church's ministers.

Now: the question is, did King make his own this advocacy of
Blunt which was clever and had no common sense, or did he only
report it as Blunt's case without committing himself to it? The
undergraduate notetaker reported King as though he made it his
own. But this is not very likely. Whatever other qualities King
lacked, he did not lack common sense. It is the less likely in that it
is put down by Blunt, and therefore by King, not in some sensible
place such as 'how can we make the laity more conscious of their
duties?', but in this particularly odd section, on how we can
interest 'the upper classes' in nearly religious conversation when
we do not yet dare to tackle them, head on, about religion.

The next place in which King cited Blunt was over the
visitation of the sick (King, pp. 54ff.; Blunt, pp. 224ff.). When
King described the use of the order for the Visitation of the Sick
in the Prayer Book, he summarized Blunt; how the service often
will not do as it stands; how the rules of the Church give the priest
or the deacon wide latitude in what he uses; how the main work
of Visitation is to produce conviction of sin with a view to
absolution. But the *spirit* of the two men on this subject is very
different.

One more case out of Blunt must be brought finally to show
the shakiness of the material with which we deal in these notes.
Naturally both teachers turn to the form of absolution in the
Visitation of the Sick in the Prayer Book. This was little used
when Blunt wrote. It was more used but therefore was controversial and roused tempers and repugnance when King wrote,
because private confession had become more controversial with
the considerable extension of the practice under the Oxford
Movement. Blunt rather beautifully said what a relief to the
priest's mind it often was to be commissioned by the Church to
make this declaration; and then he defended it, calling it a matter
for rejoicing that the Church found no more difficulty in putting
into the priest's mouth a forgiveness of *actual* sin than it did when

it put into his mouth the forgiveness for *original* sin by what it makes him say in the sacrament of baptism.

King in his lecture took this point. The undergraduate made it cruder by abbreviation and so turned it into a different point. 'Blunt says we have the right in baptism, why not here also?'

The next passage which King took out of Blunt was the advice on how to preach (King, pp. 43ff.; Blunt, lecture 5); the power of the sermon for good; the danger when so many more people are in the parish and demand pastoral time that the priest will have hours neither for general study nor for proper preparation; the necessity of knowledge, or the preacher will become a 'spin-text'; the necessity that this knowledge shall include the Scriptures, the primitive Fathers, and the records of the English Reformation; and so on; pages 43-5 are a very brief summary by King of a full treatment in Blunt of the work of the preacher. It is a good summary, and intelligible. The only odd point is the curious phrase in King, 'the mechanical part of the sermon'; which is doubtless due to the undergraduate's pen not keeping up with the speaker, for Blunt wrote 'the mechanical part of the construction of the sermon', and doubtless King would have reported him correctly in his lecture.The summary made good advice to future preachers. But it is not so good as King's advice to preachers when taken in totality, and not as a mere recorder of Blunt.

King's method cannot be called systematic. Teaching how to preach, he first gave (in sixteen pages as summarized) some good advice on preaching; then he summarized St Augustine's advice on preaching, in *De doctrina christiana*, book IV; then he summarized Gilbert Burnet in his *Pastoral Care* (as he called it, *A Discourse of the Pastoral Care* (1692)); then he summarized Blunt; then he summarized his French contemporary Bishop Dupanloup (*Entretiens sur la prédication* – not translated into English until 1890) – but with an extreme brevity, so that he need hardly have started on Dupanloup; unless, that is, the note-taker was fatigued.

To summarize Dupanloup, even in so laconic and unhelpful a fashion, if it was so laconic and unhelpful in the original version, would not have been possible for Blunt, partly because he could not have known Dupanloup's work but also because he would not think it right to use a contemporary Roman Catholic, even if he were French. One effect of the Oxford Movement was to make its adherents less insular in their attitudes to religion.

What is the difference between the forties and the seventies?

Blunt had a key passage on the village school: its value in enabling the priest to know the parents, and to learn who is sick, and who is unemployed, and who is leaving; in giving him an opening into the houses of the poor on a friendly footing; in growing him a future congregation; in forming a body of future adults with principles of morality; in giving him an agency to circulate tracts, and prayer books, and Bibles, and books from his lending library, and a knowledge of overseas missions which will also help the knowledge of geography. It will be 'a suitable area for any manifesto' (p. 185).

All this is missing from King. And it is not the only such central feature of parish work that is missing. Blunt had a section on preparing children for confirmation. It is surprisingly short in view of the importance of the subject to the individual. It does not seem to loom large in Blunt's scale of values. It is just a part of the work concerning schools. If the children have attended school, they will not *need* a preparation for confirmation, because it will have happened (p. 196). Because of the school, 'instead of a thoughtless heedless throng hastening to a holiday spectacle', the priest will be able to present to the bishop 'a well-instructed and hopeful fold seeking God's blessing at his hands and about to consecrate their lives to their Saviour in an honest and earnest heart'.

Hardly a child raises its individual head in King's notes. The word *catechizing* occurs (p. 4), taken out of a charge of Bishop Bull to his clergy of St David's diocese in 1708. He tells them not to be discouraged – 'if confirmation candidates fall away, start afresh' (p. 8). There is a warning against our losing affection for a boy as he reaches an awkward age, a 'rugged manhood'. The priest is often seen in the schools. The parish choir has boys in it, and if they are turned out for bad behaviour they resent it (p. 47). The pastor has a duty to look after the choirboys and their morals. The priest may need to deal with the complaint that the schoolmaster has been cruel to a child. King said that he was very pleased when he heard of a priest who spent four years teaching the Lord's Prayer in catechism (p. 74). And all the babes are in potentiality 'jewels in the crown of Christ' (p. 70).

This is much. But it is haphazard and in passing. Did the recorder fail to record, or did King miss out, a large area of pastoral life? In Blunt's book, which he valued, he had before him a systematic treatment of the parish school.

Of course the village school changed dramatically between 1840 and 1875. In the earlier years it was still mostly an organ of the Church to which boys and girls came bringing their pennies, and which the boys left earlier than the girls because they were needed in the fields. By 1875 there existed a national provision of schools to which boys and girls were compelled to go, and the Church's school was but a part of a wider system, and the parish priest was less powerful in the school, in that it was no longer 'his' school in the same way.

Another area of life is curiously missing, almost entirely, from the pastors of both 1840 and 1875. In Blunt brides and bridegrooms marry in church, but rather hugger-mugger, before a handful of people (p. 257), and if they have not attended school they marry like brute beasts without understanding, and if they have been to school will marry in a spirit of reverence and sobriety and with the knowledge that this is a sacrament and that their marriage is founded in religion and must be maintained in religion. King has the barest reference to marriage, as a marvellous thing which has a power, denied to the angels, of creating immortal souls (pp. 69-70); and how shocking it is to make jests about it when it has this sacredness.

Between Blunt and King came the first English divorce law of 1857. Neither in 1840 nor in 1883 do the pastors talk of any special preparation for marriage, or of what, if anything, to do about people who are divorced or whose marriage is in difficulty. The only way in which King betrayed the coming of a different age was in passing; for he warned his ordinands to be on guard if certain kinds of reading suggested evil to them – for example, 'divorce cases' (p. 20). This was the only sign of the new divorce law. It was also a sign that since Blunt wrote the national press was born. All divorce cases under the law of 1857 dealt with the adultery of one of the parties. Until reform of the press laws,

detailed reports of the adulteries made the first publicly acceptable, or at least publicly accepted, forms of press pornography.

We may infer that the reporter did not record all King's
lectures, either because he failed to attend, or because he afterwards lost some of his notes during a long life. It is hard to
imagine King, who had Blunt's book before him and valued it,
leaving out of set purpose themes which were still central to the
work of the parish priest.

Blunt was academic. He came out of a world where the main
work of the pastor was preaching, and where the sermon was
supposed to be three-quarters of an hour or an hour in length.
King was not highly academic, and came out of a world where
the main work of the pastor was care of the people, and the
sermon was supposed to last about twenty minutes. But both
expected their pastors to be learned men and to devote themselves to some very learned reading in the original tongues.

There were, however, certain differences. Blunt thought it
essential for the pastor to learn Hebrew as well as Greek and
Latin. King did not think Hebrew necessary, and did not seem to
expect an extensive knowledge of Greek, but expected an ability
to read Latin.

The world of Blunt's learning, though huge, is defined: the
Bible, the documents of the first three Christian centuries, the
documents of the Reformation – that is, in all cases, the original
documents, not modern books about them. Yet he also expected
certain 'modern' authors – Hooker, and Pearson, and Bull, and
Waterland, and S. R. Maitland on the Dark Ages, and Wordsworth's works on the Fathers, and Hardwick's *History of the
Thirty-Nine Articles*. He wished to deliver his pastor from
'vassalage to modern names and schools'. Part of the purpose of
this vast reading is defensive. He wished the pastor to be able to
defend the three orders of the ministry of bishop, priest, and
deacon; or to defend infant baptism against the Baptists; or to
justify a fixed liturgy against the independents; or to prove against
Roman Catholics that transubstantiation is not a primitive
Christian doctrine. 'I cannot promise that, simple as it is (this plan
of reading), it can be achieved in one term or two' (p. 136). 'It is a
prospectus of such an extent as not to bewilder, but enough to
require activity and patience to realise' (p. 137).

King's area of expectation was no less high. But, unlike Blunt, who thought that he asked what any active person could manage, he knew that he asked a lot – 'very great knowledge' (p. 31 from Bull). What the pastor needs to read includes, now, good sermons of different epochs and different styles – the Fathers' sermons, St Augustine or St John Chrysostom or St Bernard; famous French preachers, like Massillon or Lacordaire; a famous early Anglican preacher in Lancelot Andrewes; and the Tractarian preachers Newman, Pusey, Keble, and Liddon. Notice that King recommends Newman's Anglican sermons though Newman was now a famous Roman Catholic, just as he recommends the two French Catholics. Notice that he regards not only Newman and Pusey and Liddon as great preachers of the Oxford Movement, but also Keble, whose sermons most people thought to be less than the highest because the speaker could not be outgoing. Notice that he did not mind recommending three then living preachers, in Newman, Pusey, and Liddon. Notice that this child of the Oxford Movement did not recommend (among preachers) a single Evangelical preacher, or even an outspoken Protestant preacher. Blunt recommended Latimer's sermons as one of the documents of the English Reformation. Latimer did not appear in King.

Blunt and King were agreed in enforcing the study of primitive Christian liturgies. King, being later, had an extra dimension, the recognition that the arrangement of a church interior, and even its architecture, made an environment that can transform the nature or effect of a liturgy. Accordingly he added to the study of early liturgy the book by the lay historian E. A. Freeman, *Principles of Church Restoration* (London, 1846).

King was selective about the Fathers of the first three centuries. He was happy that his young should read 'auxiliaries', like Westcott on the *Canon of the New Testament*, or George Bull on the early witnesses for the doctrine of the Trinity, or Burton of Oxford on the same subject. There is nothing defensive in his desire to educate the priest. He has no desire to equip him to confute Baptists or Roman Catholics: except that he once talked about the need for understanding the polemical. Blunt lectured to Anglicans. King lectured to a university thrown open to the world, though doubtless most of those who went to his lectures were Anglicans. His attitude to knowledge was less controversial by reason of the situation in which he delivered his information. He might be educating Methodist and Congregationalist ministers as well as Anglican.

Part of the difference may also be due to another change in the law of the land. Blunt (pp. 254ff.) had a passage on the excellent value of the system of church rates, whereby all parishioners, and not only the Anglicans, were taxed by a local rate for the upkeep of the structure of the nave of the parish church; excellent because it brought home to everyone that the church belonged to them and that they had a responsibility for it even though they dissented from its worship; and so the local community was not divided into social groups. This system was obsolescent even in Blunt's day. Where it still survived, it was sometimes accepted peaceably as in ancient times. But in other places it caused fury and violent speeches at church meetings, and divided village communities. Gladstone finally abolished it by an Act of Parliament in 1868. King therefore does not mention it. And its abolition may be the one reason why King's attitude towards non-Anglican Protestants can be more generous than Blunt's.

This disciple of the Oxford Movement several times referred to John Wesley with much approval, in that both he and his followers had lessons to teach the Church of England. That made a contrast with Blunt thirty years before. The only reference to dissenters in the index to Blunt's book reads: 'Dissenters' arguments refuted from the Fathers.' King asked his ordinands to discover what was best and true in the teaching of the different sects of Christians, and to that end commended the reading of the Bampton Lectures of G. H. Curteis (*Dissent in its Relation to the Church of England* (London, 1872). With regard to the classical authors of the continental Reformation, Blunt commended a reading of Erasmus (*Dialogues*, and *Paraphrase of the New Testament*); and he evidently held the Reformation of the Church of England to be nearer that of Luther than that of Calvin (pp. 114, 117, 130). King nowhere mentioned Luther. He nowhere mentioned the need for time to study the continental Reformation; except – and it is a big except – he wanted his pupils to read John Calvin's *Institutes of the Christian Religion*.

The change therefore between the older high churchman and the new Oxford Movement man is this: the older man wants his pupils only to read books which will support their faith and doctrine as proper Church of England men. King wants them to read not only Anglican books but books by authors who were very much of a non-Anglican spirit. He wanted them to read – in those days they would have to read it in Latin – the moral theology of Busenhaum, who was notorious for laxity in the old battles over Jesuit morality. He wanted them to read the *Summa theologica* of St Thomas Aquinas, who, when King lectured at Oxford, was just about to be commended to the world in a famous encyclical by Pope Leo XIII. He wanted them to read Pascal – not only his beautiful *Pensées*, but the satire of the *Provincial Letters* (King, p. 31), which for all its wit no one can think a very edifying Christian document.

Above all, King wants his young men to engage in two areas of reading which it would never have occurred to Blunt to recommend; though in one area this was in part because Blunt could take it for granted that his young would read them. The first area was that of great poetry. King wanted them to read not only Dante but Homer and Aeschylus, Milton and Shakespeare, and of modern poets, Tennyson. The first four Blunt could have assumed his young men to have been forced to read at school, and knowledge of them would need no special commendation. But Blunt did commend George Herbert's poems and Keble's *Christian Year* (pp. 226 and 232). The second area commended by King was that of novels – 'good novels' – how you tell a novel from a good novel is not defined. This could never have occurred to Blunt. If it had, we are confident that he would have regarded the reading of a novel as a waste of someone's precious time and eyes. In King the intention is obvious. It is stated in these words: 'You will thus travel into the circumstances, and conditions, and situations of life.'

There is a big contrast in tone which is not only the contrast between generations, and not only the contrast between an old-fashioned high churchman and an Oxford Movement man, and not only the contrast between formal printed lectures and lectures printed informally with asides which the author, if he had printed them, might have excised.

King had an epigrammatic style; very direct. From the notes on him can be listed Dos and Don'ts for the pastor.

Don't say, I'm a spiritual person (6)
Don't keep God waiting. Study punctuality (13)
Don't begin a sermon with a platitude (34)
Don't think you have no style (36)
Don't lay on earnestness (36)
Don't sink the priest in the relieving officer (52) . . . and so on.

Or, more positively

A suffering condition of diffidence is not inconsistent with a sense of Almighty power (24)
Go round your parish, as it were, upon your knees (48)
No man is good for nothing; he is good for that something for which God intends him (17)
Make a little psalter of your own (8)
Discontent with our lot is disbelief in God's providence (13)
Humility is not making yourself humble, but knowing your relationship to great things (70) . . . and so on.

These laconic moralisms, direct, personal, make the attraction of the notes on King's lectures.

Let us define the difference between the two guides divided by a generation, and both wanting their young clergy to read a lot and be learned. Naturally, in such a demand upon time, whole areas of study are missing. Church history is missing from both. There would not be time. King includes far less than Blunt in the way of incitement to study the Old Testament. King's early Fathers are later in generation than Blunt's early Fathers – Blunt's are of the first three centuries, and his first essential author is Eusebius (p. 86). King's are of the high age, the fourth and fifth centuries. Blunt's Fathers are Origen and Clement and Justin Martyr and Cyprian and Tertullian and Hippolytus and Irennaeus and the Acts of the Martyrs. King's Fathers are Augustine and Basil and John Damascene and Gregory the Great; though Clement of Alexandria is also important to him.[2] To Blunt the study of the English Reformation is central. To King it hardly matters. To Blunt the study of monasticism or mysticism is worthless. To King, it matters that the young should know the

[2] The undergraduate reporter recorded a curious error which the editors of King allowed by some slip to pass. He made King say, 'If you are visiting a sick lawyer, you can quote from St Clement, whom he is sure to know' (p. 65).

mere outline of contemplative methods of prayer. He told them (p. 11) about the way of purgation and the way of illumination and the way of union; but it seems more as though they should know the meaning of the formulas than because he wanted to create any kind of structure of private prayer. Though he commended no special authors on prayer and the mystical way, he advised in passing the reading of the medieval mystics Richard and Hugh of St Victor, as well as St Bernard of Clairvaux. Blunt has no apparent notion that human nature can be studied. To King this is an essential part of the work of a pastor, to be done by self-knowledge, and observation, and the reading of classical moralists, and the reading of great poetry, and the reading of good novels.

Blunt's clergyman will be better armed as a controversialist. King has no interest in arming his clergyman for a fight. Blunt's clergyman will be systematically learned, better equipped to help his people by solid instruction. King's clergyman will be better equipped to help his people when hearing their confessions, and when listening to their troubles in private counselling. Blunt's clergyman will have more sense of history, King's will have more poetic and literary sensibility. Blunt's clergyman need have learned nothing from the Oxford Movement, unless he used in his devotions Keble's *Christian Year*. King's clergyman will have learned from the Anglican Newman, and Pusey, and Keble, and Liddon; especially Liddon, whose book *The Elements of Religion* (1872) was to make the fundamental book of philosophy of religion for him, and whose sermons were more warmly commended as models, and for study about method, than anyone else's. Blunt's clergyman might have a harder head, and be a more dogmatic personality and might produce a people with a clearer understanding of the faith of the Church of England. But he need understand nothing of the way of contemplative prayer. King's clergyman was likely to make prayerfulness more central to his ideals of life, and would be better equipped to help people in ways of private prayer.

For Blunt, the pastor must try to know a lot, because he is a teacher. He must have zeal, so that he can move mountains, and can kindle. He is conscious of his commission, but does not always want to use its powers. He will not seek popularity among his people by easy routes, as by laxity. He must be active among his people. He must be discreet and prudent. He must be reverent in the conduct of worship.

For King the pastor must be a person who understands quiet, and prayer, and who himself spends time on prayer. He must try to know a lot because he is a teacher. He must be discreet and prudent. He must be conscious of an ideal of saintliness. He must have a sense of his commission because that sense is the only safeguard against arrogance. He must map out his day by a rule, so that study does not get swamped by pastoral care and pastoral care is not neglected for the sake of study. He must be patient about results and care patiently about each individual. He must be accessible to everyone. He must be reverent in his conduct of worship. He must also reverence everyone. He must distrust himself and trust God.

In this way King's little book, or rather someone's book of what King said, enables us to point towards a pastoral difference made by the coming of the Oxford Movement.

Chapter 15

CATHOLICISM

Underneath the worship of God lies silence, a wordless praise, an eyeless vision. When a man gets faith, he does not get it as he gets a knowledge of England's history, or as he gets a knowledge of sparking plugs. For *gets* is the wrong word. The word which rings true is not *gets* but *receives*. If you get faith at all, you feel as though you have received it. You hardly asked for it. You may not have wanted it. It came. *Nulla fides divina nisi per infusionem* – no true faith without a descent upon you; as it were, poured out, from on high.

The Quakers say that all worship ought to be silent unless a member is moved to speak. This opinion springs from an overwhelming truth of religion: worship is deeper than the words which are spoken by a priest, deeper than the hymns which are sung, deeper than the prayers of any prayer book. Something in man's praise of God is secret, concealed in the citadel of an interior castle of the personality, the most private of possessions, though no possession.

This faith which comes does not come unclothed. No man ever received faith in God naked, unadorned, unaccompanied, unsacramentalized, unsymbolized. It comes amid things – which it makes sacred as it comes – a Damascus road, a fig tree, a garden at Milan, a lake, a haystack, a thunderstorm, a room high in a tower at Wittenberg, the customs of a home, the affection of a saint, a litany in a chapel, the poetry of a love-poet, the music of psalms, the ritual and symbol of a sacrificial offering. No true faith without associations, no true faith without a context, *nulla fides divina nisi per ecclesiam*, no divine faith without a church.

Faith, therefore, is always received in a 'historical' context – the symbols of a family, or a society, or a denomination, or a

307

people; an environment which gives symbols their context and meaning.

A 'Catholic mind' is a Christian mind with a sense of Christian history.

I seek to illustrate certain consequences of this axiom.

I THE WORD 'ECUMENICAL'

The casual world can hardly understand why it is not simple for Christians to unite. It thinks all you need is a little give-and-take, give a doctrine here and take a doctrine there. Doctrines are not like that, nor is faith. Someone receives faith as a totality of association and of communion. In the faith of a person his or her silence is as weighty as his or her utterance; sometimes weightier. In the faith of a Church its silence can be as weighty as its definitions. This is a perception of the Holy Orthodox Church of the East. In Russia and in Greece and in Rumania and Bulgaria they understand this perfectly. Once I was allowed the privilege of attending an ordination in Moscow and was invited with others to stand in the sanctuary behind the iconostasis. The church was packed with men and women standing, no room to move, no room to do anything but cross the breast. I felt powerful emotion in witnessing such a liturgy in the capital of a country where the government was hostile to that liturgy. And when the service reached the Nicene creed, the vast congregation sang it mightily, and the heart lifted almost into exaltation; until we came to the clause in the creed 'proceeding from the Father' – and suddenly we came down from the rafters with a bump, as the reproving voice of a Russian priest said in my ear, 'Nyet Filioque' – *not* from the Father *and the Son*.

Father Rudhitzky was not quite rebuking me and my Church for bad doctrine, that we followed St Augustine in the words of our creed. That was not quite what it felt like. It felt as though he attacked me not for error, but for irreverence, almost as though I walked upon the altar in my boots. Whether from his attitude or his choice of moment, he was not concerned in whether my opinions on the blessed Trinity differed from his own. His faith was totality. He did not pick or choose. The silence of his Church was as weighty in his worship as its utterance.

The casual world finds this hard to fathom. It sees that the word *Catholic* means universal; and sees that the word *ecumenical* means universal; and so thinks that the word *Catholic* and the word *ecumenical* mean the same. It is not so. Even some modern Roman Catholics, eirenic and charitable individuals, have begun to like the word *ecumenical* better than the word *Catholic*: preferring the modern word because the word *Catholic* carries too fierce a history, and gives forth a little perfume not pleasing in their nostrils, reminding people not only of *The Cloud of Unknowing* or the lepers of Damian, but of Bogside and St Bartholomew's Day.

Charles Gore would not have liked this identity between the word *Catholic* and the word *ecumenical*. Why not? Because the word *ecumenical* also has a history. It does not come to us, any more than the word *Catholic*, with all the innocence of the newborn. It has a shorter history, only a hundred years of history. But even in a hundred years words pick up smell. The word *ecumenical* suggests something contemporary; the word *Catholic* something historic. The modern word is free, or nearly free, from the association of sectarian argument. But it is free also from other, and richer associations, from the memory (for example) of St Augustine and St Paul.

No one wishes to return to the day when the word *Catholic* was treated like a sixpence in your trousers pocket – a piece of private property.

The word *Catholicism* was, and is, an easy word to 'confessionalize', to appropriate, to misappropriate, to stuff into your waistcoat. Gabriel Marcel wrote in 1961, 'If we say "we Catholics", we are already almost crossing beyond the limits of Catholicism, and almost ceasing to think like Catholics.'[1] In the Counter-Reformation Cardinal Bellarmine gave a notorious definition: 'the Church of Christ is as visible as the Republic of Venice'. Men defined Catholicity solely in terms of visible structures, of Pope, or bishops, or councils. The definitions were adapted to the needs of controversialists in a controversial age. They were smart, they bristled, they were easy for theologians to

[1] *Schöpferische Treue* (Zurich, 1961), p. 174.

handle.[2] And, like some other things that bristle, and are easy for theologians to handle, they bore small relationship to the facts of Christian life. More than a hundred years ago John Henry Newman, and Johann Adam Möhler of Tübingen, tried to present an interior kind of Catholicism: as the inward spirit, or life, or idea, of the historic Church, growing and developing through the centuries. Though they were still in the early stages of modern critical history, they had the sense of historical movement, which did not sit happily with scholastic manuals and their precise definitions of the Church. Men began to think less of a static, unchanging Church, and more of a pilgrim Church, always on the way, always in need of reform, always to be adapted to meet new needs in human society, though always with the fullness of the gospel which it received. Such thinkers were often a small minority. Pope John XXIII appropriated something of this outlook; it marked discussions at the second Vatican Council, and it was taken into the drafting of the encyclical of that Council upon the Church, *Lumen gentium*; though that encyclical neither rejected nor even modified, except by atmosphere, the tradition and structural definition of the Catholic Church. Interior renewal was what Pope John wanted. Interior renewal was what many Roman Catholics wanted. So came the transforming movement in liturgy, church life, parish and diocesan councils and finally in Roman church government, which is one of the great facts of Christian history in the twentieth century.

And then crisis, as Pope Paul VI called it. The Movement ran into a special source of conflict, which was not simply the conflict between those who love traditional ways of worship and dislike modern words, and those who want the modern words to be so modern that lovers of tradition can no longer use them. A static structure versus an inward dynamic renewal − the men of renewal were bound to question whether the structure was adequate, whether it was less like the structure of the plant which enables it to grow and bear fruit, and more like the structure of a chain which shackles the leg to a prison of the past. The inevitable questions were given point and form when the encyclical

---

[2] For the way in which the definition of *Catholic* concentrated ever more on orthodoxy and unity, see the inaugural lecture of Max Seckler at Tübingen, 'Katholisch als Konfessionsbezeichnung', in *Theologische Quartalschrift*, 145 (1965), 401ff.

Humanae vitae condemned family planning. For here was not a theoretical question about academic truth, or an aesthetic question about the language of the liturgy, but a moral question where consciences were engaged. And so the tension grew; until in 1970 the Roman Catholic professor Hans Küng of Tübingen wrote a book to slay the whole idea of infallibility and ask whether it was not time that the Roman Catholic Church got along without that doctrine. We are far from having heard the last of this argument. The Cardinal of Turin is supposed to have summed up his troubles in the words, 'Here in Turin too many have stopped at the first Vatican Council, while others are already at the third Vatican Council.'

We stand at a distance of just a hundred and twenty years from the first Vatican Council. Not so much the opening of the archives, as the healing perspective of time, has enabled students to perceive that greatest controversy of modern Christian history in more judicious and less partisan frames of mind. The infighting seems now as irrelevant and as wearisome as the infighting over the Council of Florence or the Council of Constance. The once-mighty names of anti-ultramontanes Döllinger and Acton no longer look so dominating when we see how unjust to papalists they could sometimes be; and the one-time whitewash of old papalist historians ceases to persuade anyone to see it all as quite white. Because that history has died in emotion, we are better able to attempt to say what happened and why. We see these events depending on movements deeper than the choices of individuals. We are less likely to attribute all the blame to the opinionated simplicity of Pope Pius, or to Archbishop Manning's consciousness of power, or to the failure of the French Emperor to use the only external threat which could have stopped the Council in its tracks, or to the extremism betrayed by leading German or French journalists. We see all the intellectual uncertainties of the nineteenth century coming to a point in Rome: the agonized and only partially successful quest for the union of freedom with order under democratic constitutions; the unpredictable forces of modern nationalism; the new power of the modern press, for the first time exerting its blinding public pressures upon an assembly where the meetings were supposed to be private and suddenly were not. In short, we see the unpalatable formulations of infallibility coming less from a series of rational choices by theologians than by inward and half-conscious movements of people's hearts as they struggled to adjust themselves to the events of their time and the tensions of their society.

It is certain that in the end the Catholic Church will need to get along without taking particular notice of the precise formulations of Vatican I, any more than it takes particular notice of the ecumenical Council held in the Lateran by Pope Leo X just before Luther published his theses on indulgences. But a Church cannot consciously and publicly jettison a proposition which has been so integrally associated with profound moments in its religious life and course of development. Churches cannot so turn their backs upon their past. To turn the back upon the past is not congruous with the history, indeed the nature, of Catholicism; and what must happen, and could only happen slowly, is a gradual pushing of outward expressions of it into the cellars of Vatican City, side by side with the Maundy Thursday bull of excommunications, which used to be so terrifying, but has now grown a charitable dust by disuse.

The religious need for which that old Vatican controversy was concerned was a need with which Charles Gore was concerned in his own sphere. I started with the elements in faith which are inarticulate, which underlie words, and which words never exhaust. Charles Gore stood for a different proposition: *Veritas Dei est enuntiabilis*, truths of God are speakable, they are a gospel, you can tell people about them. Because the Roman Catholic Church is now engaged in a disturbance over the nature of authority; because the Eastern Orthodox Churches are asking how they can reconcile holy tradition with meaningful dialogue with Marxism; because the Church of England is bit by bit reorganizing its self-government; because Protestant denominations are still perplexed and concerned over Christian order and freedom; because some aspects of television, and of current philosophies of education, breed in the young a sensation that religion is more a matter of trivial and superficial debate than of obedience in the will – Catholicism is hesitant, and stutters, and is humble. It is good that it is hesitant, and stutters, and is humble. It is good that it no longer treats truth as though it is a brick to throw. But whatever happens in the modern argument, authority continues; men's souls and bodies are in need. God gave a Church, and a Bible with a Word, and sacraments which are given to us and not manufactured by us, and a priesthood to consecrate. To speak only of the religious experience which is inarticulate is to open the door to superstition and credulity. That the experience of God is objective truth, Gore believed with all his being. It could be spoken. It could communicate with the modern world even when the modern world disliked it. It had something not only to feel but to say. It was not just a feeling, God meets humanity in his sacrament, but knowledge that Christ is offered in his sacrament; listening to the Word of God in the Bible and not just discussion how that Word can be spoken. Gore was a theologian with less distrust of theology than his master Newman. He was a born leader; normal, decisive, unwavering, courageous. He was not always prudent about it. No one totally wise could have done what he did – imagine Archbishop Randall Davidson, who (if it is possible to suffer from an excess in a cardinal virtue) suffered from an excess of the virtue of prudence. Gore was very clear-headed. Was he too clear-headed?

2 THE RELIGION OF NATURAL MAN

The second illustration concerns the religion of natural man. Here is a proposition: Catholicism cannot believe in 'religionless Christianity' and remain Catholic. It needs, and aims, to foster, elicit, baptize, and finally transcend, the formless religious apprehensions of society and the world.

What did Newman do for the Church of England? As with all men, the result was a mixture. If you read some of the *Parochial and Plain Sermons*, you are repelled. Why? Is it that the principles seem to you so erroneous, or the argument so tortuous? Or is it just as you might reject when you read some of the sermons by Bossuet, or by St Augustine – the thing is obsolete? But if you read others of the *Parochial and Plain Sermons*, your mind finds itself to inhabit timeless truths. The cast of thinking, the mode of expression, the principles advocated, spring from a background of thought and of ethics which has helped to condition our own minds. We feel kinship.

On the one hand Newman deepened the mystery of faith; that

is, he made English understanding of faith less shallow. He focussed it upon and around the sacrament of the Body and Blood upon the altar; a gift not depending on your faith; consecrating the natural produce of the world; a sacrament with more history to it than any other act of the modern age, and yet an act of now, here to you, taking into itself your offering of yourself and your world which is the world of now; an act private, even secret to your soul, and simultaneously an act of the universal Church; a gift which men can describe in words and speak truth about, and simultaneously a gift which, like the lilies of the field, needs no words and is beyond the level of words.

Always the Church of England appealed to the ancient and undivided Church, but usually as part of intellectual thinking, as a piece of controversy, sustaining the middle road between communions which added, and communions which subtracted, creeds. Newman appealed to that indeed, but to more: to ethical ideals, to hours of prayer, the communion of saints, the ascetic life, to nights of meditation, to self-discipline and penance. Some of this appeal we see now to have been overpressed, an immaturity or overexcitement found in the early stages of all religious movements. But what remained as a permanent possession was a lifting up of the eyes beyond the insular tradition of thought and devotion, a new sense of the history of all Christendom and its worshipping harmonies; a new ability to sympathize with holiness in the prayers of Eastern Orthodox liturgy, or in the ways of St Bernard or St Francis, or (rather later) in the devotional writers of the Counter-Reformation; an understanding of continuity in Christian tradition so that men could again define a Catholic mind as a mind with the sense of how the visible Church lives as an organized body from the apostles till now.

But this was not all that Newman did.

A quarter of a century ago a group of Anglicans, Eric Abbott, later Dean of Westminster, among them, and with Michael Ramsey, later Archbishop of Canterbury, as chairman, published a report entitled *Catholicity*. In that report they claimed that Catholicism and the true doctrine of creation went hand in hand; that Catholicism sees all the world as God's world, and as reflecting His light. They got into trouble for that claim. Men wrote pamphlets against them. Men asserted that they arrogated to Catholic Christianity something common among those who repudiated the name of Catholic. In retrospect, perhaps, the draftsman expressed himself too sweepingly. Yet the assertion witnesses to a truth. A gulf is set between an intellectual attitude to created being and a moral attitude. Newman did more than anyone to make at home in modern English religion two interwoven ideas: the indwelling of God in His world, as that idea is found in Wordsworth and others of the romantics; and Catholic sacramentalism, with all its consequences for an attitude to the material world; and to set this twin apprehension, not in an intellectual context, like proving-God-exists, but in a moral context, sending men to their knees before the nearness of a transcendent God.

If all the world is God's world, how shall we despise these erroneous, or fumbling, or inarticulate, or diffused sensations about the mystery of God, still to be found so widely among contemporaries who could not quite call themselves Christian? Or how despise (let us say) the aesthetic faculty which may lift men's minds towards things that lie beyond a workaday world?

Applying this proposition further, I illustrate it in two ways: first the nature of liturgical revision; secondly, Gore and mysticism.

a The nature of liturgical revision

How did the Church settle upon 25 December as the date of Christmas? No one knew when Jesus was born. So men like Clement of Alexandria made calculations, and guessed, and speculated, and added and subtracted, and produced different answers, a date in March, a date in November, a date in January, a date in December. It is certain that by such methods no one could achieve a feast of Christmas acceptable to the Churches. The logical method was powerless. To find a day acceptable to the Churches they must find a day congruous with their way of *worship*, not with their way of *astronomy*. They must see how the winter solstice, with the lengthening life of the sun, was perfectly fitting with their prayers which loved to see their Saviour as the sun of righteousness, rising with healing in his wings; they loved therefore to set their churches orientated towards the East, not (like the Jews) because Jerusalem was in the East, but because the sun rose in the East. They liked to lay their dead so that the light would shine upon their faces; martyrs upon the scaffold would turn towards the East to say their last committal; and so they came to feel, not very quickly, that the coming of the babe in Bethlehem was like the new coming of the sun. A great Christian feast was founded because the Church heeded the natural affections of common religious instincts, which expressed themselves in poetry and posture and mysticism. It did not achieve it, and could not achieve it, by mathematics. It had to take into account both the congruity with existing Christian prayers and the natural religious instincts which men brought with them into the Church.

That is one illustration, among many, of what happens. An innovation in worship is needed. Great innovations are possible. But such innovations are only possible where they are found congruous with existing Christian prayer and natural religious instinct. We are not dealing in the tops of men's heads, but in the elements of their religion which are hardly susceptible of words. We are dealing as much in hallowed association as in taste, or in clarity of meaning. Therefore every novelty in a way of worship needs time; digestion; reflexion. Nothing would be more unwise than for the Church of England, in ten years' time, to say that the age of liturgical experiment is over, and we must return to a uniform service in every church, so that people may always know where they are. Christmas took a hundred years or more in its establishing. And even when people establish the new, they do not jettison the old. People will perhaps say that they have got Series 2 or Series 3 or Series 4 and can jettison a 1662 Prayer Book, now obsolete. A book which, in whatever form, has once borne a people's prayers does not become obsolete in that kind of way. We are not dealing in expediency but in private inarticulate treasure that touches some people's faith. When the Church put Christmas on 25 December, some Christians thought it expedient to abolish the existing date used to celebrate Christmas. They tried therefore to drop any celebration on 6 January. They failed hopelessly. The Church insisted on keeping 6 January, and continued to remember events near to Christmas, the coming of the wise men and the baptism.

b Gore and mysticism

Gore was no admirer of the mystical tradition within Catholicism. He lived at a time when English interest reached its peak through the writings of Baron von Hügel and Evelyn Underhill. Gore was no admirer of either. Miss Underhill is not mentioned in his life, but we can imagine him disapproving much of what she wrote. He argued with von Hügel, and respected him, but distrusted the centre of his thought, and became very uncomfortable in the face of it.

'The idea that religion, in its most characteristic form, was a kind of numinous mysticism, transcending in essence all ethical considerations, was abhorrent to him.' 'After all (said Gore), the only thing certain is that we are certain we must do what is right.'[3] We know that he read *The Imitation of Christ*. But the only thing that is recorded in his biography about that reading is an outburst of laughter, in the middle of the holy silence, when he came to the sentence 'One vice must be extirpated every year' (The joke was more pointed because he was then Vice-Principal of Cuddesdon College and familiarly known as Vice).[4] That Catholic tradition which wanted to assert 'Religion is adoration' was not Gore's tradition. Adoration was not necessarily ethical. For him religion was faith in God through objective truth, and a consequent issue in a good life or attempt at a good life.

And this conviction of Gore needs modifying, as Catholicism grapples with the minds of our day. Everyone who deals in the most elementary kind of apologetic feels the vast inadequacy, even the impotence, of words. Our contemporaries can be seen in their various books to be grappling with this sense of impotence; and the trouble is, that their grappling too often resembles a mere intellectual battle, as though, in spite of all Newman said, it was by dialectic that God would at last save his people. The argument has to be carried on almost as if in the presence of God, with a religious sense of blindness and humility, with St Augustine's feeling of the gulf which divides the light of God from all our

---

[3] G. L. Prestige, *Gore*, p. 177.
[4] Prestige, p. 43. The joke is not fair to St Thomas à Kempis, who wrote (I, XI, 5) 'If it were conceivable that we could extirpate one vice every year, we should soon be perfect. But often it is the opposite we feel: that we were better and purer when we were first converted than after many years of Christian life.'

descriptions and analyses; yet with an overwhelming conviction of the purpose and the reality of that light; as a man might contemplate a wild lily of the field, flowering amid the ruins of King Solomon's temple.

FURTHER READING

Since the first chapter was published in 1960, various advances have taken place, and it is possible only to mention the chief of them.

1 A modern Oxford scholar gave a systematic treatment of the whole Movement and its ideas, especially its spiritual ideas: Geoffrey Rowell, *The Vision Glorious* (Oxford, 1983). Dean Church's classic history, *The Oxford Movement*, was edited and provided with a new introduction by G. F. A. Best in 1970.

2 Research into Newman is an industry. The publication of most of his letters edited by Stephen Dessain and others after him, *Letters of John Henry Newman at the Birmingham Oratory* (Oxford, 1961–   ; Joyce Sugg edited a selection of 155 letters, *A Packet of Letters* (Oxford, 1983)); a steady stream of articles and studies (especially valuable is *The Rediscovery of Newman*, edited by John Coulson and A. M. Allchin, 1967); the re-editing of several of his most important texts; the occasional excellent biography (especially C. S. Dessain, 3rd edn., Oxford, 1980; Meriol Trevor, *Newman*, vol. 1, *The Pillar of the Cloud*; vol. 2, *Light in Winter* (1962)). A new biography of Newman has just been published (I. T. Ker, *John Henry Newman* (OUP, 1969), which makes extensive use of the correspondence. But tucked away in numerous articles, not only in English, is a remarkable collection of good work.

3 There is still a lot of work to do on Pusey, where the archive is so plentiful. Of recent publications the most weighty is *Pusey Rediscovered*, edited by Perry Butler (1985), and cf. D. Forrester, *Young Dr Pusey* (1989), and A. G. Lough, *Dr Pusey* (1981).

4 We are still a long way from getting Manning in the right perspective, except for the agony or predicament of his mind

during the 1840s (David Newsome, *The Parting of Friends* (1966).

5 Two minor figures have received admirable treatment: Hurrell Froude by Piers Brendon, in *Hurrell Froude and the Oxford Movement* (1974), and Faber by Ronald Chapman, in *Father Faber* (1964). There is a good short life of Edward King by J. A. Newton, *Search for a Saint: Edward King* (1977). R. Addington edited selected letters of Faber (Cowbridge, Glam., 1974).

6 We know more of the ritual controversies of the sixties and seventies; and of the second or third generation of Tractarians who were priests in the slum parishes of London: Machonochie (M. Reynolds, *Martyr of Ritualism: Father Machonochie* (1965)), and Charles Lowder (L. E. Ellsworth, *Charles Lowder and the Ritualist Movement* (1982)). See also *Ritualism and Politics in Victorian Britain* by James Bentley (1978). We also know more of the sisterhoods and the monastic movement: see T. J. Williams and A. W. Campbell, *The Park Village Sisterhood* (1965). There is a good short treatment of the subject by Nigel Yates, *The Oxford Movement and Anglican Ritualism* (London, Historical Association, 1983), and an article by him on the same topic in *J. Eccl. Hist.* (1988). See also P. F. Anson, *The Call of the Cloister* (1964); P. F. Anson, *Fashions in Church Furnishings* (1965); P. T. Marsh, *The Victorian Church in Decline* (1969); J. F. White, *The Cambridge Movement* (1962).

7 Local studies, however brief and apparently limited in their matter, often afford illuminating help, by way of illustration: see Edward Royle, *The Victorian Church in York* (York, 1983).

8 Among the laymen, the most important studies are naturally of Gladstone. Colin Matthew's prefaces to the volumes of Gladstone's diary are indispensable (H. C. G. Matthew, *Gladstone 1809–74* (Oxford, 1986). There is a systematic treatment of the earlier period in Perry Butler, *Gladstone, Church, State and Tractarianism, 1809–59* (Oxford, 1982).

INDEX

Abbot, George, 10
Aberdeen, fourth Earl of, 248
Achilli, G., 102, 154, 178.
Acton, Lord, 33, 58, 116, 127, 145, 176, 189, 287, 311
Albert, Prince, 248
Andrewes, Lancelot, 8–9, 75, 83–4, 148, 195, 241, 247, 301
apostolic succession, 3, 43
Aquinas, St Thomas, 8, 12, 162, 303
Arnold, Thomas, 60, 117, 135, 139, 146, 209
Augustine of Hippo, St, 7, 14

Baxter, Richard, 10–11
Benson, Arthur, 131
Benson, E.W., 203, 253–5, 267, 270–1, 273–4, 287
Benson, R. M., 217, 287
Best, G. F. A., 63
Bible, modern criticism of, 14, 60, 283
Bickersteth, E. H., 92–4, 267–8
Blomfield, C. J., 68, 72, 74–5, 78, 80–1, 84
Blondel, Maurice, 173
Blunt, J. J., 248, 294ff.
Bramhall, John, 11
branch theory of Church, 49
Bremond, Henri, 163ff., 167ff.
Bridges, Robert, 97
Bright, William, 266, 279, 287
Bowden, J. W., 181, 190
Browne, Harold, 252–3
Bull, George, 10, 12, 15, 52, 300–1
Buonaiuti, E., 162
Burgon, J. W., 139, 144, 151, 242, 258
Burnet, Gilbert, 15
Butler, Joseph, 32–3
Butler, W. J., 226ff., 240ff., 273, 280–1, 283

Calvinism, 1, 7–13, 302
Cambridge Platonists, 11
Camden Society, 46
cathedrals, 68ff., 76
celibacy, 8, 216, 290

ceremonial, 46; see also mitres; ritual
Champneys, W., 81
Charles I, King, 3, 5, 17, 23, 61
Chichester, third Earl of, 81ff.
Church, R. W.: youth, 151; effect of Newman upon, 151, 181; attitude to Keble, 23, 58; attitude to Golightly, 237; literary critic, 53; country pastor, 250; sermons, 287; made dean, 250; Liddon and, 217; advice to Gladstone, 252–3, 267–8; book on the Oxford Movement, 23, 139, 143ff.
Church and State in England, 3, 16ff., 247ff., 266ff.
Coleridge, John Duke, 61
Coleridge, Sir John T., 55ff.
confession, private, 8, 14, 215–16, 227, 240, 242, 261, 263, 270, 296–7, 305
Copeland, W. J., 139, 141, 144
Cox, G. V., 137
Cranmer, Thomas, 6, 16–17, 247
Creighton, Mandell, 271, 284
Crowther, Samuel, 81
Cuddesdon College, 221ff., 258ff., 289ff., 317
Cyprian, St, 8

Darwin, Charles, 118–19, 160–1, 203–4, 286
Davidson, Randall, 254f., 276, 285, 287, 313
Dessain, S., 165–6, 175, 179, 196
Disraeli, Benjamin, 74–5, 249ff.
divine right of kings, 16–17
divorce law, 281
Dublin, Catholic university, 99ff.
Dykes, J. B., 96–7

eastward position, 47
Ecclesiastical Commission, 63ff.
Evangelical Movement, 1–2, 9ff., 17ff., 39–40, 81, 148, 193, 222–3, 267, 281, 288, 290; hymnody, 89, 92f.

Faber, F. W., 88, 97, 156
Fathers, study of, 7–8, 11, 29–30, 49, 304–5

Ferrar, Nicholas, 8
Fisher, Geoffrey, 72–3
Forbes, A. P., 237
Froude, Hurrell, 19, 24ff., 213; and his
    brother, 54, 139; travel with Newman, 87;
    death, 58, 143; his *Remains*, 43–4, 55
Froude, J. A., 33; thinks Keble narrow, 54;
    his history, 105, 114–15, 124; as rector of
    St Andrews, 114; memories, 139

Gibbon, Edward, 99
Gladstone, W. E.: defends Ecclesiastical
    Commission, 75; not quite approved by
    Keble, 61; choice of Cambridge professor,
    123; on Church's book, 145; diarist, 166;
    and social reform, 198–9, 203; and
    patronage of Crown, 249ff., 260–1, 280,
    289; not approved by Oxford
    undergraduates, 265; or by the *Record*, 286
Golightly, C. P., 237ff.
Gore, Charles, 51, 283, 285, 293, 317
Gorham case, 62, 218
Graham, Eric, 290ff.

Halifax, Viscount, 281
Hamilton, W. K., 248
Hammond, Henry, 11, 42, 52
Hampden, R. D., 60, 142, 178
Hardie, Keir, 101ff.
Hawkins, Edward, 28–9, 139ff., 144, 150–1
Herbert, George, 8–9, 53, 303
high church, defined, 4ff., 17ff.
Hook, W. F., 136
Hooker, Richard, 8, 10, 13, 22, 52, 58, 60,
    138, 148, 263, 300
Horsman, Edward, 69–70, 73ff.
Hort, F. J. A., 178
Howley, William, 71, 199
Hughes, H. P., 202
Hughes, Thomas, 129–30
Hume, David, 2, 103, 119
Hutton, R. H., 95, 265
hymns, 87ff., 235

Jelf, R. W., 46
Jewel, John, 6, 75
Johnson, Manuel, 217
Jowett, Benjamin, 61, 265
justification, doctrine of, 7, 11–13, 15, 17ff.,
    40

Kaye, Sir Richard, 83
Keble, John, 2, 17, 18ff.; his father, 57; his
    person, 54ff., 138; sacramentalism, 32; and
    Real Presence, 21; *The Christian Year*, 21–
    2, 52, 55, 87, 95, 303; in Oriel, 102; *Lyra*

apostolica, 87; *Lectures on Poetry*, 58, 138; on
    truth as never popular, 26; against
    originality, 27, 57; criticised for narrowness
    of mind, 54; suspects logic in religion, 33;
    in favour of tradition, 27; study of the
    primitive Church an instrument of reform,
    29–30; lover of the Bible, 30; against
    Biblical critics, 60; on faith, 35; on ritual,
    236; as confessor, 215; helps to edit
    Froude's *Remains*, 44, 55; approves of
    Tract 90, 43; writes *Life of Bishop Wilson*,
    58–60; his diligence, 59; sermon on
    Tradition, 59; writes Tract 89, 59; writes
    Eucharistic Adoration, 59; edits Hooker, 60;
    against Wesley, 60; gives dinner to Pusey
    and Newman, 61, 180; death, 143;
    memory of, 290
King, Edward, 241–4, 253ff., 273ff.
Kingsley, Charles, 105ff., 178, 190

Lansbury, George, 198, 201
Latitudinarians, 6f., 14, 40, 45, 47
Laud, William, 8–10, 247
Law, William, 138
'Lead, Kindly Light', 86ff.
Liddon, H. P.: youth, 214ff.; Pusey's close
    disciple, 50; as teacher at Cuddesdon, 41,
    228ff., ministers to murderer, 240–1; friend
    of Hamilton, 248; as able defender of the
    Bible, 50–1; in the last ditch, 50; against
    Biblical criticism, 264, 283; canon of St
    Paul's, 250; as preacher, 250, 270–1, 287,
    301, 305; as Pusey's biographer, 38, 152,
    170–1, 246; and Church, 145; offered
    bishopric, 255, 266ff.; on philosophy of
    religion, 305; memory, 290
Loisy, Alfred, 161–2
Luther, Martin, and Lutheranism, 5–8, 11–15,
    55, 60, 112–13, 127, 160, 247
Lux mundi, 51
Lyra apostolica, 87

Manning, H. E.: as archdeacon, 224; becomes
    Roman Catholic, 50, 169, 218; Strachey's
    portrait, 146; antithesis with Newman,
    156–9; accused of dogmatism, 171; against
    evolution, 204; prefers gentlemen-priests,
    213; at first Vatican Council, 311
Marriott, Charles, 95, 145, 149, 217, 224, 257,
    284, 287
Maurice, Frederick Denison, 117, 121, 122,
    130
Methodism, 23, 202; hymnody, 89
mitres, 178, 271–2
Modernism, 161ff.
monastic life, revival of, 39, 217

Monk, J. H., 69
Mozley, J. B., 51, 217, 287
Mozley, T. M., 54, 139ff., 152, 175, 217
muscular Christianity, 130ff., 244

Newman, Francis, 54, 176, 243
Newman, J. H.: his father, 141–2; his person,
143; partly Evangelical origins, 18; his
brother, 54; lover of Bible, 30; at
Hawkins's sermon as undergraduate, 28;
poetic strand, 19, 52, 87ff.; as hymn-writer,
52; friendship with Froude, 24f., 87; and
Bowden, 88; and Tom Mozley, 139–40;
and Keble, 25; refuses to write a portrait of
Keble, 56; travel in the Mediterranean, 87,
179–82; *Tracts for the Times*, 24, 30, 33;
Arians of the Fourth Century, 145; and
Whately in Oriel, 180–1; as vicar of St
Mary's, 248; *Parochial and Plain Sermons*,
32, 102, 145, 170, 179, 303, 313f.; as
orator, 143; true theologian, 51; originality,
57; astringent, 136; as controversialist, 174;
silences, 156; letter-writer, 156; at prayer,
194–5; idea of tradition, 28, 31; *Lectures on
Justification*, 40; *Lectures on the Prophetical
Office*, 30–1, 178; helps to edit Froude's
Remains, 44; distrusts too much clarity, 31–
2; idea of faith, 32ff.; charge of scepticism,
32–3; *Ecclesiastical Miracles*, 33, 50, 191–2;
friendship with the early Fathers, 36; *The
Church of the Fathers*, 190; Tract 90, 15–16,
43f.; not for an excess of ritualism, 48;
severity at Littlemore, 40; *Lives of the
English Saints*, 192; *Essay on Development*,
145, 161, 182–3; becomes Roman
Catholic, 138; at the Birmingham Oratory,
97; at University of Dublin, 99ff.; made
cardinal, 154; influence, 165, 310; later
publications: *Loss and Gain*, 189, *The
Second Spring*, 102, *The Idea of a University*,
99ff., 145, *Callista*, 189–90, *Historical
Sketches*, 190, *Verses on Religious Subjects*,
91, *Apologia*, 19f., 87, 92, 100, 102, 105ff.,
124, 137, 141, 145, 149, 174, 176, 196, *The
Dream of Gerontius*, 52, 179, *Occasional
Verses*, 86, *Grammar of Assent*, 35–6, on
Biblical criticism, 147, 193
newspapers, religious, 210
nonconformist conscience, 202–3
non-jurors, 5, 17

Oakeley, Frederick, 44, 47, 48
Oratory, Birmingham, 155, 159–60, 163, 165,
175, 184

Paley, William, 33

Palmer, William (of Worcester College), 19f.,
30–1, 43, 45
Palmerston, Lord, 106–7, 248–9, 251
Pascendi, encyclical, 162–3
Pattison, Mark, 139–41, 150–1, 217
Pearson, John, 11, 310
Perrone, Giovanni, 19, 31
Pius IX, Pope, 158, 220, 311
Pius X, Pope, 161
Pius XII, Pope, 165
Plato, Platonism, 8, 10, 39, 160, 186
poetry and religion, 1–2, 9, 19f., 23, 52, 86ff.
Prayer Book: 1549, 1552, 6; 1662, 17, 43, 47,
218; 1928, 49–50
Pusey, E. B., 2, 18–19, 21, 138; person,
170ff., marriage, 170–1, 214–15; on faith,
35; sense of sin, 214ff.; and the Tracts, 37;
Tract upon Baptism, 38, 43, 49; approves
of Tract 90, 43; but not all its language, 45;
mysticism, 37ff.; poetic strand, 52, 53;
against originality, 38; charged with
immobility, 170–3; against excess of
ritualism, 48; adaptation of Roman
Catholic books of devotion, 39; on
seminaries, 224, 237; holds branch theory
of Church, 49; against 'rationalism', 50;
and Biblical criticism, 264; commentary on
the Bible, 245; sermons, 52–3, 170, 301;
Eirenicon, 170; *Private Prayers*, 233; urges
Church to write, 143
Puseyites, 135

Real Presence, doctrine of, 21, 244
Reformation, the, 5ff., 42ff., 63, 113, 247
reserve, doctrine of, 26–7, 35, 43, 138
Revolution of 1688, 4–5, 23
Richmond, George, 260
ritual, 13, 46–7, 234–5, 269ff. see also mitres
Rogers, Frederic (later Lord Blachford), 87,
181
Robertson, F. W., 208–9
Robespierre, Maximilien, 2, 61
romanticism and religion, 2, 46–7, 52–3, 148
Rose, H. J., 21, 25, 87, 136, 144
Russell, Lord John, 75–8, 248

Sabatier, P., 163
St George's, Windsor, 83, 111; Dean of,
112ff.
St John, Ambrose, 181, 184, 190
St Paul's Cathedral, 67–9, 97, 270
Salisbury, third Marquess of, 203, 254–5, 265
Scott Holland, Henry, 51, 88, 284
secularism, 199ff.
Seeley, Sir John, 122–3
Selwyn, G. A., 60

Silsoe, Lord, 72–3
sinecures, 69, 80, 84
Smith, Sydney, 65, 69–71, 169–70
Socialism, 110
Stanley, A. P., 16, 106, 112–13, 139
Stanton, A. H., 198
Stephen, Leslie, 204
Strachey, Lytton, 146
Stubbs, William, 114, 212, 255, 287
Sullivan, Arthur, 97
Sulpician seminaries, 228
Sumner, J. B., 10

Tait, A. C., 94, 139, 249–54, 261
Talbot, E. K., 94, 255, 284, 286
Talbot, George, 219ff.
Taylor, Jeremy, 10–12
Temple, Frederick, 254, 267–8, 284
Thirty-Nine Articles, 6, 11, 14–15, 44f., 108, 139, 253, 300
Thorndike, Herbert, 10–11, 42
Three Hours devotion, 280
Tracts for the Times, 15, 22, 24; on reserve, 26; the catenas, 42–3
Tristram, Henry, 164
Trollope, Anthony, 212, 223
Tuckwell, William, 137, 152
Tyrrell, George, 160–2, 173–4, 180

van Mildert, William, 66

vestments, 47
Victoria, Queen, 94, 247ff., 266ff.

Walsham How, W., 63, 259
Ward, Mrs Humphry, 207, 266
Ward, W. G., 35, 44–5, 50, 142, 169–70
Ward, Wilfrid, 159–66, 175, 196
Webb, Clement, 11
Wellesley, Gerald, dean of Windsor, 112, 251–3
Wesley, John, 55, 278, 302
Westcott, B. F., 280, 301
Whately, Richard, 24, 25, 33, 102, 180–1
Whitaker, William, 10
Whitgift, John, 10
Whole Duty of Man, The, 17–18
Wilberforce, Robert 24, 50
Wilberforce, Samuel, 18: reviews *Lyra apostolica*, 88–9; as orator, 125; as Bishop of Oxford; prefers gentlemen-clergy, 212; forbids Pusey to preach, 219, 238; and Cuddesdon, 225ff.; and Liddon, 227ff.; King and, 258ff.
Williams, Isaac, 19, 24–6, 35, 43, 52–3, 89, 149
Wilson, Thomas, 58
Wordsworth, Christopher, 278, 282, 300
Wordsworth, William, 89, 109, 118, 148, 287
Wiseman, Nicholas, 78